John

Jacob Epstein

Sculpture and Drawings

Evelyn Silber   Terry Friedman

Elizabeth Barker   Ezio Bassani

Judith Collins   Richard Cork

Frank Felsenstein   Malcolm McLeod

Elsje Prinz

W. S. Maney and Son

In Association With

The Henry Moore Centre

for the Study of Sculpture

1989

Front cover
FIGURE IN FLENITE   1913
The Minneapolis Institute of Arts   [50*]

Back cover
SELF-PORTRAIT   *c* 1901
Walsall Museum and Art Gallery   [3*]

Page ii
Epstein at Congress House, London, in 1956, preparing to carve the TRADES UNION CONGRESS WAR MEMORIAL from a block of Roman stone

---

Page iii
Epstein, photographed by G. C. Beresford   *c* 1920

Page iv (frontispiece)
[1]   Augustus John (1878–1961)   JACOB EPSTEIN   1905–06
Etching (actual size)   Leeds City Art Galleries

Jacob Epstein
Sculpture and Drawings

An Exhibition Organised by

The Henry Moore Centre
for the Study of Sculpture
Leeds City Art Galleries

16 April – 21 June 1987

and

Whitechapel Art Gallery
London

3 July – 13 September 1987

Sponsored in Leeds by

The Henry Moore Foundation

Sponsored in London by

The Henry Moore Foundation

and

 **Midland Bank**

FOREWORD

During his lifetime Jacob Epstein (1880–1959) was for many people *the* great British sculptor. He exhibited widely and received extensive press coverage. He had often been a scapegoat for modern art and since his death changing attitudes have driven him into the wilderness. Only the large memorial exhibitions held in Edinburgh and at the Tate Gallery in 1961 offered a comprehensive overview of his tempestuous career. More recently, Birmingham Museums and Art Gallery and the Ben Uri Gallery in London have mounted shows to celebrate the centenary of his birth. These, together with the major surveys, *British Sculpture in the Twentieth Century* at the Whitechapel Art Gallery in 1981, and *British Art in the 20th Century* at the Royal Academy in 1987, have begun to reveal again his true stature as one of the two most important British sculptors of this century.

Soon after arriving in Britain from New York, via Paris, in 1905, Epstein pioneered many of the concepts central to Modernist practice — direct carving, truth to material and inspiration from 'primitive' art — which were subsequently developed by a younger generation of sculptors, amongst whom was his friend, Henry Moore. Equally, Epstein established himself as not only the outstanding portrait sculptor of his day but also one who had taken this most traditional of genres into new, expressive domains. One of the difficulties experienced by public and critics alike is the apparent contradiction between his work as a carver of monumental figures in stone and as a modeller of vividly realistic portraits in bronze, a dichotomy which existed throughout his career and which tempted people to see him as some sort of Jekyll and Hyde. Epstein consistently denied this distinction. His sculpture, whether carved or modelled, reveals an essentially humanistic vision which speaks directly and intuitively.

The time is ripe to look again at the whole range of his art and to reassess his achievement. *Avant garde* sculpture (and painting, too) worldwide is focusing on the figurative tradition, reasserting the values of intuition and expression. This reversal of the modernist ethos which prevailed for much of Epstein's career enables us to see his work in a new light. Moreover, Evelyn Silber's major study of the sculptor, the first to include a complete catalogue of works, listing some 528 sculptures, has appeared within the last year. Since it went to press, as invariably happens with such an extensive undertaking, further interesting new information has come to light and some of this has been incorporated into the present exhibition. The show also deals in more detail with the relationship between preliminary drawings and finished sculpture, with Epstein's work as an illustrator, with his sources, with the critical controversies surrounding his work, his place in contemporary society and his role as one of the greatest of all collectors of 'primitive' art. An independent catalogue of the nearly 1,000 artefacts which made up this remarkable collection is to be published this year by Ezio Bassani and Malcolm McLeod. Carlo Monzino, the present owner of a number of these works, has generously allowed some of the most important to be illustrated in our catalogue.

The two venues for the present exhibition are especially appropriate. The first sculpture Epstein ever exhibited (*Fountain Figure*, now in the Musée d'Art Moderne, Geneva) was shown at the Whitechapel Art Gallery in 1910. The links with Leeds have also been particularly strong. One of his finest portraits is of the Leeds painter Jacob Kramer, and in 1942 Epstein and his lifelong friend, Matthew Smith, exhibited side by side at Temple Newsam House. Epstein had already paid the City a compliment by telling a reporter for *The Leeds Mercury* (15 July 1939) that the 'Art Gallery there . . . is much more advanced in artistic appreciation than the London Gallery, where the trustees have no initiative and little courage'. The Leeds collection already included a number of his bronzes, and more recently it has acquired one of the sculptor's most important carvings, *Maternity*, 1910, and a unique sketchbook of 87 drawings for the Rima relief on the *W. H. Hudson Memorial* of 1925. The Henry Moore Centre for the Study of Sculpture in the City Art Gallery is in the forefront of Epstein research.

Dr Terry Friedman, the Principal Keeper of the Centre, and Dr Evelyn Silber, Assistant Director of Birmingham Museums and Art Gallery, have undertaken most of the work involved in arranging and cataloguing the exhibition, and we are grateful for the authority and dedication which they have brought to this task. Our further appreciation is due to the other contributors to the catalogue: Elizabeth Barker, Ezio Bassani, Judith Collins, Richard Cork, Frank Felsenstein, Malcolm McLeod and Elsje Prinz. The catalogue has been made possible by a special grant from The Henry Moore Foundation and, in addition, we have been most fortunate in having Midland Bank as co-sponsor of the London venue.

We owe our warmest thanks to Kitty Godley, the sculptor's daughter, and to Beth Lipkin, a lifelong friend of Sir Jacob and Lady Epstein, without whose sympathetic support and hard work the exhibition would have proven immeasurably less satisfactory. We are particularly grateful to the museums and private collectors for their magnanimous response to our request for loans. David Guy, Director of the Walsall Museum and Art Gallery, generously agreed to lend many important works by Epstein from the Garman-Ryan Collection, a collection formed by Lady Epstein and her friend, the American artist Sally Ryan. Sir David Wilson and the Trustees of The British Museum have lent a selection of outstanding ancient and primitive sculptures formerly belonging to Epstein: L. R. H. Smith, Keeper of the Department of Oriental Antiquities, T. C. Mitchell, Keeper of the Department of Western Asiatic Antiquities, and Malcolm McLeod, Keeper of the Ethnography Department (Museum of Mankind), and their staff, have helped in many valuable ways. The Museums and Galleries Commission has been, as always, unstinting in arranging for the exhibition to receive indemnity by HM Government. Phaidon Press has made available a number of excellent photographs from its archive.

We also wish to thank Dr and Mrs Abrahams, Jean Asquith, David Auchterlonie, Alasdair A. Auld, J. N. Barnes, Wendy Belsky, Vivienne Bennett, John Bernasconi, Alex Bernstein, Alan Borg, Alan Bowness, Annette Bradshaw, John Bradshaw, R. H. Bradshaw, Leon L. Bram, The British Library, Lindsay Brookes, Hilary Bruce, Richard Buckle, Adrian Budge, Mr and Mrs Stanley Burton, Helen Campbell, Janice Carpenter, Timothy Clifford, Ann Compton, The Convent of the Holy Child Jesus, Mayfield, Sussex, Raymond Coxon, R. A. Crighton, Michael Cross, Caroline Cuthbert, Alex Davis, Ian Dawson, Michael Diamond, Professor C. R. Dodwell, Anthony d'Offay, John Doubleday, Caroline Douglas, Tim Egan, Dr and Mrs Martin Evans, Funk and Wagnalls Inc., Stephen Gabriel, Dr Oscar Ghez, Francis Greenacre, Ann Gunn, Douglas Hall, David Hardwick, Harper and Row, Publishers, Inc., John Harris, The Harry Ransom Humanities Research Centre, University of Texas at Austin, Simon Haviland, Francis Hawcroft, James H. Heineman, Cathy Henderson, Kenneth Hood, Robert Hopper, Brian Hughes, Geoffrey Ireland, Michael Jaffé, T. G. H. James, Professor John R. Kaiser, Janet Kenyon, Beatrice Kernan, Norman L. Kleeblatt, T. J. Laszlo, David Lewis, The Limited Editions Club, New York, Brian Loughbrough, A. Marguiles, Jonathan Mason, Mrs Alister Matthews, Patrick McCaughley, Peter McGrath, Ian McKenzie Smith, Bernard Meadows, Barbara Miller, James Mollison, MoMart Limited, Gordon Morrison, The New York Public Library, Richard E. Oldenburg, R. L. Ormond, Liz Ottaway, Fiona Pearson, Michael Pennington, The Pennsylvania State University Library, Christopher Phillips, Ewan Phillips, The Pierpont Morgan Library, New York, L. B. Powell, Adam B. Ritchie, Norman Rosenthal, Irene Roth, John Rowlands, The Royal Society for the Protection of Birds, Crista Sammons, Stephen Sartin, David Setford, Sidney Shiff, Jacob Simon, Joanna Skipwith, Peyton Skipwith, Yonty Solomon, Julian Spalding, Sir Roy Strong, Charles Tarling, Tate Gallery Archives, Norman Taylor, Stephanie Teychenne, J. M. A. Thompson, Margaret Thornton, Claire Venner, Mrs Verasanso, Robin Vousden, Dr Martin Weyl, Adam White, Alan G. Wilkinson, Arnold Wilson, Heather Wilson, Simon Wilson, Douglas Woolf, Yale University Library and Judith Zilczer.

CHRISTOPHER GILBERT
Director, Leeds City Art Galleries

COUNCILLOR ELIZABETH NASH
Chairman, Leisure Services Committee,
Leeds City Council

NICHOLAS SEROTA
Director, Whitechapel Art Gallery

STEPHEN KEYNES
Chairman, Trustees of
Whitechapel Art Gallery

Contents

Lenders to the Exhibition

AUSTRALIA

Canberra, Australian National Museum [140]

Melbourne, National Gallery of Victoria [11, 36]

CANADA

Toronto, Art Gallery of Ontario [55]

ISRAEL

Jerusalem, Israel Museum [46]

UNITED KINGDOM

Aberdeen Art Gallery and Museums [92]

Victor Arwas [22, 75, 82]

Birmingham Museums and Art Gallery [8, 25, 60, 76, 89, 93, 111, 130, 133, 136, 151, 173, 176]

George Black [152]

Bolton Museum and Art Gallery [164, 177]

Bradford Art Galleries and Museums [18]

City of Bristol Museum and Art Gallery [159]

Christopher Bunting [146]

The Syndics of the Fitzwilliam Museum, Cambridge [19, 150]

Cardiff, National Museum of Wales [34]

Dundee Art Galleries and Museums [113]

Philip L. Dyer [17]

Edinburgh, The Scottish Gallery of Modern Art [110]

The Epstein Estate [23, 33, 168]

Frank Felsenstein [94]

Glasgow, The Burrell Collection, Glasgow Museum and Art Gallery [84]

Granada Television Ltd [134, 142]

Greenwich, National Maritime Museum [73]

P. Henriques [115]

Hull, Ferens Art Gallery: Hull City Museums and Art Galleries [154]

Hull, The University of Hull Art Collection [12]

Vane Ivanović [169]

Leeds City Art Galleries [1, 6, 13, 15, 16, 27, 37, 38, 43, 85, 86, 99, 100, 106, 114, 117, 118, 119, 120, 121, 122, 124, 125, 126, 128, 129, 153, 155, 170]

Beth Lipkin [20, 45, 78, 81, 98, 103, 116, 132, 167, 178, XV]

London, Anthony d'Offay Gallery [29, 41, 51, 53, 59, 61, 67, 68]

London, Bowater Industries plc [179]

London, British Architectural Library, The Royal Institute of British Architects [127]

London, The Trustees of the British Museum [64, VI, VIII, IX, X, XII, XIII, XIV, XVI]

London, Imperial War Museum [74]

London, The Trustees of The Tate Gallery [14, 24, 48, 63, 65, 70]

London, The Board of Trustees of the Victoria and Albert Museum [101]

Bernard Lyons [91]

Manchester City Art Gallery [79, 112]

Manchester, Whitworth Art Gallery, University of Manchester [87, 160]

Ross McInnes [2]

Newcastle upon Tyne, Laing Art Gallery, Tyne and Wear Museums Service [80]

Nottingham Castle Museum [35]

Louis Osman [171]

Oxford, Warden and Fellows of New College [180]

The Phillips Family [90]

Preston, Harris Art Gallery [58]

Mr and Mrs Peter Retey [77]

Mr and Mrs Victor Sandelson [156, 174]

Dr and Mrs Jeffrey Sherwin [104, 107, 108, 131]

Evelyn Silber [102]

Walsall Museum and Art Gallery (Garman-Ryan Collection) [3, 4, 7, 9, 10, 26, 30, 44, 47, 66, 95, 96, 161, 162, 165, XI]

Watford Museum [144, 145]

Marcus Wickham-Boynton [88, 137]

Emlyn Williams [149]

Simon and Alessandra Wilson [28]

UNITED STATES OF AMERICA

The Minneapolis Institute of Arts [50]

New York, Dr and Mrs Martin Evans [56, 57]

New York, The Jewish Museum [97]

New York, The Museum of Modern Art [52, 69]

PRIVATE COLLECTIONS

[5, 31, 42, 49, 51A, 62, 105, 109, 123, 138, 147, 148, 157, 158, 163, 166, 172, 175, 181]

Contributors to the Catalogue

ELIZABETH BARKER
is a freelance lecturer at the National Gallery and a postgraduate student at University College, London, where she is writing a doctoral thesis on *The Primitive Within: The Question of Race in Epstein's Career 1900–1939.*

EZIO BASSANI
teaches at the University of Varese. After a successful career in commerce, he began to specialise in the history of African art and, especially, of the earliest African pieces to be brought to Europe. He has published numerous articles on this subject and is the joint author, with Malcolm McLeod, of *Jacob Epstein Collector*, 1987, and, with William Fagg, of a catalogue of Afro-Portuguese ivories which accompanied a major exhibition in New York early this year.

DR JUDITH COLLINS
is Assistant Keeper, Modern Collection, at The Tate Gallery. A graduate of Edinburgh University and the Courtauld Institute of Art, she has written on Eric Gill, is the author of *The Omega Workshops*, 1983, and is currently engaged in research on early twentieth-century sculpture.

RICHARD CORK
read Art History at Cambridge. Formerly Art Critic of the London *Evening Standard* and Editor of *Studio International*, he is now Art Critic of *The Listener*. He served for several years on the Art Panel of the Arts Council and has organised many exhibitions in Britain and abroad, including *Vorticism and its Allies* at the Hayward Gallery in 1974. He is the author of *Vorticism and Abstract Art in the First Machine Age*, which won the John Llewelyn Rhys Memorial Prize in 1977. In 1979 a selection of his criticism was published under the title *The Social Role of Art*. He is a frequent broadcaster and lecturer, and his book *Art Beyond The Gallery in Early 20th Century England* was awarded the Sir Banister Fletcher Prize in 1986. His latest book, *David Bomberg*, was published earlier this year and Richard Cork is now organising a Bomberg retrospective for the Tate Gallery in February 1988. He contributed several essays, including 'The Emancipation of Modern British Sculpture', to the catalogue for the Royal Academy's *British Art in the 20th Century* exhibition in 1987.

DR FRANK FELSENSTEIN
is a Senior Lecturer in English and Bibliography at the University of Leeds. Among his research interests is the eighteenth-century Grand Tour, out of which he prepared for Oxford University Press the Clarendon edition of Tobias Smollett's *Travels through France and Italy*. He has also published works on garden history and on the history of the book. He is editor of the *University of Leeds Review.*

DR TERRY FRIEDMAN
is Principal Keeper of Leeds City Art Gallery and The Henry Moore Centre for the Study of Sculpture. After studying the history of art at the University of Michigan and the Courtauld Institute of Art, he was appointed Keeper of Decorative Art Studies at Temple Newsam House, Leeds, where he taught and organised exhibitions devoted to the sculpture of Joseph Gott and John Cheere. He has written widely on various aspects of British architecture, interior design and sculpture, and was co-organiser of the exhibitions *Henry Moore: Early Carvings 1920–1940*, 1982, and *Angels of Anarchy and Machines for Making Clouds: Surrealism in Britain in the Thirties*, 1986, held at Leeds City Art Gallery. He is the author of *James Gibbs*, 1984, and *The Hyde Park Atrocity*, a study of Epstein's *Hudson Memorial* (1922–25), to be published later this year.

MALCOLM McLEOD
has been Keeper of Ethnography at the British Museum since 1974. He previously taught at the Universities of Cambridge and Ghana, and has written extensively on the Asante of Ghana. In 1985 he organised the Museum of Mankind exhibition *Eduardo Paolozzi: Lost Magic Kingdoms and Six Paper Moons from Nahuatl*. He is the co-author, with Ezio Bassani, of *Jacob Epstein Collector*, 1987.

ELSJE PRINZ
is a graduate of the Fine Art Department of Leeds University, with a particular interest in the relationship between sculpture and architecture in early twentieth-century Britain. Born at Rotterdam, she worked for many years as a translator and interpreter, and has taught foreign language in adult education.

DR EVELYN SILBER
is Assistant Director at Birmingham Museums and Art Gallery. Following postgraduate study at the Universities of Pennsylvania and Cambridge on late medieval manuscript illumination, she worked in publishing. In 1979 she became a curator of painting and sculpture at Birmingham. Her publications include the exhibition catalogue *Rebel Angel: Sculpture and Watercolours by Sir Jacob Epstein*, 1980, and *The Sculpture of Epstein*, 1986.

Notes on the Catalogue

The catalogue, like the exhibition, is divided into fifteen numbered sections, which follow a general chronological pattern.

Numbers in square brackets [1–181] correspond to works in the exhibition.

Numbers shown as Roman numerals [I–XVI] denote ancient and primitive artefacts, formerly in Jacob Epstein's collection, shown in the present exhibition, unless otherwise stated.

Numbers prefixed by Fig. (1–100) represent material not exhibited.

An asterisk * alongside the catalogue number denotes that the work is illustrated in colour, between pages 48 and 73, or on page 97.

Dimensions are given in centimetres.

In the case of bronzes, the cast illustrated is the one exhibited, unless otherwise stated. In some cases, alternative illustrations have been used for their aesthetic or historical interest, as, for example [88], which is a studio photograph c1930 from a glass negative by Paul Laib.

EPSTEIN IN PERSON

Evelyn Silber

EPSTEIN —
Tons of God is his line
Raises tumults and dusts
Then does glorious busts[1]

This epigrammatic quip, published when the sculptor was in his mid-sixties, sums up the lifelong ambivalence of Epstein's reputation and suggests the temperamental *terribilità* which both the man and his work projected. Even in old age there hung about Epstein a Romantic aura of being 'mad, bad and dangerous to know'. The alleged barbarism of his carvings, mercilessly lampooned by cartoonists such as David Low [Figs 28–29], was complemented by the sculptor's bohemian dress and behaviour. He was a well-known figure in the West End [Figs 1–2], often to be seen at the Café Royal or dining at the Ivy, the Caprice or other well-known restaurants and clubs, either with Kathleen Garman or with an entourage of models and friends. If this caused a stir in town, it caused a sensation in the still rural surroudings of Loughton, on the edge of Epping Forest, where he rented a house from 1922 until the late Forties. The local inhabitants were regularly titillated by the sight of the sculptor himself, a powerful figure in his working clothes and heavy overcoat, of Mrs Epstein, majestic in a full-length fur coat, or by the appearance of beautiful models dressed in the height of West End fashion, parading through the village. It became the dare amongst the children to try to penetrate the hedge to see what might be going on in the house beyond, and their elders were disconcerted to discover, when they ran into Epstein in the local pub, that he was an unassuming man, approachable and easy to talk to.[2]

The passages which follow are accounts by those who knew him.

I met him in 1912 at exhibitions of the London Group . . . he was very young, very virile and very confident of himself . . . would stand no nonsense . . . he was not quarrelsome but was gentle, kind and sympathetic to brother artists.

HORACE BRODZKY
interviewed by Peter de Francia, 1960[3]

At Eric Gill's instigation, Jacob Epstein, Ambrose McEvoy and I used to gather at my studio in the King's Road, Chelsea, to discuss the question of a new religion. Gill's idea took the form of a neo-Nietzschean cult of super-humanity under the sign of the Ithyphallus. Epstein's, more simply, would be realised by an apotheosis of himself on a colossal scale, alone, and blowing his own trumpet. I was in favour of the rehabilitation of the Earth-Mother and Child, whose image installed in a covered waggon would be drawn by oxen and attended by dancing corybantes.

AUGUSTUS JOHN
Chiaroscuro, 1952[4]

Epstein is a great sculptor. I wish he would wash, but I believe Michel Angelo *never* did, so I suppose it is part of the tradition.

EZRA POUND
to Isabel Pound, November 1913[5]

Epstein was a complete artist but unlike Matisse and Picasso, who were keen businessmen, I doubt if he knew how to sign a cheque. He was incapable of striking a hard bargain over some commission he really wished to do and he would have been helpless without the devotion and care of the first Mrs Epstein and of Lady Kathleen, the beautiful Kathleen of so many works. In politics he was left of centre but I noticed he tended to be swayed by what he heard of a politician's taste in art, which is as it should be . . . his love and understanding of sculpture had its origin in religion; whether this was primitive African or highly sophisticated, he was able to identify himself strongly with the subject.

ARNOLD HASKELL
Balletomane at Large, 1972[6]

Epstein is the only artist among us who *wants* to shock. His work is definitely *épatant*.

PAUL NASH
Week End Review, 18 April 1931[7]

Epstein had an imposing presence. But this was not due to any conscious effort to impress those whom he met. On the contrary it derived from a natural propensity to engage one's direct and whole attention. His massive frame conveyed unmistakeably a sense of abounding vitality. This

Fig 1
Jacob and Peggy Jean Epstein (seated opposite) having tea at an open-air café in Kensington Gardens, 4 May 1933.

was not surprising for he was so often engaged in pitting his strength upon some great block of marble or granite . . . The muscular aggressiveness such activity entailed was speedily relinquished when work ceased and he would enter his lounge unobtrusively and at ease, ready to mix with any company. There was never a scrap of snobbery about Epstein but he had no time for small talk or mere gossip. The most striking things about him were his hands and his eyes. Fleshy and large, the hands were an embodiment of strength in recoil when they were clasped in relaxation or at rest on his knees. I never saw him in the act of modelling or carving, for he would always stop work and enter upon conversation in which the subject, as likely as not, would be the latest diatribe from one of his detractors, and it was then that his eyes would blaze with anger and contempt. That he was often prone to anger was, I thought, the obverse side of an extremely sensitive nature. There would be some relief from this state of mind when he discussed the characteristics . . . of the most recent sitters [and] on these occasions he would reveal a degree of psychological insight as acute as his modelling. When these discussions in the studio turned to the work in hand it was remarkable how little Epstein had to say by way of elucidating or amplifying his attitude to the sculptor's art. He never tired of insisting that any example must speak for itself. The

beholder, he would affirm, must bring something of himself or herself to the act of assessing the emotive quality conveyed. If there was nothing to give in this way the reaction would be one of emptiness, frustration or irritation. Epstein showed his own quality of sympathetic awareness at no time more readily than when he would bring out an example from his many pieces of primitive . . . sculpture. It was a tactile education to see him handling this or that example, telling of its origin, and turning it around so its plastic significance could be fully appreciated.

L. B. POWELL
Unpublished reminiscence, March 1983

Once after a full day's work on a huge fifteen or sixteen foot-high figure — climbing — lifting — visualising — I found him sitting the wrong way round on a small chair, painting a watercolour of a fairy and decorations on a Christmas tree. Another moment he would bark out his disapproval of some work or other — then swing around with enthusiasm over something else as emphatically as a student. He had a great affinity with much younger people. I was never once conscious of his age, and he was then seventy-five or six.

GEOFFREY IRELAND
'Eye Witness', 1961[8]

One hears many criticisms of Epstein which are merely contemptible . . . but I know few artists who, being given a commission of a fixed but generous sum, deliberately discarded a work of great distinction [the first project for the Tomb of Oscar Wilde] already nearing completion and proceed to work on a vast new project involving large expenditure on material, transport and erection at a cost amounting to what was probably as much as the whole commission. That was the work of a sincere artist wholly devoted to his art and thinking nothing of the profit. Epstein is annoying, he has not a spot of gratitude in his make-up, he is quarrelsome and stupidly suspicious. He knows how to get publicity whenever he wants it (he would probably hate popularity like the devil) but he has the secret of making his work live.

CHARLES HOLDEN
Unpublished notes on sculpture, 1940[9]

He was a man of great physical strength, whose broad shoulders and sturdy limbs retained signs of vigour to the end of his life. Indeed he changed very little and never seemed to grow old. I have seen him carry heavy pieces of stone and large bronze busts in a way that not only astonished a small man like myself but surprised our staff at the Galleries who were used to heavy burdens . . . He was more insulted and abused than any artist I have ever known, but Epstein was indomitable. The trivial and vulgar attacks of the gutterpress left him indifferent; hostility from serious critics — such as the Bloomsbury Group — made him perhaps more bitter in private talk with friends but seldom led him to reply in public. On the other hand anyone who did not treat him with personal respect, or might appear to act so, made him flare up with surprising wrath.

OLIVER BROWN
Exhibition, 1968[10]

I remember that on one occasion he jumped into a taxi with a piece of sculpture of mine he had just bought from me, even though I did not regard it as completely finished, because it was his and therefore he wanted it then and there — [this] was perhaps one of the most attractive qualities of the man. He was strong and immediate in his likes, and also in his dislikes . . . And few men can have loved sculpture purely for its own sake more than Jacob Epstein . . . His warmth and his vitality and his courage will not be quickly forgotten. We have lost a great sculptor.

HENRY MOORE
obituary notice, The Sunday Times
23 August 1959[11]

Fig 2
Esther Garman, Mark Joffe, Kathleen Garman and Jacob Epstein (left to right) at the opening of the Battersea Park Open Air Sculpture Exhibition, 13 May 1948.

Epstein
and his Patrons

Evelyn Silber

It is indicative of the directly communicative power of Epstein's work as well as the vicissitudes of his reputation that his patrons included not only two of the most important collectors of early twentieth-century art — John Quinn and Charles Rutherston — but also many people whose 'Epstein', possibly bought by instalments, was the first (maybe the only) work of art they possessed. Typical of the latter was a young Irish school-teacher, Helen Campbell, who first encountered his work in the mid-Twenties. She was on her way to a job in the South of England when she decided to go and see for herself what the recent hullabaloo in the newspapers was about. Leaving her suitcase at the station, she set off for Hyde Park and the notorious *Rima* [Figs 80–81*], only to discover that, far from being a monstrosity, it struck her as a great work of art. Miss Campbell became a dedicated admirer but it was only twenty years later, after the War, that she actually bought a bronze from Victor Waddington's Gallery in Dublin. After repeated visits to contemplate the portraits in the exclusive atmosphere of the gallery, it abruptly dawned upon her that the considerable sum of £160 for a bronze head was not beyond her. Her life insurance policy had just matured! Until then, 'it had never occurred to me that an ordinary person like myself *could* own an Epstein'. The Director of the Dublin National Gallery told her, 'I do not know whether to congratulate you more on the ownership of an Epstein, or upon your enterprise in daring to buy one'.[1]

A kindred sense of adventure informs a letter written by J. B. Manson, a curator of the National Gallery at Millbank (Tate Gallery), to the then Director of Leicester Corporation Art Gallery, early in 1924, soon after they became, so he believed, the first provincial gallery to acquire an Epstein:

> I must congratulate you on acquiring Epstein's Weeping Woman. It is a magnificent work. How did you manage to get it? I envy you too! We have three Epsteins [*Bust of Nan* (24), *Euphemia Lamb* (14) and *Jacob Kramer* (85)] but nothing so fine as yours . . . There is stuff in his present exhibition as great as anything that has been done at any time![2]

Although most clients, like these, bought work through Epstein's dealers, others, including of course all the portrait sitters, came to the studio. There they could see bronzes, watercolours and drawings, and a multitude of plasters stacked on shelves or on the floor in the corner of the studio,

from amongst which a cast could often be commissioned. Many of those who came to sit for their own portrait ended up buying something else as well, just as others who began by collecting Epstein's work through the galleries ended up commissioning a portrait.

For the sculptor visitors to the studio could be supportive, appreciative, and rewarding to talk to, but his autobiography makes clear his sympathy with Rodin, who had to be polite to the numerous time-wasters, tourists and amateur artists who 'had the impudence to impose on him'.[3] He himself frequently found such visits irritating; on occasion a potential patron was unceremoniously shown the door for making belittling or offensive remarks, or for revealing tastes in art of which the sculptor vehemently disapproved.[4] There was a latent tension between the acute cash crises to which the Epstein household was subject and the concomitant desirability of encouraging any buyer, and the sculptor's overriding need to avoid wasting time on social pleasantries in order to concentrate on the work in hand.

Between 1905, when he arrived in England, and the Twenties, when his shows at the Leicester Galleries brought widespread fame and an increasing number of portrait commissions, Epstein was heavily dependent on a small, close-knit network of artists and art-lovers, all more or less closely connected with the New English Art Club, where he exhibited his first work in England, a painting called *Konhong Sarah*, in December 1906.[5] Armed with a letter of introduction from Rodin he had gone first to George Bernard Shaw who, though he never commissioned anything, proved a useful supporter for more than thirty years.[6] Shaw's equivocal enthusiasm for his work was more than outweighed by his willingness to back a promising young artist on principle and by his alacrity in repelling ill-conceived attacks on Epstein's sculpture in the press with caustic stabs of the pen.[7] He, in turn, introduced Epstein to the prominent NEAC member, William Rothenstein, and to Oscar Wilde's literary executor Robert Ross, who also happened to be a co-director of the Carfax Gallery. Though no exhibition resulted, Rothenstein bought a *Calamus* drawing and both were to play a major part in arranging for Epstein to receive the commission for the *Tomb of Oscar Wilde* [Fig. 46] three years later.[8]

William Rothenstein was an artist so tirelessly helpful in encouraging the work of others that he became more important as an administrator than as an artist, and his protégés not infrequently ended up rebelling against his assiduous interest in their affairs, as Epstein eventually did.[9] Out of faith in his talent and from a desire to help a fellow Jewish artist, Rothenstein aided the impoverished American with a small monthly payment from his own pocket, and solicited a Jewish aid society to enable Epstein to return briefly to America. Later, Rothenstein did not hesitate to advise the sculptor on his work; after seeing one of the BMA figures being modelled in the Cheyne Walk studio, he wrote:

> I admire the conception enormously, and some parts of the figure seem to me excellent, but other parts very incomplete . . . I cannot rid myself of the idea that sculpture . . . occupies itself with the perfection of form . . . You have an unusually fine, robust and fundamental vision of what your work should be . . . But unless you can get more nervous simplicity into your limbs for instance, your conception must suffer.[10]

Epstein may have heeded this advice in working on his studies of *Euphemia Lamb* and *Nan*. Rothenstein was both stimulated and disturbed by Epstein's 'strange, uncouth power' and admitted that he felt more admiration for his work 'when it is not too forceful'.[11] Nevertheless he seems to have been instrumental in bringing Epstein and Gill together and took a paternal interest in the progress of the *Oscar Wilde Tomb*, as well he might, having had a hand in Epstein receiving the commission.[12] Despite a row in June 1911, when Epstein exploded, 'I want no more of your damned insincere invitations. This pretence of friendship has gone on far enough',[13] Rothenstein retained his basic respect for Epstein's work. In 1924, when he was head of the Royal College of Art, he recommended Epstein to be Professor of Sculpture, only to be frustrated by the timidity of the Board of Education.[14]

The importance of Jewish patronage later in Epstein's career is easily established by looking at the commissions he received for the portrait of Chaim Weizmann and from numerous Jewish collectors, businessmen, and friends. Less well known is the support he received and gave to others during his early years in London. There were undoubtedly many who were prejudiced against him because of his background, but there was also solidarity among some Jewish artists and patrons to support him, notwithstanding his rejection of formal religious observance. The artists Horace Brodzky and Alfred Wolmark are now better known for their friendship with Henri Gaudier-Brzeska than with Epstein.[15] However, between 1913 and 1917 Epstein sold three early works — *Baby asleep* [6], *Lillian Shelley*, and the cast of *Romilly John* exhibited here [31] — with Wolmark's active assistance to two of the painter's most faithful backers, Alfred and Rudolf Kohnstamm, leather manufacturers in Beckenham.[16] They were especially sympathetic to needy artists, particularly if they were Jewish, though as the postscript to an undated letter from Epstein to Wolmark shows, they got a good price too: 'Do not mention the prices of the heads I sold to Mr Kohnstamm to others as in selling them singly I

shall ask for more'.[17] A few years later Epstein asked Wolmark whether his friends might be able to help a young and penniless Mexican Jewish artist, Benjamin Coria (whom he had befriended and with whom he remained on good terms for some years).[18] Epstein's contacts with Brodzky were more tenuous, but he gladly supplied the painter with a reference when he was after a teaching job in 1925, and Brodzky later tried to do a book on Epstein's drawings, though this project fell through owing to the wide dispersal of the works he wanted to reproduce.

Augustus John, another of the NEAC circle, was, strictly speaking, less a patron than a comrade-in-arms. Until they fell out during the Great War, their relationship had the easy give and take of fellow bohemians who employed the same models and who shared the same keen interest in the opposite sex. In 1905–06 John drew and etched portraits of Epstein [frontispiece and Fig. 42] and, in 1907, Epstein's first outstandingly original portrait, which foreshadowed much of his subsequent development, was of one of John's sons, *Romilly John* [31]. During the BMA controversy John proved a perceptive supporter, writing to Robert Ross, 'Epstein's work must be defended by recognised moral experts. The Art question is not raised. Of course they [the BMA sculptures] would pass the *moral* test as triumphantly as the artistic, or even more if possible. Do you know an intelligent *Bishop* for example?'[19] They did, and Cosmo Lang, then Bishop of Stepney, duly mounted the scaffolding and pronounced the works inoffensive. John came to the rescue again soon afterwards when the Epsteins found themselves in a desperate financial plight, almost starving, because the unanticipated costs of the BMA figures had left them deep in debt. John produced a fiver on the spot, and followed up by bringing that doyenne of patronesses, Lady Ottoline Morrell, to visit the studio, where she commissioned a marble garden statue for £25. Epstein responded gratefully, 'A garden figure sounds delightful; sculpture outdoors among trees and shrubs; it is reminiscent of Italy and Greece'.[20] The resulting work, in which classicism and naturalism felicitously combine, developed some of the life studies of *Euphemia Lamb* [13] into *Fountain Figure* [Fig. 3], which Lady Ottoline in 1910 lent to 'Twenty Years of British Art 1890–1910', at the Whitechapel Art Gallery, thus making it the first sculpture by Epstein to be exhibited in a public gallery.

Epstein retained the plaster model from which he had carved the garden sculpture and showed it the following year under the title *Euphemia*, at the first annual exhibition of the National Portrait Society, held at the Grafton Gallery. The sculptor probably decided it was well worth the two-guinea subscription in order to show suitable work at a respectable venue where it might well attract commissions.[21] In addition to *Euphemia*, he showed the stone head of *Rom* [34] and the stone bust of *Mrs Chadbourne* [Fig. 52], a wealthy Chicago collector to whom John or Rothenstein had probably introduced him. It is not known whether any commissions resulted and the reviews were hostile, at least to *Rom*, but the show did attract the attention of C. Lewis Hind, whose

The Post Impressionists, published in 1911, picked out these works for special praise and drew attention to the archaism and truth to materials which united the work of Epstein and Gill.

The painters and etchers Francis Dodd and Muirhead Bone formed, with the architect Charles Holden, an influential triumvirate linked by family ties and common interests; Bone, a Scot who had turned to draughtsmanship after a period as an apprentice architect, had arrived in London in 1901, encouraged by Holden. Subsequently he married Dodd's sister, while Bone's brother, James (London editor of *The Manchester Guardian*) married Holden's sister. All three were major supporters of Epstein's early work. In 1907 Dodd brought Holden to Epstein's studio where the life-size wax *Girl with a dove* [9] immediately convinced him that he had found the artist he was looking for to work on the BMA building. Holden's partnership with Epstein over the BMA and the London Underground Electric Railways Headquarters [127] gave the sculptor almost the only opportunities he received before 1950 to demonstrate and develop his powers as an architectural sculptor, a field in which the sculptor is necessarily entirely dependent on patronage.[22] Dodd's brilliant etched portrait of Epstein [Fig. 51] shows him poised for action beside a huge unsquared block of stone which seems to reflect his ruggedly elemental character; several years later, while working on the *Tomb of Oscar Wilde* [Fig. 46], Epstein returned the compliment with a charmingly naturalistic portrait of Mrs Dodd.[23] The two men remained on close terms and, in 1916, it was Dodd who arranged with the Duchess of Hamilton for him to sculpt *Admiral Lord Fisher* [73].

The bohemian young American, with his courteous but direct manner, strong opinions, and Brooklynese accent, was still very much an outsider. Augustus John, Ambrose McEvoy, and Dodd were middle-of-the-road artists, reflecting the growing conservatism of the once radical NEAC; already busy with society portraiture, they possessed contacts in fashionable London which Epstein initially lacked. Once introduced he not only made a favourable impression ('un génie qui est jeune', as Gladys Deacon [75] joyfully reported) but also began to receive portrait commissions. He developed two strategies for exhibiting his work, the annual exhibitions of the National Portrait Society for his portraits and the London Group shows for his experimental *avant-garde* carvings and drawings. In 1914 he showed a *Carving in Flenite* [50* or 56–57] and the lost *Bird Pluming Itself* at the London Group, while exhibiting a couple of old bronzes, *Head of a Girl* and his second portrait of *Euphemia Lamb* (lent by Muirhead Bone) at the NPS. In April 1917, with the increase in his private commissions, he was able to show seven portraits at the NPS, including early examples, such as *Lady Gregory* [27], and more recent studies —*Admiral Lord Fisher* [73?], a portrait of *Meum Lindsell-Stewart*, the head of Bernard van Dieren (model for the head of *Risen Christ* [110]) and the *Countess of Drogheda*. This last sitter was unusual in that, while her portrait was orthodox to a degree, she was committed to the most extreme modernism in interior décor and

had recently employed Wyndham Lewis to produce an extraordinary black mirrored dining room with Vorticist decoration for her London home.[24] In 1914, she also held a small private show of Epstein's sculpture, including one of the provocatively daring pairs of mating *Doves* [46, 48*], the mere sight of which caused her husband to exclaim, 'I won't have those fucking doves in here — I'll throw them out of the window!'[25] Other patrons, lulled by the naturalistic vigour of Epstein's modelled portraits into a false sense of security, were equally outraged by Epstein's one-man show at the Leicester Galleries in 1917. Here, too, were portraits of *Fisher* and *Meum*, together with *The Tin Hat* [74] and earlier works such as the *Bust of Nan* [24], but they were dominated by the towering presence of the marble *Venus* enthroned, standing on her mating doves [Fig. 68].

Though his portraits were receiving increasing acclaim (Lawrence Binyon in *The New Statesman* hailed 'the hand of a master', while P. G. Konody of *The Observer* found them 'almost uncanny'),[26] there were only two patrons seriously interested in carvings such as *Venus*, *Doves* and the Flenite pieces — T. E. Hulme and John Quinn. The philosopher and aesthetician of the *avant-garde*, T. E. Hulme [62], was preparing a book on Epstein's work when he and it were lost in France in September 1917. At the time of his death, Hulme was purchasing two of the carvings — *Flenite Relief* [56] and *Female Figure in Flenite* [Fig. 69] — by instalments. Having reverted to the sculptor, they remained in the studio where they were discovered abandoned in the bottom of a trunk after his death.[27] Hulme had purchased from a deep conviction that Epstein's carvings heralded an entirely modern, geometric art. Though the works may briefly have influenced Henry Moore in the Twenties, and are now highly prized, there is no sign that much attention was paid to them when Epstein exhibited them again in 1933. It is not surprising, therefore, that the sculptor treasured the only article that Hulme had published on his work, 'Mr Epstein and the Critics', and lamented the loss to his cause which Hulme's death represented. In an unpublished draft review of Epstein's very first one-man show at the Twenty-One Gallery in 1913, Hulme had argued that the flenite pieces showed the sculptor using elements drawn from primitive art as a stepping stone to the abstract geometric forms of the new art he prophesied:

Take the smaller 'Carving in Flenite' [?], which seems to me the best thing he has done so far. Technically it is admirable. The design is in no sense empty but gives an impressive and most complete expression of a certain blind and tragic aspect of its subject. The archaic elements it contains are in no way imitative. What has been taken from African and Polynesian work is the inevitable and permanent way of getting certain effects.[28]

Less analytical in his approach to contemporary art, but far richer, more ambitious and voracious as a patron of modern literary and artistic talent, was the Irish-American lawyer, John Quinn. Between 1910 and his death in 1924 Quinn

Fig 3
FOUNTAIN FIGURE (EUPHEMIA LAMB)
1908–10   (S14)
Marble   H 134.5
Musée d'Art Moderne, Geneva

amassed an extraordinarily distinguished collection, which took in not only the British *avant-garde* — Epstein, Gaudier-Brzeska, Wyndham Lewis and the Vorticists, Augustus and Gwen John — but also the Futurists and the most important young artists then working in Paris — Brancusi, Duchamp-Villon, Picasso, Matisse and Gris.[29] The only comparable collectors of contemporary art then active in the United States were the redoubtable Dr Barnes of Merion, Pennsylvania, and Walter and Louise Arensburg of Baltimore, none of whom was at all interested in British art. Quinn's Epsteins — twenty-six in all — was the most important collection formed during the artist's lifetime (though many larger ones, such as those of E. P. Schinman and Eisenberg-Robbins have been formed since).[30]

Augustus John had first recommended Epstein to Quinn in 1910, when he picked out the sculptor, Wyndham Lewis and his own sister, Gwen John, as young artists whose work deserved backing. Quinn recorded an exceedingly merry evening (3 September 1910) spent at the Café Royal in the company of John, Epstein and his wife, the painter J. D. Innes, and the Irish dramatist, George Moore.[31] Three years were to elapse before Quinn began to buy Epstein's work; his taste was still conservative, centring on the work of Lucien Pissarro, John and Irish artists such as Hone, Shannon, and Yeats. However, on his return to England in autumn 1911, Quinn visited Epstein's Cheyne Walk studio and was impressed by the carving for the *Oscar Wilde Tomb* [Fig. 48] which was then in progress; a few months later he responded to a plea for financial assistance ('advance money for stone bust') with a cheque for £60 towards a sculpture which he assuredly never received.[32] In March 1912, alerted by John to Quinn's potential as a generous patron, open to persuasion, Epstein confided to him his large ambitions: 'I don't want to rest with the Oscar Wilde but go on and do large new things: no work no matter what the scope would appal me, the larger the better; I want to carve mountains.'[33] Quinn responded at once by trying to get him a commission to work on the New York pavilion for the San Francisco World Fair and, when this did not come off, was supportive during the rumpus which attended the installation of the *Tomb*, sending the sculptor £50 to enable him to remain in Paris and battle with the authorities. He was not, however, a soft touch and when Epstein appealed to him the following year for £200 to buy the cottage at Pett Level, where he was working with intense concentration, Quinn refused, suggesting rather that he should send him £100–150 to buy African sculpture for Quinn in Paris.[34] Nothing seems to have come of this offer, which may be symptomatic of Quinn's increasing interest in the Paris art world and which certainly indicates that Epstein's expertise on 'primitive' sculpture was already well known.

Quinn was so busy with his law practice (which funded his collecting fever) that he was rarely able to visit Europe again. In his approach to Epstein over the African sculpture, and in many of his subsequent transactions, he bought at long distance, relying on exhibition catalogues, photographs and the recommendations of artists and

agents whose judgement he trusted. Early in 1913 he purchased his first sculpture — Epstein's bust of *Euphemia Lamb* [14], which he shipped over just in time to include in the famous Armory Show.[35] His motives were sentimental rather than purely aesthetic since he had met Euphemia and another model, Lillian Shelley, subsequently portrayed by Epstein but then in the company of John, during his London visit in 1910; he and John had invited both women to accompany them on a tour of France, though they had not turned up. Nevertheless, Quinn's admiration for them was undiminished, for he later purchased Epstein's first portrait of *Lillian Shelley* as 'a companion piece', writing nostalgically: 'She was a beautiful thing four or five years ago, red lips and hair as black as a Turk's, stunning figure, great sense of humor'.[36] Quinn's robust and somewhat predatory interest in women surfaces more than once in their correspondance. He bought a portrait of the flamboyant *Iris Tree*, another of the Café Royal regulars whom he had met in London and who subsequently visited him in the States, but turned down the modestly decorous bust of *Mrs McEvoy* [15*] with the cool remark, 'I don't like that type of Englishwoman'.[37] In 1916, after he had received photographs of the unfinished *Maternity* [37], he was not slow to recognise the ripe sexuality of a work which he described as 'the woman with big breasts exposed, which might be called "Maternity" or "Paternity" or "Fecundity" or "Whoring" or "A Chinese Goddess". She might be a Kwanin or a madame of a house or the mother of a patriarchal family or a Venus; and anything but a virgin'.[38] Despite the coarse jocularity, his summary aptly captures Epstein's powerful fusion of female mystery, sexuality and maternal protectiveness.

Quinn's interest in the international *avant-garde* had been quickened by the revelation of the Armory Show, where he was both the most important single lender and purchaser; amongst his many acquisitions were two pieces by Raymond Duchamp-Villon (he was eventually to own eighteen). In 1914 he also bought the first of his twenty-seven Brancusis, *Madame Pogany*, 1912, from the one-man show at the Steiglitz Gallery.[39] In the same year, possibly realising that Epstein's latest work represented a trend analogous to that of the Brancusi, he began to buy the British sculptor's carvings, picking items unseen for the most part, and leaning on Augustus John and the American poet, Ezra Pound, for expert advice. The *Doves* [48*] was commissioned in Spring 1914, soon after two pairs of *Doves*, the sculpture now in the Hirshhorn Museum and [46] had been exhibited at the Twenty-One Gallery and the London Group. Pound wrote urging him 'For God's sake, get the two that are stuck together, not the pair in which one is standing up on its legs', to which Epstein testily replied that Pound should mind his own business, and yes, Quinn was getting the 'stuck together' pair.[40] Epstein's irritation is probably explicable; he may already have sold one if not both the earlier pairs, and now began work on a third group, which he described to Quinn as a replica, but which was, in fact, very different from either of the other two, and which he completed late in 1915.[41]

By then Quinn had also almost bought *Rock Drill* [70–72], which was exhibited alongside three other innovatory pieces — *Cursed be the Day Wherein I Was Born*, the exquisite marble *Mother and Child* [Fig. 66] and *Figure in Flenite* [50*] — at the 1915 London Group show. That he had in the end decided not to buy this, the most revolutionary of all Epstein's pre-War works, was entirely due to Augustus John, who wrote to Quinn that it was 'altogether the most hideous thing I've seen. He's turning the handle for all he's worth and under his ribs is the vague shape of a rudimentary child or is it something indigestible he's been eating?'[42] In spite of this Quinn bought all the other London Group pieces, together with three bronzes, for a grand total of £550 in May 1916, by which time he was becoming embroiled in the tortuous campaign designed to keep Epstein out of the army and away from the fate which had already befallen Gaudier-Brzeska and was soon to befall Duchamp-Villon. Pound had been doing his utmost to interest Quinn in Gaudier's work and, hearing that John also considered him 'a man of talent', he embarked on protracted negotiations, eventually acquiring six sculptures and numerous drawings.

As these episodes demonstrate, Quinn was a man of strong loyalties towards those artists whom he chose to back. He continued to correspond with and buy from John, long after his interest in his art had begun to wane. Similarly his loyalty to Epstein survived a series of angry letters and cables from the sculptor and his wife accusing him of unsympathetic interference after he had taken endless trouble to help Epstein stay out of the War. In October 1917 he confided to a friend, 'I am accustomed to ingratitude, large and small, right and left, but I have never had such a case as that of Jacob Epstein!'[43] With supreme irony, this occurred not long after Quinn had purchased the controversial *Venus* [Fig. 68] and the unfinished granite *Mother and Child* [Fig. 59] for £700, and at the very moment when Quinn's article on Epstein's sculpture, illustrated with photographs by Alvin Langdon Coburn, was appearing in *Vanity Fair*.[44] There had been other minor irritations, quickly sorted out, over the number of casts Epstein might take from his work, but all these tempests were weathered successfully, and by the end of 1917 Quinn was buying again — bronzes of *T. E. Hulme* [62] who had been killed in September, and *Muirhead Bone* [113].[45] Their correspondance resumed after Epstein had been invalided out of the army, and by August 1918 the sculptor was writing of his depression at the pusillanimous English art market: 'If I produced Babe's heads to the end of my days I would be thought wonderful, but anything large, grand, and terrible, fit for our times, is timidly shrunk away from in the timid and tepid atmosphere of our art world here . . . There are too few like you in the world. Scarcely one out of a million has insight and courage.'[46]

However, by 1918 Quinn's taste was veering ever more strongly towards Paris under the influence of the purchases he had already made and the works he saw exhibited by a number of dealers in New York. By 1919 he was beginning to discourage Epstein from sending him any more bronzes, a blow to the sculptor since he was working on portraits and on the 'grand and terrible' image of the *Risen Christ* [110]. Quinn's growing disinterest in English art was brought into focus by an exhibition of Canadian and English War Art in New York, of which he wrote to Epstein: 'In fact I don't care too much for English art at all. It is too domestic, too heavy, and it lacks the brilliance and style and chic quality of the best French art'.[47] Effectively Quinn was now collecting sculpture only by Brancusi, Epstein and from the estates of Duchamp-Villon and Gaudier-Brzeska. Although he purchased two final bronzes from Epstein in 1920 on the recommendation of Pound, who confessed he was 'damned hard hit' by three works in the Leicester Galleries show, he had really finished with English art, apart from Gwen John.[48]

In 1922, an exhibition of recent British art, much of it drawn from Quinn's collection, was held at the Sculptors' Gallery, New York. It included twenty-two Epsteins and six Gaudier-Brzeskas, in addition to works by Gwen and Augustus John, J. D. Innes, and Wyndham Lewis. Visiting the exhibition and seeing the work displayed instead of stacked up all over his apartment or in the basement, Quinn was dismayed. As he wrote to his French agent, H. P. Roché, 'My second visit to the Sculptors' Gallery made me rather angry that I had bought so many Epsteins, about ten times too many; so many things by Lewis, twenty times too many; so many things by John, forty times too many.'[49] His preoccupations were now French and amongst sculptors, Brancusi interested him almost to the exclusion of anyone else. In 1923, in order to get the capital to buy more French works, he consigned most of his English pictures for sale, and in 1924 sent twenty-three Epsteins, the entire collection except for *Venus*, *Cursed be the Day* and the granite *Mother and Child* (which was allegedly disposed of with Epstein's permission by dumping into the Hudson River) to Scott and Fowles in New York for sale.[50] He wrote to the dealers, 'I will fix my prices at not only reasonable figures but at figures making losses to me after deducting your commission.' The prices were modest, with many of the bronzes valued at the same price as the carvings: *Doves*, the first portrait of *Euphemia Lamb*, *Iris Tree*, the first portrait of *Meum* and the *Duchess of Hamilton*, shared the top price of $1,000, while the marble *Mother and Child* only rated $500. In fact, Quinn appears to have quailed at the thought of losing all his Epsteins, for within a month he had requested the return of six works, including all the carvings.[51] By this time Quinn was dying of cancer, though he continued collecting to within four months of his death, Rousseau's great *Sleeping Gypsy* being his last triumphant acquisition.

After Quinn's death in July 1924, the entire collection was dispersed; five of the Epsteins (all portraits) entered public collections in the United States and Canada, but the remainder vanished into private collections or remained in the hands of dealers, such as Stevenson Scott.[52] The fact that many of the works sold for less than Quinn had paid Epstein indicated the exceptional character of Quinn's patronage. Though Epstein returned to the United States only three years later for an exhibition of his work at the Ferargil Galleries, and was able to undertake three portrait commissions during that visit, the trip and the show were not financially successful, so that American patrons had to continue coming to London if they sought his work until well after the Second World War.

Soon after Epstein's first one-man show at the Leicester Galleries had opened in 1917, Quinn had written to him in a cautionary vein: 'I still believe in you and your work even though you are apparently well on the way to popularity, which generally ruins most artists.'[53] There must have been many moments during the Twenties when, attacked by the press and acutely short of cash so that he was driven to write solicitous letters to past clients and get advances on future sales from the Leicester Galleries, Epstein thought wryly of these words. The enthusiastic reviews which greeted the bronzes and the controversy which surrounded *Venus* (bought by Quinn) and the *Risen Christ* (refused by Quinn) at the Leicester Galleries shows of 1917, 1920, 1924, certainly attracted some new patrons. Apsley Cherry-Garrard, the Antarctic explorer, purchased *Risen Christ* for £2,000, adding it to Rodin's *The Walking Man* in the music room and, later, the garden of his home at Ayot St Lawrence (where Shaw was his neighbour). In Bradford, William Rothenstein's brother, Charles Rutherston, was forming an outstanding collection of British early twentieth-century art which he presented in 1925 to Manchester City Art Gallery.[54] During the early Twenties he purchased six Epsteins — *Baby asleep* [6], the head of *Cunninghame Graham* [112], portraits of *Kathleen*, *Dolores*, and *Sunita* amongst them — which took their place alongside sculpture by Gaudier-Brzeska, Frank Dobson, Eric Gill, and Henry Moore, whose first patron he was. In 1923 Moore, invited up to stay for a few days, sent an account of the collection to a friend:

He has probably one of the most important collections (outside museums) of ancient Chinese art in England — besides which he has examples of negro, Scythian, Siberian, Archaic Greek and Egyptian art — three or four Epstein busts, about the same number of busts by Dobson and several Eric Gill carvings and most of his woodcuts and an unknown quantity of paintings and drawings by contemporary artists — French and English.[55]

Nevertheless, this did not prevent Epstein from being 'very hard up', as he confessed to Rutherston that very year, explaining that he had already received an advance on the sale to him of *Kathleen* from the Leicester Galleries but, not having had a show there that spring, was finding it hard to contact patrons. Since Rutherston had expressed an interest in another piece, would he perhaps like to buy it now?[56]

Though Quinn had no real successor, there were forms of patronage other than money. In the immediate aftermath of the Great War and throughout the Twenties no patron did more for Epstein than his old friend, Muirhead Bone who, though a conservative artist himself, had a ready sympathy for work quite different from his own and who was a consistent supporter of two mavericks — Epstein and Stanley Spencer. He owned at least one bronze before 1914, and sat for his own portrait [113] in 1916, shortly before being appointed the first war artist.[57] In spite of being overworked and in considerable danger as he drew indefatiguably on battlefronts at home and abroad throughout 1917, he did not lose touch with Epstein's abortive efforts to join the war artists. At the end of 1918 he presented £2,000 to set up a fund for the acquisition of works of art for the Imperial War Museum — works to be chosen by himself. He purchased several of Epstein's most distinguished wartime portraits — *The Tin Hat* [74] and *Admiral Lord Fisher* — and even tried to commission a relief, akin to those already requested from Jagger and others for the projected Hall of Remembrance, depicting the Moeuvres incident at which Sargeant Hunter of the Highland Light Infantry had won his VC. An ill-timed article in the *Dundee Advertiser*, suggesting that the commission came from the Imperial War Museum itself, led to a hasty denial, and the whole project was dropped, though Bone still got from Epstein a portrait bust of Hunter, which is one of his most grimly impressive works.[58]

A few years later it was Bone who arranged for Epstein to undertake one of his most memorable portraits, of *Joseph Conrad* [93*], during an interval in his work on the *Hudson Memorial* [Figs 80–81*]. Bone was a prominent member of the memorial committee and the extensive minutes and letters which survive, enabling us to trace the progress of this tortuous commission, leave no doubt that Bone, strongly supported by the Chairman, Cunninghame Graham (who had known Hudson well), was the guiding spirit of the entire project. Not only did he press for Epstein to receive the original commission for Hudson's portrait, but once that scheme was turned down, it was he who continued to support Epstein's involvement, patiently resisting his colleagues' timidity. He took the initiative in getting Rima as the theme, a theme chosen explicitly because 'I am as anxious as ever to get something really strikingly imaginative and beautiful from Epstein'.

When Epstein's design was finally accepted in February 1924, Bone produced the bird's-eye-view artist's impression of the *Memorial* and its surroundings [Fig. 82], which was published to raise money for the scheme. When, after the unveiling, there were demands that it should be removed from the Park, it was Bone who masterminded the letters in its defence to *The Times* (23 November 1925) and got his brother, James Bone, London editor of the *Manchester Guardian*, to publish an editorial defending it. Finally, he ensured its survival with a well-argued memorandum to the Office of Works, proving that they had been fully consulted and that the Memorial Committee's conduct had been entirely correct.

The intelligent support of men like Bone and Charles Holden was the more valuable to Epstein because in such large projects the execution of sculpture, Epstein's only consideration, was always essentially secondary to the management of the whole scheme, the political, administrative, and financial aspects of which were all foreign to the artist, who wanted only to be left alone (and paid) to get on with the job without interference.

In such circumstances Holden and Bone played a vital diplomatic role in persuading the official patron, whether individual or group, that the sculptor could and should be entrusted with a commission; thus Bone advised and suggested to the Hudson Committee, Holden persuaded Frank Pick, against his original decision, that Epstein should be employed on 55 Broadway, and in the Fifties, the architects Louis Osman and Basil Spence cajoled and implored *their* patrons to employ Epstein at Cavendish Square [Fig. 93] and Coventry Cathedral [Fig. 96] respectively.

Between 1929 and 1950 there were no patrons for Epstein's services as an architectural sculptor and virtually none for the large carvings and bronzes, most of which, by virtue of their subjects and the naturally tectonic character of Epstein's sculpture, were implicitly designed to function best in large architectural settings. Of *Consummatum Est* [Fig. 9] Epstein wrote, 'I even imagine the setting for the finished figure, a dim crypt, with a subdued light on the semi-translucent alabaster', although he had little hope of its ever being placed 'in a cathedral or basilica'.[59] On the one hand, this was the tragedy of Epstein's career, for his monumental carvings and bronzes have rarely been placed in appropriate settings. *Visitation* at least was purchased by the Tate Gallery, and the contemporary *Madonna and Child* [Fig. 74], bought by Epstein's admirer, the American sculptor, Sally Ryan (who also acquired *Sun God* [Fig. 57] and *Primeval Gods* [Fig. 86]) has gone to the Church of Riverside Drive, New York, though it is placed where few notice it. Other works, including *Genesis* [134*], *Adam* [Fig. 88], and *Jacob and the Angel* [143*], were for some years part of a sideshow at Louis Toussaud's in Blackpool. Shortly before his death, Epstein was unable even to give away the totemic *Behold the Man* [Fig. 6] to Selby Abbey, where the Rector wanted it but others objected.[60] Yet, on the other hand, Epstein also demonstrated that he could and would resist the need for patronage; by using the income from his portraits and watercolours, he demonstrated repeatedly throughout the Thirties that he need not depend upon a patron for the most ambitious carving projects; deeply personal, dramatic works like *Behold the Man*, *Adam* and *Jacob and the Angel* followed only the dictates of his own creative need. At the end of his life he even found a patron to share one of his visions, when the historian, A. H. Smith, Warden of New College suggested, during a portrait sitting, that the carving, *Lazarus* [Fig. 10], which he had been contemplating in the studio, would adorn the cloisters of the college. It was eventually placed in New College Chapel where it was, wrote Epstein, 'miraculous . . . that the sculpture should harmonise so completely with the ancient stone walls. The lofty soaring arches seemed to continue the upward thrust of my figure'. How often, he concluded, does a sculptor find 'the ideal setting for his work?'[61]

Even with portraiture, where the success of the work is heavily dependent upon the rapport between sculptor and subject, Epstein was able to a considerable extent to dictate his own terms by choosing so many of his models — children, beggars, prostitutes, adventurers, ordinary men and women — whose features were their only distinction. *Old Pinager* [92] and the *Girl from Senegal* [87] are typical of such works, egalitarian and humane themes in which subject and technique are perfectly united. It was perhaps for these qualities of communication, beyond any narrow aesthetic, that Epstein portraits achieved their broad popularity, being bought by galleries and individuals all over the country.[62] The complex humanity of the sitters, miraculously brought to life by the sculptor, exerted a peculiar fascination, not least on writers. When bronzes belonging to John Gibbins, deceased proprietor of the Ruskin Galleries, Birmingham, were auctioned at Sotheby's in 1932, press interest in this, the first sale of Epstein's work on the open market, was considerable, and it was noted that Hugh Walpole and Mrs J. B. Priestley each purchased two works. Walpole told the *Daily Mail* reporter, 'I've coveted the head of Dolores for a long time and I was determined to get it.' Asked why he admired Epstein's work, he replied that the 'poetry and character expressed in these heads must appeal to a novelist'.[63] Both Walpole and Priestley sat for portraits within the next five years, neither very successful; Walpole, at least, seems to have allowed his awareness of 'poetry and character' to lead him into self-dramatisation, which as Epstein observed, was disastrous:

> He insisted in sitting to me like a Pharoah, with head held high and chin stuck out. In reality, Sir Hugh is the most genial of men, with sparkling twinkling humour in his eye, and his mouth wreathed in a kindly and genial smile. But with the rigidity of [his] pose I could do nothing . . . it was Sir Hugh Walpole in the role of Benito Mussolini.[64]

Priestley was no better, but through cynicism rather than pretending to be what he was not; he looked upon the work as an insurance policy; 'If you get forgotten, there is your bust of *me*. If I am forgotten, there is *your* bust of me.'[65] Clearly some patrons were designed to be collectors, while others, like the composer, Ernest Bloch, and the philosopher, Bertrand Russell 'whose fawn-like head I had long wanted to portray', were cut out to be sitters rather than collectors.[66]

The see-saw balance between producer and consumer is necessarily fraught with innumerable complicating factors; in Epstein's case they varied from dealers, the press, and the income tax, to the allure of a Gabon head, or the behaviour and demeanour of a sitter or model. Despite working in an expensive medium and being unusually dependent upon models for the bronzes which make up the bulk of his output, Epstein retained an astonishing degree of independence. As a boy in New York, he had been proud that while many of his fellow students had to earn money at the 'hateful work' of enlarging and hand-colouring photographs, he 'could always sell [his] drawings'.[67] When he did not, as Hutchins Hapgood reported in his account of the young Epstein's garret studio in New York, he would go 'to bed' until something turned up.[68]

THE PASSIONATE COLLECTOR

Ezio Bassani and Malcolm McLeod

Epstein was an eager and passionate collector; acquiring and possessing sculpture from other cultures was a central activity for much of his life. When he died in 1959 he had a collection of about one thousand items drawn from a wide range of cultures and from many periods.[1] It was an incomparably rich collection, containing some of the greatest, most famous and widely illustrated works of African and Pacific sculpture ever to reach Europe. It is possible that no other British home ever held so many masterpieces of 'primitive' art [Figs 4–5].[2] After his death, about a third of this astonishing collection, previously seen only by friends, was exhibited by the Arts Council.[3] The whole was then dispersed by private sale and at auction.[4] Works from it are now among the most prized possessions of many of the world's great museums and private collections.[5]

The collection was essential to Epstein's life and it filled many parts of his house, dominating the rooms where it was displayed. While the best pieces were given a little space to themselves, placed at intervals on mantle shelves or on the tops of cupboards and chests of drawers, lesser works were literally heaped together on the floor or crammed into cabinets, as is evident in the photographic record made just before his death.[6] It gives an overwhelming impression of rich clutter, of African, Ancient Egyptian, Pacific, and American figures, masks, vessels, textiles, jewellery and weapons mixed together with only one or two of the sculptor's own pieces carefully and unobtrusively placed in their midst. Epstein's bedroom, for example, contained nine of the greatest Fang sculptures from Gabon (one previously owned by André Derain),[7] what is almost certainly the most famous carving from Madagascar (first illustrated by Carl Einstein in 1915),[8] very fine Dogon wood sculpture, a major Maori standing figure,[9] Maori feather boxes with elaborately carved surface decoration, Egyptian, Classical and pre-Columbian pieces, woven raffia cloth from the Bakuba of Zaire, pre-Cycladic items and a standing figure from Mesopotamia [VI]. The room contains, as far as one can estimate from the photographs, about seventy items. In another room, at the base of a unique double figure from Lake Sentani, New Guinea, now one of the great treasures of the Australian National Museum,[10] lies, in a jumble of other pieces, a Fijian Kava bowl, full of African ivory bracelets, with a bark-cloth beater and what seems to be a Pacific weapon edged with shark's teeth.

The way the collection was displayed provides clues to its importance to Epstein. It was not only a source of delight and contentment for him but also a repertory of sculptural forms, of solutions to the problem of representing the human figure or head. Arnold Haskell, who saw the collection in 1930, emphasised that it 'had none of the deadness of the Museum [because] the works had not lost their individuality' and he recounts Epstein's pleasure in showing the collection.[11] Works were displayed — and, we believe, acquired — because of their formal qualities and for no other reason. There was no concern to display them by tribal origin, or to acquire material to give a comprehensive coverage of particular tribal groupings or styles.

Epstein, while he was proud of his large collection and the many famous and superb pieces it contained, seems to have allowed only close friends to see it, perhaps because he was scorned for collecting the products of 'savages' and accused of plagiarising such 'crude and primitive' sculptures in his own works.[12] The American art historian, Robert Goldwater, recorded that Epstein would fetch out a few pieces at a time to examine with friends,[13] and William Fagg, later the keeper of Ethnography in the British Museum, has emphasised this aspect of Epstein's pleasure, the close and delighted scrutiny of a few pieces from the collection, when he would 'spend hours in silent contemplation or animated discussion of them, considering always the sculptural problems with which the artist confronted himself, or was confronted by tradition, and the solutions which he had found for them'.[14]

The composition of the collection provides some indication of what and why Epstein collected. Out of the thousand pieces left on his death, over four hundred came from the cultures of sub-Saharan Africa, about two hundred from the islands of the Pacific and a hundred and thirty from pre-Columbian Central and South America; ninety-five items originated in Ancient Egypt, forty-five in Archaic and Classical Greece and Rome, while the remainder came from North America, India, China, Indonesia and Medieval Europe. These crude numbers cannot, of course, indicate the importance and aesthetic worth of the pieces from each area nor how Epstein regarded them. Many of the African pieces, for example, were undeniably minor: ivory armlets, brass anklets, stools, a wooden milk pot, a mortar. And, while the majority were works of sculpture, Epstein also collected other sorts of items which pleased or interested him: pottery or stone vessels, weapons, textiles, items of personal adornment and so forth.

It cannot be over-emphasised that this was one of the greatest, perhaps the greatest, private collections of 'primitive art' ever formed. Epstein was able to recognise masterpieces and was ruthless in pursuing and acquiring them. He also had contacts, especially in Paris, the centre of the

I
SEATED HERMAPHRODITE, Dogon, Mali
Wood H 69
Carlo Monzino (not exhibited; formerly Jacob Epstein collection)

trade in primitive art, which gave him many opportunities for acquisition. It is impossible to list all the major pieces in the collection in the space available here. The African section was undoubtedly the strongest, the heart of it being the five heads and eleven reliquary figures from the Fang of Gabon. At least ten of these pieces must be included among the greatest works of African sculpture known. Lady Epstein recalled that a damaged Fang figure, cut off at the waist, was his first acquisition and if so, this was probably the truncated figure still in the collection at his death.[15] Most of these Fang pieces must have been acquired through Paris where, as Gabon was a French colony, such sculpture was more readily available than in England. It is probably also through this French Colonial connection that Epstein acquired his great pieces from the Dogon of Mali [I].[16] Also of exceptional importance were a Dan mask [III],[17] the double funerary sculpture from Madagascar [Fig. 4],[18] a Tabwa (Zaire) figure [II],[19] a Bakongo head (illustrated first in 1915),[20] a pair of female figures with children on their backs from the Idoma of Nigeria [XIV],[21] a figure of a woman and child from Cameroun [Fig. 5] and a double ivory bell and striker from Benin, now in the Nigerian national collections.[22] The Oceanic collections contained fewer masterpieces but, among these, were two wooden double figures from the Marquesas [V], a Grade Society figure from Vanuatu,[23] the unique double figure from Lake Sentani, New Guinea [Fig. 5], and a human figure in wood from Easter Island.[24] From Central India came the superb stone standing figure of a woman [IX] and a Gandhara Buddha.[25]

Everything indicates Epstein acquired most items in his collection for their aesthetic qualities and because they were of direct relevance to his own preoccupations as a sculptor. The pieces provided evidence for the existence of virile and successful traditions different from those which had held sway in Europe since Classical times or the Renaissance, showed the possibilities of the non-naturalistic representation of the human form and demonstrated the virtues of direct carving. At the same time, we believe, they served to comfort and reassure Epstein when he was under attack from critics of his own sculpture: the size and quality of his collection showed how discriminating was his own taste and how sharp his own perception, and served to prove to him that the naturalistic aesthetic had no overriding claim to superiority.

Not everything in the collection was a masterpiece; Epstein acquired second rate and even fake pieces but, as he explained to his friend and fellow collector, the painter Joseph Herman, such works could still suggest ideas and solutions to him.[26] It is this underlying concern with sculptural form which explains the overwhelming preponderance of African and Oceanic works. Not only were such carvings newly available in considerable numbers, and comparatively inexpensive, in the first half of this century, but they stood as splendid evidence of a great diversity of sculptural traditions which, until then, had been unknown and were perhaps otherwise inconceivable to Europeans.

Fig 4

View of Epstein's bedroom, 18 Hyde Park Gate, London, *c* 1959

1   SEATED FEMALE FIGURE, Fang, Gabon (*BML*261), C. Monzino (formerly G. de Miré)

2   RELIQUARY HEAD ('THE GREAT BIERI'), Fang, Gabon (257), Metropolitan Museum of Art, New York (formerly P. Guillaume)

3   HEAD AND TORSO, Baulé, Ivory Coast (62), C. Monzino

4   RELIQUARY HEAD (BIERI), Fang, Gabon (256), C. Monzino (formerly J. Brummer)

5   RELIQUARY HEAD (BIERI), Fang, Gabon (254), C. Monzino (formerly C. Ratton)

6   STANDING FEMALE FIGURE, Dogon, Mali (2), formerly T. Tzara

7   STANDING MALE FIGURE, Fang, Gabon (268)

8   RELIQUARY HEAD (BIERI), Fang, Gabon (253), C. Monzino

9   STANDING FEMALE FIGURE, Fang, Gabon (259), Metropolitan Museum of Art, New York (formerly André Derain)

10   TOP OF MORTUARY POST, Madagascar (349), C. Monzino (formerly E. Brummer)

11   STANDING MALE FIGURE, Fang, Gabon (260), C. Monzino (formerly G. de Miré)

12   STANDING WOMAN WITH CHILD, Dogon, Mali (3), C. Monzino

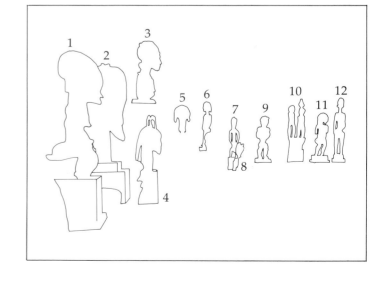

Fig 5

View of an upstairs room, 18 Hyde Park Gate, London, c 1959

1 STANDING FEMALE FIGURE SUCKLING CHILD, Grasslands, Cameroun (BML247), R. Withofs
2 HELMET MASK IN FORM OF BIRD, Grasslands, Cameroun (250), C. Monzino
3 FOOD BOWL, Solomon Islands (461)
4 SEATED WOMAN WITH CHILD, Idoma, Nigeria (230), P. Goldman
5 DANCE MASK (NIMBA), Baga, Guiné (13), C. Monzino
6 STANDING FEMALE FIGURE, Bambara, Mali (4), C. Monzino (formerly Sadler)
7 STANDING MALE AND FEMALE FIGURES, Lake Sentani, Papua New Guinea (420), Australian National Gallery, Canberra (formerly P. Loeb)

As with all great collectors, there seems to have been an element of compulsion in Epstein's collecting. He gloried in his acquisitions, perhaps even exaggerating his determination and sagacity in finding and getting certain of these works, or over-praising their qualities at the expense of better known similar pieces. Sometimes, friends have recounted, he would buy without really having sufficient cash available to pay for them or to meet his other needs. Richard Buckle records that he was loaned money by the American oil magnate, Hiram Halle (who also sat for his portrait in 1934), after spending an unusually large amount on buying sculpture.[27] The money was paid back only after the sculptor's death. Epstein admitted that he had mortgaged his future earnings for a long time to buy the Lake Sentani figures [Fig. 5].[28]

The exact date when Epstein began to acquire non-Western art is still not known but it may well have been in the first decade of the century. Certainly, in later years, he was eager to establish that his interest began very early, at the same time, or even earlier, than that of other artists like Picasso, Derain and Matisse, and well before collecting 'negro art' became an affair of opportunistic dealers and collectors eager to follow the current fashion. Unfortunately, no evidence except that given or suggested by Epstein himself has been found to show exactly when and how he acquired his first pieces, and this small evidence is not as consistent as one would like. Thus, in talking with Haskell in 1930, Epstein dated the start of his collecting to about twenty-five years previously and emphasised he had 'discovered' African art at about the same time as Picasso and Derain.[29] However, Buckle, writing three decades later, suggested an even earlier date, 1902, following a visit to the Trocadéro, and also implied that Picasso made his discovery of African art at a later date, by which time Epstein had already left Paris.[30] The sculptor's autobiography seems to indicate that it was only in 1912 that he became aware of 'the vast and wonderful collections from Polynesia and Africa' in the British Museum.[31] Early in that year, C. J. Holmes, Director of the National Portrait Gallery, wrote of Epstein's 'Neo-Papuan enthusiasm'[32] and it was also in 1912, while in Paris, that he first encountered Paul Guillaume, soon to become one of the most influential dealers in both 'primitive' and modern art. In 1913, the distinguished American collector, John Quinn, was asking Epstein to purchase such pieces for him[33] and certainly by 1914 it was fairly well known that he was interested in African carvings and 'South Sea idols' [2]. By the early Twenties Epstein's collection was already considerable. Henry Moore stated that when he got to know him about this time, his bedroom (a favourite place for hoarding treasures, some of the most precious pieces were said to have been kept under the bed) was already overflowing with negro sculptures.[34] By 1930, the collection then contained some two hundred 'statues, masks and ivories'.[35]

In England Epstein was exceptional in collecting primitive art. There existed very large public holdings: the British Museum, the Pitt Rivers Museum at Oxford, and the University Museum of Archaeology and Ethnology at Cambridge, among others, and a few pieces were beginning to appear in the homes of the more advanced private collectors by 1914, but no English contemporary of Epstein seems to have been so voracious or well informed, or to have started so early in the century. In the Twenties Michael Sadler, Vice Chancellor of Leeds Univeristy, began to form his own collection and later, of course, Robert and Lisa Sainsbury acquired superb African and Pacific material as well as examples of ancient and modern art.[36] In France, the link between modern art and 'art nègre' was far stronger and established far earlier, and it was from Paris that Epstein acquired many of his most important pieces. That city was the first in which dealers in African and Pacific carvings and masks became firmly established, some of them successfully combining that activity with selling contemporary painting and sculpture. British dealers in 'Ethnographica', such as Beasley and Oldman, were well established in England in the 1890s, and issued illustrated catalogues, and exotic sculptures were also sold in junk and curio shops and at miscellaneous auctions; but it was in Paris, in the second decade of the century, that dealing in primitive art became an activity which was central to the wider trade in *avant garde* art.

Visiting Paris in 1912, Epstein recalled, he had seen an advertisement seeking African carvings in a colonial paper.[37] It had been inserted by the dealer Paul Guillaume, whom Epstein now met. Guillaume had a gallery on Rue Miromesnil, which intersected Rue de la Boétie, a centre of modern art dealing. Later, he moved to the more prosperous Faubourg St Honoré (where he sold both primitive art and works by Derain, Picasso, Vlaminck, de Chirico and Braque).[38] The two men remained in contact for long after 1912; several of Epstein's most prized pieces passed first through the dealer's hands, and he noted Epstein's importance in spreading interest in African art in London.[39] Guillaume also sold material to many other important collectors, including Dr Barnes of Philadelphia where, in 1927, Epstein saw African pieces formerly owned by the French dealer.[40]

Another Paris dealer who was beginning to be important and who also handled pieces that eventually entered Epstein's collection, was the Hungarian Joseph Brummer. Brummer had begun dealing from a shed on the Rue Falguière, made money and, with his brother Ernest, opened a gallery on the Boulevard Raspail. In 1913 Joseph may have loaned material to an exhibition in Prague, where paintings by Picasso, Braque and Derain, from the dealer Kahnweiler, were exhibited with those carvings: the first such exhibition to associate modern and negro art.[41] Brummer seems to have been the sponsor and main source of illustrations for Carl Einstein's enormously influential *Negerplastik* of 1915, the first publication devoted entirely to African art. Epstein, who must have known the book well and may even have used it as a sort of shopping list, was later to own several pieces illustrated there.

Although it was still possible to buy excellent African sculpture for a few pounds until the Fifties, by the Twenties some of the prices asked by

French dealers were already reaching extraordinary heights. In 1923, Ernest Brummer had insured for 50,000 francs each a funerary post from Madagascar [Fig. 4] and a bust from the Bakongo people, which he loaned to an exhibition; both were subsequently owned by Epstein.[42] In 1925, Guillaume had asked 40,000 francs for a Fang head of the sort Epstein subsequently owned; this sum would then have bought a decent house in Paris. Values varied, however; Hessel, then the owner of an important double figure carving from the Marquesas [Fig. V], which was in Epstein's ownership by 1931, perhaps earlier, valued it only at 10,000 francs in 1923.

Documentary evidence from the Thirties shows Paris as the source of a number of Epstein's best primitive pieces. Two of these, a Bakongo nail fetish[43] and the Marquesas double figure, were sold at auction at the Hotel Drouot in December 1930. Epstein also acquired an excellent Fang figure,[44] which was in the sale of the collection of André Breton and Paul Eluard in 1931.[45] In December of that year, George de Miré's collection (which Epstein called 'undoubtedly the finest collection of African art outside a museum')[46] was sold. From this came four of his most important acquisitions: a large Fang male figure [Fig. 4],[47] the seated Fang female figure,[48] a superb Dan mask [III][49] and a great Dogon figure [I].[50] Some of these works first passed through the hands of the Paris dealers, Louis Carré and Charles Ratton. It must be stressed that a number of the examples Epstein was acquiring about this time were already famous in collecting circles and were soon to become more widely known. The catalogue written by the collector J. J. Sweeney for the great 1935 exhibition of *African Negro Art* at the Museum of Modern Art in New York, depicted several Epstein pieces: the de Miré Dogon figure and Fang female figure mentioned above (then owned by Carré and Ratton respectively) and the Bakongo bust, owned by Brummer.[51] In another 1935 publication, Carl Kjersmeier's influential *Centres de style de la sculpture nègre africaine*, the Fang male bust from de Miré is illustrated as now belonging to Epstein.[52] Here, too, he is given as the owner of the famous 'Black Venus' Fang figure, formerly in the possession of Carré and now in the Metropolitan Museum, New York [Fig. 4], and the outstanding Fang head, formerly owned by the Brummer brothers [IV].[53] Epstein was exceptionally proud of having acquired this masterpiece and said he had first seen it in Brummer's shop in 1913, and then rediscovered it by chance in a dealer's in 1935 when 'all Paris was seeking it'.[54] It seems that it was also about this time that he acquired from Guillaume another Fang piece, now known as 'the great Bieri', which is very probably the most frequently illustrated of all African sculptures [Fig. 4].[55] Another major acquisition of this period was the double figure, recovered by 1929 from Lake Sentani in New Guinea, which was owned by Pierre Loeb before Epstein got it.[56]

Epstein's acquisitions in England, probably because they were mainly of less famous pieces, are not so well documented. Between 1914 and his death there are only a handful of records which show that he made purchases at the

London auctions. From time to time, he bought considerable numbers of things at a single sale, then his name vanishes from the lists of auction purchasers for several years. There may be several reasons for this paucity: he could have left bids under another name, had dealers bid for him or generally been content eventually to buy from the dealers who made the successful bids. Thus, at Sotheby's in April 1930, he paid just over £300 for eighteen lots, some of which he kept until his death.[57] At other times he acquired items that had been through the auction rooms but it is unclear how long afterwards they came to him. Thus, a pre-Columbian cast gold rattle, probably Mixtec, from the collection of William Randolph Hearst,

II
STANDING MALE FIGURE, Tabwa, Zaire
Wood H 62
Carlo Monzino (not exhibited; formerly Jacob Epstein collection)

III
MASK, DAN, IVORY COAST
Wood, fibre H 26.5
Private collection (not exhibited; formerly Jacob Epstein collection)

was sold by Sotheby's in 1939. It was bought for £39 by 'Martineau' and subsequently entered Epstein's collection.[58]

Most of the acquisitions he made in London must have come from dealers, and a few may have been got by exchanges with fellow collectors. The late John Keggie, a London dealer, recalled that when Epstein became depressed in the Forties his wife, Peggy, would telephone and ask him to take round interesting pieces. John Hewett, a well-known dealer, recalls selling Epstein the great Tabwa figure [II].[59] He obtained a major North-west Coast sculpture from the collector Hooper[60] and, according to Hewett, the sculptor acquired over seventy per cent of his Maori jade *tikis* [XI] and several Cycladic figures from the dealers and collectors, Webster and Armitage. He seems also to have obtained small items from the shop owned by the jeweller Hakym, off Bond Street and, after the Second World War, from Gallerie Apollinaire off the Charing Cross Road.[61]

Epstein was both proud of and defensive about his collection. He was at pains to emphasise that he, and other artists, were the first to 'discover' African art when previously it had been regarded only as of anthropological interest: 'Of course, it was the artists who first saw the sculptural qualities of African work and they were followed by the dealers who saw money in it'. He stressed also that in this field the eye of the artist was of crucial importance, for the collector had to rely upon himself: 'each work must be taken on its merits. There can be none of the magic of the artist's name . . . The work is either good or bad'.[62] However, once African art began to become popular he despised those who dealt or collected for reasons of fashion. When Duveen asked him to loan to a New York exhibition he found the 'idea of Lord Duveen taking an interest in an Art so alien . . . ludicrous, and just another example of the facile and unthought-out opinions of the opportunists of Art'.[63]

He also tended to emphasise his own perspicacity in collecting, claiming, as we have seen, to have discovered and secured the Brummer Fang head 'much to the chagrin of the Paris dealers'.[64] He was particularly attached to an Egyptian stucco head of Nefertiti (now thought to be a fake), which he found in an English collection, where all but he had overlooked its importance. He believed this to have been the model for the famous head in Berlin and by examining photographs of the Berlin version decided his was superior: 'It is one of the most wonderful works in the world'.[65]

Some of Epstein's recorded remarks about pieces in his collection are perceptive, others simply wrong. He was sure that primitive art was not something separate from the concerns of other traditions: 'It is governed by the same considerations that govern all sculpture',[66] and he was among the first to note that the best specimens of African art were not the products of carvers working blindly and uncreatively within a rigid tradition but the work of 'highly individualised artists'.[67] His pronouncements on the reasons for the forms of particular masks and carvings, however, are less accurate. He seems to have

believed that many of these were 'fetishes', used in emotionally charged rituals to 'impress, terrify and impart to the beholders a state of mind bordering on, or actually, hallucinatory'.[68] It was this function that governed form: 'the directness and simplification are a result of this: the necessity of producing a feeling of awe and fear'.[69] Since there was little accurate information about the beliefs and ideas of tribal societies at the time he wrote, Epstein's conviction that so many of these pieces had a profound religious significance probably suggests as much about his attitude to his own work as it does to his collection. He may have been incorrect about the indigenous use of some of the pieces in his vast collection; he may have misconceived the motives of their makers: it is of little importance. He collected so he could experience directly sculptures from other traditions. What ever is eventually decided about his own stature as a sculptor, there is absolutely no doubt that his passion and sensitivity made him, in his chosen field, one of the world's greatest collectors.

IV

RELIQUARY HEAD (BIERI), Fang, Gabon
Wood   H 63
Carlo Monzino (not exhibited; formerly Jacob Epstein collection)

V

TWO STANDING FIGURES (TIKI), Marquesas Islands, Polynesia
Wood   H 155.5
Carlo Monzino (not exhibited; formerly Jacob Epstein collection)

IMAGE FROM STONE: EPSTEIN AS CARVER

Richard Cork

At the stone-yard I see a tremendous block of marble about to be sliced up and used for interior decoration. When I see these great monoliths lying ready for the butcher's hands, as it were, I instantly have sentimental feelings of pity that the fate of a noble block of stone should be so ignominious. Knowing that this stone could contain a wonderful statue moves me to purchase it and rescue it, even though at the moment I have no definite idea for it. Never mind — that will come.[1]

When Epstein died in August 1959 Henry Moore wrote a generous tribute to his friend and described him as 'a great sculptor'.[2] Moore had good reason to feel grateful to Epstein, who gave the younger man much-needed support and patronage at an early stage in his career. They shared at that time an obsession with the theme of maternity, an omnivorous enthusiasm for the sculpture produced by cultures far outside the classical and Renaissance tradition, and a passionate belief in the importance of 'carving direct', cutting from the stone or marble an image that honoured the intrinsic identity of the original block. Moore's early carvings owe a considerable debt to the example set by Epstein, most notably in works like the flenite figures [50* and Fig. 69] which showed how much primal dignity could be invested in subjects of enduring importance to Moore himself. In his obituary appreciation, however, he did not mention these innovative carvings at all. Far from emphasising how important Epstein's pioneering implementation of 'truth to material' had been, Moore declared that 'he was a modeller, rather than a carver', and then drove the point home by asserting: 'Of the sculptor's media, his was surely clay.'

Elsewhere in this tribute, Moore provided a great many sensitive and understanding insights into the nature of Epstein's work. He was surely right to describe that triumph of the modeller's art, the *Madonna and Child* in Cavendish Square [Fig. 93], as one of Epstein's 'best and last works'; and he was especially acute in arguing that Epstein, 'an intensely warm man', created a body of work which 'transmitted that warmth, that vitality, that feeling for human beings immediately'. But Moore was wrong to ignore Epstein's achievement as a carver, and to claim that the 'warmth' was responsible for producing 'his greatest work, which I believe to have been his portraits'.[3] However substantial Epstein's merits as a portraitist may have been, the heads he modelled during the last forty years of his life

should not be allowed to overshadow the carvings he continued to execute throughout his career. Although few in number compared with the plethora of portraits, they constitute on their own an impressive *œuvre* which in many ways represents Epstein at his most ambitious, consistent and profound. It is a pity that he became known primarily as a portraitist, and that the same reputation endures today.[4]

Some critics, blinded by this aspect of his fame, have claimed that the success of the portraits led to a deterioration in Epstein's work as a whole. But they ignore the fact that he did continue to produce large-scale figure carvings whenever an appropriate public commission arose, refusing to be disheartened by the vilification which often attended their unveiling. Indeed, he expended an enormous amount of thought and energy on other massive carvings as well, stubbornly working on them with little hope of adequate remuneration or a sympathetic reception. Subsidised by his work as a portraitist and painter of landscapes and flowers, these carvings emerge from the most personal and obsessive side of Epstein's imagination. The largest of them, *Behold the Man* [Fig. 6], occupied him over an extended period and never found a purchaser during his lifetime. Several others were sold to a showman who treated them as sensational and even pornographic oddities in a Blackpool sideshow; while *Adam* [Fig. 88], into which Epstein thought he had 'merged'[5] himself more than any other sculpture, was installed for a while in a peep-show by a New York promoter. Their humiliating fate poignantly contrasts with the acclaim enjoyed by the portraits, and Epstein must have felt that he was doomed never to be respected for the work which ultimately embodied his most impassioned and aspiring impulses.

The time to make amends for this injustice, and stop seeing Epstein primarily as a portrait modeller whose carvings occupy a secondary place in his art, is therefore long overdue. Epstein the carver deserves to be honoured in his own right, as the maker of consistently 'heroic works' which, as he pointed out, were produced 'from time to time in my studio without commissions and with little or no encouragement from official bodies'.[6] The urge to carve occupied a central place in his vision as a sculptor, and from the outset it was bound up with the sense of release Epstein discovered in tough, manual exertion among surroundings which emphasised the most epic and untamed aspects of the world. It is surely significant that he first became convinced of the desire to shape three-dimensional form when, as a youth, he escaped from 'the teeming East Side where I was born', whose streets 'were the most densely populated of any city on earth'.[7] He was stimulated by the close-packed, boisterous vitality of the Hester Street neighbourhood, where the constant press and surge of humanity prompted him to draw from a very early age. However attached he felt to the 'moving mass' observable from the 'wooden, ramshackle building'[8] which afforded him a mesmerising daily view of market life, it was a claustrophobic activity. 'I had been drawing and reading to excess, sometimes in dim light, and my eyes had suffered from the strain', he remembered, describing how his first attempts at sculpture 'gave me relief'.[9]

The relief was associated above all with 'a delight in outdoors' engendered by a Whitmanesque expedition Epstein undertook one winter with his artist friend, Bernard Gussow. The adventure remained vivid in his mind for the rest of his life, and decades later he recalled how they had 'hired a small cabin on the shores of Greenwood Lake, in the State of New Jersey. In this mountain country I spent a winter doing little but tramping through snow-clad forests, cutting firewood, cooking meals and reading. To earn a little money we both helped to cut ice on the lake.' It was, perhaps, Epstein's first experience of carving into natural substances of outsize dimensions, and his work at the lake must have encouraged him to regard the act of cutting as a large-scale endeavour. He afterwards described the fortnight's labour on the ice as 'very hard but congenial work', explaining that it was 'a physical life full of exhilaration and interest'.[10] The consequences were profound, for after returning from this winter at Greenwood Lake he decided to become a sculptor.

Epstein would always see the challenge of carving as an activity as demanding, vigorous and close to nature as the ice-cutting had once been. But he seems to have found his student years disappointingly constrained and frustrating in comparison with the lakeside venture. In New York his studies concentrated on work in a bronze casting foundry, and a modelling class in the evenings under the paternal eye of George Grey Barnard. Epstein 'longed to see the originals of Michelangelo and Donatello',[11] but America could provide him with little experience of the sculpture he valued most. Paris did, and he relished the opportunity provided by the Louvre to become familiar with 'early Greek work, Cyclades Sculpture, the bust known as the Lady of Elche, and the limestone bust of Akhenaton'.[12] He also remembered enjoying 'a mass of primitive sculpture none too well assembled'[13] at the Trocadéro, although it is doubtful whether the work displayed there had any direct effect on Epstein's carvings at this early stage in his career.

The academic instruction he received at the Ecole des Beaux Arts laid more emphasis on modelling from life and drawing Michelangelo casts. 'In carving there was practically no instruction,' he recalled, 'and we were left alone to do pretty well what we pleased.'[14] His subsequent period at Julian's also seems to have stressed the importance of working in clay from the model. A visit to Rodin's studio, arranged with the help of Frederick Cayley Robinson, would have confirmed the pre-eminence of modelling when Epstein encountered the prodigious energy of the bronzes on show there. The dynamism and spiritual intensity of Rodin, whose 'quiet, confident manner' Epstein contrasted 'with the *cabotin* pose of other artists of great reputation I met later',[15] left a permanent mark on his early work. With Rodin, he realised, 'modelling became interesting and individual for its own sake',[16] and the outspoken urgency of the Frenchman's bronzes impressed itself on Epstein's mind. But he did manage to see one significant carving in Rodin's studio, 'the large Victor Hugo in marble, still unfinished'.[17] Although he afterwards decided that the *Balzac* was the finest of Rodin's public sculptures, Epstein would have been predisposed to admire the exclamatory Hugo monument. Indeed, the only works from the Paris period he regretted destroying were projects on a monumental scale — a 'group of "sunworshippers"' and the 'Temple of Love'.[18] Since they were 'heroic-sized', and one of them bore 'a remarkable resemblance' to 'early Egyptian figures', it may be that they were carved out of stone.

A brief visit to Florence, where Epstein would surely have admired Michelangelo's *Captive* figures struggling to emerge from the mass of marble which still partially contains them, did not inspire a further period of carving. His first years in London were marked by hesitation and destruction rather than positive achievement, and the small marble relief of a *Mother and Child* [8] executed during this difficult period is an awkward and tentative exercise. The mother's stance, straining as she lifts her wriggling infant, does, however, reveal Epstein's determination to explore surprising and expressive poses based on close observation of life itself.

A similar resolve lay behind his eagerness to work from posed models when he commenced the British Medical Association commission in 1907. But the outcome reveals just as much indebtedness to classical, Renaissance and Rodinesque precedents as it does to empirical scrutiny of the naked bodies he employed to pose for him.[19] Moreover, these statues were initially modelled in clay, and so in conception at least they cannot be counted as works which reveal how Epstein would have approached a straightforward carving venture. Photographs of the plaster casts standing in their niches in his Cheyne Walk studio [Fig. 36] prove that the figures were, essentially, complete before their translation into stone began. There was little chance of permitting the final character of the statues to be influenced by the stone itself. Besides, Charles Holden gave the commission to Epstein not on the strength of his existing carvings, but because the sculptor was working on 'a delicate and sensitive figure of a young girl holding in her hand a dove — it was in black wax, life-size or slightly over, and was approaching completion' [9].[20] The 'small model'[21] which Epstein prepared for the BMA Council was likewise made from either wax or clay, and he later admitted that the carving of the final statues had largely been carried out by a firm of architectural carvers. The execution of eighteen over-life-size figures in little more than a year necessitated such extensive technical assistance that Epstein 'had only "touched them up" in the stone'.[22]

Nevertheless, it is still significant that the carving was carried out, not in the studio, but on scaffolding attached to the building itself. For Epstein shared Holden's conviction that sculpture should be integrated as firmly as possible with the structure of the building, and not resemble an afterthought. Indeed, he went further than his architect in ensuring that the Portland stone for each statue be cemented into position as an undivided block. 'I in my inexperience yielded to Epstein's desire to work the figures in one single stone each', Holden recalled, 'although my own original intention was to build up the blocks in two or three stones, which would have offered greater resistance to the weather.'[23] Even at this early stage in his career Epstein was fired by the notion of tackling monolithic stone lumps and, as Michelangelo had done with the *Captive* figures, liberating the statues from their boulder-like confines. The existence of the fully-worked-out plasters [11] meant that he could not take his cue from the blocks in a very substantial way, but one of the BMA figures contains an eloquent pointer towards Epstein's future *modus operandi*. The second statue in the sequence, *Matter* [Fig. 7], deals with the theme of birth and protection by placing in the hands of a bearded patriarch a conspicuously rugged fragment of stone. Cut into the face of this primal substance, which Epstein described as 'a mass of rock',[24] is the embryonic form of a child. This tender image bears witness to the sculptor's fascination with the seemingly miraculous feat involved in generating a living body from the rough stone. The broken, uneven quality of the 'rock' has been preserved, so that Epstein can dramatise the extraordinary metamorphosis which his chisel enables it to undergo. 'Form and life emerge from the inchoate and lifeless', he wrote of *Matter* in 1908,[25] and the very title of the statue reveals his preoccupation with the wonder of shaping human forms out of inert material.

Epstein never lost that fundamental sense of wonder, and after the completion of the BMA scheme he set about exploring how to make the relationship between untouched stone and carved image a central issue in his sculpture. While he deployed a delicate form of attenuated naturalism in modelled figures like the now-destroyed *Narcissus* [Fig. 43], his carvings became more robust and asserted the geometrical primacy of the original block. The second version of *Rom* [34], a portrait of Augustus John's small son, is among the most uncompromising declarations of this growing interest in rectangular grandeur. Although the child's face could hardly be more chubby, with a roundness accentuated by the enclosing helmet of hair, he grows out of a stone cube which may well represent the dimensions of the stone before Epstein started work. If this is the case, *Rom* can be seen as an almost programmatic declaration of the connection between the completed image and the raw material from which the sculpture was fashioned. The two elements, held in a balance, enjoy a symbiotic relationship which Epstein would examine in a multitude of resourceful ways over the next six years.

During that period carving became far more important than modelling, most obviously in a visionary plan for a vast sculptural temple set in six acres of the Sussex countryside. Eric Gill, who collaborated with Epstein on the venture, emphasised its megalithic character by describing it in the autumn of 1910 as 'a great scheme of doing some colossal figures together (as a contribution to the world), a sort of twentieth-century Stonehenge'.[26] Since Epstein had previously executed some 'temple' sculpture of his own, and had been inspired by epic outdoor locations ever since his formative trip to Greenwood Lake, he was probably responsible for the initial conception of this ambitious idea. Financial obstacles frustrated it, but several carvings can be associated with the scheme. *Rom* [34] is among them, for C. Lewis Hind reported that it was intended as 'one of the flanking figures of a group apotheosising Man and Woman, around a central shrine, that the sculptor destines in his dreams for a great temple'.[27]

Another carving which might well be linked with the 'Stonehenge' venture is the *Crouching Sun Goddess* [35*], a figure that announces Epstein's renewed enthusiasm for the Egyptian inspiration behind his earlier 'temple' sculpture. The form of the block, announced in the plinth, is retained throughout this remarkable image. Unlike *Rom*, where the base's rectangularity gives way to a rotund head, the *Sun Goddess*'s entire body is governed by the shape of the oblong stone beneath her feet. As our eyes travel round her, we become acutely aware of the block's straightness still obliging her back, sides and front to conform to its cubic identity. Although modest in size, *Sun Goddess* is sufficiently powerful to suggest a figure 'colossal' enough for the temple plan outlined by Gill. Indeed, Epstein would himself use this little carving as the starting-point for his massive *Elemental* [138*] two decades later; and despite its scale, it is more monumental in its implications than the far larger *Sun God* relief [Fig. 57], which can also be related to the Sussex temple project. Epstein continued to deepen the relief of this brazenly naked figure long after he commenced it,[28] but in 1910 the *Sun God* must have been shallow enough to look as if he was growing out of the enormous expanse of Hoptonwood stone. He is as dependent on this vast backdrop as the sun goddess appears to be on the plinth below her. The umbilical link between figure and ground is most spectacularly dramatised in the great mane of Egyptian hair, which flows back from the god's imperious face until its tendrils merge with the stone behind.

When Epstein was photographed with his *Maternity* in 1910 [Fig. 62], her hair likewise appeared to be growing out of the roughly-hewn mass of stone. Although he subsequently refined the back of her head until it achieved an unusual degree of smoothness [40], large expanses of this major carving were left incomplete. Since he exhibited it as *Maternity* (*Unfinished*) two years later,[29] Epstein presumably liked the figure in this

Fig 6
BEHOLD THE MAN (ECCE HOMO)
1934–35   (S246)
Subiaco stone   H 300 (studio photograph)
Coventry Cathedral

state. Its large areas of broken chisel-marks gave onlookers a startingly raw idea of the passionate physical engagement which informed Epstein's cutting of the stone. He never explained why *Maternity* was abandoned: an ambiguously defined garment on the right of the pigtail, and the oddly dislocated thumb on the left hand, suggest that he encountered difficulties which proved impossible to resolve. But looking at this figure today, with its eloquent evidence of Epstein's struggle so honestly exposed, we suspect that he was right to leave it unfinished. The principle of 'carving direct', which gave early modernist sculpture so much of its power and vitality, is implemented here with formidable conviction. Epstein's cutting is supple enough to master the delicacy of the skin-fold above her right breast as well as the vigorously handled sweep of the robe beneath her buttocks. The whole figure is a testament to the wide range of expressive possibilities opened up by Epstein's pioneering audacity.

If *Maternity* was intended originally for the Sussex temple, and perhaps even regarded as the figure of *Woman* positioned in 'the central shrine',[30] she could hardly have provided a more brazen celebration of fecundity. Compared with the *Maternity* completed two years earlier for the BMA building [Fig. 39], which calmly adhered to the European tradition, this new carving unequivocally rejects the Western norm. Instead, it embraces alternatives culled from Indian and African sources, and most of the viewers who scrutinised *Maternity* at the Albert Hall in 1912 were still quite unprepared for Epstein's disturbing new interpretation of womanhood. They would have been shocked above all by the seemingly wanton flaunting of her sexuality. Scandalised attention doubtless centred on the erect nipples thrusting out from her globular breasts, and the ripe pair of buttocks curving so provocatively above the low-slung drapery behind. Never before had a British sculptor dared to present such an inescapably voluptuous image of fertility. Although this serene mother lowers her Asian eyes to contemplate the roundness of her stomach, she exudes the intensely physical allure which brought about her impregnation. However oblivious she may be to everything except the foetus burgeoning within, her body offers itself like a delectable fruit while loose strands of garment slide round her breasts, curve over her shoulders and course down the white smoothness of her back. Even the heavy plait descending from her helmet-like head in a sequence of plump folds is eminently graspable, and far more swollen than its predecessors falling from the hair of the old woman in the BMA's *New-Born* [Fig. 38]. No wonder that Gill incorporated a smaller yet similar plait in his 1911 'statue of the Virgin' carved for Roger Fry's garden, where she stretched her hands behind her and 'appreciated' the view.[31]

But *Maternity* is not just a celebration of the ardent feelings Epstein harboured for nubile women in their procreative prime. Although Gill was scarcely exaggerating when he wrote in his diary that Epstein was 'quite mad about sex',[32] this carving also possesses a considerable amount of tenderness and dignified restraint. The feet peeping out so modestly from the strange arch-like opening at the base of her robe indicate that she is standing in a very formal, upright position. No distracting curves are allowed to disrupt the sober sequence of vertical folds in the drapery enclosing her legs. They signify the more chaste side of the figure, and seem determined to give the lower half of the mother a privacy she so conspicuously lacks above her waist. But the robe's flatness and strong upright direction are also the outcome of Epstein's desire to honour the identity of the block he had carved. When seen from the sides in particular, the statue discloses Epstein's urge to retain the form of the tall Hoptonwood stone slab which had confronted him at the outset.

The desire reaches its apogee in *The Tomb of Oscar Wilde* [Fig. 46], by far the largest and most lengthily considered carving Epstein ever produced. Indeed, he might have been inspired to settle on the memorial's final form when confronted by the titanic stone chosen for the purpose.[33] His previous modelled study for the tomb, probably the elongated and decidedly *fin-de-siècle* figure of *Narcissus* [Fig. 43] gazing in tremulous admiration at his own reflection, no longer satisfied Epstein's wish for a resounding statement carved according to his new-found respect for his material. 'I went to Derbyshire to the Hopton Wood stone quarries', he remembered, 'where I saw an immense block which had just been quarried preparatory to cutting it up into thin slabs for wall-facings.' Epstein could not bear to contemplate the desecration awaiting this noble form, and so he acted with speed to save it from such a humiliating fate. 'I bought this monolith, weighing twenty tons, on the spot, and had it transported to my London studio', he explained, describing how 'I began the work immediately and without hesitation continued to labour at it for nine months.'[34]

Charles Holden, who prepared drawings for the plinth, recognised that the *Tomb* presented a 'most unusual problem demanding an unusual solution'.[35] For Epstein had created a 'flying demon-angel'[36] floating entirely free of its plinth, emerging from the side of the block. He had arrived at this ingenious hovering position by applying the same principle that had recently informed his *Sun God* relief [Fig. 57]. For the angel grows out of his ground in a similarly organic manner, and the streamlined Assyrian sweep of his wings remains wholly faithful to the flank of the stone itself. The extended horizontal rush of these majestic wings gives the figure beneath a sense of irresistible momentum, reinforced in the parallel thrust administered by his own outflung arm. The wings seem to describe 'lines of force' in space as well, evoking an energised motion which the Futurists would surely have savoured.

The spectacular simplification of the wings could hardly be further removed from the concentrated richness of the figures signifying *Intellectual Pride, Luxury* and *Fame* on the angel's headdress. Ezra Pound considered such details to be 'over-ornate',[37] and it is certainly true that their dense concentration of decorative detail seems wasted on a position so high above the viewer's head. But the contrast between this relatively small area of elaboration and the bareness of the angel's principal masses, is finely judged. To walk round the *Tomb* is to be made aware of the stark planar austerity displayed by its other surfaces. A large part of this awesome carving relies on the potency of unadorned slabs, and in June 1912 two remarkably percipient reviewers seized on the *Tomb*'s fidelity to the Derbyshire 'monolith' which had so enthralled Epstein at the quarry.

After surveying the newly-completed carving in the sculptor's studio, the *Pall Mall Gazette*'s (6 June 1912) critic declared that

> imitation of Nature, either in bronze or marble, becomes mere futility and ape-work unless it be illuminated by a plastic idea, not only closely associated with and deriving all its beauty from the medium in which it is worked, but suggested by it. As the painter's idea lies, not in literary suggestion or imitation, but in the perfection of the paint, so the carver's idea must be born in the marble and spring directly from it.

In its emphasis on truth to materials, primal emotion and direct manual cutting, the writer's response was so close to Epstein's thinking that it must have been influenced by the explanation which the sculptor had offered in his studio. But the *Tomb* itself seems to have immediately impressed its maker's priorities on those who examined it at 72 Cheyne Walk that summer. 'The first thing that strikes one is Mr. Epstein's regard for his material and its purpose', declared the *Evening Standard*'s (3 June 1912) reviewer.

> From the earliest ages it has been the almost universal instinct of humanity to set up a stone over the dead, but modern sculptors are too apt to forget that every touch of the chisel, though justified by the craving for expression, is a destruction of the monumental character of the stone. Mr. Epstein has not forgotten this, and his work, though an expression of human emotion, recognises the rectangular solidity implied in the idea of a tomb. It is not executed but conceived in stone.

The notion that the Hoptonwood block had almost engendered the inevitability of this image impressed itself very forcibly on the reviewer's mind. He concluded by stressing that the figure's

> muscular divisions are suggested by linear treatment rather than by aggressive modelling, and a vertical plane would enclose the carved surface of the monument. Thus there is nothing to destroy the effect of a rectangular block of stone that has felt itself into expression.

No phrase could more vividly describe the sense of profound animism in Epstein's carvings of the period, the feeling that the material he employed was responsible for decreeing the form assumed by the final sculpture. Far from exhausting himself over the Wilde tomb, Epstein was emboldened by its achievement. In March 1912 he was still exhilarated enough to tell his patron John Quinn that 'I want to carve mountains.'[38] Having rejected a modelled figure in favour of a stone alternative at an early stage in the tomb project, he now devoted all his best energies to carving alone.

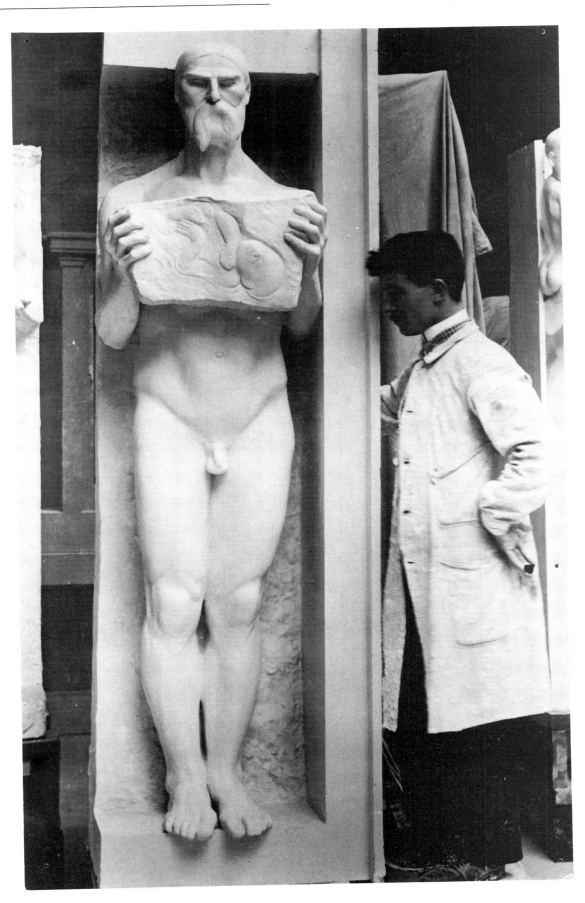

Fig 7
MATTER   British Medical Association Building, 1907–08   (S9:2)
Plaster   H 210–15 (studio photograph)
Destroyed

The friendships Epstein made in Paris, where he stayed in the latter half of 1912 and at various times the following year, encouraged him to approach the stone in an even more radical manner than before. Modigliani, like him a Jewish artist far from home, proved especially congenial, and Epstein seems to have forged a relationship almost as close as he had previously achieved with Gill. The two men saw each other 'for a period of six months daily', and tried to find a 'shed' they could share on the Butte Montmartre. The idea, according to Epstein, was to 'work together in the open air' — always a desideratum after his experience at Greenwood Lake. He may even have been tempted to revive the notion of a grand collaborative venture, for the mesmerising sight of the work gathered in Modigliani's 'miserable hole' of a studio reminded him of his old obsession with an architectural ensemble. 'It was then filled with nine or ten of those long heads which were suggested by African masks, and one figure' [Fig. 64], Epstein recalled. 'They were carved in stone; at night he would place candles on the top of each one and the effect was that of a primitive temple.'[39]

Modigliani was a man after his own heart, even if the extreme elongation of these masks would never have recommended itself to Epstein in his attempt to find a similarly pared-down formal vocabulary. The closest he ever approached to Modigliani's attenuated *Heads*, one of which came to London after Epstein had been instrumental in encouraging a British collector to purchase it,[40] was *Sunflower* [36*]. The almond eyes are incised in the San Stefano stone with an elegant economy worthy of Modigliani, and Epstein resists the temptation to add any more facial features other than the nose. Compared with the head of the *Sun God* relief, which must always have possessed eyebrows, mouth and prominent chin even in its original, shallow-cut state, *Sunflower*'s face is sparing indeed. But its circular head, squat nose and sturdy neck are far removed from Modigliani's characteristic attenuation. Robust form was of prime importance to Epstein when he carved: his feeling for slimmer and more bony limbs found its principal outlet in modelled sculpture. So rather than following Modigliani's example in a slavish way, he remained faithful to his own predilections when making *Sunflower*. Moreover, Modigliani would never have wanted to produce anything as aggressive as the double row of zigzag hair segments exploding from the head of this hallucinatory sculpture. Reminiscent of the dogtooth carvings which embellish the arches of so many Romanesque churches in Britain, they appear positively menacing after the mellifluous linear rhythm of the tendrils flowing from the head of the *Sun God* relief.

Contact with Brancusi and his work likewise impressed Epstein during his French sojourn, but the Rumanian's influence only surfaced after he returned to England. 'This period in Paris was in itself, from the point of view of working, arid', he explained afterwards, blaming his exasperation on practical difficulties and neighbours complaining about his incessant hammering. But the encounter with Brancusi may have had an inhibiting effect, for his intense singlemindedness hel-

ped to convince Epstein that a ruthless degree of simplification was now necessary. The chance to examine *The Kiss* in Montparnasse Cemetery [Fig. 8] probably led Epstein to reflect that his own tomb sculpture seemed over-elaborate in comparison. Nothing, after all, could be more purged of sculptural superfluities than Brancusi's embracing lovers. The block of stone seems scarcely interrupted by the eyes, lips, arms, hair and breasts chiselled so delicately into its surface. This extreme purification of form, which succeeded at the same time in retaining a remarkable amount of sensuous tenderness, soon bore fruit in Epstein's carving. He realised that the last vestiges of his earlier enthusiasm for Michelangelo must be jettisoned, leaving behind only the absolute essentials permitted by the stone itself. Decades later Epstein still remembered how Brancusi 'would pluck at the back of his hand and pinch the flesh, "Michelangelo", he would say, "beef steak!"'[41]

Only after leaving the orbit of this immensely persuasive and dedicated man did Epstein manage to divest his sculpture of the last vestiges of superfluous flesh. Impressed by the 'saintly' commitment to work shown by Brancusi, who 'would exclaim against café life and say that one lost one's force there',[42] he decided to settle in a remote location where his carving could be carried out with a similar amount of devotion. It was a welljudged move. Freed from the constant distractions of metropolitan life, Epstein was able to settle into 'a solitary place called Pett Level, where I could look out to sea and carve away to my heart's content without troubling a soul'.[43] This secluded Sussex coastal village, exposed to the stimulating immensity of the English Channel, was perhaps the most rural location Epstein had inhabited since his time on the shores of Greenwood Lake. The cottage he rented was a small one, and he worked in a shed in the back garden.[44] But the surroundings inspired him to think in terms of grander and more elemental forms than he had ever imagined before.

Even the smallest of his Pett Level carvings have a largeness of spirit which transcends their true dimensions. In a little *Birth* carving [55], unfinished enough to suggest that it was one of the first and most tentative of the images he produced there, Epstein is at pains to stress the inviolate, cubic presence of the stone. It appears to play as prominent a part in the genesis of the child as the mother's legs and vagina, parting to allow the new-born baby to emerge from the womb. Although the same moment is re-enacted on one side of the related *Flenite relief* [57], the infant this time holds an ovoid form in his hands. The frankness and gravity with which he displays this germinating egg of creation before him recalls the BMA *Matter* statue; but the 'inchoate and lifeless' lump of stone held by the patriarch in the earlier carving is now transformed into an eloquent, living force. The dark flenite is still indisputably a primal slab, with which Epstein has interfered as little as Brancusi did when he carved the Montparnasse tomb sculpture. Nevertheless, it has been transformed by the most minimal means into the body of a woman. The other side of the relief [56] bears her inverted torso and head, topped by forearms which cross each other with a diagonal neatness reminiscent of the arms in Brancusi's *The Kiss*. Her arms also encompass the erect phallic columns installed like virile sentinels on the edges of the block, for Epstein was always eager to incorporate reminders of the part played by the male member in the procreative mystery.

Just how mysterious he wanted the fructifying process to appear in his flenite pieces can be discovered by examining the two pregnant women he also carved from this dark green serpentine. The very word 'flenite', Epstein's own nickname, evoked not only the hardness of granite but the prehistoric associations of flint. And both these women inhabit a primeval world as surely as the archaistic mother and baby in the *Flenite relief*. The larger of the two, *Figure in Flenite* [50*] adopts a defensive attitude to the life swelling inside her stomach. She cranes her Polynesian face forwards in an apprehensive way, but the sheer block-like solidity of her dress counteracts some at least of the anxiety she transmits. Epstein honoured the integrity of his flenite in order to convey sturdy resilience as well as awesome primeval trepidation. *Figure in Flenite* seems unshakeable as she asserts a stony strength in the face of whatever dangers may confront her.

When Epstein revealed the legs of a similar woman in *Female Figure in Flenite* [Fig. 69], her limbs turned out to be indomitably stocky. Viewed from the side, the figure's upper half sways back from her legs in an extraordinarily dramatic arc. It culminates in the great head hanging with solicitous solemnity over her pregnant belly, but the legs need to be strong in order to support this astonishing curve as it extends from the base of the spine round to her bulbous brow. In Paris, Brancusi had counselled Epstein against imitating the 'primitive' carvings they both admired, and *Female Figure in Flenite* avoids that danger by fusing its Polynesian inspiration with a wholly personal response to a woman's body. This mother, for all her prehistoric 'barbarity', is absorbed in a poignant concern for the baby growing in her stomach. One angry critic accused the flenite figures of 'rude savagery, flouting respectable tradition — vague memories of dark ages as distant from modern feeling as the lives of the Martians'.[45] But Epstein evokes these 'dark ages' only in order to recover atavistic truths about motherhood, birth and sexuality which 'modern feeling' was in danger of forgetting. By showing the *Female Figure in Flenite* bestowing such loving concentration on the bulge in her belly, he wanted to remind his viewers that fertility was a miracle lying at the very core of human existence.

All the figures in his carvings of this period share the same sense of unfathomable strangeness. In the exquisite marble *Mother and Child* [Fig. 66], facial features are minimally defined so that Epstein can explore the full contrast between the baby's convex rotundity and the woman's concave elongation. And as if to emphasise the enigma of existence, the face of the first marble *Venus* [Fig. 67] remains impenetrably blank. She keeps her secret, and affirms complete serenity even though she maintains a precarious poise on the sloping back of the dove beneath her feet. This amply built *Venus*, with her dangling African breasts and heavy buttocks, seems to be encouraging the doves in their copulation below. She would, in reality, crush them with her colossal weight, but Epstein proposes a dream-like correspondence between birds and woman which allows them to coexist in an eerily calm union. He may, however, have been dissatisfied with the elements of ungainliness in this carving. Seen in profile, the *Venus* does appear to be sliding awkwardly down towards the male dove's head, and the bend in her legs seems a painful posture for her to adopt.

That, surely, is why he then set to work on a second version of the statue [Fig. 68], twice as tall and far more satisfactorily integrated with the birds below. Displaying smaller and more compact breasts, a less drooping face and an expanse of falling hair more sensuous than its bunched counterpart in the first version, this cool personification of fertility is able to lean against the cock's comb for support. Her legs part as if in pleasurable appreciation of this meeting, and the dove in turn raises his tail to register his delight at such beguiling contact with the slender goddess. He is far more satisfactorily integrated with his partner than the doves in the first *Venus*, where Epstein produced a pair of birds whose disjointed forms suggest that he had not yet learned how to amalgamate their bodies as well as Brancusi had done in *Three Penguins*.[46] Working on the final and more unified pair of *Doves* [48*] for Quinn helped him to resolve these difficulties, and the experience he gained there paid dividends in the tightly-knit design of the doves below the second *Venus*.

Despite its commanding height, which suggests a very public statement on Epstein's part, this refined and self-assured carving retains a potent sense of privacy. He seems to have developed an unusual feeling of intimacy with the *Venus* as he carved her in the quiet isolation of Pett Level. When it finally went on view in February 1917, the sculptor confessed to a friend that 'few will see what I've expressed or aimed to express in it; and if they did they would be unholily shocked. What sacrilege to present to public view that work which I for a long summer privately and almost in secrecy worked at for my own pleasure'.[47] Epstein was more than a little in love with his chaste yet quietly seductive *Venus*, which should be seen as the culminating image in the prodigious sequence of Pett Level carvings. At once virginal and voluptuous, this subtly ambiguous creature extends her pale body upwards in a column which, from front and back, exudes a phallic rigidity. But as well as reaffirming Epstein's obsession with sexual potency, this 'beautiful tower of white marble'[48] represents the crowning manifestation of his youthful desire to remain faithful to the tall block which initially confronted him in his garden studio by the sea. As if to retain a reminder of the original marble, Epstein deliberately left it broken and unfinished at the base of the statue. But he hardly needed to: its form is everywhere apparent in a carving which pays tribute to the governing inspiration of the stone at every turn.

With hindsight, we can see that the second *Venus* marks a turning-point in Epstein's carving

Fig 8
Constantin Brancusi (1876–1957)
MONUMENT TO TANIA RACHEVSKAIA (THE KISS) Montparnasse Cemetery, Paris, 1909–10
Stone H89.5

career. It takes simplification to such a pitch of distilled quiescence that he must have realised he could push it no further. Nothing more, in his opinion, ought to be shed in the search for extreme purity of form. He mistrusted the whole notion that the more artists proceeded towards an abstract ideal, the better their work became. Epstein was an instinctive rather than a programmatic sculptor, and he had reserved the right to model in more figurative ways even at the height of his pre-war innovation. 'My own essays into abstract art have always been natural and not forced', he told Quinn in 1917. 'I make no formula, and only when I see something to be done in abstract form that better conveys my meaning than natural form then I use it. There is a solidity in natural forms though that will always attract a sculptor, and great work can be done on a natural basis.'[49] If it is true that Epstein ordered the dumping of his vast granite *Mother and Child* [Fig. 59] in the Hudson, after the carving had mistakenly been sent to Quinn, then the episode may reflect a certain ambivalence on his part towards the stylistic extremism it embodied. Judging by a photograph of the work taken at an early stage, this massive work was an impressive summation of the ideas previously explored in the three flenite pieces. The child is related to his predecessor on the *Flenite relief*, and the rest of the roughly prepared carving promises to respect the material identity of the whole block in the most monumental manner imaginable. Epstein certainly stressed its role as an assertion of materiality when he exhibited it in 1917, for the title in the catalogue commenced with the words *Carving in Granite*, and only then added 'Mother and Child.' *Unfinished*. Perhaps he left it incomplete because of his waning interest in the smoothed-out finality of the *Doves* and *Venus* carvings. He undoubtedly disapproved of Quinn's zealous enthusiasm for *avant-garde* art, telling him with robust directness that 'I think you are inclined to overrate what you call advanced work; not all advanced work is good, some of it is damn damn bad.'[50]

It certainly did not satisfy Epstein's changing perceptions now that a world war had begun. After all, he charged the fearfully amputated final version of *Rock Drill* [70–72] with his most tragic feelings about the slaughter in France. Epstein abominated war so fiercely that he equated enlistment with creative extinction. It was a traumatic period for him, and in 1920 his haggard *Self-Portrait with Beard* still implied that he had not fully recovered his old composure after the 'complete breakdown' suffered two years before.[51] The broken, pitted surface and agitated handling of this furrowed bronze head testify to a spiritual turbulence that could not be expressed in terms of carving at all.

Six years elapsed between the completion of the second *Venus* and Epstein's next carved sculpture, and even then the outcome was a pair of *Marble Arms*, 1923,[52] so dutiful in their anatomical propriety that they excluded too much of Epstein' individual vision as an artist. Only in the *Memorial to W. H. Hudson* [Figs 80–81*], commenced in the same year, did he recover his earlier fire as a carver, and even here the most apparent source of inspiration was a Greek carv-

ing far removed from the African and Oceanic work which lay behind his pre-war figures. The debt to *The Ludovisi Throne*,[53] which Epstein later acknowledged, constituted a significant return to the classical tradition. It showed that he shared the widespread renewal of interest in Greek and Roman art felt by many erstwhile innovators during the Twenties. But the importance of *The Ludovisi Throne* should not be exaggerated. Epstein's final carving has a wild harshness and insistent angularity which depart considerably from the Hellenic Aphrodite and her attendants. A superb sketchbook [117] filled with exceptionally exalted studies for the panel show how the theme of Rima and the birds stimulated his inventiveness. In style and composition alike, some of these vigorously brushed drawings look back to the *Rock Drill* period, as if he felt impelled to review the formal possibilities discovered during those heady pre-war years. Well over a decade had passed since Epstein had last received a public commission, and he gave it as much intensity of concentration as the *Wilde Tomb* had once attracted.

The sublime rapport between the dryad Rima and the South American forest was bound to awaken, in Epstein's mind, memories of his own response to the environment at Greenwood Lake. As if to recapture the mood of that expedition to the New Jersey countryside, he decided to work 'in Epping Forest, in a shed, on the direct carving of the panel from a block of Portland Stone'. Here, for seven months, he laboured 'through the winter, solitary, surrounded by silent and often fog-laden forest'.[54] This lonely, hermit-like dedication, so different from the London portraiture sessions when Epstein depended on his interaction with the sitters who frequented the studio, enabled him to recapture the mood he had cherished at Pett Level. Looking back on that Sussex period later, he regretted his departure from a place he associated with happiness and fruitful work: 'were it not for the war and the impossibility of living in the country and making a living, I would have stayed there forever'.[55] The sojourn in Epping Forest must have been an attempt to find surroundings as congenial as Pett Level, and the Rima panel does indeed possess the spirit of personal fervency which had marked the second *Venus* carving. Just as the *Venus* enjoyed an almost mystical relationship with her doves, so the nature-spirit heroine of Hudson's *Green Mansions* delights in her intimacy with the birds of the forest.

In every other respect, though, she differs from her marble predecessor. Where the *Venus* was static, reserved and contained within a severe columnar structure, Rima flings her arms out at either side and lets her hair fly in corrugated waves through the air. Her body, for all its distortions, is more naturalistic in conception than the schematic *Venus*, and the yearning glance she casts towards the sky is wholly at variance with the blank placidity of the Pett Level goddess. Moreover, the impassioned Rima wants the denizens of the forest to come far closer than the *Venus* would ever have desired. She kept the copulating doves firmly beneath her feet, whereas this ecstatic wood nymph revels in her proximity to the birds who brush their feathers against her forearm, nestle in her abandoned tresses or playfully stretch their expectant beaks towards her torso and outflung fingers. Rima's harmony with her winged attendants is even more complete than the sensuous rapport between pigeon and boy explored by Frank Dobson in a small carving a few years before, or the gentle affection between boy and rabbit celebrated by Gaudier in 1914.[56] Both she and the birds are caught up in a feverish communion with each other and the forest around them.

The *horror vacui* in this closely packed composition, filled with the press of limbs, feathers and hair, was offset by the calm planar austerity of the surrounding block. Designed by Charles Holden's firm, it continued the dialogue between monumental figure carving and bare architectural masses which he and Epstein had previously conducted at the BMA building and the *Wilde Tomb*. Emboldened by the success of the *Hudson Memorial*, and not at all cowed by the savage hostility it provoked, Holden now proceeded to present his old ally with the finest and most prominent sites allotted for carvings on the new head offices of the London Underground Electric Railways. Although the preliminary model for the building proves that Holden conceived it devoid of significant sculptural decoration,[57] the two sites above the entrances to the Underground Station proved felicitous for Epstein. While Moore, Gill and four other sculptors were given remote positions high up on the building, he was able to place *Day* and *Night* [Fig. 84] in throne-like settings which suit both carvings admirably. Epstein's looming groups chime well with Holden's gaunt architecture [127]. 'However much people may dislike *Day* and *Night*,' the sculptor said soon after their completion, 'no one can deny that they form very definitely part of the mass of the building. I would have done something entirely different had I intended them for exhibition in a gallery or museum.'[58]

The severity of the carvings' structure bears out Epstein's claim. Over twenty years separate them from the first architectural statues he made for Holden, and *Night* and *Day* reveal a far more audacious willingness to strip the human figure of everything other than the broadest masses. Surviving photographs of the BMA carvings [Figs 38–39] disclose a surprising amount of detail, especially in the plaits adorning the old woman in *New-Born* and the elaborate musculature of the male nudes at the corner of the building. But for the Underground Railways project, Epstein dispensed with everything other than the most essential lines and volumes. By this time, Holden was as much of an advocate of direct carving as Epstein himself, and the architect ensured that none of the sculptors working on the building prepared himself for the task by executing full-scale models of his contribution. Although a small bronze study for *Night* does exist [131], it is a *Pietà* group which Epstein had already been planning and differs in many respects from the final work. In 1907 Holden had presided over the careful modelling and casting in plaster of all Epstein's BMA figures. Now, by contrast, he explained to the *Manchester Guardian* (3 August 1929) that

it was a condition that the figures were to be carved direct in the stone without the use of the pointer or any mechanical means of reproduction from a preliminary clay or plaster model, the objection to this being that the resulting sculpture is not as a rule the work of the artist's own hand, that it is usually dull and lifeless as a result of its translation from one medium for which the model is suitable to another medium for which it is unsuitable. It was preferred to preserve all the virility and adventure brought into play with every cut of the chisel, even at the expense of some accuracy of form.

Epstein further attempted to instil a sense of 'adventure' in his carvings, as well as ensuring their compatibility with the building, by executing them on site. If he was unable to escape to Pett Level or Epping Forest, he could at least instal himself on scaffolding at Westminster and hammer away for six months 'through the entire bitter winter . . . of 1928, working out of doors and in a draught of wind that whistled on one side down the narrow canyon of the street'.[59] It was a heroic feat of endurance for a man approaching fifty, and the carvings themselves have a similar heroism. *Day*, with a child standing in front of a parent, develops an idea first explored by Epstein when he produced the granite *Mother and Child* [Fig. 59] during the war. But the woman has now become a father who presents his son to the world and simultaneously encloses him with a powerful pair

Fig 9
Epstein in the studio with CONSUMMATUM EST (*S275*) and an unidentified sculpture in the first stage of preparation, around 21 October 1937.

of hands. A range of sources, encompassing Mexican, Assyrian and Egyptian precedents, does not prevent this group from proclaiming Epstein's very individual vision. At once beneficent and sinister, it is as ambiguous in meaning as *Night* on the other side of the building. There, in a group more deeply cut to compensate for the lack of direct sunlight,[60] a mother lays her 'child-man' to rest under the shadow of a massive arm. The inevitable associations with a *Pietà* give this limp figure a suggestion of death, and in both groups Epstein's persistent involvement with atavistic emotion lends an almost sacrificial *frisson* to the parent-child relationship. They haunt the imagination precisely because of this richness of meaning, half protective and half menacing. But Epstein, to his credit, does not allow these layers of primal symbolism to impair the formal grandeur displayed by both carvings. 'I wanted to keep a simple bulk and let nothing distract the big lines of the design', he explained,[61] and the tenacity with which he adhered to this aim allowed him to produce here the most satisfying and powerful of his architectural sculpture.

The extraordinary fusion of influences as disparate as the Mongolian and the Michelangelesque is so complete, in *Night*, that we cannot finally tell where one ends and the other begins. They are all subsumed in Epstein's singular vision, for he was now a fully mature artist able to impose his own personality on a project as demanding as the Underground Railways façade. But the success of this venture did not mean that he always managed to reconcile the different strains of inspiration feeding his complex and omnivorous awareness of sculptural achievements from so many cultures of the past. In *Genesis* [134*–135], on which he worked 'with no hesitations, and with no preliminary studies', the very clarity of his preconceptions led to a flawed outcome. 'I attacked the stone with my aim very clearly defined in my mind, and with a sympathetic material',[62] he remembered, and this ease of execution made him rather too complacent about the sculpture. Behind most of Epstein's finest carvings lies a considerable period of gestation, during which he pondered the task ahead with drawings or maquettes and a great deal of searching in the untouched block to ascertain how best to free the image latent within it. The rapid completion of *Genesis* seems to have contributed to its failings, for there is an unresolved clash between the heavily African treatment of the head and the far more naturalistic approach to the rest of this swollen body. Epstein's passion for acquiring 'primitive' carvings reached its height around this time, and his immense collection was especially remarkable for its holdings of West African sculpture. The face in *Genesis* reflects that enthusiasm all too literally, in the hope of conveying what he later described as 'the eternal primeval feminine, the mother of the race'. His overall aim in this brazen image was to produce a 'serene and majestic' alternative to all the 'coquetries and fanciful erotic nudes of modern sculpture'.[63] It was an admirable objective, but here his handling of anatomy is altogether too predictable to marry convincingly with the harshly stylised head. Her face and body are incompatible, the products of

two divergent cultures which look as if they have been jammed together without enough subtlety on Epstein's part.

In order to ascertain how deficient this sincere yet jarring sculpture really is, it has only to be compared with the two outstanding images he produced in 1932. In this *annus mirabilis* of Epstein's carved work, comparable in achievement with 1913, both *Elemental* [138*–139] and *Woman Possessed* [140*–141] showed him at his best. Compressed, raw and still bearing the marks of a chisel that has not been prevented from registering the immediacy of the sculptor's attack, *Elemental* is the more impressive of the two. True to his title, Epstein shows a figure still emerging from the alabaster rather than fully defined. The embryonic implications of his hunched posture identifies him as a product of the same obsession which had previously produced so many images of babies growing inside the womb or seated, newly born, within their mother's protection. But *Elemental* is closest of all in stance to the small *Crouching Sun Goddess* [35*] carved over two decades before, and the contrast between them shows how much Epstein had gained in authority and expressive force since those early days. *Elemental* appears to be striving to release itself from the material which still flows down the back of its head and encases the body in a mass of pale veined alabaster. If the flattened face bears witness to the pain involved in the struggle, there is stoicism as well as anxiety in this primordial figure. Caught halfway between yearning and resignation, it exemplifies Epstein's ability to absorb 'primitive' influences and carve an image which no longer proclaims an overt indebtedness to a specific source.

The same is true of the dramatic *Woman Possessed*, where he achieves the unity of head and body which he had striven for in *Genesis* but failed to attain. From her bunched fists to her stubby feet, this carving presents a woman transported by an ecstasy which seems orgasmic in implications. It is surely no accident that the great De Miré sale was held in the same year as the making of *Woman Possessed*, for Epstein acquired, from the collection on offer at the Hôtel Drouot, a standing figure from the Gabon River [Fig. 4:11] which he claimed 'equals anything that has come out of Africa.' In his view, this towering wooden man with hallucinatory eyes 'has the astounding attitude of being held spell-bound by sorcery',[64] an observation that applies equally well to *Woman Possessed*. The De Miré figure may even have helped Epstein to construct his superbly taut and disciplined carving, for it contains an extreme of heightened emotion within a body from which every trace of superfluous frenzy has been ruthlessly expunged. But it would be unwise to search for close connections between the two images. By this time, Epstein was capable of absorbing African inspiration within his individual form-language, an achievement which becomes still more striking when *Woman Possessed* is compared with the mother in *Flenite relief* [56]. Although her body was arrested in a similarly arched position, the little flenite woman was far more 'archaic' in structure than the 1932 carving. Just as Brancusi would have wished, Epstein now succeeded in

Fig 10
LAZARUS 1947–48   (S391)
Hoptonwood stone H 254
(studio photograph)
New College Chapel, Oxford

establishing complete independence while continuing to rely on the African example as a yardstick for his own attempts to arrive at the heart of human experience.

He must have been aware of the consistency of purpose behind works as far apart in date as *Flenite relief* and *Woman Possessed*, for both carvings were included in his 1933 one-man show at the Leicester Galleries. Other early flenite and dove pieces were displayed there as well [46 and Fig. 69], alongside the vast *Sun God* relief [Fig. 57] which he had finally completed after twenty-three years of neglect. His readiness to exhibit these images proves that he considered them worthy of his recent work, and there was indeed a striking continuity linking the pre-war carvings with the latest products of his chisel. However much these images earned him the respect of younger sculptors like Moore, who at that time regarded direct carving as the pinnacle of his ambitions, they did not earn Epstein any praise from a wider public. His carved work was either ignored or regarded as merely 'shocking' by most visitors, who as usual reserved their admiration for the modelled portraits.

It is a tragedy that Epstein's undoubted ambitions as a carver did not receive any stimulus from further public commissions in the Thirties. Although *Night* and *Day* had shown how distinguished a contribution he could make to contemporary buildings, no more invitations to collaborate with architects on carved work were issued until the end of his life. Holden, who would have liked to employ him on the Senate House of London University, was told that Epstein must on no account be employed there. The furore aroused not only by his Underground Railways work but also by subsequent carvings like *Genesis* [134*], which a *Daily Express* (7 February 1931) headline had denounced as a 'MONGOLIAN MORON THAT IS OBSCENE', meant that Holden would have lost the University appointment if he enlisted the services of this reviled sculptor.

The loss is ours, for Epstein the carver could have been encouraged to stamp his humane mark on buildings whose bleakness urgently needed to be alleviated by grand and affirmative images. But he persisted, with admirable fortitude, in applying his chisels to stones vast enough to inhabit the most monumental of locations. Even though he knew there was little chance of finding an appropriate site for such work, Epstein could not resist the temptation to take up the challenge implicitly issued by epic slabs whenever he came across them at the quarry. The block of Subiaco stone which eventually became *Behold the Man* [Fig. 6], the largest carving he had executed since the *Wilde Tomb*, was also 'the toughest, most difficult piece of stone I had ever tackled. All the tools I had broke on it, and it was only after trying out endless "points", as they are called, with different tool-makers that I finally hit upon a "point" that resisted, and began to make an impression on the stone'.[65] The arduous labour involved in carving this obdurate monolith did, however, suit the theme Epstein wanted to tackle. *Behold the Man* is a sculpture concerned above all with suffering and endurance. So the travail

experienced by its maker, as he continued to work on it intermittently for more than a decade, informed the meaning he conveyed.

His choice of such a subject demonstrated how far Epstein had wandered from the orthodox Jewish beliefs espoused by his family. But he was still deeply interested in religious feeling and, as Anthony Blunt remarked when the unfinished stone was first exhibited in 1935, Epstein's interest in 'primitive' carvings sprang from a belief that their makers

> offered a new way of making statements about the supernatural. True, the religious and superstitious ideas which they sought to express were remote from those of Christianity, but at any rate they both existed on the same supernatural plane, and it would be worth trying whether their methods could not be adapted to the needs of European art.[66]

An amalgam of 'primitive' and Renaissance styles does indeed account for *Behold the Man*'s overbearing power. If the carving appears simplified to the point of crudeness, it does at least remain faithful to the massive stone which prompted Epstein to expend so much energy on its creation. It is as totemic, in its way, as the tall marble *Venus* [Fig. 68], even if the coolness of the latter statue was now replaced by a more turbulent mood. There is about this bruised yet resilient face a hint of self-portraiture, suggesting that Epstein identified himself with a man battered by hostility and ridicule but stubbornly undismayed by the humiliation he had suffered. *Behold the Man* is a partially autobiographical work, evincing the sculptor's determination to continue carving in the face of the most dispiriting antagonism. In that respect, it seems appropriate that the statue remained in Epstein's studio until his death — even though, as Blunt pointed out, it deserved 'to be placed in a church, where it would be seen from a distance and would make its appeal instantly'.[67]

All the same, it should be remembered that *Behold the Man* contains this sentiment within a very severe composition of large, flat planes. The sculptor himself insisted that 'the plastic aim was always of paramount importance and the "preaching" side secondary, or rather the idea, the subject, was so clear and simple to me, that, once having decided on it, I gave myself up wholly to a realisation of lines and planes'.[68] The formal discipline he had acquired early in his career guided him still, and when Epstein addressed himself to his next major carving he remained close to his old respect for the identity of the material he selected. Convinced that he should 'do no violence to it as stone',[69] he left the huge block of alabaster which became *Consummatum Est* [Fig. 9] unworked in his studio for a whole year. After wondering whether to raise it to a vertical position, or fashion a whole group of figures from its vastness, he decided in the end to leave it lying horizontally. Then, quite suddenly, music provided him with the solution which this much-scrutinised slab seemed to deserve. Listening to the 'Crucifixus' section of Bach's *B Minor Mass*, he experienced 'a feeling of tremendous quiet, of awe. The music comes from a great

distance and in this mood . . . I see the figure complete as a whole. I see immediately the upturned hands, with the wounds in the feet, stark, crude, with the stigmata. I even imagine the setting for the finished figure, dim crypt, with a subdued light on the semi-transparent alabaster'.[70]

Although this predominantly Egyptian figure sports an Assyrian beard, Epstein's reference to a 'dim crypt' indicates that he was also affected by the medieval alabaster tradition of his adopted country. The title, 'It Is Finished', is redolent of death's finality; and yet Epstein, with typical stubbornness, refuses to produce a quiescent image of extinction. The patriarch's outstretched hands have the vigour of life about them; the head seems to be raised up in defiance of mortality; and even the feet are protruding enough to recall Stanley Spencer's *The Last Supper* of 1920, where the sacramental proceedings are upstaged by the disciples' obtrusive toes thrusting out from the end of their robes. Epstein could not prevent his innate sense of physical vitality from declaring itself even in a sculpture as sepulchral as *Consummatum Est*.

Despite his melancholy realisation that no one wanted such a deeply-pondered work, that 'it came from me and returns to me in a world where it is not wanted',[71] he refused to be defeated by the ignominy of neglect. On the contrary: just over a year after he finished this magisterial memorial to the departed, the irrepressible carver set to work on a titanic celebration of man at his most alive and potent. The alabaster block must have been roughly the same size as the slab that generated *Consummatum Est*, but this time he stood it on end and made a figure of *Adam* [Fig. 88] who became the embodiment of indomitable virility. Although the alabaster had been resting in his studio for a number of years, there is nothing torpid about the image he discovered inside the stone. 'The conception, fairly clear in my mind in its general outlines, developed a law of its own as it proceeded', he wrote soon after its completion, 'and I managed to get a tremendous movement within the compass of a not very wide, upright stone.'[72] This dynamism is the most conspicuous quality of a carving that surges upwards, gathering power as it moves in an expansive momentum towards the arching pectorals and aspirant head above. Without indulging in any outflung gestures, which would have impaired the figure's compressed energy and flouted the integrity of the original block, Epstein infuses *Adam* with a Whitmanesque vivacity. He personifies the principle of exuberant masculinity which his maker had first explored in *Man* on the BMA façade, and now the sculptor had managed to invest him with all the striving ambition which Epstein himself had continually tried to instil in his carved work. Earthbound and yet determined to push as far towards the sky as possible, *Adam* represents the most restless and indeed reckless side of Epstein's temperament. No wonder he admitted that 'into no other work had I merged myself so much'.[73]

He made this confessional remark, however, before going on to execute the most turbulent, complex and personal carving of his later years. If Epstein identified himself with Adam, he seems to have projected himself even more ardently into the human protagonist who strives against divine opposition in *Jacob and the Angel* [143*]. The two Jacobs shared the same first name, after all, and throughout his life Epstein had regarded carving essentially as a prolonged struggle with the massive blocks of matter he liked best. The alabaster employed for *Jacob and the Angel* was one of the most enormous he had ever handled, and the effort he expended on its shaping was as prodigious, in its way, as the long nocturnal wrestling match which Jacob undertook with the winged figure. Moreover, the structure of the carving reinforces the idea that Jacob is battling, not only with a divine agent but also with the megalithic slab of stone itself. Epstein makes sure that the angel's wings, viewed from behind, present a flat expanse of alabaster directly evocative of the material which confronted him before the cutting began. So it is reasonable to see Jacob as a man pitting his strength against the formidable size and toughness of matter hewn from the bedrock of the planet — matter which Epstein doubtless saw as the creation of God.

Since the angel eventually overcame Jacob, does this carving therefore imply that Epstein felt vanquished by his attempts to impose his sculptural will on the 'inchoate and lifeless' stones[74] with which he had striven? I think not. For *Jacob and the Angel* was never conceived as a simple battle between two antagonists. Unlike Jacques Lipchitz, who had modelled a sizeable sculpture on the same theme almost a decade before, Epstein saw this struggle as much a matter of fierce, sensual affection as muscular combat. Lipchitz explained that 'to me, this [the story] meant that God wants us to fight with him',[75] whereas Epstein's preliminary studies stress the erotic nature of their embrace. A pencil drawing [142] makes clear that alongside the aggressive strain of conflict, the angel and Jacob enjoy the intimacy of lovers. In the sketch of standing figures, they stretch out one pair of arms in a gesture suggestive of an amorous dance. Then, in the study outlined beside it, the two protagonists fall to the ground in a rapturous union filled with frankly sexual overtones. Epstein must have known that these wild and fervent visions, reminiscent of the illustrations he had made for *Calamus* [98*] forty years before, could not be carried over directly into alabaster. But he drew them in order to ensure that the final carving contained the full ambiguity of Jacob's Whitmanesque involvement with the powerful stranger.

He succeeded magnificently. The carving concentrates on the moment when Jacob, caught in the angel's tight embrace, lets his own arms go slack. His limp body, almost lifted off the ground by the adversary's irresistible grip, contrasts with the coiled tension of the limbs holding him in their thrall. There is, however, scant suggestion of humiliation or defeat in his stance. Jacob's body seems to merge willingly with the angel's, and he throws his head back in an attitude of heightened satisfaction which recalls the orgasmic ecstasy of *Woman Possessed*. The angel's face, far more clearly defined than his own, bears down on him as intimately as the mother who once nestled with her child on the façade of the BMA building

[Fig. 39]. For these two figures are embroiled in a union of exceptional intensity, and the resemblance between the faces of the angel and Epstein's Rima [Figs 80–81*] indicates that a straightforward homoerotic relationship is not being dramatised here. Rather is the angel's sexuality as ambiguous as the meaning of the carving itself. Caught halfway between submission and fulfilment, Jacob surely embodies the duality of Epstein's own relationship with the stones he chiselled. He recognised their redoubtable authority, and must often have felt overwhelmed by the difficulties involved in struggling with the looming bulk of his apparently intractable material. But he was happy, at the same time, to let his shaping impulses be governed by the powerful imperative of the block. Hence the rapture of Jacob's expression as he allows his massive alabaster contestant to impose the full force of divine will on his human exertions. The figures ultimately convey a sense of physical and spiritual consummation which reflects a profound truth about Epstein's creative tussle to wrest the image from the stone.

After completing this climactic and deeply personal masterpiece, Epstein appears to have felt emptied of the need to make another carving for some time. The amount of energy such a work required was formidable for a man now in his sixties, and several years passed before he again addressed himself to another major statement in stone. The choice of *Lazarus* [Fig. 10] as a theme should not be considered in isolation from the historical moment at which it was commenced. In 1947 Britain had yet to recover from the battering and traumatic effects of a World War. Although victory had finally been attained, it left the country exhausted and near-bankrupt. If Epstein saw his *Lazarus* as a personification of resurgence after the tragic waste of conflict, he must also have been aware that the recovery would be slow, tentative and in no sense dramatically triumphant. Thirty years before, his abomination of war led him to create a similar monument to the hope of resurrection, and *Risen Christ* [110] had taken on an appropriately gaunt, muted air. It refused to hold out any facile prospect of instant redemption. Epstein adopted the same unrhetorical course with *Lazarus*, permitting the dead man to emerge almost hesitantly from the bands swathing his body.

The statue once again honours the towering expanse of Hoptonwood stone, taller than *Jacob and the Angel* or *Adam* had been and correspondingly slimmer in proportion. Although the reawakened figure begins to lift his arms, they are still constrained by bands oddly reminiscent of the strands of garment encircling the torso of the 1910 *Maternity* [40]. And lower down, his limbs look as if they are incapable of sundering the thick cat's-cradle binding him like dressings on a patient whose wounds have yet to heal. *Lazarus* entirely eschews the bombast which sometimes mars Epstein's later bronze work, and its refusal to indulge in melodrama enables him to convey an altogether more subtle and compassionate order of feeling. For this figure is still embroiled in a sleep close to the death he once suffered. His head may be turned at a surprisingly sharp angle, thereby fighting against the temptation to droop down on his chest in terminal weariness. But he still cannot open his eyes, and leans cheek against shoulder as if to rest after the gruelling strain involved in emerging from extinction. Compared with Michelangelo's *Captives*, which had once again surfaced in his memory forty years after they first helped to inspire some of the BMA figures, *Lazarus* is barely able to sustain the life which has so miraculously returned to him. Even though frailty is not a characteristic to be found in most of Epstein's carved work, the ageing sculptor's awareness of mortality allowed him to give this superb statue a quite new apprehension of the ultimate vulnerability of man.

The tenderness and restraint of his poignant carving finally led to its sale to the Warden of New College, Oxford, whose felicitous decision to instal it in the chapel was described by Epstein as 'one of the happiest issues of my working life.'[76] This gratifying event did not, however, prompt him to set to work on another carving for a further eight years. Part of the reason for this long delay can be found in the plethora of commissions for large-scale bronzes which suddenly began to descend on him in the post-war period. There was hardly time to carry them all out, let alone embark on a large stone image as well. Besides, Epstein was by now an old and partially infirm man whose physical capacities simply would not allow him to undertake too many arduous commitments; and the wonder is that he finally felt willing, at the age of seventy-five, to accept an invitation from the Trades Union Congress to carve a colossal *War Memorial* for its new London headquarters [Fig. 98]. The man who had once confessed that he wanted 'to carve mountains'[77] could not resist this last great challenge.

Although the bronze maquette [177*] accepted by the Congress promised a conventional work, in a direct line of descent from the *Pietà* which had become a preparatory study for *Night* [131] almost three decades before, he must have known that the eventual carving would be a far more resounding affair. The height of the block of Roman stone 'provided by the architect'[78] militated against the horizontal projection of the corpse in the maquette, and Epstein's preference for the primordial led him to dispense with the body's army helmet when carving commenced. Physical weakness obliged him, for the very first time in his long career, to let assistants prepare the stone. But when he was photographed in 1956, standing on the scaffolding and gazing up at the awesome megalith,[79] he certainly appeared to be bracing himself for one final heroic engagement with the material which had yielded so many of his finest works. It was a taxing ordeal, and may have contributed to his death soon after the monument's completion. 'I have let myself in for some devilish hard work', he admitted in March 1956, 'as this particular block is as hard as granite and tools just break on it'.[80] But Epstein had refused to be defeated by the exceptional hardness of Subiaco stone when chiselling *Behold the Man*, and he did not let this new obstacle deflect him now.

The TUC *War Memorial* turned out to be just as impressive as *Night* had been, and the obvious similarities between the two carvings did not mean that he now merely reiterated a formal solution arrived at in its essentials so long ago. The woman in the TUC statue is as elemental as her forerunner, certainly, and the figure below her owes some of its structure to the body sleeping on *Night*'s lap. But she is no longer content to remain seated. Roused by the terrible anger and grief of bereavement, she stretches to her full imposing height on the plinth. The desire to protest, and expose the tragedy of a young man's slaughter, gives her enough strength to hold the corpse in her arms. Epstein had been preoccupied with the notion of one figure presenting another ever since he made the old woman in *New-Born* hold out the baby on the BMA façade [Fig. 38], and there is a moving correspondence between these two works even though half a century separates them. The old woman's resignation has here been replaced by a furious indignation, however. Remembering no doubt the distress he suffered when two of his own children died in 1954, Epstein gave his sorrowing matriarch eyes forceful enough to transfix the onlooker. They stare down from the high plinth as if daring us to evade the harrowing reality of death. Her gaze is made doubly inescapable by the brusque simplification of the carving, which reduces features, draperies and prone limbs to a sequence of raw, elemental components. Epstein forces us to focus on what matters most: the hands gripping torso and thigh with absolute conviction, the dangling arm and legs of the inert victim, and supremely the woman's hard, accusing stare. Nothing else counts, and the entire carving is fired by a fury which refuses to be associated in any way with the genteel mourning of so many War Memorial statues erected elsewhere in the country. Epstein is determined not to forget the cold horror of war, and he has no intention of evading it by resorting to decorous symbolism or melancholy platitudes.

The TUC carving hits out with the vigorous conviction of a fist, and yet its ultimate achievement is to interpret the abstraction of its theme in the most personal manner imaginable. The sight of a woman clasping a corpse has the gruelling and timeless inevitability of Greek tragedy. From the gauntness of the stone block, which Epstein has retained more overtly than ever before in the lower half of his statue, he cut a painfully desolate elegy. 'The deeply intimate and human were always sought by me', he declared in the concluding pages of his autobiography, 'and so wrought, that they became classic and enduring.'[81] It was a noble ambition, and in this final carved testament he fulfilled it to the last defiant blow of his chisel.

'EPSTEINISM'

Terry Friedman

During Autumn 1921, the young Henry Moore, who had recently arrived in London to begin his training at the Royal College of Art, visited Epstein, then regarded as the leading sculptor of the *avant garde* in Britain. 'In the years before and just after the . . . war', Moore later recalled, 'while he was perhaps the sculptor most admired by the perceptive, he was undoubtedly the most loathed by the philistines.'[1] Moore brought with him on that first visit a letter of introduction from Charles Rutherston (an important Epstein collector living in Bradford, whose brother, William Rothenstein, was then Principal of the College).[2] The young Yorkshireman and the burly Epstein,[3] who retained his Brooklyn accent, hit it off from the start and during the next ten years kept in close contact, Moore being a frequent guest at the Epstein's Sunday afternoon gatherings.[4] During this period Epstein became increasingly prominent through his two controversial public commissions — the *W. H. Hudson Memorial*, 1925 [Figs 80–81*], and the groups of *Day* and *Night*, 1928–29, for the London Underground Electric Railways headquarters [Fig. 84], and regular exhibitions of his bronzes at the Leicester Galleries. Moore rapidly established himself as the star pupil of the RCA, where he became an instructor in 1924. He began to receive recognition through exhibitions at the Warren Gallery in 1928 and the Leicester Galleries in 1931, from both of which Epstein made purchases. During the early Thirties Moore emerged as the leading *avant garde* sculptor in the eyes of progressive critics. Epstein remained the more prominent in the popular press as a scapegoat for modernism. 'The word "Epsteinism"', reported the *Liverpool Post and Mercury* (20 January 1932), 'is a synonym for "art atrocity".' Moore later wrote: 'He took the brickbats, he took the insults, he faced the howls of derision . . . As far as sculpture in this century is concerned, he took them first. We of the generation that succeeded him were spared a great deal, simply because his sturdy personality and determination had taken so much.'[5]

It was while Moore was a student at Leeds College of Art (1919–21) that Epstein re-emerged into the public eye. The critic, Frank Rutter, who was curator at Leeds City Art Gallery, proclaimed in the *Sunday Times* (25 February 1917) of his exhibition of carvings and portraits at the Leicester Galleries: 'The astounding revelation is . . . not so much the sculptor's strength, which has long been recognised, as his extraordinary range and his unerring perception of the appropriate treatment by which each emotion should be expressed.' This was confirmed by P. G. Konody (*The Observer*, 8 February 1920), who acclaimed

Epstein as a 'sculptor of exceptional power and daring, a leader among modern artists'. This view was far from being shared by the art establishment. The painter, Walter Horsley RA, mentioned Epstein when he wrote to the distinguished academic sculptor, Sir Hamo Thornycroft in 1917, congratulating him on receiving a knighthood, which he regarded as 'quite a refreshing breather in the poisonous gas wave Art is struggling with in these days'.[6] The critic, A. L. Baldry, also wrote to Thornycroft, in 1919, that he was

quite ready to accept Epstein, [Ivan] Mestrovic, and all the rest of that set, as great masters when they begin to show the spirit by which all the great masters in sculpture have been guided. At present they seem to me to be merely clever men who are throwing away their chance of greatness by adopting deliberately affectations in which they really do not believe. I hear a creed in art matters which induces me to believe that the aesthetic instinct is really at its foundation the same as the sexual inclination and that therefore the love of beauty is merely the educated and developed form of the natural selection idea. It follows from this that the men who worship ugliness, distortion, perversion of type, and so on, are men with vicious and unnatural feelings and immoral minds, and, as such, are to be avoided by decent people. One does not knowingly count a sodomite among one's personal friends, and one should not reckon a man whose artistic sentiment is depraved as one of the company of great artists. I daresay all this from the 'advanced' point of view would seem very old-fashioned but the old fashions in art have produced many supreme masterpieces and I am quite content with them until some new man can give us some more novel and better statement of the old, fundamental truths. I most certainly do not find this statement in Epstein, and Co. — they seem to me to be men who have mixed primitive savagery with modern vice and call the mixture art. If it is art — if it is the true manifestation of the artistic sense — I can only say that for the sake of my own cleanliness of soul I do not want to have anything more to do with art.[7]

Although Moore had read Roger Fry's important essay on African sculpture published in *Vision and Design*, 1920, in Leeds Reference Library early in 1921,[8] it may well have been the initial contact with Epstein later in that same year that prompted him to begin a systematic exploration of the Egyptian, Assyrian and Ethnographical collections in the British Museum, with their 'ecstatically fine

Fig 11
Henry Moore (1898–1986)
Seven studies for full and half figures,
No. 2 Notebook 1921–22, p.22
Pencil 22.4 × 17.1
The Henry Moore Foundation

Fig 12
Henry Moore (1898–1986)
MATERNITY 1924
Hoptonwood stone H 22.9
Leeds City Art Galleries

Fig 13
Henry Moore (1898–1986)
THREE STUDIES FOR 'CHILD RIDING ON
MOTHER'S BACK', No. 4 NOTEBOOK 1925, p. 23
Pencil 22.7 × 17.5
The Henry Moore Foundation

negro sculptures', as he reported to a Yorkshire friend.[9] At some time during this period Moore became one of the favoured friends who was shown Epstein's collection of primitive art.[10] Both sculptors shared this passion for primitive and archaic sculpture, avidly studying examples in the British Museum and the Musée de l'Homme in Paris, believing that such sources could lead to a new aesthetic which offered modern sculptors an inspiring alternative to the traditional European ideal of classical beauty favoured by many of their older contemporaries. This doctrine is reflected in Moore's earliest London carvings which, perhaps not unexpectedly, share ideas in common with Epstein's work.

In the *No. 2 Notebook* of 1921–22 Moore sketched figures [Fig. 11] related to one of the *Dancing Girls* [Fig. 36] on the British Medical Association Building in the Strand, which Epstein carved in 1907–08.[11] The partial figures mounted on canted blocks, drawn on the same sheet, have an Egyptian appearance recalling the *Figure in Flenite* [50*], which was illustrated in Bernard van Dieren's monograph published in 1920.[12] In August 1923 Moore visited Charles Rutherston in Bradford, where he saw 'probably one of the most important collections (outside museums)' of ancient, primitive and Oriental art in England, as well as several Epstein bronzes — *Mrs Epstein with earrings* [79], *Head of Meum, Betty May* and *R. B. Cunninghame Graham* [112], all purchased at the Leicester Galleries in 1922 and 1923, and *Baby asleep* [6], which had been bought directly from the artist in the latter year.[13]

By 1924 Moore had turned for inspiration to specific Epstein carvings, in particular, the over-life-size Hoptonwood stone figure of *Maternity* [37], begun in 1910, but left unfinished and still remaining in the studio, where Moore may have seen it. His much smaller Hoptonwood stone group, also known as *Maternity* [Fig. 12], shows the mother with similarly broad, flat facial features and huge, spherical breasts and cradle-like arms and hands. Such features, combined with Epstein's monolithic treatment of the skirt and bare, protruding feet, became the starting point for a group Moore called 'Child riding on mother's back' sketched in the *No. 4 Notebook, 1925* [Fig. 13]; this was modified into the magnificent Green Hornton stone torso group of the same year, now at Manchester City Art Gallery.[14] However, these two works are certainly not slavish imitations, since by the distinctive cropping of the mother at the waist, thereby omitting the procreative aspect of her anatomy, Moore has greatly strengthened the maternal character of the groups.

Other early works, a *Figure* of 1923 and the 1927 *Head and Shoulders*, both in Verde di Prato, a variety of serpentine (or flenite, as Epstein called it), are finished with a polished, Epsteinian sophistication.[15] These were carved at a time Brancusi's sculpture was becoming more widely known outside France (he was represented, for example, in the Exhibition of Tri-National Art held at the New Chenil Gallery in London in October 1925).[16] Two years later, in October 1927, while Epstein was in America (an article in *The New York Times* was headlined 'Epstein, Stormy

Petrel of Sculpture Returns'),[17] he testified on behalf of Brancusi's polished bronze *Bird in Space*, 1926, which had been impounded by United States Customs and taxed as a metal utensil on the grounds that it was not art because it 'left too much to the imagination'. Epstein defended the sculpture on the modernist ground of form alone: 'It is a matter of indifference to me what it represents, but if the artist calls it a bird so would I.'[18] *The New York Evening Post* described Epstein on this occasion as a 'famous American sculptor and one of the most embattled of the modernists'.[19] The government, in fact, lost its case and the episode, widely reported in the press, was hailed as a 'stunning victory for modern art'.[20]

After Epstein's return to London, later in 1927, he acquired the small, cast-concrete *Suckling Child*, 1927 [Fig. 14] from Moore's first one-man exhibition (42 sculptures and 51 drawings) held at the Dorothy Warren Gallery in Maddox Street in January 1928.[21] *The Times* (26 January) critic commended this carving for its 'immense vitality' and the sculptor's general 'stability [and] refusal to be seduced from his loyalty to the capacities of his materials'. P. G. Konody, writing in *The Observer* (29 January) thought Moore 'at his best where he approaches realistic treatment, as in the "Suckling Child" . . . which is realised with passionate intensity', and he placed him squarely within the 'extreme modernist' camp. *The Daily Herald* ('Miner's Son as Artist | Sculptures That Are Staggering | His Genius', 26 January) also cited this 'superb' work in a 'very advanced show [containing] much sculpture of almost overwhelming power'.[22] The attitude of the press towards Moore as a 'new apostle of "architectural form"' in the mould of Epstein (*The Evening Standard*, 27 January) may have encouraged the older sculptor to recommend him to the architect, Charles Holden. This resulted in Moore being invited to join Epstein and five other sculptors (Eric Aumonier, A. H. Gerrard, Eric Gill, Frank Rabinovitch and Allan Wyon) to carve a series of monumental figures on the Underground Electric Railways headquarters (now Transport House) at 55 Broadway, St James's [127].[23]

Epstein's inclination towards the integration of sculpture and architecture had been apparent since 1907–08 [Fig. 37], but Moore, working on his first architectural commission and apprehensive about it, undoubtedly felt a special kinship with Epstein, who believed that in 'Egypt can be found the perfect example of the alliance' between the two Arts.[24] Moore had also expressed this opinion about Egyptian architecture and sculpture while a student in Leeds:

> The statues had to be so as to correspond to the magnificence & extent of the building [and are] not to be judged as if they were all sufficient & independent; if taken in connection with the monuments of which they form part it will be found that they are in complete harmony with their surroundings. Vertical & horizontal lines echo those of the building to which they were attached. The rhythm of the long colonade was carried out by the repetition of a single attitude. Their colossal dimension & immovable solidity brought them into complete harmony with the huge structures of which they form part.[25]

Child riding on mother's back.

(23)

Size of figure
15" x 11" x 10"

Carving *West Wind* high up on the façade of the building [Fig. 15], Moore seems to have kept an eye on what Epstein was doing in his carefully protected hut (locked to keep the prying press away) far below, and an intriguing photograph of him completing *West Wind* shows a small sketch on the stone block of what appears to be Epstein's design for *Day* [Fig. 84] over one of the main entrances.

Although Gill, at least, was a national figure, the press directed its attention almost exclusively to the contributions of Epstein and Moore.[26] An *Evening Standard* article (31 January 1929) headlined 'Our Art Critic Interviews Epstein Up a Ladder', shows Moore and his relief, accompanied by Epstein's praise of it as 'one of the most successful' of the series because it suggested 'volition in space remarkably well'. *The Yorkshire Post* (1 February 1929) thought *West Wind* 'somewhat in the manner' of the *Rima* relief on the *W. H. Hudson Memorial* [Figs 80–81]. In fact, its links with the *Oscar Wilde Tomb* [Fig. 58][27] and Moore's own *Standing Woman*, a destroyed stone carving of 1926, seem stronger.[28]

R. H. Wilenski's verdict, that *Night* [Fig. 84] was 'an immensely interesting contribution to the sculpture movement of to-day'[29] and the support of a few other critics, was shouted down by the majority of the press, which condemned all the work as 'modern monstrosities' and 'distorted deformities' (*The Times*, 6 and 10 April 1929), 'permanent examples of this age of ugliness! [and] a warning to future generations when England awakens from its nightmare and appreciates real beauty' (*The Morning Post*, 15 April 1929). *The Sheffield Independent* (14 April 1931) observed that Epstein was 'generally blamed' for *West Wind* when 'he is, in fact, not guilty'.

In the early Thirties the critical perception of the relationship between Epstein and Moore within the *avant garde* began to shift, and its progress was well charted in the contemporary press. In 1928–29 Moore had come increasingly under public scrutiny: *The Manchester Guardian* (21 April 1928) referred to him as an 'artist who has already begun to establish a reputation for his work in stone [and] wood'. He was, however, still seen as Epstein's protégé and, therefore, suffered the same vilification by the art establishment. Wilenski reported indignantly in 1929 that the Royal Academy, which 'claims . . . to be representative of British Art', once again failed to show work by either sculptor, or for that matter by other modernists like Frank Dobson, Eric Gill and Barbara Hepworth.[30] One remedy for this was an independent show called the Young Artists' Exhibition held at The New Burlington Galleries, just behind the RA, in March 1930. *The Daily Herald* (13 March) included a photograph of Epstein but pointed to Moore as one of the 'moving spirits behind the scenes'. The selection committee, all under the age of forty, enlisted the support of Epstein (then fifty), who exhibited his bronze bust of *Mrs Godfrey Phillips*, 1928 [90]. Moore showed the alabaster *Seated Figure*, 1930 (which was photographed with the artist in *The Daily Herald*, 17 March, and captioned 'Grotesque Carving by Mr. Henry Moore, an English sculptor, who has attained fame in Paris') and the Brown Hornton

stone *Reclining Figure*, 1929 (illustrated in *The Sunday Chronicle*, 30 March, accompanied by photographs of four young society women and the caption 'Feminine Beauty — As Modern Art Sees It!').[31] Work by Dobson, Hepworth and John Skeaping was also noted. *The Times* (15 March) critic concluded his review by observing that while the *Phillips* bust was 'one of [Epstein's] best recent works', it appeared to be an anomaly among those by the younger generation, who were 'primarily carvers making the architectural organisation of form the first consideration'. *The Evening Standard* (15 March 1930) also stressed the group's 'monumental aims', which could 'hold their own in the British Museum's array of monumental sculpture of past times'. In fact, although both Moore and Epstein rooted their art in the figurative tradition,[32] the former deplored the influence of Italian Renaissance sculptors (except Michelangelo) because of their reliance on pictorial illusion, whereas Epstein turned regularly to Donatello and his contemporaries for inspiration.[33] Perhaps it was this growing dichotomy between the carving and modelling aesthetic which led *The Times* critic to ask: 'Who is to blame our young sculptors if they choose to rival the carvers of antiquity rather than the modellers of the Italian Renaissance?' The same point was made by the London correspondent of *The Scotsman* (3 June 1930), reviewing an exhibition by sculptors of the London Group, which included Moore, held in the open-air roof-garden of Selfridge's Store in Oxford Street. The 'main interest' of the show lay in its 'revelation of the new tendencies in sculpture'. Epstein and Dobson were represented by already well-known works and it was felt that these 'giants of modern English sculpture had been brought in to give distinction to a group consisting chiefly of eager young ladies with a passion for stone-carving'. The article was appropriately entitled 'Modern Sculpture. Passing of the Traditional'.

If these and other articles of the time were intended as indirect attacks on Epstein's more traditional activities as a portraitist in bronze, he answered his critics in 1931 in the series of conversations on art with Arnold Haskell, published as *The Sculptor Speaks*: 'As I see sculpture it must not be rigid. It must quiver with life . . . carving often leads a man to neglect the flow and rhythmn of life.'[34] Nevertheless, hidden away in the Hyde Park Gate studio in 1930 was a monumental, aggressive stone carving, *Genesis* [134*], which was to burst upon an unsuspecting and outraged public in the following year. During the Thirties, Epstein returned to large-scale carving of a type which had established him as the *enfant terrible* of pre-War British sculpture. In 1931, he began to rework the large stone relief of *Sun God* [Fig. 57], begun in 1910, and exhibited at the Leicester Galleries in May 1933 a pair of *Doves*, perhaps the first version of 1913, and two flenite carvings from the same year [56–57 and Fig. 69], together with his latest monumental carvings, *Woman Possessed* [140*] and *Primeval Gods* [Fig. 86], which was carved on the back of the *Sun God* relief. *The Jewish Chronicle* (5 May 1933) considered the latter technically beautiful and evidence of Epstein's 'increasing ability to deal with the colossal

Fig 14
Henry Moore (1898–1986)
Suckling child   1927
Cast concrete   L 43.2
Whereabouts unknown (formerly Jacob Epstein collection)

Fig 15
Henry Moore carving West Wind on the London Underground Electric Railways Headquarters, Westminster, 1928–29.

difficulties, both ideal and material, of this kind of work'. The press, however, seems to have totally ignored the pre-War carvings. Epstein's enthusiasm for working stone once again could have been encouraged, perhaps even compelled, by Moore's recent successes in this field.

The controversial issue between the merits of carving and modelling, and the attitude of the two chief protagonists towards it and, therefore, of their respective rôles in the *avant garde*, was brought into focus by events in 1931.

The press now actively encouraged a reversal of their positions. Where, in 1930, Epstein had told an *Evening Standard* (19 May) reporter that he regarded himself 'without any conceit [as] the greatest sculptor in this country', while Moore was the 'undoubted second',[35] in 1931 *The Birmingham Evening Dispatch* (13 April) proclaimed Moore 'a serious rival' to Epstein who 'still reigns supreme . . . only because . . . Moore has not yet mastered the art of disregarding Nature entirely and of concealing the last shreds of his appreciation of beauty of form'. He 'really seems to have come into his own and to have become, as far as the public is concerned, a second Epstein' (*The Yorkshire Post*, 16 April 1931). *The Jewish Chronicle* (1 May) was unqualified in its praise of Moore's 'tremendous display of genius'; at 32 he had 'achieved results which set him beside the three or four greatest of his contemporaries . . . Three of the greatest names in present-day sculpture are Jewish names — Epstein, Zadkine and Lipschitz. No admirer of these should neglect this opportunity of seeing [work] which constitutes the most serious challenge they have yet received'. 'EPSTEIN'S RIVAL HAS ARRIVED' (*The Sheffield Mail*, 13 April 1931).

In April Moore exhibited 34 sculptures and 19 drawings in a one-man show at the Leicester Galleries, one of the most active commercial galleries in London to promote modernism, and Epstein's dealers since 1917. He not only lent the *Suckling Child* [Fig. 14], purchased in 1928, and the Cumberland alabaster of *Mother and Child* of 1931 [Fig. 16],[36] but also, in what Wilenski called an act of 'splendid generosity',[37] Epstein contributed the prefatory note to the catalogue. This begins with the oft-quoted remark, invariably misinterpreted by the press: 'Before these works I ponder in silence'. He went on:

> Henry Moore by his integrity to the central idea of sculpture calls all sculptors to his side. What is so clearly expressed is a vision rich in sculptural invention, avoiding the banalities of abstraction and concentrating upon those enduring elements that constitute great sculpture . . . Here is something to startle the unthinking out of their complacency. Sculpture in England is without imagination or direction. Here in . . . Moore's work are both qualities. Bound by the severest aesthetic considerations, this sculpture is a liberation of the spirit . . . For the future of sculpture in England Henry Moore is vitally important.[38]

Epstein repeated the note in *The Sculptor Speaks*, 1931, and added that Moore 'is the one important figure in contemporary English sculpture'.[39] *The Sunday Dispatch* (12 April 1931) reckoned such

'praise from one of the greatest living sculptors to a fellow artist is praise indeed'. Wilenski proclaimed the show 'a landmark in the history of English sculpture' (*The Observer*, 12 April). At the same time, the Yorkshire critic Herbert Read, in *The Meaning of Art*, 1931, identified Moore as responsible for the rebirth of sculpture in England, which Read rather exaggeratedly claimed had been lost since the fifteenth century and which by virtue of the sculptor's 'sureness and consistency [places him] at the head of the modern movement'. This panegyric was impaired by his reference to the 'Semites [who], in fact, are not expressive at all in plastic modes — that is to say, they are not original or "creative" in them . . . [their] art has not the same respect for form as Aryan art.'[40] This was surely an attempt to force Moore's case at Epstein's expense.

The Leicester Galleries exhibition was a sort of official coming-out. Although the conservative press 'howled in derision' – Lady Brassey, confessing her ignorance of modern art to *The Hastings Observer* (25 April 1931), nevertheless regarded it as an 'insult to be asked to look at even a newspaper print of some of Mr Epstein's or Mr Henry Moore's productions. It cannot be good for young people to study such monstrosities'[41] — the exhibition was financially successful: sales amounted to £385. Dr Max Sauerlandt, Director of the Museum für Kunst und Gewerbe at Hamburg, purchased the small ironstone *Head*, Moore's first work acquired by a foreign gallery,[42] while Epstein bought the powerful Ancaster stone *Half-figure*, 1930 [Fig. 17].[43] Moore later recalled that he had 'showed an excitement in my work [and] encouraged me by buying my sculpture . . . which pleased me enormously'.[44] *The Scotsman* (13 April 1931) was quick to point out that when 'word goes around that Epstein has bought a brother artist's work, dealers begin to look upon it with new interest', just as when he writes such an appreciation 'it may safely be presumed that the work is of the type that produces letters to editors on the "Cult of Ugliness"'. The exhibition propelled Moore, whose work in the previous year was 'still mainly known to collectors and students of the arts' (*The Daily Express*, March 1930), into prominence.[45] *The Nottingham Journal and Express* (13 April 1931), in an article entitled 'Epstein's Protege', reported that the departure of the monumental marble *Genesis* [134*] from the Leicester Galleries immediately before Moore's show did not signal 'the end of the reign of Epstein. Indeed he formally introduces his successor to the same building [and his preface to the catalogue] will probably be the battleground of another artistic controversy'.[46]

Epstein's premier position in the *avant garde* was now seriously threatened, partly by the very enthusiasm with which he had championed the younger man. 'Nobody anxious to discover what the modern sculptor is trying to achieve should miss [Moore's] exhibition . . . He is more uncompromising, indeed, than Mr. Epstein, whose occasional ironic half-concessions to the public undermine the artist's proper magisterial authority and lay him open to impertinent attack' (*The Manchester Guardian*, 13 April 1931). The alabaster *Mother and Child* [Fig. 16], which Epstein had

bought from Moore in 1931, featured in a notice in *The Bulletin and Scots Pictorial* (15 April 1931) with the headline 'Putting Epstein in the Shade'.

By the time of Moore's exhibition at the Lefevre Galleries in November of that year, where he demonstrated his 'superb' and 'extremely sensitive' talent as a direct carver, it was noted that both Epstein and Read looked upon him as 'the greatest sculptor England has yet produced' (*The Yorkshire Post*, 10 November 1931). Epstein's work now seemed 'almost conventional by comparison' (*The Newcastle Evening Chronicle*, 29 December). Although they remained coupled as leaders of the modern movement (*The Yorkshire Post*, 5 March 1932, described them, with Dobson, as the 'greatest English sculptors of the day',[47] and Epstein and Moore alone represented England in the international anthology by Paul Fierens, *Sculpteurs D'Aujourd'hui*, 1933),[48] Epstein was excluded from the important survey show, the first in Germany since the end of the War, held in Hamburg and Berlin in July 1932, which included work by Moore and Maurice Lambert.[49] This was also the case with regard to the modern English art exhibition held at Krefeld in September of that year (*The Times*, 5 September). At the same time, some British critics, advocates of a purer abstractionism, attempted to divorce Epstein altogether from the mainstream. In *A Short History of English Sculpture*, 1933, Eric Underwood suggested that his ancestry and early environment accounted for his 'essentially oriental' art in which 'there is practically nothing English. He is with us but not of us. It is vigorous, dynamic [but] wholly exotic, and for this reason cannot appropriately be dealt with at length' in such a survey.[50]

This is not to suggest that Moore was now free of the 'howls of derision' and 'popular fury' previously reserved for his friend.[51] The earlier optimism expressed in the press for the younger sculptor's work now quickly vanished. His 'crude mis-shapen images . . . look like a conscientious attempt to get back to the art standards of the troglodyte man . . . A visit to the Elgin Marbles, after the Leicester Galleries show, is like jumping from the Oval gasometer to the Alhambra in Spain' ('Out-Heroding Epstein', *The Bolton Evening News*, 15 April 1931).[52] J. G. Moody, in his presidential address to the National Society of Art Masters in January 1931, refuted Wilenski's article 'Ruminations on Sculpture and the Work of Henry Moore', published in *Apollo* (December 1930), and believed that an artist who produced such 'vulgar and repulsive distortions' should not be entrusted with training students.[53] This was a sore point. In 1924, following the resignation of Derwent Wood as Professor of Sculpture at the Royal College of Art, Epstein's name had been put forward both by Moore and William Rothenstein, but to no avail. The Permanent Under-Secretary at The Board of Education wrote that to 'appoint [him] would be a very perilous experiment and might cause us considerable embarrassment'.[54] In fact, Epstein never received a teaching post.

What is particularly interesting about the press attacks against Moore is that they were often expressed in Epsteinian terms of primitivism and barbarism. He is frequently referred to as working

Fig 16

Henry Moore (1898–1986)
MOTHER AND CHILD   1931
Cumberland alabaster   H 47 (from H. Read, *Henry Moore Sculptor*, 1934)
The Hirshhorn Museum of Art, Washington DC (formerly Jacob Epstein collection)

Fig 17

Henry Moore (1898–1986)
HALF-FIGURE   1930
Ancaster stone   H 50.8 (from H. Read, *Henry Moore Sculptor*, 1934)
National Gallery of Victoria, Melbourne (formerly Jacob Epstein collection)

Fig 18

'Epstein Out-Epsteined', *The Daily Mirror*, 14 April 1931, illustrating Henry Moore's RECLINING FIGURE, 1929, now in Leeds City Art Galleries.

in the 'Epstein vein'. An article published in *The Daily Mirror* (14 April 1931) entitled 'Woman As She is "Sculpted" | Monstrosities in Stone', is headlined 'EPSTEIN OUT-EPSTEINED' (an oft-repeated phrase) and illustrated with the Brown Hornton stone *Reclining Figure*, 1929, which is described as a 'monostrosity . . . which surpasses in repulsiveness even that of Epstein' [Fig. 18].[55]

The anti-Leftist *Morning Post* (13 December 1930), which had been responsible for launching the attack on the *W. H. Hudson Memorial* in 1925, now turned its wrath on Moore, in an article entitled 'Ugliness in Art | "An Easy Road to Notoriety"', in which his work is criticised as 'unconventional or what is called "Bolshevist" art'. The additional information that he was employed at the RCA, which was 'controlled' by William Rothenstein, who had championed the sculptor since the mid Twenties, suggests a sinister anti-semitic prejudice to the article. During the *Hudson Memorial* controversy, *The Evening News* (26 November 1925) condemned the relief as 'a revolt against civilisation', and suggested ties with people who had a 'sympathetic bias towards every movement coming within the scope of the "Left" wing of political action . . . where their preference lay in the policy to be pursued towards the Soviet state'. *Rima* [Figs 80–81*], therefore, 'comes as a dramatic and concentrated piece of evidence of the spirit of anarchy . . . so constant a factor in modern life that it links [with] the Red Flag [and] Jazz music . . . leading us backward to barbaric conceptions of life'. *The Morning Post* (28 December) suggested enshrining Epstein's 'hideous masterpiece' near Lenin's Tomb as 'a new Temple to Rimmon, seventh in order of the hierarchy of hell'. In the early Thirties, the press associated this 'grotesque ugly phase of art [with a] considerable uneasiness [that the] younger generation may be induced to foresake the great and progressive traditions of art for the crude manifestations which are termed "modern"' (*The Morning Post*, 16 December 1930), just as it was feared it might also do in the political arena. By inference, Epstein (and, therefore, Moore) — the radical modernists — were associated with Baldwin's Socialist government (it was Baldwin who unveiled the *Hudson Memorial* in 1925), and ultimately Bolshevism. This was a less dangerous though potentially no less harmful form of bigotry than the Nazi equation between the domestic architectural style professed by the Bauhaus and the alien orientalism of Jewishness, which resulted in the closure of the great design school in Berlin in 1933 because it was a 'breeding place of cultural Bolshevism'.[56] It was perhaps in the light of this attitude that *The Evening Standard* (11 April 1931) mentioned the otherwise innocuous fact that Moore's wife, Irina, née Radetsky, whom he had married in 1929, was a Russian-born artist. The Bolshevik theme was renewed at the time of the 1931 Leicester Galleries exhibition. *The Graphic* (10 January) illustrated the Leeds *Reclining Figure* as an example of 'Bolshevism in Modern Art', and a correspondent to *The West Sussex Gazette* (7 May 1931), deploring Moore's position as an instructor at the RCA, recommended that some 'influential public movement . . . be set on foot to oppose

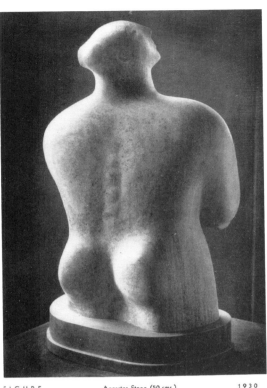

FIGURE   Ancaster Stone (50 cms.)   1930
(Collection: JACOB EPSTEIN ESQ.)

EPSTEIN OUT-EPSTEINED
MORE SCULPTURE MONSTROSITIES

A monstrosity at an exhibition of sculpture by Mr. Henry Moore which surpasses in repulsiveness even that of Epstein.

what is nothing more or less than Bolshevism in art'. *The Bournemouth Echo* (12 May 1931) argued more extremely that the aim of Bolshevik art was 'to bring us back to the level and standards of the cave man. And as Communism and Bolshevism did not grow out of native soil in these islands, but were foisted upon us in malice prepensed by foreigners, so this perverted and diseased form of "art" did not grow out of English soil. It has been, from the beginning to now, taught and spread by foreigners; the critics and writers who uphold it are in almost every instance aliens'.

In 1933 *The Yorkshire Post* (26 June) speculated that the architect, Charles Holden, who had already collaborated with Epstein on several major commissions, would again choose him to work on the new Senate House of London University. In fact, Holden was only offered the job on condition that Epstein was *not* employed. Moore was approached but the project was not pursued beyond a few sketches.[57] About this time the critics began to detect Moore's influence on the older sculptor. *Chimera*[58] and *Woman Possessed* [140*], both of 1932, were cited as examples by *The Jewish Chronicle* (5 May 1933) when they were exhibited at the Leicester Galleries in that year. It is true, as we shall see, that the latter piece at least owes something to Moore, but the two sculptors' works were distinct.[59]

Herbert Read had begun promoting Moore in *The Meaning of Art*, 1931, and *Art Now*, 1933, and in 1934 published the first monograph, *Henry Moore Sculptor: With an Appreciation . . . and Thirty-Six Full Page Plates*.[60] (Three of the illustrations are of carvings then owned by Epstein: the *Half-figure* and *Mother and Child*, which had featured in the 1931 show, and a Dark African wood *Composition* of 1932 [Fig. 19], acquired in the following year.)[61] Beginning in 1920, with Bernard van Dieren's polemical *Epstein*, there had been a series of substantial, well-illustrated publications on the sculptor: Hubert Wellington's in 1925, Arnold Haskell's in 1931 and L. B. Powell's in 1932. Thereafter, nothing of this sort appeared until Epstein's autobiography, *Let There Be Sculpture*, in 1940. In the second half of the Thirties, Moore became the most written about of modern British sculptors. He contributed to several of the most important books on progressive art: *Unit 1: The Modern Movement in English Architecture Painting and Sculpture*, 1934, edited by Read, Myfawny Evans's *The Painter's Object*, 1937, and *Circle: International Survey of Constructivist Art*, also 1937, edited by Leslie Martin, Ben Nicholson and Naum Gabo. Moore wrote important articles for *The Listener*, on Mesopotamian and primitive art (5 June 1935 and 24 April 1941 respectively) and on his own work ('The Sculptor Speaks', 18 August 1937), while respected critics also began to write about him: Graham Bell, Geoffrey Grigson, Arnold Haskell, William Rothenstein, Adrian Stokes, R. H. Wilenski. Moore also exhibited abroad more regularly and his sculpture appeared on the covers and in the pages of foreign art journals.[62]

It is ironic that many of the developments which the younger generation of sculptors were making their own, had their origins in Epstein's own work before the Great War. He was,

however, now isolated both by his outspoken hostility to abstract and constructivist art and by the frequently expressed critical cliché which depicted him as a modeller whose carving was inept.[63] Moore himself came to regard him as 'scarcely an innovator, let alone a revolutionary', apart from a brief period before 1914, and classed him as a 'modeller rather than a carver', whose art was 'visual rather than . . . mental', with an emphasis on 'subject rather than on form'.[64] Epstein clearly resented being passed-over and it may have been at this time that their friendship cooled. In Haskell's view 'It was only when the critics began to use Moore to denigrate Epstein that the friendship suffered', although the younger sculptor played no part in this.[65] In 1937, when Roland Penrose installed the extraordinary Brown Hornton stone *Mother and Child*, 1936, which he had just purchased from Moore, in the front garden of his Georgian terraced house in Downshire Hill, Hampstead, the press ridiculed it as an 'Epstein the Morning After the Night Before' (*The Star*, 29 December 1937).[66]

In one important respect, however, the two men's aims did remain constant: to fight for the cause of progressive sculpture against philistinism. When, in August 1937, the High Commission for Southern Rhodesia, the new owner of the British Medical Association Building in The Strand, mutilated Epstein's eighteen Portland stone figures carved on the façade in 1907–08, there was an outcry among many artists, but it was, as Richard Cork records, the President of the Royal Academy's refusal to lodge an official protest which so incensed Moore that he vowed never to exhibit at Burlington House.[67]

Although Epstein, unlike Moore, maintained no artistic links with the Surrealists, he shared their anxiety about the alarming spread of Fascism in Europe, particularly the recent political events in Spain, and what Moore described as the 'Brute force and the imminent fear of torture and death . . . set up as the keystone of national organisation . . . with an inhuman totalitarian ferocity which may well make us despair' (*The Yorkshire Post*, 31 March 1938). In November 1935 Moore, Epstein, Dobson and a number of painters in revolt against war, had contributed to a highly successful exhibition in aid of the International Column in Spain.[68] The cinema-going public may have been alerted to this resistance movement among British artists in Alexander Korda's 1936 Futurist film, *Things To Come* (Britain's first million-dollar movie), about the world at war and the abominable aftermath of destruction and pestilence. They may even have identified Epstein with the character of Ariston Theotocopulos, whom Korda had transformed from the gifted painter in H. G. Wells's prophetic dream novel *The Shape of Things to Come*, 1933, into the sturdy, rebellious sculptor resisting the totalitarian state by haranguing a crowd before his colossal, modernist carved figure of a woman.

In 1937 Epstein and Moore, with Read, Eric Gill, Paul Nash, the architect, Serge Chermayeff, and the cartoonist, David Low, announced the formation of a National Congress organised by the British Section of the International Peace Campaign to galvanise the public to 'energetic action

Fig 19

Henry Moore (1898–1986)
COMPOSITION   1932
Dark African wood   H 38.7
Private collection (formerly Jacob Epstein collection)

Fig 20

Henry Moore in Grove Studios, Hammersmith 1926–27, with the large, unfinished standing female figure with upraised arms (whereabouts unknown).

on behalf of world peace'.[69] In January 1938, the
Foreign Office refused to issue visas to Epstein,
Moore, Rose Macaulay, Stephen Spender, Paul
Robeson and others to permit them passage to
Spain at the invitation of the Republican Govern-
ment. Epstein reckoned this reflected British
Government policy: 'If the invitation had come
from Franco we should probably have got the
visas' (*Reynolds News*, 30 January). During the
same month he met with a group of Jewish artists,
among them David Bomberg, Horace Brodzky,
Hans Feibusch, Mark Gertler, Jacob Kramer and
Bernard Meninsky, to discuss this situation.[70] On
5 December 1938, Epstein, Moore, Gertler, Nash,
Augustus John, the Rothensteins and other artists
forming an emergency committee, signed a letter
to the press drawing attention to their German
confrères who had found asylum in Czechoslovakia from Nazism but who were still in imminent
danger of being sent to concentration camps (*The
News Chronicle*, 8 December). And, in the following February, the two sculptors showed at the 4th
annual exhibition held at The Whitechapel Art
Gallery of the Artists International Association
(AIA), a left-wing organisation aimed at unifying
the profession in the cause of peace.[71] It was,
however, too late and within the year, the Spanish Republican Government collapsed, Italy
invaded Albania, Germany marched into
Czechoslovakia and Poland, and the Second
World War erupted.

Moore reacted immediately by drawing a group
of figures sinking in a quagmire below a cliff,
which he called *September 3rd 1939*, and modelling
the first of the *Helmet Heads* in lead.[72] Epstein's
reaction was less overtly war-like: a seven-foot
high, three ton alabaster figure of *Adam* [Fig. 88].
Nevertheless, it was quickly associated with these
events and appeared in *Lilliput* (August 1939), a
popular British journal of photography, opposite
a photograph of a brutish, barking Mussolini,
stripped to the waist, fist aggressively upraised
[Fig. 32].[73] At the time, *Adam* was on display
at a Blackpool peep-show. The critic of *The
Daily Sketch* found it 'Stupendous, staggering,
colossal, overwhelming . . . Adam is certainly no
Tarzan . . . Squat, thick, malformed, he strides
vigorously forward on enormous feet, with clenched arms and uplifted head, sunlight pouring on
his ugly pink face and outthrust chin.'[74]

Adam had evolved from a bold and aggressive
figure style (cruelly diagnosed as 'elephantiasis'
by *The Sheffield Independent*, 14 April 1931), which
Epstein developed earlier in the Thirties when the
press attacks were most vituperative and his
friendship with Moore at its closest. *The Jewish
Chronicle* (5 May 1933) had suggested that *Woman
Possessed* [40*–41] owed something to the younger
sculptor. It can be compared to a large stone
carving of a standing female figure with upraised
and clenched fists [Fig. 20], which Moore had
been working on in 1925–26 but abandoned
around 1930.[75] This carving was illustrated in *The
Evening News* (1 January 1931) as an example of his
'vulgar and repulsive distortion' of the human
body, and *The Northern Echo* (14 April) particularly
drew attention to the 'monstrous hands such as
Epstein favours'. (It is perhaps pertinent that the
Dark African wood *Composition*, 1932 [Fig. 19], the

last of Moore's works Epstein acquired, is an
especially vigorous carving with the shoulders
and arms boldly emphasised.) Moore's stone
figure would also seem to be the prototype for
Adam.

Although Epstein still had twenty years more
work in him, he was already, in 1939, being
relegated to the perspective of history. The American sculptor, Malvina Hoffman, wrote of him as
one of a group, which included Dobson and Gill,
Bourdelle, Despiau and Maillol (the last having
been born in 1861), which had led the way
'through the early years of the twentieth century
to the battlefield of contemporary sculpture'.[76]

THE PRIMITIVE WITHIN
THE QUESTION OF RACE
IN EPSTEIN'S CAREER 1917–1929

Elizabeth Barker

In a 1934 review of the religious sculpture of Epstein and Eric Gill, published in *The American Magazine of Art*, a critic pointed to the 'deep-seated racial influences' that, consciously or unconsciously, influenced their interpretations. She contrasted Gill's 'sturdy Anglo-Saxon heritage' with the cosmopolitan and 'Hebraic' strain of Epstein's background, asserting that Epstein had turned 'Negroid exaggerations to design purpose not so much because of his very real interest in Negro sculpture but because the primitive in Negro sculpture answers the primitive in Epstein.'[1]

A new emphasis on Epstein's racial identity emerged in the widespread public criticism which followed each new exhibition of his work in the Twenties. Analogies were frequently drawn between his artistic interests in 'savage', non-Western cultures and his own ambivalent status as a Jewish immigrant in Britain; positioned on a cultural borderline between 'inside' and 'outside', 'civilised' and 'savage', the 'primitive' and 'modern'. After the First World War, moreover, there was an increasing tendency to explain Epstein's artistic primitivism as the inevitable expression of his own 'alien' mentality and racial instincts rather than the product of any purely formal motivation. One anti-Semitic critic asserted that the primitivist style of his *Hudson Memorial* [Figs 80–81*] was the outcome of an 'atavistic yearning of like for like'.[2]

An analysis of the history and various responses to Epstein's work between 1917 and 1929 provides an opportunity to examine the ways in which public debates about racial difference, notions of 'self' and 'other', became focused on and merged with aesthetics in Britain. Whilst the more extreme anti-Semitic outbursts and acts of vandalism against Epstein's sculpture were widely condemned as alien to the British tradition of toleration and moderate behaviour, deviations from this norm of toleration, in the form of verbal assaults, gained wide publicity through the popular press and respectable art criticism.

The overtly racist remarks and official censorship of Epstein's art in the Twenties are, in many respects, less disturbing than the so-called 'disinterested', purely aesthetic, responses to his sculpture which have continued to shape his artistic reputation in Britain. The most intriguing aspect of Epstein's career during this period is the way both the champions and Modernist critics of his work, such as Roger Fry, R. H. Wilenski and Herbert Read, enlisted various concepts and vocabulary from racial discourse to characterise it as a form of 'outsider' art.

Eric Underwood refused even to discuss Epstein's work in his *Short History of English Sculpture*, published in 1933, because he claimed it was 'wholly exotic' and unassimilable within British culture. Underwood asserted that 'Epstein's ancestry and early environment go far to explain his art. This is essentially oriental . . . Epstein is with us but not of us'.[3] Stanley Casson criticised Epstein's 'alien' genius in *Some Modern Sculptors*, published in 1928. He interpreted his syncretic primitivism as a form of artistic 'rootlessness': 'Wherever his taste roams it always seems to hit on the same type of thing. From Maya, or Aztec, or Negro art Epstein extracts what is most Epsteinish in character . . . He is in origin one of an oppressed race, and his most personal expression of feeling is in sympathy with the grief and agony of oppression.'[4] Read went further in his discussion of 'The Racial Factor in Art', published in 1933, stating that there was a clear distinction between the art of the 'Aryan' and 'Semitic' races. He considered that the Semites were 'not expressive at all in the plastic modes, that is to say they are not original or creative in them'. He dismissed 'Jewish art' as the late product of a 'culturally dispossessed race' which did not have the same 'respect for form' as Aryan art: 'It avoids the definite and static. It is essentially romantic, it is not ashamed of its romanticism. It sees in painting, not a means of interpreting the outer world, but a means of expressing the inner self.'[5] By utilising a traditional aesthetic opposition between Romantic and Classic art, Read effectively exiled 'Jewish art' from the Modernist camp. Throughout the Twenties, other Modernist critics were to dismiss Epstein in similar ways, unfavourably comparing his 'eccentric Romanticism', 'subjective' and ill-disciplined approach with the 'rationalism' and objectivity of carvers such as Frank Dobson, Henri Gaudier-Brzeska and Henry Moore.

It is only when one considers the more extreme vocabulary and ideological background of British anti-Semitism during the Twenties that the racist implications of this genteel practice of art criticism becomes apparent and recurrent descriptions of Epstein's post-War art as 'instinctive', 'tragic', 'idiosyncratic', 'eclectic', 'expressionist', 'Romantic', 'Oriental', 'Eastern' and 'primitive' are revealed as loaded terms.

An examination of the process whereby racist attitudes could be tolerated, defended and perpetuated within the context of art criticism, exposes the more deeply-entrenched prejudices and subtle forms of racism which existed behind the mask of British tolerance and which have continued to shape attitudes to outsiders in this country.[6]

A significant feature of the 'racial aesthetics' applied to Epstein's art in the Twenties is the widespread notion that there was something fundamentally 'primitive' within the artist himself. Critics discovered primitive qualities in his realistically modelled portraits and religious bronzes despite the fact that few of these works betrayed tribal or archaic influence. 'The Primitive' was a particularly mobile concept which was used in various ways to define notions of 'self' and 'other' rather than any specific formal relationships in Epstein's art.

Epstein was always acutely conscious of his social marginality and despite occasional bids for assimilation within British society, deliberately promoted his image as a cultural outsider, free from the restrictions of any single artistic or national identity. This attitude was reflected in his bohemian life-style and left-wing views, his known passion for primitive art, the overt sexuality of much of his sculpture, and use of non-white models, some of whom became members of the Epstein household. It is important, therefore, to question the ways in which the cross-cultural dialogues, intrinsic to artistic primitivism, could have functioned for Epstein as a means of countering the racial tensions he experienced as a Jewish artist in Britain. There is a curious irony in the contrast between Epstein's own ideal of the primitive, as something which could transcend the boundaries of race and time, and the notion of primitive used by his critics to score racial and cultural divisions.[7]

1. The Effects of War and the Growth of Anti-Semitism in Britain

The abrupt shift in public attention from artistic to military fields of battle in 1915 transformed the way Epstein's artistic identity was conceived and articulated in Britain. As his Vorticist colleagues adjusted themselves and variously assimilated the nationalist values of war-time culture, Epstein found himself increasingly isolated and subject to virulent anti-alien prejudice. He was branded and persecuted as an 'enemy within' and the question of his Jewish identity, which first became an issue of public debate on conscription and national security, began, in 1917, to affect the nature of aesthetic response to his sculpture.[8]

The first indications of a change in attitude to Epstein's work emerge from the reviews of his first major retrospective show at the Leicester Galleries in February 1917. This exhibition, in which Epstein included twenty recent bronzes to establish better public relations,[9] generated a new form of criticism which attempted to rationalise the increasing variety of his artistic output in terms of his foreign culture and essentially primitive instincts. The reviews of this show are marked by equivocal language and by a sense of confusion about Epstein's motives. Most critics focused on the apparent dichotomy between the carved and modelled works and made various attempts to explain this in terms of an inner contradiction between Epstein's tamed and untamed instincts. Whilst some welcomed the greater naturalism of the portraits as evidence of Epstein's efforts to become assimilated within British society, others drew analogies between the enigmatic primitivism of the carvings and an equally primitive quality in the bronze portraits. Whereas Lawrence Binyon expressed anxiety about Epstein's borderline position between civilised and savage, criticising his primitivism as an 'acutely self-conscious' effort,[10] Lewis Hind argued that Epstein's instincts were essentially primitive. He qualified his description of the modelled works as examples of Epstein's 'tamed' side: 'by tamed, I do not mean that he is ever tame. He is never that. I mean that he has begun to realise, as all must, that civilisation has its own mission, as well as savagery'. The primitivist carvings, in his opinion, revealed 'the real Epstein, the untamed Epstein, the South Sea Island Epstein, with hard brain and caustic insight, aghast at civilization'.[11]

One of the most striking attempts to position Epstein outside contemporary Western culture was made by a critic of The Jewish Chronicle, who detected a single spiritual concept underpinning both aspects of Epstein's art. He asserted that Epstein's expression was 'entirely Hebraic' and claimed him as 'the first great Jewish sculptor'.[12] It is significant that Jewish critics only began to identify with Epstein's works in this way as the Great War drew to a close and the question of their own racial identity had become a focus of public debate and anxiety in Britain. After the War there was a sense of cultural dislocation and loss of the traditional values upon which British identity had been based. The awareness of social and cultural fragmentation at the heart and periphery of Empire, in the form of labour strife at home and revolution in Ireland, Egypt and India, all provided a receptive climate for Spenglerian beliefs about the decline of Western civilisation and return to a primitive condition in the modern age. Oswald Spengler's Decline of The West (1918 and 1922, published in English 1926–29), enjoyed a wide currency in Britain during the Twenties. It provided an appropriate ideological framework and vocabulary for projecting anxieties about modern culture and fears of social regression onto Jewish outsiders, who were cast as the instigators of both International Capitalism and Bolshevik revolution, remorseless technological progress, and social regression.

The affiliation established between Einstein and Epstein in the popular press provides one example of the way Jewish identity was used as a counterpoint to the idea of British character and symbol of the changes believed to threaten its security in the new post-War world. Modern scientist and artistic primitive were frequently coupled as barbarian iconoclasts, intent on breaking down the established order of civilised thought through their respective forms of relativity. A recurrent theme of the jokes which articulated their relationship was that they 'misused figures', making their work 'incomprehensible' to that trustworthy representative of British culture, 'the man in the street'.[13]

Bolshevik was another adjective, compounding notions of modernity and the primitive, used by Epstein's most hostile critics to denote his Jewish identity and iconoclastic intentions. The identification of Jews and Bolsheviks, popular in the British press after the Russian Revolution, intensified the belief that Jewish immigrants were a dangerous force within the nation, working to achieve social, cultural and even racial regression. General Pitt-Rivers, for example, attributed to Bolsheviks a 'mad desire for a return to the primitive', and Winston Churchill expressed his belief that Bolshevism was 'a world-wide conspiracy for the overthrow of civilisation and for the reconstitution of society on the basis of arrested development'.[14] A cartoon which appeared in *Punch* on 1 July 1925 [Fig. 26] is interesting as an example of the way Epstein was represented as a subversive

revolutionary whose artistic practice paralleled the type of social regression which, it was feared, would follow the Bolshevik revolution. The cartoon is also striking for the way his features have, by an unflattering exaggeration, been cast into a Jewish stereotype; unpleasant insinuations about his immoral way of life and sexual relationships with his 'white' models are also present.

The publication of *The Protocols of The Elders of Zion* in *The Times* in 1919 was a major catalyst in the growth of anti-Semitism and, despite later proof of forgery, the document provided the focus for a wide range of socio-economic grievances directed against the Anglo-Jewish population during the Twenties.[15] The most concentrated form of anti-Semitic propaganda based on the *Protocols* was disseminated by *The Britons* in their periodical, *The Hidden Hand or Jewish Peril*, and they published several articles about Epstein's work in the Twenties to illustrate their theory of an international Jewish conspiracy in the Arts. Stressing the sinister implications of Epstein's cosmopolitanism, *The Britons* argued that Epstein's use of non-European sources and models was a form of cultural miscegenation, designed to corrupt the moral and even racial purity of the British people.[16]

2. RESPONSES TO EPSTEIN'S MODELLED WORK IN THE TWENTIES

The first direct references to Epstein's 'racial art'[17] appeared in 1920, when his modelled life-size *Risen Christ* [110] was exhibited at the Leicester Galleries. Paradoxically, Epstein's foray into more familiar stylistic and thematic territory with this work only served to accentuate his 'otherness'. By representing Christ, Epstein, consciously or unconsciously, drew attention to his Jewish identity. However submerged, the ancient religious prejudices dividing Jew and Gentile continued to provide a basis upon which racial and cultural boundaries were drawn and the figure of Christ represented the most potent symbol of this divide. For a Jew to depict Christ was like an act of reclamation, a denial of prohibitions and a challenge to the accepted British notions of 'self' and 'other'.[18] Whether hostile or supportive, critics shared the opinion that Epstein's *Christ* was the expression of an alien mentality and constituted a direct challenge to the moral and aesthetic values native to contemporary Christian art. Their reviews were based on a common set of terms, such as 'archaic', 'barbaric', 'Oriental', 'Egyptian', 'aesthetic' and 'revolutionary', signifying the otherness of Epstein's *Christ* and offering a counter-image to the gentle divinity of Christian convention. Sensation-seeking press articles frequently combined assertions of the *Risen Christ*'s non-Western racial identity, with descriptions of his 'monstrous', 'revolutionary', 'insane', 'criminal', 'simian' and even 'Satanic' appearance.[19] The irony of this criticism was compounded by the fact that the head had developed from a portrait of Epstein's Dutch composer friend, Bernard van Dieren. Father Bernard Vaughan's diatribe was perhaps the most extreme in tone although the basic images he used were common

to other hostile reviews. He described the 'degenerate' racial characteristics of Epstein's figure, which suggested 'some degraded Chaldean or African, which wore the appearance of an Asiatic-American or Hun-Jew, which reminded me of some emaciated Hindu, or a badly grown Egyptian swathed in the cerements of the grave.' Father Vaughan declared that Epstein's *Christ* was Bolshevik in appearance and concluded his article with the insinuation that local pornographic shops in Soho provided the appropriate setting for such artistic immorality.[20] Other critics emphasised Epstein's psychological unsuitability, as a Jew, to depict Christian themes. In a letter to *The Daily Graphic*, 'an artist' questioned: 'Is Mr Epstein of British blood, and is he by faith a Christian? The name Epstein is no guide but it suggests a possibility that this sculptor is addressing an audience of British Christians without the necessary psychic equipment.'[21]

Staunch defenders of Epstein's work did not disregard the significance of his Jewish background and alien mentality. John Middleton Murry, for instance, asked whether there was 'any chance of insulting a nation if we say that it is, after all, a Jewish Christ and not the Christ of the Western World'.[22] Articles in Jewish newspapers also hailed the work for its 'Jewish expression'; defining this 'Jewishness' in terms of the humanity and vigour of Epstein's conception.[23]

Associations between the primitive and Jewish qualities of Epstein's work were a common feature of the responses to another religious bronze, the *Madonna and Child* of 1926 [Fig. 74], which was perhaps Epstein's most radical reclamation of prohibited Christian subject-matter, since he

directly challenged the Aryan monopoly of Christian art by modelling the figures on his Indian model, Sunita, and her son Enver. Reviewing the bronze when it was exhibited at Knoedler's in 1930, one critic stated that 'Epstein lacks the European mind, and feels no urge for the refined types of an aristocratic society. When, as now, his muse feeds on Oriental mysticism, it has much of the gloom, sadness and cramping spirit of the ghetto.' He detected an ancient quality in the faces of Epstein's figures 'that is older than man, as old as the sun. Something of the brooding quiet that first swept over the cradle of the world'.[24]

Epstein's portraits were frequently described as primitive not because they showed evidence of any stylistic borrowing from tribal or archaic sources but because they revealed Epstein's own predilection for non-European models and his indifference to Western norms of female beauty. One critic, in his account of Epstein's sympathetic portrayal of the 'animal' features of a young Senegalese girl [87], even cited the belief that 'the Jew forms a missing link between the black and white races'.[25] Epstein commented to Arnold Haskell on this tendency to ascribe primitive qualities to his traditionally modelled portraits: 'If any work of mine takes them out of their depth they rely on some easy generalisation, and talk of the oriental influence on my work, lumping African, Chaldean or Indian together quite loosely, merely to signify something that does not enter into their experience. I think that the chief reason that they hit upon the supposed African influence is the fact that I have modelled so many African types . . . I am interested in the negro type of beauty, but the results are purely traditional and European in technique.'[26] He also protested against the 'racism in art' evident in responses to the portraits which were exhibited at the Venice Biennale in 1924, and which had been held up on arrival in Italy because of Mussolini's Aryan decrees. Epstein cited a particularly extreme example of anti-Semitic art criticism, published in *The New Age*, as proof of the 'early growth of hatred and propaganda against Jews in art'.[27]

After questioning why Epstein should choose to express his 'alien genius' in the 'portrayal of such savage types' or project 'bestial characteristics [onto] ordinary good-looking models', the *New Age* critic declared his belief that 'the soul of the race speaks' through artistic genius and that Epstein's portraits expressed his 'subconscious racial Hebraic life'. Surrounded by Epstein's sculptures, the critic assumed 'European civilization has vanished. Balance, self-poise, control, proportion — the gifts of ages — have been swept away. He transports us anew to the twilight of early Jewry, where power is the motive force of man, and woman is but an instrument of sensuality.'[28]

In 1924, *The Britons* published an article entitled 'Epstein's Art and The Learned Elders of Zion', citing a favourable review of Epstein's portraits by P. J. Konody as evidence of the Jewish threat to 'English womanhood'. This quotation is striking not only for the way it illustrates the overt racism of *The Britons*, but for the direct analogies it reveals between their notions of race as a determining factor in Epstein's art, and those of Konody, a Jewish critic supportive of *avant garde* art in Britain. Konody praised Epstein's bust of *Ferosa Rastoumji* [Fig. 21], 'a Parsee woman, whose racial characteristics are observed and recorded with a subtlety and sympathy that Mr Epstein rarely brings to bear upon his interpretation of Western womanhood. Indeed, a curious perversity seems to make him search among his white models for the high cheekbones and protruding lips and eyes of the dark races'.[29]

Modernist preoccupations with the principle of 'truth to materials' forced critics, such as Roger Fry, to pay formalist lip-service to Epstein's directly-carved public commissions of the Twenties, such as the *W. H. Hudson Memorial* [Figs 80–81*]. His support of this work against the threat of ignorant public prejudice and official censorship was, however, more tactical than truly appreciative.[30] It is striking how frequently not only Fry but also the more sympathetic Wilenski resorted to arguments about Epstein's racial difference in an attempt to marginalise his work and place it outside the field of true aesthetic experience.[31] In 1929 Wilenski was vociferous in his defence of the formal power of *Day* and *Night* [Fig. 84] but he later had misgivings about Epstein as a stone carver, suggesting that he was too much of a 'romantic' to be capable of the 'discipline which the modern concept imposes on its disciples'. Wilenski argued that Epstein's carving *Genesis* [134*], perhaps his most racially provocative work, could not have been produced by any other sculptor living in England, since 'no other is mentally so removed as to be able to arrive at this primaeval conception and to rest upon it as sufficient'.[32]

In contrast, a more typical splenetic reaction to the Underground carvings was expressed by Sir Reginald Blomfield, President of the Royal Institute of British Architects: 'Bestiality still lurks below the surface of our civilisation, but why grope about for it in the mud, why parade it in the open, why not leave it to wallow in its own primaeval slime?'[33] This outcry, like so many of the responses to Epstein's work in the Twenties, indicates a deeply-rooted anxiety about the 'primitive within'; a fear of the tenuous borderline separating the forces of civilisation and savagery. It is significant that Sir Reginald, in the process of defending Britain's civilised values from the primitive invasion of Epstein's work, should, however, have acknowledged that the forces of barbarism were inherent in his own culture. His only concern seems to have been that the mask of civilisation remain intact, the primitive concealed!

15 ◁
Mary (Mrs Ambrose) McEvoy 1909–10 (S18)
Bronze H 41.5
Leeds City Art Galleries

Fig 49
Tomb of Oscar Wilde Père Lachaise Cemetery,
Paris (S40, detail)
Hoptonwood stone

35
Crouching Sun Goddess 1910? (S28)
Limestone H 37.5
Nottingham Castle Museum

36
SUNFLOWER 1912–13 (S42)
San Stefano stone H 58.5
National Gallery of Victoria, Melbourne

39
MATERNITY 1910 (S23, detail)
Hoptonwood stone H 206
Leeds City Art Galleries

44
Amedeo Modigliani (1884–1920)
CARYATID c1912
Pencil and blue crayon 41.5 × 55
Walsall Museum and Art Gallery (Garman-Ryan
Collection, formerly Jacob Epstein collection)

48
DOVES (third version) 1914–15 (S55)
Marble H64.8
The Trustees of the Tate Gallery

59
STUDY OF A WINGED FIGURE c 1912–13
Blue crayon 52 × 63.5
Anthony d'Offay Gallery, London

50
FIGURE IN FLENITE 1913 (S46)
Serpentine stone H 60.9
The Minneapolis Institute of Arts. Gift of Samuel H.
Maslon, Charles H. Bell, Francis D. Butler, John
Cowles, Bruce B. Dayton, and anonymous donor

96
'Lunch in the Shop' or 'The Sweat-
shop' 1900–02
Black chalk 43 × 53
Walsall Museum and Art Gallery (Garman-Ryan
Collection)

93
Joseph Conrad 1924 (S148)
Bronze H 48.2
Birmingham Museums and Art Gallery

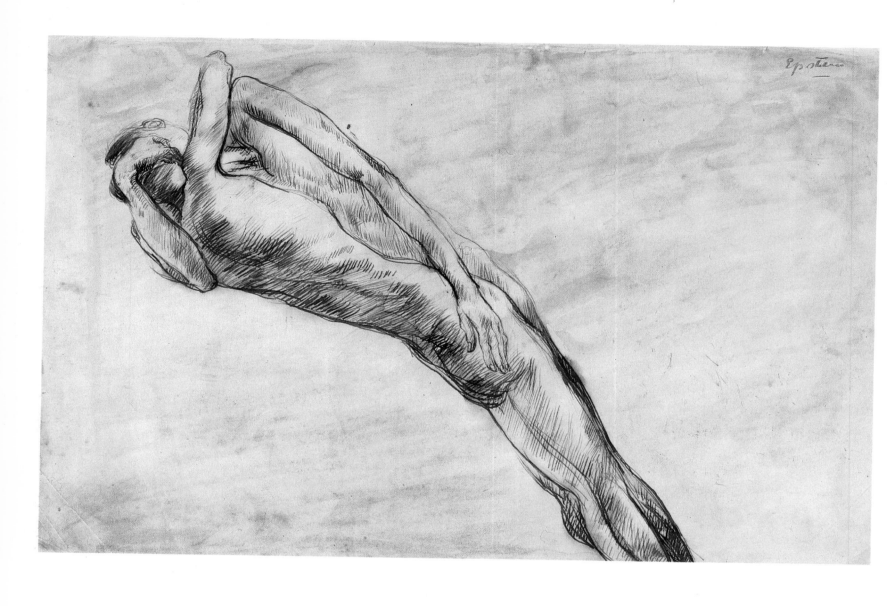

98
'We Two Boys Together Clinging' for
W. Whitman, Calamus, in *Leaves of Grass*, *c* 1902
Pen and ink and coloured wash   35.8 × 23
Beth Lipkin

109
STUDY FOR THE CENTRAL PANEL (DETAIL) OF THE
DROP-CURTAIN FOR THE BALLET DAVID   1935
Pencil and watercolour   57 × 44·3
Private collection

Fig 81
W. H. Hudson Memorial   Hyde Park, London
1923–25   (*S*147)

124
STUDY FOR THE RIMA RELIEF 1923
Pencil and watercolour 58.7 × 45.1
Leeds City Art Galleries (HMCSS)

116
EPPING FOREST 1933
Watercolour 56 × 43.2
Beth Lipkin

134
GENESIS 1929–30 (S194)
Seravezza marble H 162.5
Granada Television Ltd

143
JACOB AND THE ANGEL   1939–40   (S312)
Alabaster   H 213
University of Liverpool: on permanent loan from
Granada Television Ltd

138
ELEMENTAL   1932   (S225)
Alabaster   H 81
Private collection

140
WOMAN POSSESSED 1932 (S226)
Hoptonwood stone L 101.6
Australian National Gallery, Canberra

157
GIRL FROM BAKU 1944 (S354)
Bronze H 55.9
Private collection

164 ▷
LEDA HORNSTEIN (fourth portrait: with coxcomb) 1940 (S311)
Bronze H 19
Bolton Museum and Art Gallery

177 ▷▷
MAQUETTE FOR TRADES UNION CONGRESS WAR MEMORIAL 1955 (S489)
Bronze 53.2
Bolton Museum and Art Gallery

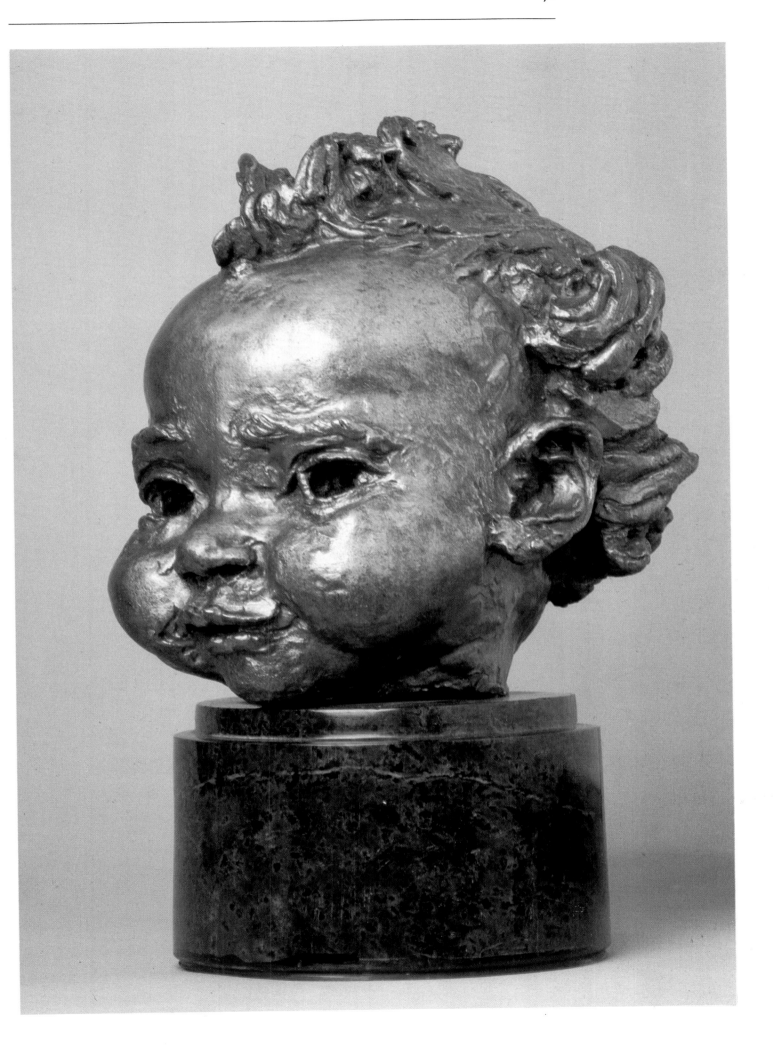

EPSTEIN LAMPOONED

Einstein and Epstein are wonderful men,
　　Bringing new miracles into our ken.
Einstein upset the Newtonian rule;
　　Epstein demolished the Pheidian School.
Einstein gave fits to the Royal Society;
　　Epstein delighted in loud notoriety.
Einstein made parallels meet in infinity;
　　Epstein remodelled the form of Divinity.[1]

I don't like the family Stein.
　　There is Gert, there is Ep, there is Ein.
Gert's writings are punk,
　　Ep's statues are junk,
Nor can anyone understand Ein.[2]

PROGRESS.

Post-Elliptical Rhomboidist: "Him a modern! Bah! He paints in the old-fashioned manner of last Thursday!"

Fig 22
Will Dyson
PROGRESS　1914
Pen and ink
Seated left, Epstein and right, Augustus John, with
Wyndham Lewis, background, in hat.[3]

2
Adrian Allinson
EPSTEIN DOUBTING THE AUTHENTICITY OF A
SOUTH SEA IDOL   1914
Pen and ink   20 × 20
Ross McInnes[4]

Fig 23
Charles Sykes
THE VENUS OF EPSTEIN   1917
Pencil
Private collection[5]

FOR THIS RELIEF NOT MUCH THANKS.

EPSTEIN'S FEMALE. "KAMERAD!"
GILBERT'S EROS. "I THINK NOT."

There once was a sculptor of mark
    Who was chosen to brighten Hyde Park;
Some thought this design
    Most uncommonly fine,
But more liked it best in the dark.[8]

Fig 24
Edmund Dulac
ECCE HOMUNCULUS: EPSTEIN ADMIRING A BUST
OF NAPOLEON   1920
Pen and ink
Private collection[6]

Fig 25
Anonymous
From *Punch*   3 June 1925[7]

Fig 26
Frank Reynolds
From *Punch*   1 July 1925[9]

Fig 27
Anonymous
From *Punch*   1 July 1925[10]

Fig 28
David Low
BUDGET GODS. MR. CHUMPSTEIN'S LATEST
Ink and crayon
For *The Evening Standard*, 27 April 1933
The Centre for the Study of Cartoons and Caricature,
University of Kent at Canterbury[11]

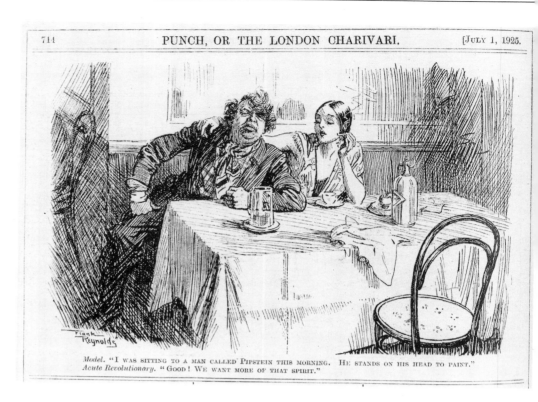

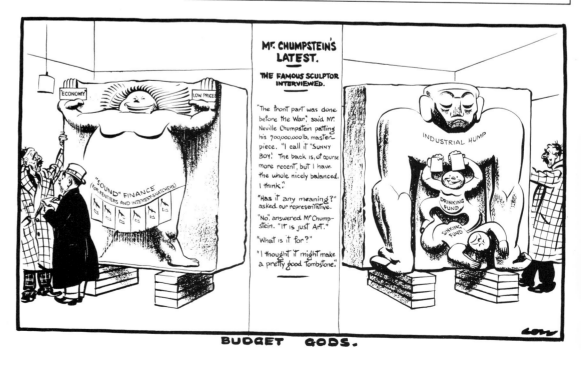

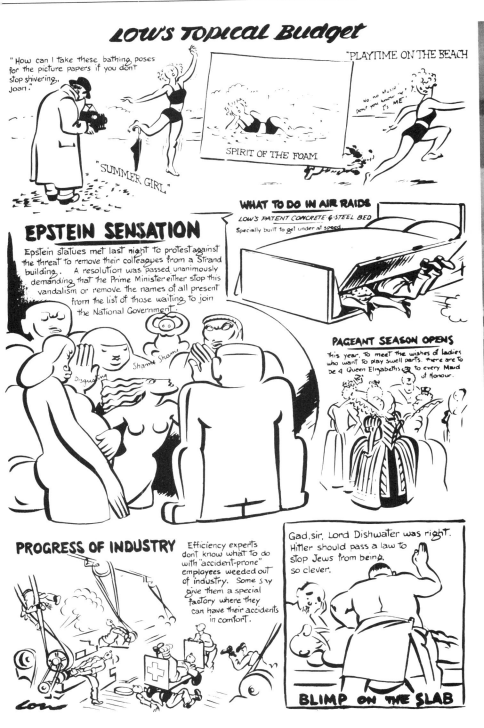

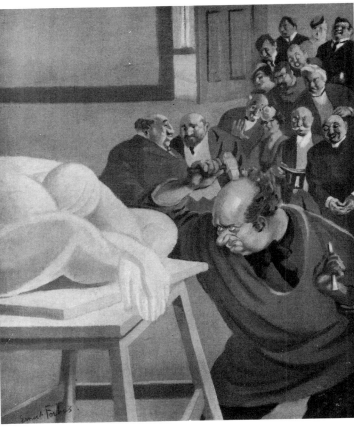

Fig 29
David Low
LOW'S TOPICAL BUDGET: EPSTEIN SENSATION
Ink and crayon
For *The Evening Standard*, 25 May 1935
The Centre for the Study of Cartoons and Caricature,
University of Kent at Canterbury[12]

Fig 30
Ernest Forbes
THE CONFRONTATION: SCULPTOR JACOB
EPSTEIN PREPARES A FRESH PROBLEM FOR HIS
PUBLIC
From *The Sketch*, 17 March 1937[13]

Fig 31
Will Dyson
MR NOEL COWARD 'OF COURSE MR EPSTEIN, I
SPEAK AS A LAY MAN — FOR THE MOMENT I HAVE
DONE NO SCULPTURE'
Etching
The Fine Art Society Ltd, London

Fig 32
Press Topic
MODERN CAESAR: MUSSOLINI SPEAKING
and Felix Man
MODERN ADAM: EPSTEIN'S SCULPTURE
From *Lilliput*, August 1939[14]

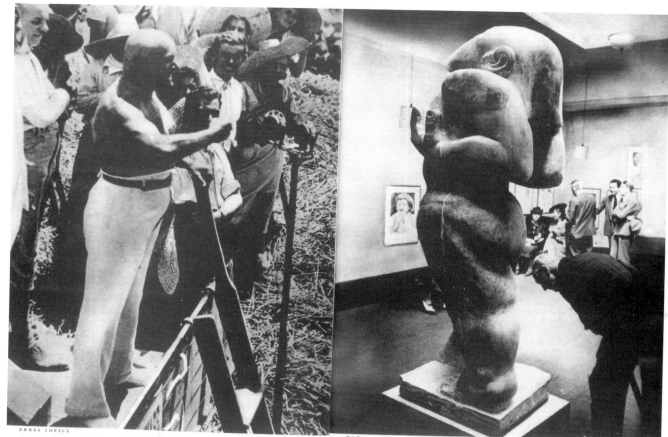

MODERN CÆSAR
Mussolini Speaking

MODERN ADAM
Epstein's Sculpture

Jacob Epstein: A Chronology 1880–1959

Compiled by
Elsje Prinz and Terry Friedman

The main events of Epstein's life are associated with contemporary cultural events which bear on his work and place it in wider art contexts, public and press attitudes towards sculpture, and world events. Following the first entry, Epstein is referred to as JE. Works of art and literature are generally listed under the year of completion or, in the case of music, of a first performance. Epstein's sculpture, drawings and illustrations carrying bracketed numbers coincide with works in the exhibition. The chronology must necessarily be brief, and the reader seeking more detailed information is directed to: Epstein's autobiography, *Let There Be Sculpture*, 1940 (reprinted 1942, 1955); R. Buckle, *Jacob Epstein Sculptor*, 1963; E. Silber, *The Sculpture of Epstein: with a complete catalogue*, 1986 (includes list of exhibitions *c*1898–1986); also J. Clapp, *Art Censorship: A Chronology of Proscribed and Prescribed Art*, 1972; R. Cork, *Vorticism and Abstract Art in the First Machine Age*, 1976; S. Nairne and N. Serota, eds, *British Sculpture in the Twentieth Century*, 1981; E. Lucie-Smith, *Cultural Calendar of the 20th Century*, 1979; A. Palmer, *Dictionary of Twentieth Century History 1900–1982*, 1985; and standard biographies.

The New York Years 1880–1902

1880	Jacob Epstein is born on 10 November at 102 Hester Street, New York City, the third child of Max and Mary Solomon Epstein, Jewish-Polish immigrants	Auguste Rodin, *The Gates of Hell* begun Edgar Degas, *The Little Ballet-dancer, 14 Years Old* Birth of André Derain	
1881		Metropolitan Museum of Art school (opened 1880) introduces drawing, modelling and carving classes Births of Wilhelm Lehmbruck, Pablo Picasso	Louis Pasteur discovers rabies virus Jewish emigration from Russia following pogroms provoked by Tzar Alexander II's assassination
1882		Births of Umberto Boccioni, Eric Gill, Gaston Lachaise, Elie Nadelman Death of Charles Darwin	
1883		Birth of Ivan Meštrović Deaths of Edouard Manet, Karl Marx, Richard Wagner	
1884		Birth of Amadeo Modigliani	J. K. Huysmans, *A Rebours* Fabian Society founded in Britain

1885		Prince Kropotkin, *Paroles d'un révolté* (later read by JE)	Death of Victor Hugo
		Le Révolté, anarchist review, established in Paris	
		Birth of Henri Laurens	
1886	JE contracts pleurisy, ill for several years	F-A Bartholdi, *Statue of Liberty* erected in New York harbour	
		300 Impressionist paintings ('lumpy and obnoxious creations') shown at George Petit Gallery, New York	
		George Seurat, *La Grande Jatte*	
		New English Art Club founded as reaction to Royal Academy conservativism	
		Birth of Frank Dobson	
1887		New York Society for the Suppression of Vice seizes 117 'lewd and obscene' illustrations of modern French masterpieces at Knoedler Gallery	
		H. H. Richardson, *Marshall Field Store*, Chicago	
		Births of Alexander Archipenko, Jean Arp, Marc Chagall, William Zorach	
1888		Rodin, *The Kiss*	
		Nabis founded in Paris	
		Leeds City Art Gallery opened	
1889		Educational Alliance Art School founded on Lower East Side, New York	
		Gustave Eiffel, *Eiffel Tower*, Paris	
		Vincent van Gogh, *The Starry Night*	
1890		Augustus Saint-Gaudens's mixed life-drawing classes at Art Students' League, New York, discontinued	
		Births of David Bomberg, Naum Gabo, Leon Underwood, Ossip Zadkine	
		Death of Vincent van Gogh	
		James Fraser, *The Golden Bough*	
		William James, *The Principles of Psychology*	
1891	JE wins a Cooper Union art competition about this time	Births of Henri Gaudier-Brzeska, Jacques Lipchitz	
		Paul Gauguin moves from France to Tahiti, carves *Hina and Te Fatou* (1892)	
		Bernard Meninsky emigrates from Ukraine to Liverpool	
		Oscar Wilde, *The Picture of Dorian Gray*	

1892		*Munich Secession* founded Death of Walt Whitman	
1893	JE attends PS Seven, Christie Street, and the East Side Settlement (until age thirteen); he registers at the Art Students' League, giving his address as 102 Hester Street	World's Columbian Exposition, Chicago Alfred Gilbert, *Shaftesbury Memorial (Eros)*, London	
1894	JE studies at the Art Students' League (until 1902)	*Yellow Book* founded in Britain Claude Debussy, *Prélude à l'Après-Midi d'un Faune*	Dreyfus Case causes widespread anti-semitism in France
1895		Adler and Sullivan, *Guaranty Building*, Buffalo Rodin, *Burghers of Calais* Paul Cézanne's first one-man show in Paris	Guglielmo Marconi invents wireless telegraphy Sigmund Freud and Joseph Breuer, *Studies on Hysteria* Oscar Wilde on trial in London
1896	JE is living at 26 Delancey Street and attending James Kirk Paulding's classes at the Community Guild, where he is introduced to the writings of Conrad, Ruskin, Turgenev and Whitman	Anton Chekhov, *The Sea-Gull*	Klondike Gold Rush First modern Olympic Games held at Athens
1897		Frederick MacMonnie's 'licentious' *Baccante and Infant Faun*, removed from Boston Public Library (1896), presented to Metropolitan Museum of Art, New York George Grey Barnard's *Pan* rejected by New York Superintendent of Parks Alfred Stieglitz founds *Camera Review* in New York Eric Satie, *Gymnopédies* *Vienna Secession* founded Tate Gallery opens	Queen Victoria's 60th Jubilee
1898	JE organises an exhibition of work by local artists at the Hebrew Institute, New York and spends the winter with the painter, Bernard Gussow on Greenwood Lake, New Jersey, where he decides to be a sculptor	Rodin's plaster *Monument to Balzac* attacked as 'formless lava' by outraged public Lachaise studying at Académie Nationale des Beaux Arts, Paris (until 1905) Cézanne begins *The Great Bathers* Kathe Kollwitz's 'gutter art' condemned by Kaiser Wilhelm II Leo Tolstoy, *What is Art?* Births of Alexander Calder, Henry Moore Death of Aubrey Beardsley Wilde, *The Ballad of Reading Gaol*	Spanish-American War

1899	JE remains in rented rooms overlooking Hester Street after his family moves to 1661 Madison Avenue; he is employed as a physical education instructor and tenement inspector, and begins to sell his drawings	Aimé-Jules Dalou, *Triomphe de la République*, Paris Paul Bartholomé, *Monument aux Morts*, Père Lachaise Cemetery, Paris Frederick Delius, *Paris-Song of a Great City* Joseph Maria Olbrich, *Secession Building*, Vienna Charles Rennie Mackintosh, *Glasgow School of Art*	Boer War
1900	JE is employed in a New York bronze foundry, draws the Lower East Side scene [95–97], illustrates Hutchins Hapgood's 'Four Poets of the Ghetto' (*The Critic*, March issue) and 'The Foreign Stage in New York' (*The Bookman*, August issue), and turns down an offer to work with Thomas Eakins in Philadelphia	Universal Exposition, Paris Hector Guimard, *Métro stations*, Paris Jacob Kramer emigrates from Ukraine to Leeds Edward Elgar, *The Dream of Gerontius* Joseph Conrad, *Lord Jim* Giacomo Puccini, *Tosca* Death of Wilde	Freud, *The Interpretation of Dreams* Max Planck publishes quantum theory British Labour Party founded Boxer Rising in China
1901	JE attends Barnard's modelling classes at the Art Students' League (1901–02) and receives the commission to illustrate Hapgood's *The Spirit of the Ghetto* *Self-portrait* [3]	M. H. Spielmann, *British Sculpture and Sculptors To-Day* Picasso's first Paris exhibition Birth of Alberto Giacometti Death of Henri Toulouse-Lautrec Thomas Mann, *Buddenbrooks* H. G. Wells, *The First Men on the Moon*	Assassination of President McKinley Death of Queen Victoria

THE PARIS YEARS 1902–1905

1902	*The Spirit of the Ghetto* [94] is published; JE is working in other premises as a result of his first studio burning down; he is issued with a passport on 10 September and sails for France, arriving in Paris on 3–4 October to witness the anti-semitic demonstrations attending Zola's funeral; he shares a studio with Gussow in the Rue Belloni (near Antoine Bourdelle's studio in the Impasse du Maine), attends the modelling atelier at the Ecole des Beaux Arts, visits the Louvre, Musée Guimet (Indian and Far Eastern art), Musée Cernusci (Chinese art) and a 'mass of primitive sculpture' at the Trocadero; probably begins the drawings for Whitman's *Calamus* [98]	Aristide Maillol exhibits at Durand-Ruel, Paris Toulouse-Lautrec retrospective, Paris Georges Meliès, *Voyage to the Moon* Debussy, *Pelléas et Mélisande*	Royal Commission on Alien Immigration into Britain appointed
1903	JE ('ce sauvage Américain') studies for eighteen months under Jean Paul Laurens at the Académie Julian; about this time he visits Rodin, meets Margaret ('Peggy') Dunlop and makes a brief trip to Florence	Death of Gauguin (the first European sculptor inspired by 'primitive' art) in the Marquesas Islands; major exhibition at Vollard, Paris Gertrude Stein arrives in Paris	Pierre and Marie Curie awarded Nobel Prize for discovering radium First Ford motor factories established in Detroit

		Auguste Perret, *Rue Franklin apartment block* Birth of Barbara Hepworth Henry James, *The Ambassadors* George Bernard Shaw, *Man and Superman* Delius, *Sea Drift* (text by Whitman) Edwin S. Porter, *The Great Train Robbery*	Wright brothers fly first self-propelled aircraft at Kitty Hawk, North Carolina Emmeline Pankhurst founds the Womens' Social and Political Union in Britain
1904	JE living at 5 Rue Campagne Première, Montparnasse; models or carves his first sculptures, including the *Temple of Love* and *Sun Worshippers* (destroyed by 1905) and probably visits England and the British Museum *Baby asleep* [6] *Baby awake* [7]	W. H. Hudson, *Green Mansions*	

THE LONDON YEARS 1905–1959

1905	JE destroys the contents of his Paris studio and moves to London with Peggy Dunlop, bringing a commendatory letter from Rodin; he lives and works at 219 Stanhope Street, St Pancras and is introduced to Shaw, Robert Ross and the artists James Muirhead Bone, Francis Dodd, Augustus John [1] and William Rothenstein *Mother and child* [8]	Zadkine moves from Sutherland, County Durham, to Paris Maillol, *L'Action Enchainée* shocks French officials *Les Fauves'* work at Salon d'Automne enrages public French Impressionists show at Grafton Gallery, London Derain painting in London *Die Brücke* founded in Dresden Antonio Gaudi, *Casa Milá*, Barcelona	Albert Einstein, *On the electrodynamics of moving bodies* (*Special Theory of Relativity*) Freud, *Three Treatises on the Theory of Sex* Max Weber, *The Protestant Ethic and the Spirit of Capitalism* St Petersburg workers form the first Soviet Russo-Japanese War
1906	JE visits New York briefly, returns to London, marries Peggy Dunlop, settles at the Stamford Bridge Studios, Fulham and exhibits at the New English Art Club *Girl with a dove* [9]	Rodin exhibition, International Society, London Jewish Exhibition, Whitechapel Art Gallery Gaudier-Brzeska visits England Constantin Meunier's *Monument au Travail* refused by Belgium government Frank Lloyd Wright, *Unity Temple*, Oak Park, Illinois Death of Cézanne	
1907	JE moves his studio to 72 Cheyne Walk, Chelsea, and begins work on the eighteen statues for Charles Holden's British Medical Association Building in the Strand *Romilly John* [31]	Death of Saint-Gaudens Brancusi, *The Kiss* (first version), *Torment*, *Wisdom of the Earth* Derain, *Crouching Figure* Picasso, *Les Demoiselles d'Avignon* Ralph Vaughan Williams, *Towards the Unknown Region* (text by Whitman) Conrad, *The Secret Agent*	

1908

JE's BMA statues [10–12], unveiled to unprecedented public and press hostility, are defended by Bone, John, Frank Harris and the Bishop of Stepney; Eric Gill claims JE is 'raising modern sculpture from the dead'; the commission for the *Tomb of Oscar Wilde* is announced

Euphemia Lamb [14]

Fountain Figure (Euphemia Lamb)

Gaudier-Brzeska revisits England

Wyndham Lewis moves from Paris to London

Roger Fry defends Cézanne in *Burlington Magazine*

Henri Matisse, *Two Negresses*

E. B. Havell, *Indian Sculpture and Painting*

A. Coomaraswamy, *Medieval Sinhalese Art*

Peter Behrens, *AEG Turbine Factory*, Berlin

Mass-production of Model T Ford in Detroit

Union of South Africa established

1909

Mrs Ambrose McEvoy [15]

Nan Condron [25]

Rom [33]

Narcissus

Picasso, *Head of a Woman: Fernande* (cubist sculpture)

Matisse, *The Back* (first version), *The Serpentine*

George Braque, *Piano and Mandola*

Thomes Brock, *Victoria Memorial* London

Barnard's symbolic figure for Pennsylvania State Capitol ordered draped at official unveiling

Ezra Pound arrives in London

F. T. Marinetti, *The Foundation and Manifesto of Futurism*

Sergei Diaghilev's *Ballet Russes* in Paris

Louis Blériot crosses Channel in aeroplane

1910

JE becomes a naturalised British subject on 22 December, exhibits at the Allied Artists' Association and the Whitechapel Art Gallery. With Gill he attempts unsuccessfully to establish an artists' commune, with monumental sculptures, 'a modern Stonehenge', at Asheham House, Sussex; the marble bust of *Mrs Ambrose McEvoy* is purchased by Johannesburg Art Gallery (his first work to enter a public collection)

Lady Gregory [27]

Rom [34]

Crouching Sun Goddess [35]

Maternity [37]

'one of the hundred pillars of the Secret Temple' [41]

The Flame of Life [42]

Marie Rankin [45]

Mrs Emily Chadbourne

Sun God

Gill begins carving in stone (*Cocky Kid, Ecstasy, Votes for Women*)

Frank Rutter, *Revolution in Modern Art*

Roger Fry's first Post-Impressionist Exhibition, Grafton Galleries, London

Sir Arthur Evans begins Knossos excavations

Brancusi, *The Kiss* (*Monument to Tania Rachevskaia*, Montparnasse Cemetery, Paris)

Matisse, *Head of Jeannette I, The Dance*

Boccioni and others, *Manifesto of the Futurist Painters*

Henri Rousseau, *The Dream*

Chagall arrives in Paris from Vitebsk

Igor Stravinsky, *The Firebird*

Der Sturm founded in Berlin

Adolf Loos, *Steiner House*, Vienna

Strauss, *Salome* (first performance in London)

Vaughan Williams, *A Sea Symphony* (text by Whitman) premiered at Leeds Musical Festival

Plastic invented

1911	JE exhibits at the National Portrait Society, London *Nan seated* [17] *Nan the Dreamer* [18, 22] *Standing Mother and Child*	Gaudier-Brzeska settles in London Albert Toft, *Modelling and Sculpture* *Camden Town Group* founded in London Duncan Grant, *Bathing* Brancusi, *Maiastra* (first version) Raymond Duchamp-Villon, *Head of Baudelaire* Matisse, *The Red Studio No 1* Kaiser Wilhelm II proclaims Impressionists and Van Gogh 'too depraved for the Prussians' *Blaue Reiter* group founded in Munich Walter Gropius and Adolf Meyer, *Fargus Factory*, Alfeld Mahler, *Das Leid von der Erde*	Roald Amundsen reaches South Pole
1912	JE begins the first of a series of portraits of his wife [78], introduces Mark Gertler to Egyptian art at the British Museum, meets Wyndham Lewis while decorating The Cave of the Golden Calf in London (destroyed 1914), completes the *Tomb of Oscar Wilde*, which Gaudier-Brzeska and others see in the London studio, before its installation in Père Lachaise Cemetery, Paris; there JE meets Modigliani (with whom he considers sharing a studio, and from whom he acquires *Caryatid* [44]), as well as Brancusi, Picasso and the collector, Paul Guillaume; JE probably purchases his first pieces of primitive sculpture [2], before returning to London in November; there he exhibits *Maternity* at the Allied Artists' Association, his friendship with Gill breaks up and he moves to Pett Level, Sussex, while keeping rooms above Harold Munro's Poetry Bookshop in Devonshire Street *Tomb of Oscar Wilde* [30] *Sunflower* [36]	George Frampton, *Peter Pan*, Kensington Gardens Bomberg, *Vision of Ezekiel* Lewis, *Kermesse* Fry's Second Post-Impressionist exhibition Stanley Spencer, *The Nativity* Brancusi, *Mlle Pogany* (first version, acquired by John Quinn 1914) Marcel Duchamp, *Nude Descending a Staircase* Maison Cubiste, Salon d'Automne, Paris Italian Futurist Painters exhibition, Paris and London Giorgio de Chirico, *The Enigma of the Hour* Maurice Ravel, *Daphnis et Cloé* Chagall, *Hommage to Apollinaire*	*Titanic* sinks in North Atlantic Charles Pathé produces first newsreel First Balkan War Manchu Dynasty collapses in China
1913	In January JE travels with Bomberg to Paris, where he sees the *Brummer Fang reliquary head* (which he purchases in 1935); returning to London in August, he begins *Rock Drill* [61, 65–69], shows sculpture and drawings in his first one-man exhibition at the Twenty-One Gallery; the first version of *Doves*, studies for *Rock Drill* and the flenite carvings [50] appear in the Post-Impressionist and Futurist Exhibition, and the bust of *Euphemia Lamb* [14] at the International Exhibition of Modern Art (Armory Show) in New York; JE is defended by T. E. Hulme in *The New*	Rodin, *The Kiss*, on loan to Lewes Corporation, hidden from public by tarpaulin Gilbert, *The Leeds Chimneypiece* Gill, *Stations of the Cross*, Westminster Cathedral Gaudier-Brzeska, *Horace Brodzky*, *Alfred Wolmark* Brancusi shows *Sleeping Muse* at Allied Artists' Exhibition, London *Omega Workshop* founded Post-Impressionist Room, Ideal Home Exhibition *Rebel Art Group* formed in London	Alfred Whitehead and Bertrand Russell, *Principia Mathematica* Niels Bohr discovers structure of atom

Age (25 December); his mother dies in New York	Lady Drogheda's London dining room decorated by Lewis	
Venus (first version) [49]	Matthew Smith, *Lilies* [153, later owned by JE]	
Figure in Flenite [50]	Shaw, *Pygmalion*	
Birth [55]	Matisse, *The Back* (second version)	
Flenite relief [56–57]	Duchamp makes the first 'ready-made' sculpture	
Rock Drill [60]	Lipchitz, *Mother and Child*	
Totem [63]	Guillaume Apollinaire, *The Cubist Painters*	
Study for Man-Woman [64]	Stravinsky's *The Rite of Spring* causes riot in Paris	
Doves (first version)	Marcel Proust, *Swann's Way*	
Female Figure in Flenite	Boccioni, *Unique Forms of Continuity in Space*	
Cursed Be the Day Wherein I Was Born		
Mother and Child		

1914	JE travels to Paris for the unveiling of the *Tomb of Oscar Wilde*, which receives a hostile reception; he returns to London, exhibits in the Jewish section of *Twentieth Century Art: A Review of Modern Movements* at the Whitechapel Art Gallery; his studies of birth are illustrated in the first issue of Lewis's periodical *BLAST* and he exhibits work at the Wilton Crescent home of the Droghedas': Lord Drogheda threatens to throw 'those fucking doves' out the window!	Gaudier-Brzeska, *Red Stone Dancer, Seated Woman, Bird Swallowing Fish, Hieratic Head of Ezra Pound*	Panama Canal opens
		Gill, *Mulier*	Archduke Franz Ferdinand of Austria assassinated at Serajewo
		Meštrović working in London	First World War breaks out
		Vorticism's official coming-out	First Battle of the Marne
		Bomberg, *The Mud Bath*	
		Velazquez's *Rokeby Venus* (National Gallery, London) damaged by suffragette	
	Doves (second and third versions) [46, 48]	Renoir, *Venus Victorious*	
	Venus (second version)	Brancusi, *Two Penguins, The First Cry*	
		Picasso, *Glass of Absinth*	
		Ernst Barlach, *The Avenger*	
		Metropolitan Magazine suppressed by New York City postmaster for illustrating Paul Manship's sculpture	
		Edgar Rice Burroughs, *Tarzan of the Apes*	
		James Joyce, *The Dubliners*	

1915	JE's *Doves* is purchased for £60 by John Quinn (a New York lawyer who defined 'art' for the United States Tariff Law)	*BLAST 2*	Battle at Gallipoli
		Gaudier-Brzeska killed on Western Front	*Lusitania* sunk by German submarine in Atlantic
		Meštrović exhibition, Victoria and Albert Museum	Edith Cavell executed by Germans for spying
	Mother and Child (destroyed 1923)	Brancusi, *Caryatid II*	
		Duchamp, *In Advance of a Broken Arm, The Bride Stripped Bare by Her Bachelor, Even* begun	
		Gabo, *Constructed Head No 1*	
		Carl Einstein, *Negerplastik*	
		D. W. Griffith, *Birth of a Nation*	
		Franz Kafka, *Metamorphosis*	

1916	JE returns from Pett Level to London, moves to 23 Guildford Street, Bloomsbury and exhibits *Rock Drill*	Pound, *Gaudier-Brzeska: A Memoir*	Conscription introduced in Britain
		Ben Uri Society founded in London	First British tanks used on Western Front

Torso [70]; Quinn purchases *Female Figure in Flenite*

T. E. Hulme [62]

Admiral Lord Fisher [73]

The Tin Hat [74]

Mrs Jacob Epstein with earrings [79]

James Muirhead Bone [113]

Joyce, *Portrait of the Artist as a Young Man*

Matisse, *The Back* (third version)

Dada group formed in Zurich

Leo Janáček, *Jenufa*

Battles of Verdun and the Somme

Easter Rising in Dublin

Alfred Binet, *The Development of Intelligence in Children*

Murder of Rasputin

1917

JE sells £1,600 worth of bronzes at his first Leicester Galleries exhibition ('the most remarkable ever given by a British sculptor', *The Weekly Dispatch*, 18 February) and begins *Risen Christ*, which is interrupted when he is forced to enlist as a Private in the Jewish 38th Battalion of the Royal Fusiliers, stationed at Crownhill, Plymouth; he fails to gain an appointment as Official War Artist; Hulme is killed in France; Quinn purchases *Venus* (second version) for £400, the granite *Mother and Child* and portraits of the *Duchess of Hamilton*, *Countess of Drogheda* and *Meum*; some of the Ghetto drawings made in New York in 1900–01 appear in *The Century Magazine*

Self-portrait in a Storm Cap [58]

Gladys Deacon [75]

T. S. Eliot, *The Love Song of J. Alfred Prufrock* ('In the room the women come and go | Talking of Michelangelo')

Deaths of Rodin, Degas, Duchamp-Villon

Apollinaire and Guillaume, *Sculpture Nègres*

Police remove Modigliani's nude paintings from Paris exhibition

Tony Garnier, *Cité Industrielle*

De Stijl (periodical) founded in Netherlands

Barnard's *Statue of Abraham Lincoln* for Parliament Square, London, rejected by British Parliament in favour of Saint Gaudens's

United States enters War

Battles of Ypres and Verdun

Tzar Nicholas II of Russia abdicates, October Revolution

Balfour Declaration supporting establishment of Jewish State in Palestine

Lion Feuchtwanger, *Jew Süss*

Carl Jung, *The Psychology of the Unconscious*

1918

JE, absent without leave on the eve of his regiment's departure for the Middle East, is hospitalised at Mount Tovey, Plymouth, and invalided-out in July; he begins a series of portraits of his first child, Peggy Jean (born 1918); Quinn purchases the portrait mask of *Mrs Epstein* [79] for £80 and the bust of *Muirhead Bone* [113] for £70

Corporal Harry Kosky [76]

Sargeant-Major Mitchell [77]

Mrs Jacob Epstein in a mantilla [80]

Mask of Meum [82]

Meum with a fan [84]

Gaudier-Brzeska memorial exhibition, London

Meninsky appointed Official War Artist

Lehmbruch, *Praying Woman*

Women over thirty given vote in Britain

Oswald Spengler, *The Decline of the West*

Russian royal family executed

Union of Soviet Socialist Republic proclaimed

Armistice Day (11 November)

1919

Moore enters Leeds College of Art as sculpture student

Deaths of Lehmbruch, Renoir

Bauhaus established at Weimar

Vladimir Tatlin, *Monument to the Third International*

Robert Wiene, *The Cabinet of Doctor Caligari*

Treaty of Versailles

League of Nations established at Geneva

Murders of Rosa Luxemburg and Karl Liebnecht

Benito Mussolini founds Fascia di Combattimento

Adolf Hitler founds National Socialist German Workers Party

John Maynard Keynes, *The Economic Consequences of the Peace*

1920	JE contemplates modelling a *Deposition* group [86], becomes a focus of attention when *Risen Christ* [110] is seen by huge crowds at the Leicester Galleries and is reviled by Father Vaughan as having 'the appearance of an Asiatic-American or Hun-Jew' (*The Graphic*, 14 February); JE visits Paris and Florence; Quinn purchases *An American Soldier* for £80; Bernard van Dieren, *Epstein* (with 50 illustrations, the first monograph), is published *Self-portrait with a beard*	Vorticism ends Fry, *Vision and Design* (essays on ancient and primitive art) Frampton, *Edith Cavell Memorial*, London Brancusi, *King of Kings*; *Princess X* removed by police from Salon des Indépendants in Paris on grounds of indecency Death of Modigliani Gabo and Antoine Pevsner expelled from Russian Communist Party Max Ernst organises 'First Dada Event' in Cologne; Arp's sculpture causes riot Otto Dix, *Skat Players*	American women given vote Prohibition legislated in United States Trial of Sacco and Vanzetti
1921	JE's work is discussed in Kineton Parkes, *Sculpture of To-Day* and attacked as 'crudities' in Lorado Taft, *Modern Tendencies in Sculpture*; he meets Kathleen Garman, a music student, and Moore, who begins training at the Royal College of Art *Jacob Kramer* [85] *Madeleine Béchet: Girl from Senegal* [87]	Dobson, *The Man Child* Spencer, *Christ's Entry into Jerusalem* Gustave Holst, *The Planets* Erich Mendelsohn, *Einstein Tower*, Neubabelsberg Ludwig Wittgenstein, *Tractatus Logico-philosophicus* Luigi Pirandello, *Six Characters in Search of an Author*	
1922	JE is commissioned to carve the *W. H. Hudson Memorial* in London; he rents a cottage at 49 Baldwyn's Hill, Loughton in Essex [116] *The Weeping Woman*	Dobson, *Portrait of Sir Osbert Sitwell* Deaths of Brock, William Henry Hudson Howard Carter discovers Tutankhamen's tomb Joyce, *Ulysses* MacMonnies's nude sculpture *Civic Virtue* causes public outrage in New York Chicago *Tribune Tower* competition Le Corbusier introduces International Style in architecture and design	Defeat of Coalition Government in Britain BBC established in London Mussolini becomes Italian Prime Minister (March on Rome)
1923	JE's first design for the *Hudson Memorial* [114–15] is replaced by one based on the character of Rima [117–22, 124–25] from *Green Mansions*, which is approved by the Memorial Committee and the Office of Works; the relief is begun; he criticises the British Museum's 'restoration' of Greek and Roman sculpture (*The Times*, 21 February); his granite *Mother and Child*, bought by Quinn in 1917, is apparently destroyed in New York on the sculptor's instructions *Old Pinager* [92] *R. B. Cunninghame Graham* [112] *Dolores* [123]	Gill, *Leeds University War Memorial* Brancusi, *White Negress* Gerrit Rietveld, *Schroeder House*, Utrecht George Grosz, *Ecce Homo*, charged with 'defaming public morals' in Germany	Stanley Baldwin becomes British Prime Minister Hitler begins *Mein Kampf* in prison

1924	JE is rejected as a candidate for the Chair of Sculpture at the Royal College of Art, Fry attacks his work in *The New Statesman* (26 January), an anti-semitic article appears in *The New Age* (14 February); he writes the Foreword to Hulme's *Speculations* (edited by Herbert Read); his son, Theo, is born and he meets Sunita and Anita, who become his models; Quinn dies in New York *Joseph Conrad* [93]	Death of Frederick William Pomeroy Births of Anthony Caro, Eduardo Paolozzi André Breton, *Manifesto du Surréalisme*	First Labour Government in Britain Death of Lenin Leon Trotsky, *Literature and Revolution*
1925	The *Hudson Memorial* in Hyde Park is unveiled by the Prime Minister, sparking-off the most virulent attacks of JE's career, including anti-semitic letters to the press, cartoons in *Punch* and questions in Parliament; he is praised by Sybil Thorndike for making 'me more like what I really am' (*The Evening Standard*, 27 May); Hubert Wellington, *Jacob Epstein*, with 35 plates, is published; at about this time JE meets Matthew Smith, a lifelong friend	Death of William Hamo Thornycroft Charles Sargeant Jagger, *Artillery Memorial*, Hyde Park Corner Brancusi exhibits at New Chenil Galleries, London Florence Mills' Blackbirds Revue, first show with all-black cast in London Exposition des Arts Décoratifs, Paris Gropius, *Bauhaus*, Dessau Alban Berg, *Wozzeck* Kafka, *The Trial* Sergei Eisenstein, *Battleship Potemkin* F. Scott Fitzgerald, *The Great Gatsby*	Scopes's 'monkey trial' in Tennessee (teaching evolution in schools)
1926	JE exhibits *Visitation* at the Leicester Galleries *Sunita* [88] *Rabindranath Tagore* [91] *Madonna and Child*	Death of Francis Derwent Wood T. E. Lawrence, *Seven Pillars of Wisdom* Calder, *Josephine Baker* Lang, *Metropolis*	General strike in Britain First public demonstration of television in Britain
1927	JE gives up the Guildford Street studio, visits New York for four months to attend a highly successful exhibition of his work, which includes *Madonna and Child*, at the Ferargil Gallery; during this time he meets William Zorach, visits the Barnes Collection in Philadelphia and defends Brancusi's *Bird in Space* at a Customs' hearing; his daughter, Kitty, is born	Sir Leonard Woolley excavates Ur of the Chaaldeas Virginia Woolf, *To the Lighthouse* Barlach's *Hovering Angel* is destroyed by Nazis as 'un-German' Hermann Hesse, *Steppenwolf* Abel Gance, *Napoleon* Lachaise, *Standing Woman* Buckminster Fuller, *Dymaxion House* *The Jazz Singer* (with Al Jolson)	Charles Lindberg's first transatlantic solo flight Execution of Sacco and Vanzetti *Mein Kampf* published in Germany
1928	JE returns from New York in January (on shipboard, Lord Rothermere hails him as 'the greatest sculptor in the world'), moves into 18 Hyde Park Gate, Knightsbridge and Deerhurst at Loughton, Essex; Holden invites him	Gill and Moore carving *Wind* reliefs on London Underground headquarters Death of Sir George Frampton D. H. Lawrence, *Lady Chatterley's Lover*	Alexander Fleming discovers penicillin

to carve *Day* and *Night* on the London Underground Electric Railways headquarters [128–133]; JE purchases *Baby Suckling* from Moore's first one-man show; JE's work is discussed in Stanley Casson, *Some Modern Sculptors*

Mrs Godfrey Phillips [90]

Peggy Jean: The Sick Child [160]

Congrès Internationaux d'Architecture Moderne (CIAM) founded

Luis Buñuel and Salvador Dali, *Un Chien Andalou*

Paul Schulze-Naumberg, *Art and Race* (Nazi concept of degenerate art based on hereditary determinism)

Kurt Weill, *The Three Penny Opera*

1929

JE begins carving *Genesis*, his studies of Sunita, negresses [99] and other models are published in *Epstein. Seventy-Five Drawings* [100], with an introduction by Hubert Wellington; his daughter, Esther is born; 'Statues — Mr Epstein and the Man in the Street' (BBC talk by Osbert Sitwell, 31 May)

Day and *Night*

Moore, *Reclining Figure*, Brown Hornton stone

J. Thorpe, *Eric Gill*

Death of Bourdelle

Mies van der Rohe, *German Pavilion*, Barcelona

Museum of Modern Art opens in New York

Ramsay Macdonald's Labour Government in power

Wall Street Crash

1930

JE brings a court case against plagiarists (*The Daily Telegraph*, 17 October)

Genesis [134–36]

Lydia [137]

Theodore Garman [161]

Hepworth, *Figure of a Woman*

H. S. Ede, *A Life of Gaudier-Brzeska*

William Aumonier, *Modern Architectural Sculpture*

Wells Coates, *Isokon Flats*, Lawn Road, London

Le Corbusier, *Villa Savoye*, near Paris

Shreve, Lamb and Harmon, *Empire State Building*

Grant Wood, *American Gothic*

Alfred Rosenberg, *Myth of the Twentieth Century* (Nazi doctrine on art)

Amy Johnson flies solo from Britain to Australia

1931

JE exhibits *Genesis* to a vituperative press; he proclaims Moore 'vitally important [to] the future of sculpture in England' in the prefatory note to his one-man show at the Leicester Galleries, from which JE purchases *Half-figure* and *Mother and Child*; he resumes work on the *Sun God* relief, begun in 1910, and on the reverse carves *Primeval Gods*; his work is discussed in Parkes, *The Art of Carved Sculpture* and *The Sculptor Speaks* (a series of conversations with Arnold Haskell, who notes that JE owns some 200 pieces of primitive sculpture, including probably the Lake Sentani standing figures)

Gill, *Prosper and Ariel*, Broadcasting House, London

Ede, *Savage Messiah* (life of Gaudier-Brzeska)

Edwin Lutyens, *Viceroy's House*, New Delhi

Matisse, *The Back* (fourth version)

Dali and Giacometti invent 'surrealist objects with symbolical functioning'

Calder begins making mobile sculpture in Paris

James Whale, *Frankenstein* (with Boris Karloff)

Spanish Republic proclaimed

1932

JE exhibits *Old Testament* watercolours [101] at the Redfern Gallery, London, purchases the Fang reliquary figure from the De Miré sale and Moore's

Gilbert, *Queen Alexandra Memorial*, London

Alfred Drury, *Statue of Joshua Reynolds*, London

Mosley's British Union of Fascists founded

	Composition; his work is described in L. B. Powell, *Jacob Epstein* and R. H. Wilenski, *The Meaning of Modern Sculpture*; Emlyn Williams calls him the 'best-known living sculptor' *Elemental* [138] *Woman Possessed* [140] *Emlyn Williams* [149] *Isobel Nicholas* [154]	Spencer, *Burghclere Chapel* murals Rothenstein, *Men and Memories 1900–1922* Ford Madox Ford, *Return to Yesterday* Aldous Huxley, *Brave New World* Giacometti, *Woman with Her Throat Cut* Association of Soviet Artists formed to control art in Russia along Stalinist lines ('All art must be propaganda') Nazis dissolve Bauhaus: 'one of the prominent centres of the Jewish-Marxist art programme'	
1933	JE illustrates Moysheh Oyved, *The Book of Affinity* [102] and paints nearly one hundred watercolours of Epping Forest; he is excluded, as an 'alien', from Eric Underwood's *A Short History of English Sculpture* *Albert Einstein* [150] *Lydia laughing* [155]	Moore, *Composition* (first sculpture with holes) *Unit 1* established in London to encourage abstract art Read, *Art Now* Wells, *The Shape of Things to Come* Julio Gonzalez, *Large Maternity* Gropius, Mendelsohn and Mies van der Rohe flee Nazis Max Beckman, *Departure*	Hitler becomes German Chancellor Berlin Reichstag burnt First Nuremberg Rally Dachau and Oranienburg concentration camps open Spanish Fascist Party founded Prohibition repealed in United States Long March of Chinese Communists
1934	JE begins carving *Behold the Man* (*Ecce Homo*)	Death of Gilbert and Jagger Read publishes *Henry Moore* (first monograph) and edits *Unit One* Dollfuss orders nude statues removed from Austrian streets	Hitler appointed German Führer
1935	JE's son, Jackie, is born; he purchases the Fang reliquary head from Joseph Brummer and begins painting the drop-curtain for the ballet *David*; the Southern Rhodesian Government announces its intention to remove the BMA statues, the *Hudson Memorial* is defiled by the Independent Fascist League and *Behold the Man* is attacked by the Catholic press but defended by Anthony Blunt in *The Spectator* (15 March); Gill calls JE 'the greatest portraitist of our time' and he is the subject of an essay in Louis Golding, *Great Contemporaries* *Kathleen Garman* [159]	Gabo moves from Paris to London David Gascoigne, *A Short Survey of Surrealism* J. J. Sweeney, *African Negro Art* Carl Kjersmeier, *Centres de Style de la Sculpture Nègre Africaine* Death of Lachaise: 'violently sexual' sculptures excluded from Museum of Modern Art, New York retrospective George Gershwin, *Porgy and Bess* Hitler stigmatises German modern artists as 'corruptors of art' and 'insane'	Nuremberg Laws deny German citizenship to Jews Italy invades Abyssinia (JE models portrait of *Haile Selassie*, 1936)
1936	JE carves *Consummatum Est* and begins his illustrations for Charles Baudelaire's *Les Fleurs du Mal* [103]; Cunninghame Graham dies *David* ballet drop-curtain [109]	Dobson, *Margaret Rawlings* International Surrealist Exhibition, London Read, *Surrealism* Maxwell Fry, *Sun House*, Hampstead	Spanish Civil War begins Federico Garcia Lorca assassinated Germany hosts Winter Olympic Games, occupies the Rhineland *Queen Mary* launched Abdication of Edward VIII

Alexander Korda, *Things to Come*

16,500 modern art works purged from German museums

Wright, *Falling Water*, Pennsylvania

Charlie Chaplin, *Modern Times*

1937	JE (with Gill, Moore, Read and Paul Nash) signs a letter of co-operation with the International Peace Campaign against Fascist aggression in Spain; the BMA statues are mutilated despite widespread public protest, *Consummatum Est* is attacked by the press and clergy, Moore's *Mother and Child*, 1936, is described as 'Epstein the Morning After the Night Before' (*The Star*, 29 December) *Pola Givenchy* [156] *Kitty Garman* [162]	Roland Penrose, *Winged Domino: Portrait of Valentine* *Circle: International Survey of Constructive Art* British artists refuse to exhibit in Berlin due to Nazi edict against 'specific reservations as to race and political faith' Degenerate Art Exhibition, Munich Picasso paints *Guernica* following bombing of Basque capitol Brancusi, *Endless Column*, Tîrgu Jiu, Rumania	A. M. Turing, 'On computable numbers'
1938	JE receives an honourary degree from Aberdeen University; with Moore, Stephen Spender and others, he is refused a visa to visit Republican Spain; the carving of *Adam* begins and *Les Fleurs du Mal* drawings [104–07] are shown, without success, at Tooth's, London *Adam and Eve* [144] *Burial of Abel* [145]	Gill, *Creation*, League of Nations, Geneva Moore begins making 'stringed' sculpture Arp, Brancusi, Calder, Gabo and Pevsner sculptures at Guggenheim Jeune Gallery, London, ignite Customs' row Death of Barlach Robert Goldwater, *Primitivism in Modern Art* Breton and Trotsky, *Manifesto: Towards a Free Revolutionary Art*	Austrian *Anschluss* German occupation of Czechoslovakia and Sudetenland Hitler and Chamberlain meet at Berchtesgaden Anti-Jewish legislation in Italy Jean Paul Sartre, *La Nausée*
1939	*Adam* is exhibited at the Leicester Galleries, acquired by a showman and toured, making 'pulpits seethe, strong men blush, and the public flock to look'; financial difficulties force JE to sell his collection of Matthew Smith paintings *Jackie: Ragamuffin* [163]	Uli Nimptsch settles in England Death of Gertler Lehmbruck's *Kneeling Woman* condemned for deriding Nazi ideal of Woman Fig-leafed copy of Michelangelo's *David* displayed at Forest Lawn Cemetery, California Christopher Isherwood, *Goodbye to Berlin* Antoine de Saint-Exupéry, *Wind, Sand and Stars* John Steinbeck, *The Grapes of Wrath*	Jung, *The Integration of the Personality* Spanish Republican Government collapses Italy invades Albania Russia invades Finland Germany invades Poland Second World War begins (3 September) Freud dies in London
1940	JE begins carving *Jacob and the Angel* [142], *Adam* is exhibited at The Famous Gallery, New York; *Flowers of Evil* [108] and JE's autobiography, *Let There Be Sculpture*, are published *Leda with coxcomb* [164]	Death of Gill Hepworth and Ben Nicholson move to St Ives, Cornwall Moore moves to Much Hadham, Hertfordshire Lascaux Caves discovered Ernest Hemingway, *For Whom the Bell Tolls*	Winston Churchill becomes Prime Minister Evacuation at Dunkirk Blitzkrieg Battle of Britain Germany invades Scandinavia, Holland, Belgium, Luxembourg

		Arthur Koestler, *Darkness at Noon* Charlie Chaplin, *The Great Dictator* Walt Disney, *Fantasia*	Fall of France (Paris occupied) Trotsky assassinated in Mexico
1941		Moore begins *Shelter Drawings*; first retrospective exhibition held in Leeds Gill, *Autobiography* Orsen Wells, *Citizen Kane*	Germany invades Russia Japan attacks Pearl Harbour United States enters War Herbert Marcuse, *Reason and Revolution*
1942	JE exhibits *Jacob and the Angel* [143] at the Leicester Galleries; he shares a two-man show with Matthew Smith at Temple Newsam House, Leeds (the City Art Galleries purchase *Lady Gregory* [27] and *Peggy Jean Laughing* for £100 each); Robert Black, *The Art of Jacob Epstein* is published *George Black* [152]	Death of González John Huston, *The Maltese Falcon* Albert Camus, *L'Étranger*	Battles of El Alamein and Stalingrad Burma Campaign
1943	*Lucifer, Belial and Beelzebub* [146–47] *Nude* [148]	Piet Mondrian, *Broadway Boggie- Woogie* *Casablanca* (starring Humphrey Bogart and Ingrid Bergman)	German army surrenders at Stalingrad Warsaw Ghetto uprising Mussolini toppled and Italy surrenders to Allies
1944	JE begins work on *Lucifer*; he is not represented in A. T. Broadbent, *Sculpture Today in Great Britain* *Girl from Baku* [157] *Esther Garman* [165]	Moore, *Northampton Madonna and Child* Death of Maillol Francis Bacon, *Three studies for the Base of a Crucifixion*	D-Day Battles of Arnheim and Monte Cassino Paris liberated IBM builds first electro- mechanical computer
1945	JE is welcomed by Picasso at a party given by Felix Topolski in London, *Lucifer* is exhibited at the Leicester Galleries and then rejected as a gift by both the Tate Gallery and the Fitzwilliam Museum, Cambridge	Evelyn Waugh, *Brideshead Revisited* Benjamin Britten, *Peter Grimes* Marcel Carné, *Les Enfants du Paradis* Roberto Rossellini, *Roma, Città Aperta*	Hiroshima and Nagasaki destroyed by Atomic bombs Hitler commits suicide Mussolini is hanged Second World War ends United Nations founded
1946	JE models the portrait of *Winston Churchill*	Moore's first major retrospective held at Museum of Modern Art, New York Deaths of Despiau, Nadelman Jean Cocteau, *La Belle et la Bête* Allied Military Government orders destruction of Nazi memorials in Germany	Nuremberg Trials begin
1947	JE begins carving *Lazarus*, *Lucifer* is presented to Birmingham Art Gallery; Margaret Epstein dies	Institute of Contemporary Art (ICA) founded in London	Indian Independence Act Marshall Plan

1948	*Girl with Gardenias* (Kathleen Garman) is shown at the first 'Sculpture in the Open Air' exhibition at Battersea Park	Moore awarded International Sculpture Prize, 24th Venice Biennale	State of Israel established Gandhi assassinated Stalin cracks-down on non-realist art in Russia
1949	JE visits New York briefly; *Youth Advancing* is commissioned for the Festival of Britain *Ralph Vaughan Williams* [151] *Ann Freud* [166] *Roland Joffe* [169] *Victor* [170]	Moore, *Family Group* Graham Sutherland, *Portrait of Somerset Maugham* George Orwell, *Nineteen Eighty-Four* Arthur Miller, *Death of a Salesman* Simone de Beauvoir, *The Second Sex*	Claude Lévi-Strauss, *Elementary Structures of Kinship* NATO established Apartheid set up in South Africa Mao-tse-tung proclaims Communist People's Republic of China
1950	JE is commissioned to make the *Madonna and Child* for the Convent of the Holy Child Jesus in Cavendish Square, London [171] *Marion Abrahams* [158] *Marcella Barzetti* [172]	Moore, *Three Standing Figures* unveiled in Battersea Park	Korean War starts McCarthyism in United States
1951	JE models the portraits of *T. S. Eliot* and *W. Somerset Maugham*, visits Philadelphia to discuss the commission for *Social Consciousness* [173]; *Youth Advancing* is shown at the Festival of Britain, *Lazarus* is displayed at Battersea Park	Picasso, *Baboon and Young* David Smith, *Hudson River Landscape* Arnold Schoenberg, *Moses and Aaron*	
1952	JE retrospective, organised by the Arts Council, is held at the Tate Gallery, *Lazarus* is unveiled in New College Chapel, Oxford *Annabel Freud* [167] *Cavendish Square door handles* [168]	Moore, *King and Queen* Kathleen Kenyon excavates Jericho Metropolitan Museum of Art exhibition of *Contemporary American Sculpture* attacked as furthering 'aesthetic leftism' Samuel Beckett, *Waiting for Godot*	
1953	JE opens the London County Council Sculpture School at Camberwell, receives an honorary doctorate from Oxford University and refuses an offer of membership to the Royal Society of British Sculptors; he is commissioned to make *Christ in Majesty* for Llandaff Cathedral [174] and *Field Marshal Smuts* for Parliament Square, London; the Cavendish Square *Madonna and Child* is unveiled; Muirhead Bone dies	Moore, *Time and Life Screen*, London Reg Butler wins international competition for *Monument to the Unknown Political Prisoner*	Coronation of Elizabeth II Edmund Hillary scales Mount Everest Death of Stalin Execution of Julius and Ethel Rosenberg Korean War ends
1954	JE is knighted, begins the *Liverpool Resurgent* for Lewis's Store and speaks on BBC Radio ('Sir Jacob Epstein on Modern Art'); his son Theodore (Theo) Garman dies, and a few months later his daughter Esther commits suicide	Zadkine, *Monument to the Destroyed City of Rotterdam* Deaths of Matisse, Derain Basil Spence begins Coventry Cathedral	Roger Bannister runs 3 minute 59.4 second mile Algerian War Battle of Dien Bien Phu

1955	JE marries Kathleen Garman (Lady Epstein); they travel to Philadelphia for the unveiling of *Social Consciousness* and take a holiday in Paris; the *Trades Union Congress War Memorial* in London [177] and *St Michael and the Devil* for Coventry Cathedral are commissioned; *Epstein: An Autobiography* is published	Death of Carl Milles Robert Rauschenberg, *Bed*	
1956	*Liverpool Resurgent* and *Field Marshal Smuts* are unveiled, the *Memorial to William Blake* is commissioned for Poets' Corner, Westminster Abbey *Hon Wynne Godley* [175] *Studies for St Michael and the Devil* [176]	Paolozzi, *Shattered Head* Richard Hamilton, *Just what is it that makes today's homes so different, so appealing?* John Osborne, *Look Back in Anger*	Suez Crisis Sinai Campaign Hungarian National Rising
1957	JE takes a short holiday in Scotland, *Christ in Majesty* is unveiled at Llandaff Cathedral and *William Blake* in Westminster Abbey; *Epstein: A Camera Study of the Sculptor at Work by Geoffrey Ireland* (introduction by Laurie Lee) is published	Death of Brancusi Jack Kerouac, *On the Road*	Russia launches Sputnik
1958	JE, ill in hospital with pleurisy and a thrombosis, is unable to attend the *TUC War Memorial* unveiling; he convalesces in France and Northern Italy, visiting Padua, where he sees Donatello's *Gattamelata*; the *Ascension of Christ* is commissioned for Crownhill Church, Plymouth; HRH Princess Margaret sits for her portrait, the parishioners of Selby Abbey, Yorkshire, petition to reject as a gift the 'ugly heathen' *Behold the Man*; the *Bowater House Group* is started [178–79]	Moore, *UNESCO Reclining Figure*, Paris Jasper John, *Three Flags* Mies van der Rohe and Phillip Johnson, *Seagram Building*, New York	European Economic Community (EEC) established Campaign for Nuclear Disarmament (CND) launched
1959	JE models a postumous portrait of *David Lloyd George* for the Houses of Parliament, takes a short holiday in Italy and completes the *Bowater House Group* on the day of his death, 19 August, at 18 Hyde Park Gate; he is buried at Putney Vale Cemetery, with a memorial service at St Paul's Cathedral. 'We have lost a great sculptor' (Moore's obituary notice, *The Sunday Times*, 23 August)		

'CE SAUVAGE AMÉRICAIN'

Evelyn Silber

An air of self-conscious rebellion pervades Epstein's earliest known self-portrait drawing [3*]. The dishevelment of the open-necked shirt and the hair, flowing back, uncombed, from the broad forehead suggest impatience with convention, while the direct penetrating gaze under lowered brows hint at wilful determination. Though the relation of figure to paper is slightly misjudged, the draughtsmanship is assured, rapid diagonal strokes of the chalk modelling the figure and spreading beyond it as if to suggest the radiating impulses of the artist's creative energy and confirming the impression he made in Paris, where one of his teachers at the Académie Julian called him 'ce sauvage Améicain'.[1] The portrait dates, according to Lady Epstein, from shortly before the twenty-one year old artist left New York to train in Paris in the Autumn of 1902.[2] Since about 1893 he had been studying drawing and, more recently, sculpture at the Art Students' League, and living in a garret studio, earning a precarious living as a draughtsman and illustrator. Since 1897 he had lived apart from his family, who had moved to a more respectable area uptown. Hutchins Hapgood, author of a pioneering study of the Jewish community and one of the first to spot Epstein's talents, described a visit to his studio:

> On the corner of Hester and Forsyth streets is a tumble-down rickety building. The stairs that ascend to the garret are pestiferous and dingy. In what is more like a shed than a room, with the wooden ribs of the slanting roof curtailing the space, is a studio . . . A miserable iron bedstead occupies the narrow strip of floor beneath the descending ceiling. There is one window, which commands a good view of the pushcart market in Hester Street. Near the window is a diminutive oil-stove, on which the artist prepares his tea and eggs. On a peg on the door hang an old mackintosh and an extra coat — his only additional wardrobe. About the narrow walls on the three available sides are easels, and sketches and paintings of Ghetto types . . . he pays $4 a month, and he cooks his own meals, $12 a month is quite sufficient to satisfy all his needs. This amount he can usually manage to make through the sale of his sketches; but when he does not he 'goes to bed,' as he puts it, and lies low until one of his various art enterprises brings him in a small cheque.[3]

Given Epstein's lifelong preoccupation with the theme of motherhood, there is a certain poetic justice in the fact that drawings of new-born babies [4–5, Fig. 33], the two modelled studies [6–7] and the carved relief of a mother and child [8] are probably the only works to survive from his time in Paris and his early months in London, as well as being his earliest extant sculptures and drawings for sculpture. Their precise dates are uncertain; according to Lady Epstein's account the drawings and heads were done in Paris in 1904, when a model with her child in her arms came to the studio asking for work.[4] Epstein himself, however, dated the *Baby asleep* [6] to 1907.[5] It may also be indicative of a later dating that he did not apparently take either of the modelled studies to show George Bernard Shaw, when he was seeking an exhibition of his work soon after he arrived in London in 1905.[6]

Epstein recalled his time in Paris, from Autumn 1902 to Spring 1905, being 'passed in a rage of work; I was aflame with ardour and worked in a frenzied, almost mad manner, achieving study after study, week after week, always destroying it at the end of the week to begin a new one the following Monday'.[7] During six months at the Ecole des Beaux Arts and then in the less formal surroundings of the Académie Julian, he drew and modelled both from life and after Michelangelo casts, and began to carve in marble. However, when he left Julian's and worked alone he tried to do too much too soon and abandoned two 'heroic-sized' groups.[8]

The tenderly observed realism of the surviving works recalls the Lower East Side drawings [94–97]; these are much more intensely studied and he has dropped the mannerisms derived from Théophile Steinlen and other contemporary illustrators which characterised the Ghetto drawings in favour of a more direct, tactile approach. When he first began to sculpt in New York, Epstein had been stimulated both by the physicality of making sculpture and by a desire to 'give greater reality to my drawings'.[9] These are some of his first truly sculptural drawings, the fragile solidity of the child's body and head contrasted with the boneless delicacy of its limbs. The maternal presence is evoked only by cursory indications of the mother's breast, lap and hands as she supports and nurtures the infant.

The absolute trust and repose of a baby asleep is vividly captured in a related sheet containing five drawings of sleeping babies [Fig. 33], at least two of which closely resemble the sculpture [6]. Formally succinct and silkily smooth, this piece already points to the creative dialogue between naturalism and formal simplicity which was to

3
SELF-PORTRAIT c1901
Red chalk 29.5 × 22.5
Walsall Museum and Art Gallery (Garman-Ryan Collection)

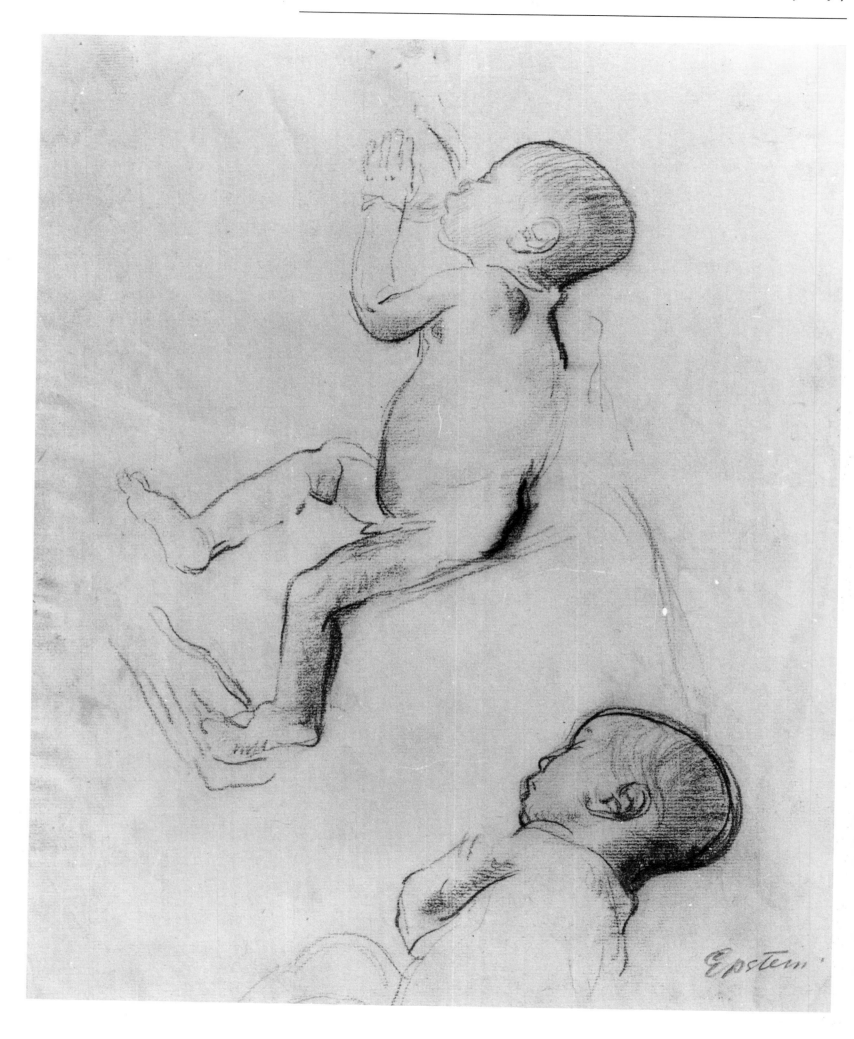

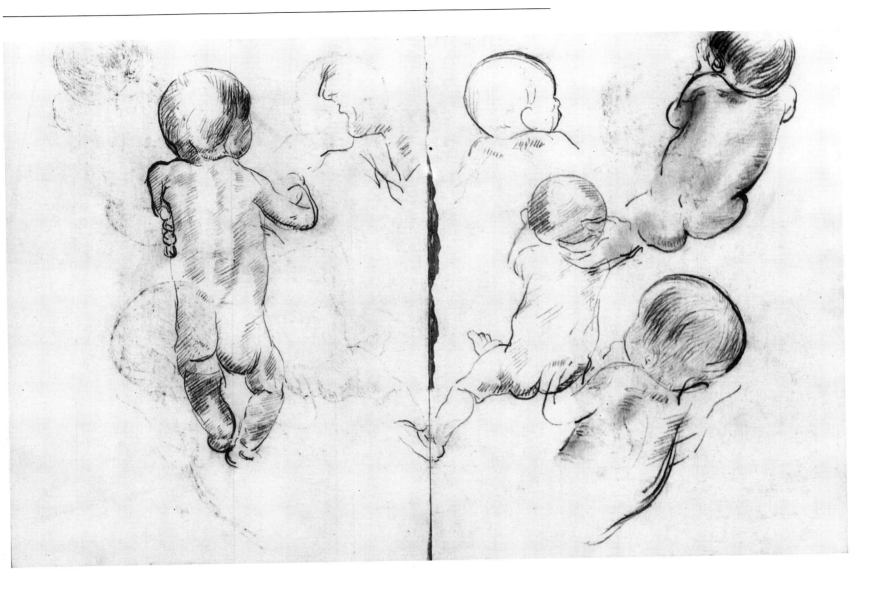

4 ◁
TWO STUDIES OF A BABY *c*1904
Black chalk 37.5 × 30
Walsall Museum and Art Gallery (Garman-Ryan Collection)

5 △
FIVE STUDIES OF A BABY AND MOTHER *c*1904
Black chalk 45.1 × 28.3 (two sheets from a lost sketchbook)
Private collection

Fig 33
FIVE STUDIES OF A BABY ASLEEP *c*1904
Black chalk 47.7 × 30.7
Whereabouts unknown

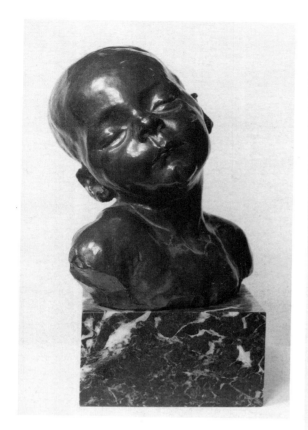

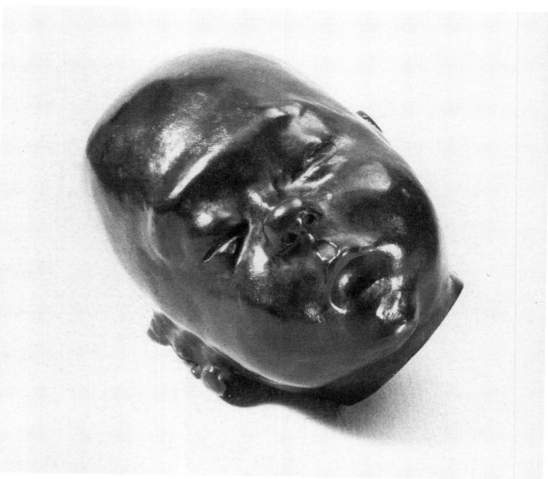

Fig 34   △
Aimé-Jules Dalou (1838–1902)
HEAD OF A SLEEPING CHILD   c1878
Bronze   H 19.7
Museum of Art, Carnegie Institute, Pittsburgh

6
BABY ASLEEP   c1902–04   (S3)
Bronze   H 11.5 (cast by A. A. Hébrard, Paris)
Leeds City Art Galleries

Fig 35
Michelangelo (1475–1564)
MADONNA OF THE STEPS   1489–92
Marble   55.5 × 40
Casa Buonarroti, Florence

7   ▷
BABY AWAKE   c1902–04   (S4)
Bronze   H 18.5
Walsall Museum and Art Gallery (Garman-Ryan
Collection)

characterise much of Epstein's work over the next ten years. There are clear analogies with the contemporary work of Jules Dalou, such as his *Head of a sleeping child*, c 1878 [Fig. 34].[10] Epstein's conveys a comparable mood of placidity while simplifying and unifying the shape of the skull. It is perhaps significant of the nascent interest amongst younger sculptors in organic but simplified shapes that the pure, subtle form of a newborn child's head attracted both Epstein and Brancusi. The latter, inspired by the same work of Dalou, based his own *Tourment*, 1906, on it.[11]

Mother and child [8] is a carver's apprentice piece, tentative in technique and revealing uncertainties over how to foreshorten figures in low relief. Nevertheless, the uncompromising nudity and naturalism of both figures represents a radical rethinking into modern terms of the classic Renaissance image of the Madonna and Child. There is good reason to suppose that Epstein had studied the available examples of the Renaissance *relievo schiacciato* technique, such as Donatello's *Christ giving the keys to St Peter* in the South Kensington Museum.[12] A still more important source was probably Michelangelo's early marble relief, *Madonna of the Steps* [Fig. 35], which Epstein may have known only from photographs but which he perhaps also saw during a brief visit to Florence in 1903 or 1904. The left hand sketch [5], from which the figure of the child is clearly derived, also has a female profile and other faint indications which strongly suggest a conscious reworking of Michelangelo's composition, a suggestion supported by the mother's straddled stance, which

seems derived in part from the boy on the stairs in the same relief. The work is unfinished and Epstein probably planned to repeat it on the reverse of the marble slab, where the traced outline of the composition can still be seen.

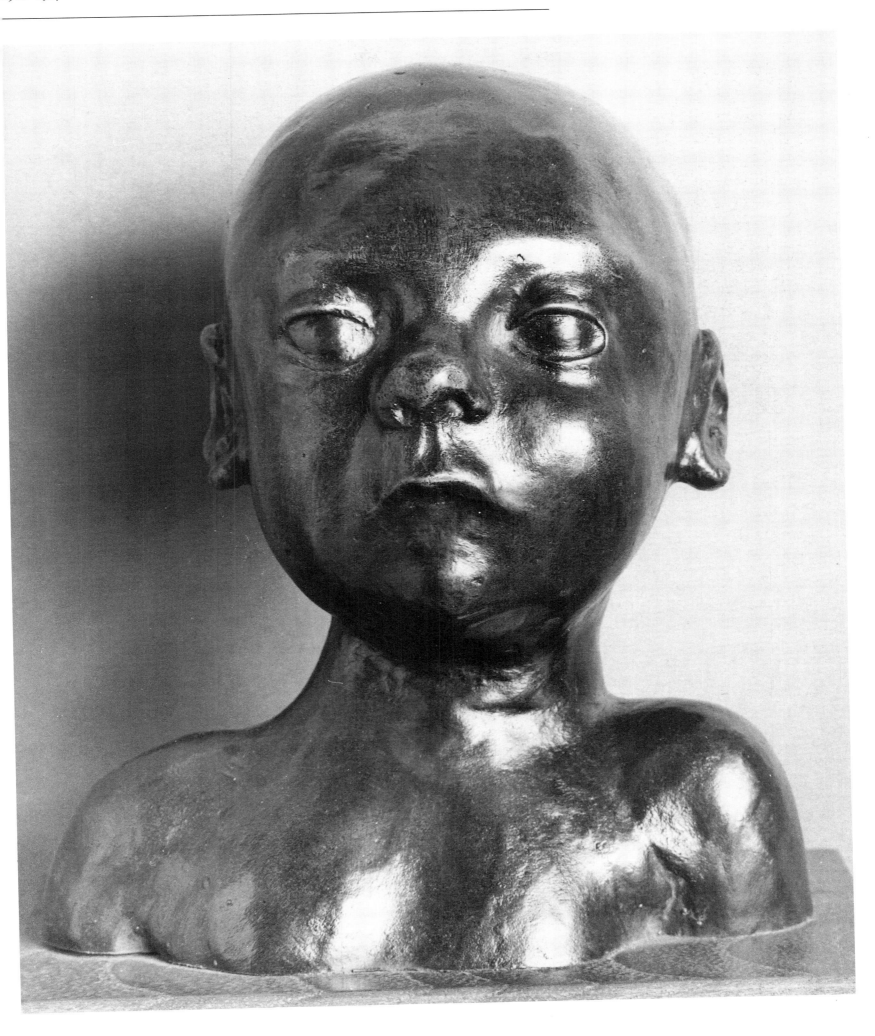

8
MOTHER AND CHILD   1905–07   (S5)
Marble 35.5 × 35.5
Birmingham Museums and Art Gallery

2 · 1907–1908

THE BRITISH
MEDICAL ASSOCIATION
BUILDING

Richard Cork

Although the statues executed for the British Medical Association ultimately suffered a tragic fate, the young Epstein was fortunate indeed to have been given such a remarkable commission [Fig. 37]. Newly settled in London, plagued by misgivings about his own abilities, and as yet unknown outside a small circle of fellow-artists, he can hardly have expected an architect to invite him in 1907 to make eighteen over-life-size figures for a building on a prominent metropolitan site. But Charles Holden, who had just won a limited competition to design the British Medical Association's new headquarters in the Strand, decided to ask the painter, Francis Dodd, about a suitable sculptor for the project. Dodd, a friend of Epstein's, was perceptive enough to realise that the American emigrant might be enormously stimulated by such an opportunity. He may have known that Epstein already harboured ambitions to work on a monumental scale, planning and partially making figures for a *Temple of the Sun* and a *Temple of Love*.[1] Chronic dissatisfaction with his own work prompted him to destroy a group of 'sun-worshippers'[2] from one of the Temples, but Holden had little hesitation in deciding that Epstein was the sculptor he required after a visit to the studio. There, Epstein was working on the life-size figure of *Girl with a dove*, for which only an exquisite drawing now survives [9].[3]

Holden wanted to produce a building that proclaimed his admiration for C. R. Cockerell's Westminster Insurance Company offices of 1832, which used to occupy the site, and at the same time design an audacious edifice bare enough to reflect his passionate belief that 'only the aboriginal force in any building can be called architecture, and to introduce any form that is not contemporary, is to hinder progress and the true expression of the modern in architecture'.[4] The lower half of his design, which paid tribute to Cockerell in granite, was therefore combined with an altogether more modernist upper half in Portland stone. Holden saw the statues as a crucial structural device, for he 'conceived the idea that the series of white sculptural figures, on each side of the windows and set in a framework of dark granite, would serve to weave the two materials together like white stitching joining a dark to a light material'.[5]

But he also hoped to discover a sculptor whose work chimed with his Whitmanesque conviction that 'we are ashamed of our nakedness — and yet it is in the frank confession of our nakedness that our regeneration lies'.[6] Epstein did not disappoint him. He shared Holden's enthusiasm for Whitman, and soon after they met the architect felt certain that Epstein's admiration for *Calamus* [98*] and *The Leaves of Grass* would infuse the statues with the ardency he desired. 'I remember how in a very few days he was able to lay down a programme as wide in scope as Whitman', Holden remembered later, 'which was in fact exactly what I was hoping to find in him'.[7] Determined to ignore a suggestion from a member of the British Medical Association, who wanted the figures to portray 'their historically famous medical men',[8] Epstein pursued Holden's vaguely stated idea of encompassing the 'seven ages of man'.[9] The final scheme, which includes figures symbolising Medicine and Health as well as Chemical Research, indicates that he arrived at a compromise between his patrons' demands and the plan he would ideally have liked to implement. But Epstein's statues, taken as an entirety, still bear out the essential truth of his claim in July 1908 that, 'apart from my desire to decorate a beautiful building, I have wished to create noble and heroic forms to express in sculpture the great primal facts of man and woman'.[10]

The four figures on The Strand frontage initiate the progression he sought, starting with *Primal Energy*, who turns to the left and breathes life into the foetal form held by the next statue, *Matter* [Fig. 7]. The delicate contours of the foetus, enclosed in a rough-hewn lump of stone, are contrasted with the robust palpability of the bearded sage who holds the stone in his hands. The emergent life looks far more fragile than his guardian, and the hieratic solemnity of the old man's stance shows how seriously he takes his responsibilities. He inaugurates the theme of protection which runs through the scheme, and the foetus is Epstein's first surviving expression of an image which would reappear several years later nestling in the angular, machine-like forms of *Rock Drill* [70]. The British Medical Association was doubtless gratified to find the importance of nurturing stressed with such gravity on the

Fig 36
Epstein with the plaster model for DANCING GIRL (S9:12, destroyed) for the British Medical Association Building, Westminster, 1907–08 (from *Epstein: An Autobiography*, 1955, frontispiece)

Fig 37
British Medical Association Building, Agar Street front, Westminster, photographed in 1908 during construction.

9
STUDY FOR GIRL WITH A DOVE   1906–07   (S6)
Pencil   48 × 21
Walsall Museum and Art Gallery (Garman-Ryan Collection)

façade of its building. But *Matter* also demonstrates that Epstein was able to charge this theme with a very personal intensity, and the relationship between awakening life and parental care remained of central importance throughout his later work.

The next figure on the Strand frontage did not, admittedly, give him the opportunity to make a very individual statement. *Hygieia*, the Goddess of Medicine and Health, looks very aloof as she holds her symbolic attributes, the cup and serpent, like votive offerings before her. The statue shows how conscious Epstein was, at this early stage in his career, of the Hellenistic tradition, and a similar veneration for hallowed classical precedent marks the musculature of the two nudes who flank the corners of the buildings as it turns into Agar Street. Representing *Chemical Research* and *Academic Research*, they swing their bodies away from the viewer in order to concentrate on their allotted tasks. The activities they pursue seem less important, however, than the structure

of their mighty physiques. All the way through the BMA venture Epstein was bent on paying tribute to the magnificence of the mature nude. But there is nothing ostentatious about his readiness to display nakedness. The well-developed man who personifies *Mentality*, and inaugurates the finest group of statues within the entire sequence, is a retiring and even introspective figure. Clasping a skull with wings, he stares down at this strange and almost surrealistic attribute in a state of rapt absorption.

As for *Youth*, who comes next in the Agar Street sequence, he is one of the most vulnerable of all Epstein's male nudes. The power of growth is implicit in his upward-straining stance, but the raised arms appear to be shielding him from full exposure to daylight. He seems to need the shelter of the architecture around him, and the conspicuous narrowness of the spaces which Holden gave Epstein suggests that the notion of enclosure was an important consideration. Although the recesses are shallow and the cornice above

provides no protection for the figures, the building manages to contain its statues with the same
kind of firm solicitude that the BMA's members
wanted to offer their patients. Epstein certainly
sympathised with this priority, for the statue he
placed after *Youth* is explicitly engaged in a nurturing role. He called it the *New-born* [Fig. 38], and
the old woman who holds a baby in her hands is
sombrely conscious of her duties. Epstein invested her gaunt face and bony body with an unusual
amount of emotional commitment. She is among
the very finest of the BMA statues, and he
explores with great sensitivity the poignant contrast between her haggard stoicism and the spontaneous vivacity of the baby's smoothly rounded
limbs.

Man, who continues the Agar Street progression, is one of the few figures to burst out of the
confines of his niche. A vigorously sinewed
embodiment of Whitmanesque potency, he
thrusts a foot and an elbow outwards as if to stride
towards the woman on the opposite side of the
window. Epstein described him as a 'figure of
man in his energy and virility', lamenting the fact
that 'today the use of great words like "virility"
has become so smirched by coarse shame that it
becomes a hazardous thing for an artist to use
them in a description of his work'.[11] *Man* seems to
be aroused by the sight of *Maternity* [11 and
Fig. 39] in the next niche, but she does not return
his glance. Far too involved with her offspring to
pay him the attention he desires, she leans her
head towards the child in order to savour physical
intimacy and, perhaps, a few affectionate words.
The rapport between them is the hallmark of this
superbly gentle and appealing statue, without
doubt the masterpiece of the whole sequence.
None of the succeeding figures on the Agar Street
façade, which Epstein intended to 'represent
Youth, joy in life, youths and maidens reaching
stretching arms towards each other',[12] matches
the heartfelt quality of this carving. More than any
other BMA statue, *Maternity* fulfils Epstein's
declared wish that his work should be 'possessed
of an inner life',[13] and it is ironic indeed that this
modest image of womanhood became the initial
focus of the controversy which suddenly overcame the entire venture.

In the early summer of 1908, the arrival of
Maternity was noticed by the National Vigilance
Association, whose offices happened by some
bizarre coincidence to be directly opposite the
Agar Street frontage of Holden's building. They
were incensed by the figure's generously propor-
tioned body, and lost little time in reporting this
outrage to the press. *The London Evening Standard*
was happy to present the 'scandal' to its readers
as the leading story on the front page, announc-
ing on 19 June 1908 that Epstein's carvings 'are a
form of statuary which no careful father would
wish his daughter, or no discriminating young
man, his fiancée, to see'. It was a farcical assertion, and no attempt was made to reveal precisely
why a mother with child should be considered so
obscene. But the *Evening Standard* writer did
maintain that Edwardian society expected its
artists to observe a strict sense of decorum
whenever they moved outside the gallery and
executed work for an open-air city site. 'Nude

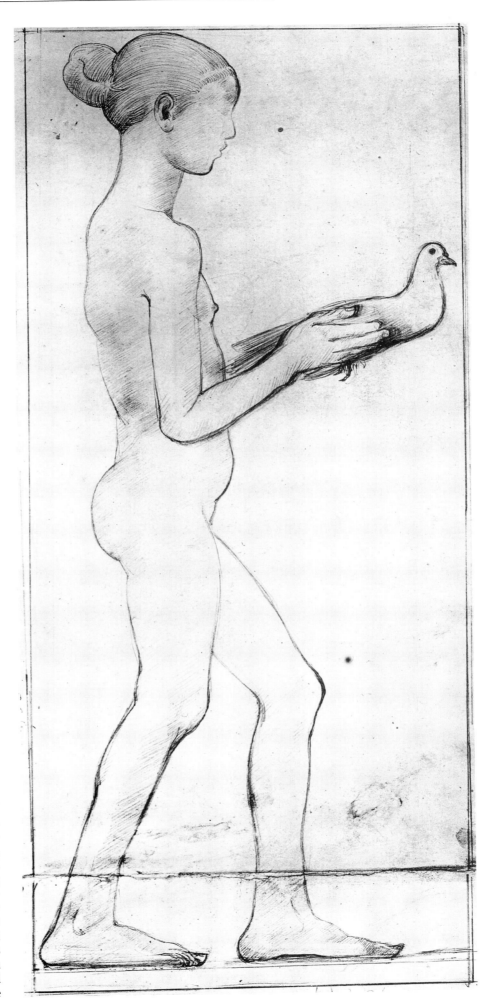

statuary figures in an art gallery are seen, for the most part, by those who know how to appreciate the art they represent', declared the journalist, 'and it is in only the most exceptional cases that they afford subjects for the vulgar comment of the inartistic, who visit art galleries out of purposeless curiosity, or with the object of whiling away an idle hour — people for whom art galleries are never intended. To have art of the kind indicated, laid bare to the gaze of all classes, young and old, in perhaps the busiest thoroughfare of the Metropolis of the world . . . is another matter.'[14]

Without *The Evening Standard*'s prompting, the probability is that nobody would have considered Epstein's statues indecent at all. But the combined efforts of Fleet Street and the National Vigilance Association ensured that they soon became notorious. Epstein found himself visited by the police on site, while the Editor of the *British Medical Journal* described with astonishment how 'the whole Strand opposite was packed with people, most of them girls and young men, all staring up at the statues'.[15] The BMA took fright, and the Chairman of its Council, Edmund Owen, opined after a quick tour of the carvings that 'they ought never to have been put there'.[16] He added that an emergency meeting of the BMA's building committee would be held very soon to debate the fate of the statues, and the Church contributed a note of ecclesiastical indignation when Father Vaughan accused Epstein of attempting to 'convert London into a Fiji island'. The enraged prelate even declared that the carvings were provoking 'vulgarity and unwholesome talk, calculated to lead to practices of which there are more than enough in the purlieus of the Strand already'.[17]

By this time the accusations had become patently absurd, and the perplexed young sculptor must have been very relieved when an impressive array of artists, critics and museum directors came to his aid. The sculptors ranged from F. W. Pomeroy of the older generation to Eric Gill, who was about to embark on a fruitful career with many interests in common with Epstein himself. Augustus John, Walter Crane, Roger Fry and Sir Charles Holroyd, the Director of the National Gallery, also joined the chorus for the defence, and they all stressed the dignified restraint and severity of the figures. A crucial intervention was made by another member of the religious establishment, Dr Cosmo Gordon Lang, then Bishop of Stepney and later Archbishop of Canterbury. He took the trouble to climb the ladders to Epstein's scaffolding and absolve the statues of all immoral intent. Since the Home Secretary refused to join in the condemnation when a question was tabled in the House of Commons, the BMA finally decided on 1 July 1908 that Epstein should be permitted to complete his original commission.

It was a victory both for sound aesthetic judgement and for common sense, and the remaining figures were soon finished. But they lacked the singular character of their predecessors, and signs of repetition in their poses suggest that Epstein was now in a hurry to put the project behind him. One statue in particular, a dancing 'maiden' [Fig. 36] which surely owes a debt to a figure by the Viennese sculptor, Richard Lüksch [Fig. 40] reproduced in *The Studio* not long before,[18] is used twice on the Agar Street façade in different positions. Shaken by the acrimony his work aroused, and doubtless wondering whether he had been right to settle in a country where philistine anger was so easily aroused, Epstein grew bitterly aware of his controversial status. The unease would linger throughout his life, aggravated at regular intervals by renewed outbursts of popular indignation over his subsequent work. Although he was robust enough to withstand the opprobrium, the BMA scandal ensured that he did not receive another architectural sculpture commission for twenty long years.

The furore also contributed to the eventual downfall of Epstein's statues. In 1935 Holden's building was purchased by the Southern Rhodesian Government, and soon afterwards its High Commissioner announced that all the carvings would be taken down. His official reason was that 'they are not perhaps within the austerity usually appertaining to Government buildings',[19] but beneath the diplomatic camouflage lay the same objection which the National Vigilance Association had expressed in 1908. Epstein's frank representation of nudity was considered embarrassing for an Embassy, and once again an elaborate campaign had to be mounted in the statues' defence. This time, Sickert, Kenneth Clark and H. S. Goodhart-Rendel, the President of the Royal Institute of British Architects, were at the forefront of the support for Epstein. When the President of the Royal Academy, Sir William Llewellyn, refused to sign their letter of protest, on the dubious grounds that it was 'not an Academy affair',[20] an apoplectic Sickert resigned from the Academy. His admirable efforts, combined with many other letters published in the national Press, eventually won the day. By July 1935 the statues seemed safe.

The respite, however, was sadly short-lived. Nearly two years later a piece from one of the carvings detached itself after decorations had been placed on them for King George VI's coronation procession. The stone fragment crashed onto the pavement, almost hitting one pedestrian and bruising another passer-by on the foot. The Government of Southern Rhodesia seized on the incident at once, and were happy to obey the London County Council's injunction to render the building safe. But they refused to consult Epstein, ignoring Holden's plea that the sculptor be invited to oversee the removal of unsafe portions and the restoration of the figures. The repair of decayed stonework should not have presented any insuperable problems, and Epstein was understandably eager to help. The Southern Rhodesia Government would not have anything to do with him, though, and they likewise dismissed the campaign mounted by Epstein's admirers to ensure the survival of the carvings. They would not even allow the sculptor's own moulder to make full-size replicas of the statues, employing instead an inferior team who, according to the mortified Epstein, 'hustled through a wretched job and made moulds which were complete travesties of the originals. The battle was lost'[21] [Fig. 41]. Nothing could now prevent a

Fig 38

NEW-BORN   British Medical Association Building, Westminster, 1908   (S9:8, detail)

Portland stone   H 210–15

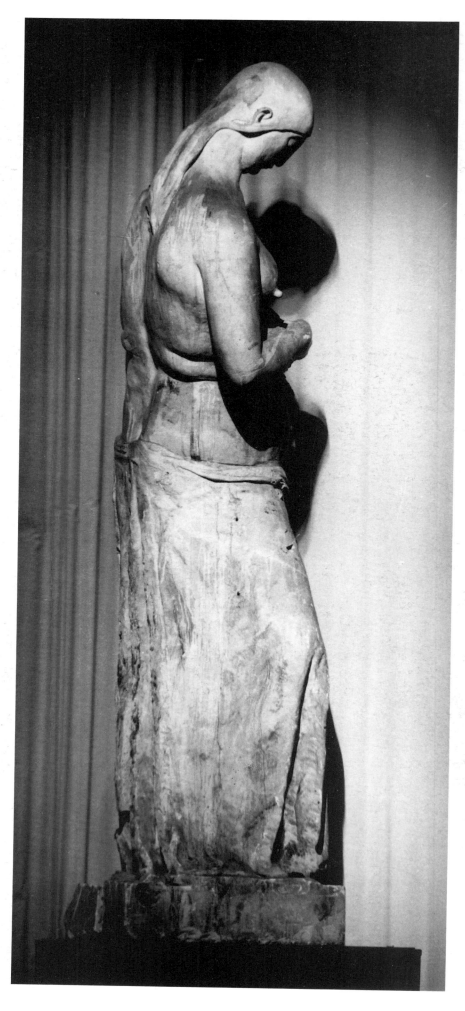

10
STUDY FOR MATERNITY British Medical
Association Building, Westminster, 1907
Pen and ink and pencil 50 × 30.5
Walsall Museum and Art Gallery (Garman-Ryan
Collection)

11
FULL-SIZE MODEL FOR MATERNITY British
Medical Association Building, Westminster,
1907 (S9:10)
Plaster H 215.5
National Gallery of Victoria, Melbourne
(Presented 1971)

Fig 39
MATERNITY British Medical Association Building,
Westminster, 1908 (S9:10, detail)
Portland stone H 210–15

12

STUDY FOR DANCING YOUTH   British Medical
Association Building, Westminster, 1907   (S9:18)
Pencil   33 × 50.8
The University of Hull Art Collection

Fig 40

Richard Lüksch (born 1872)
Wiener Werkstätte Exhibition, Miethke Gallery,
Vienna, from *The Studio*, vol. 37, 1906

group of callous inspectors, including Holden, from examining each figure and hacking away any section considered to be dangerous. No attempt was made to repair the butchered carvings, and their terrible mutilations are still exposed in all their rawness on the building today.

The destruction was inexplicably savage, ruining a scheme which can now be seen as the most impressive sculptural sequence ever made for the façade of a London building. Epstein was not a fully mature artist when he carried it out, and surviving photographs reveal an eclectic range of stylistic sources at work there. Some of the figures, like *Hygieia*, are profoundly indebted to classical precedent, and show how the Greek collections at the British Museum exerted their hold over Epstein's imagination. Others, most notably *Youth*, demonstrate his respect for Michelangelo and Rodin, the latter of whom had written him a 'commendatory letter'[22] when he left Paris for London. But the uncompromising realism deployed in the head of the old woman in *New-Born* [Fig. 38] shows how important Donatello's example had also become, while an undulating ink and pencil study for *Maternity* [10] indicates that Epstein was already beginning to look with avidity at the voluptuousness of Indian carvings.

All these heady sources of inspiration ensure that the BMA scheme is marked by unusual diversity. It lacks the homogeneity which an older sculptor might have achieved, but the venture as a whole gives a fascinating insight into the early flowering of Epstein's inventive resources. Rather than feeling overwhelmed by the sheer scale of this monumental commission, he was immensely stimulated by the opportunity it presented. Holden gave him the chance to create 'large figures on which I could let myself go', and Epstein explained later that 'I had been like a hound on a leash, and now I was suddenly set free'.[23] Statues as memorable and, in the end, as personal as *New-Born* and *Maternity* prove that he did manage to establish his own individuality as a sculptor on the BMA project.

The execution of the scheme involved a complex process, modelling the images from figures posed in the studio, casting them in plaster [11] and then transporting them to The Strand where they were carved in Portland stone [Fig. 39] with the considerable help of assistants from a firm of architectural carvers, John Daymond of Westminster Bridge Road. This elaborate procedure was far removed from the ideal of 'carving direct' which Epstein would later espouse, and there are no traces on the BMA façade of the Assyrian, Egyptian and African sources which would fire

him in the creation of so many later carvings. All the same, Epstein did succeed in establishing on Holden's building the primacy of the great humanist themes he would spend the rest of his life exploring with such intensity. His achievement in the BMA project rested, fundamentally, on his ability to fuse the curative side of the commission with his own most deeply-felt preoccupations: erotic delight, mortality, birth, virility and above all a celebration of men and women in their unashamed nakedness. The fury aroused by these austere, graceful, impassioned and tender figures is hard to understand, just as their final dismemberment is still impossible to forgive.

Fig 41
Removing the plaster cast of YOUTH, Rhodesia House (formerly British Medical Association Building), Westminster, 18 August 1937, prior to the mutilation of the Portland stone original (S9:7).

3 · 1908–1910

EARLY PORTRAITS

Evelyn Silber

Nina Forrest, usually known as Euphemia Lamb, and the gypsy, Nan Condron were by far the most important of Epstein's early models. Drawings, portrait busts and sculpted figure studies of both women survive. With the exception of Kathleen Garman (Lady Epstein), Amina Peerbhoy, known as Sunita, and the black woman, Betty Peters, no other women attracted such sustained and varied interest.

Euphemia Lamb, so called by her husband, the painter Henry Lamb, because of her likeness to Mantegna's *St Euphemia*, became model and companion to several artists — Lamb himself, Augustus John and J. D. Innes. Her gregarious personality and classic English beauty could hardly be a greater contrast to the lanky taciturn Nan Condron. A professional artist's model who had posed for Orpen and Rothenstein, Nan rarely spoke and demanded only to be taken to the music-hall once a week. She devoted herself entirely to Epstein for some time and, as the sculptor's daughter, Kitty Godley recalls, turned up to help around the house at Hyde Park Gate during a period of domestic crisis in 1953–54. Even then she made a strong physical impression with her tall, lean figure, whispy grey hair, great dignity and unusual bone structure. Nan was in many respects the prototypical 'Epstein model', a loner and outcast who, nevertheless, projected a touching strength and inner composure in the face of the world's hostility. *Dolores* [123] and *Old Pinager* [92] are amongst her successors, the people of the Lower East Side her ancestors.

The drawing [13] dates from 1907 or 1908, when Euphemia first began to model for Epstein and relates closely to the first portrait bust [14]. Her natural physical grace and ebullience are immediately apparent, and the close kinship between the standing figure, with its exploratory handling of the head, and the two *Dancing girls* on the BMA Building [Fig. 36][1] convince the present writer that Euphemia was their model. In the drawing the naturalistic handling of pelvis and legs is also remarkably close to that of a lost sculpture, the so-called *Narcissus* sculpted in 1909–10 [Fig. 43]; this may have been the first but it was not the last time that Epstein was to use studies from a female model for a male figure. (He did so again in *Lucifer*, 1945),[2] and so marked were his preferences that there are few instances of his

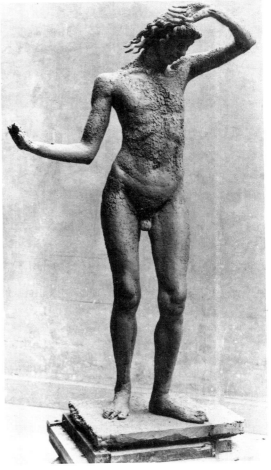

13
THREE STUDIES FOR THE FIGURE AND HEAD OF
EUPHEMIA (MRS HENRY) LAMB   1907–08
Black chalk   50.5 × 35.4
Leeds City Art Galleries (HMCSS)

Fig 43
MODEL FOR NARCISSUS   1909–10   (S21)
Clay or wax, near life-size
Destroyed

14
EUPHEMIA (MRS HENRY) LAMB
(first portrait)   1908   (S13)
Bronze   H 37.5
The Trustees of the Tate Gallery

Fig 44
MARY (MRS AMBROSE) MCEVOY   1909   (S19)
Marble   H 47.2
The Johannesburg Art Gallery

16
STUDY FOR NAN CONDRON KNEELING   1911
Pencil   50.5 × 35.5
Leeds City Art Galleries (HMCSS)

17
NAN SEATED   1911   (S38)
Bronze   H 47 (another cast illustrated)
Philip L. Dyer

18
NAN THE DREAMER   1911   (S36)
Bronze   H 26.7
Bradford Art Galleries and Museums

20
TWO STUDIES OF NAN CONDRON
RECLINING   1911
Chalk   50.6 × 35.4
Beth Lipkin

21   ▷
TWO STUDIES FOR NAN THE DREAMER   1911
Pencil   35.6 × 50.8
Whereabouts unknown

nploying men to model after the completion of
e BMA Building in 1908.

These naturalistic drawings and portrait
udies were part of the sculptor's continuing
elf-education.

After so much that was large and elemental I
had the desire to train myself in a more inten-
sive method of working . . . I began a series of
studies from the model, which were as exact as
I could make them. I worked with great care
and followed the form of the model by quarter
inches, not letting up on any detail of construction of plane.[3]

n later years Epstein's many nude studies were
haracteristically rapidly and carelessly executed,
uthlessly used to capture an expression or mood.
Often he would do as many as twenty in a day.[4]
These early drawings, self-consciously naturalis-
ic and unusually closely related to the sculptures,
are, therefore, rare in Epstein's work.

The first portrait bust of *Euphemia Lamb* [14] is
exceptionally pictorial and spontaneous in comparison with the more studied formality of the
second portrait of three years later.[5] It develops
directly from the life drawing; the provocatively
direct glance, untranslatable into bronze, is modified to a demurely downcast gaze which,
nevertheless, contrives to suggest the sitter's
coquetry, while the characteristic turn of her
head, with its hanging curtain of hair, and her
parted lips suggest an articulate, vivacious presence. Like the contemporary portrait bust of
Mary McEvoy [15], wife of the painter Ambrose
McEvoy, it looks back to early Renaissance
prototypes, even in the modestly downcast gaze,
but that tradition is revitalised by its unforced
realism. With her stylised, severe hairstyle and
handsome medallion, *Mrs McEvoy* curtsies to the
conventions of Edwardian portrait sculpture,
while rejecting its formality and impervious polish.
There are areas of uncertainty; the descriptive treatment of the eyelashes is not successful, and when
Epstein repeated the portrait in marble [Fig. 44], he
softened the modelling and left the eyes closed. The
comparison between the two versions is fascinating; the genteel reserve and controlled vivacity of
the bronze yields to a subtle if melancholic repose in
the marble. It was only at this period of his career
that Epstein attempted portraiture in stone, but his
technique was still traditional. Just as he had with
the BMA sculptures and Lady Ottoline Morrell's
Fountain Figure [Fig. 3], based on Euphemia
Lamb, he modelled in clay before transferring the
figure to marble using traditional pointing devices
(the 'points' are still visible).

Significantly, both the *McEvoy* and *Lamb* portraits enjoyed immediate success when they were
exhibited in 1913 and 1917. Two casts of *Euphemia
Lamb* were purchased at once; one by the Contemporary Art Society, which presented it to the Tate
Gallery in 1917, the other by the American collector, John Quinn, Epstein's most important patron, who lent it to the now legendary Armory
Show in New York. The marble version of *Mrs
McEvoy* became the first work by Epstein to enter
a public collection, being purchased on the
recommendation of Robert Ross and Sir Hugh
Lane for Johannesburg Art Gallery in 1910.

19
STUDY FOR NAN THE DREAMER   1911
Chalk   H 32.9
The Syndics of the Fitzwilliam Museum, Cambridge

22

NAN THE DREAMER, HEAD AND
SHOULDERS 1911 (*S37*)
Bronze H 14
Victor Arwas, London

23

NAN CONDRON, HEAD FROM A MAQUETTE FOR
THE FIGURE *c*1911
Wax H 9
The Epstein Estate

---

24 ▷

NAN CONDRON 1909 (*S17*)
Bronze H 44.5 (earrings lost)
The Trustees of the Tate Gallery

The portraits and drawings of Nan are far more
extreme in their disregard for conventional
canons of beauty. Balletic in pose, the study of
Nan kneeling [16] defers to the grace inherent in
her slender limbs, a characteristic explored both
in *Nan seated* [17] and *Nan the Dreamer* [18]. In the
latter, the sequence of gangly, folded limbs
evokes the subtle, natural rhythms of her body.
The descending clockwise rotation of head,
shoulders, breasts, waist, hips and bent left leg is
balanced by the extended right leg and arms. It
was probably a hard pose to hold, but the grace-
fully extended right arm, so exquisitely placed
within the composition, counteracts the tension
of the braced left arm on which the whole pose
depends. This complex, contrapuntal composition was worked out in a series of exceptionally
brilliant life drawings [19–21]. Epstein also modelled a variant head and shoulders of *Nan the
Dreamer* [22], wonderfully pert and bony, and a
head in wax never previously exhibited [23]
appears to have belonged to a maquette of yet
another figure, now destroyed.

Henri Gaudier-Brzeska saw *Nan seated* [17] during 1913; he had met Epstein the previous year
and been impressed by the *Oscar Wilde Tomb*,
which was then in the studio. Now he wrote to
Sophie Brzeska, 'he showed me a little bronze,
very beautiful, quite the nicest work of his I have
seen — alive and sincere — a seated woman with
her arms above her head'.[6] A memory of it
was absorbed, developed and emerged from
Gaudier's hand a year later as *The Dancer*.[7]

Outstanding though these figure studies are,
they are rivalled by the portrait bust of *Nan* [24].
This and the bust of *Lady Gregory* [27] can be seen
as Epstein's first great mature portraits in which
the sitter's very psyche seems indelibly written in
the body's language, so that the set of the shoulders, the tension of the neck and every contour
and shadow of the face speaks. *Euphemia Lamb*'s
demure glance is a social ploy, a momentary
gesture; but for *Nan*, whose eyes are downcast or
closed in both the drawings and the final bronze,
they are inherent to her, the guardians of her
proud, unshakeable reserve and inner life. In the
drawings, Epstein emphasises, on the one hand
[25], the bony irregularity of her profile and, on
the other [26], the underlying symmetry and
repose of her features. He simplified the ovoid
shape of the skull and treated the hairline,
eyelashes and eyebrows as a subtle interplay of

25
STUDY OF NAN CONDRON   *c*1909
Pen and ink   26 × 40.7
Birmingham Museums and Art Gallery

26
STUDY OF NAN CONDRON   1909
Pencil   27.5 × 43.2
Walsall Museum and Art Gallery (Garman-Ryan
Collection)

arcs. It is Epstein's tremendous grasp of the
essential purity of natural forms which sets portraits such as these and *Marie Rankin* [45] apart
from anything produced in Britain up to that date.
This was probably what the painter, William
Rothenstein was getting at when he contrasted
Epstein's 'unusually fine, robust and fundamental vision' with 'the smooth characterless
decadent modelling of most contemporaneous
sculpture'.[8]

Unlike *Nan*'s native dignity, *Lady Augusta
Gregory*'s imperviousness was to the manner born
[27]. Co-founder of the Abbey Theatre in Dublin
and an author in her own right, she was, as
Epstein recalled in his autobiography, an 'intellectual, somewhat "schoolmarmish" person
[whose] usual appearance was all of a piece and
quite dignified'. Thus, he planned the portrait —

severe, alert, a doughty fighter. He was greatly
irked by Lady Gregory's sudden appearance,
mid-way through the sittings with 'the most
astonishing head of curls' and at her insistence
that she would appear much finer with bare
shoulders in evening dress. 'It is amazing how
English women of no uncertain age fancy themselves dressed as Venus', Epstein grumbled to
himself, and refused to alter it. Sir Hugh Lane
exclaimed, 'Poor Aunt Augusta. She looks as if
she could eat her own children.'[9] Later, however,
she recalled that while sitting she had become
animated in conversation about the theatre; 'he
had cut through the clay throat; tilting head and
chin in an eternal eagerness. Hugh grumbled at it,
and it was thought too revolutionary for the company of the serene marbles at Coole. It is very
clever and I do not quite dislike it'.[10]

27
LADY AUGUSTA GREGORY   1910   (S24)
Bronze   H 38
Leeds City Art Galleries

4 · 1908–1912

THE TOMB OF OSCAR WILDE

Evelyn Silber

Within six months of the completion of the British Medical Association Building in the Strand, Epstein received a still more important public commission, for the tomb of Oscar Wilde in Père Lachaise Cemetery in Paris. Robert Ross, Wilde's literary executor and co-director of the Carfax Gallery, had been one of Epstein's first contacts in England. George Bernard Shaw had written to him in 1905 introducing the young American,[1] so Ross, like Shaw and William Rothenstein, had been shown the emotionally charged drawings of male nudes intended to illustrate Walt Whitman's poem, *Calamus* [98*].

After Wilde's death in exile in 1901, Ross had spent years promoting publication of his writings and clearing his heavily indebted estate. This had finally been achieved late in 1908 and at a dinner given in Ross's honour at The Ritz on 1 December 1908 (the 8th anniversary of Wilde's death), he announced that an anonymous patron had donated funds (£2,000) for the tomb on the condition that Epstein was the sculptor. It is now known that the benefactor was a friend of Wilde's, Mrs James Carew. Recent research has also indicated that it was Rothenstein who first suggested that Epstein could do the job.[2] The patron's anonymity was probably a device of pure political caution, since the employment of Epstein was certain to be controversial, especially since the young American was being chosen ahead of well-known British sculptors.[3] One in particular who might have felt justifiably aggrieved was Charles Ricketts, who had been a friend of Wilde's and visited him during his imprisonment in Reading Gaol.[4] In about 1906 he had even modelled a Symbolist maquette of a cloaked and hatted figure with two fingers sealing its lips, entitled *Silence*, apparently intended as a design for the tomb.[5] Such was the desire for secrecy in the formulation of the project that Epstein himself knew nothing of it. When people called up to congratulate him the day after the dinner he thought he was being hoaxed.[6]

Unlike the BMA affair, where controversy resulted from Epstein's sculpture rather than from the nature of the task, the creation of a tomb for Wilde, tried and imprisoned for homosexuality in 1895 and still execrated by many, was fraught with difficulties from the outset. Later Epstein recalled the pressure put upon him by Wilde's admirers who 'would have liked a Greek youth standing by a broken column, or some scene from the Young King, which was suggested many times'.[7] Others thought it abominable that Wilde should be commemorated at all.

After taking some time to get going, Epstein began to consider the possibilities of a classically-conceived mourning figure which would, through its archaic character, allude to the platonic ideal of male comradeship and love [28]. The draped figure on the right (male or female, is not clear), leaning on a column, reflects the expectations of the Wilde lobby, but appears to have been developed no further. Epstein seems more interested in the idea of a facing pair of male figures seen in profile as if carved in high relief. The central pair, with hands touching, springs directly from the abandoned figure of *Girl with a dove* [9], which had so impressed Charles Holden in 1907. However, it is not clear how this pair would have fitted on the site in Père Lachaise or how inscriptions could have been accommodated. This difficulty is solved by the group on the left: the youths stand symmetrically confronted, heads bowed in grief over a plain stone stele upon which the words OSCAR WILDE can be discerned. The slender figures echo the sinewy forms of the *Calamus* drawings of c 1902 [98*]. Had this design been carried out it would have aligned Epstein stylistically not with an emergence of an English *avant garde*, but with Sir Alfred Gilbert and Rodin's more symbolic works, such as *The Prodigal Son*, 1889,[8] though there can be little doubt that nude male figures employed for sepulchral sculpture would have caused more than raised eyebrows, especially since Wilde was the subject.

Epstein came near to completing a figure related to these studies.[9] He himself recalled only that 'I made sketches and carried them out, but I was dissatisfied and scrapped quite completed work.'[10] However, Charles Holden who, at Epstein's request, was designing the architectural elements of the tomb, recalled seeing 'a fine figure — over-lifesize — in wax I believe — with something of a Havard Thomas's *Lycidas* about it'.[11] (This can plausibly be identified with a clay or wax figure known as *Narcissus* [Fig. 43].) It was probably abandoned soon after the end of July 1910, when Eric Gill spent several hours designing an inscription for the plinth; work on this architectural setting stopped at the sculptor's request, only a few days after Holden had received the commission. What Ross thought about Epstein's sudden decision to start again from scratch one can only guess. Although 'there were slight disagreements about the length of time I took to do the monument', there is no evidence that Epstein was under pressure from Ross or his friends to alter it.

On the contrary, his first design was close to their suggested interpretation.

However, throughout this period Epstein was also working closely with the stone-carver, Eric Gill. Both men had carved versions of *Rom* [33–34, and Fig. 53], after the bronze *Romilly John* [31–32], and they were exploring non-European archaic traditions of carving — the art of Egypt and India. The growing divergence between the idealised male nudes of the first tomb project and the directly carved, ample volumes of *Rom* and the contemporary figure of *Maternity* [37] may have become impossible to reconcile.

The transformation of the *Wilde Tomb* into a massive flying figure [Fig. 46], integrated into its architectural setting is ultimately enigmatic since the sculptor himself left no written clue about how he reached his decision. From his first years in Paris, the sculpture of the Ancient Near East had fascinated him and the Assyrian and Egyptian collections at the British Museum were favourite haunts. However, the immediate source of inspiration was certainly Wilde's poem, *The Sphinx*, first published in 1894, with illustrations by Ricketts. The artist considered these illustrations his best but Wilde was less enthusiastic: 'You have seen them through your intellect not your temperament'.[12]

The Sphinx was a recurrent symbolist image, explored by Moreau, Rops and Toorop amongst others; her fascination lay in her equivocal balance between the physical and spiritual — seductive but world-weary and endlessly sceptical — an equivocation aptly symbolic of Wilde himself.[13] The first hint of Epstein's interest in *The Sphinx* is a rough pencil drawing of a winged female figure raised on a tall plinth, sketched on the verso of the sheet bearing the first tomb studies [Fig. 47]. The splendidly detailed, if unsculptural, drawing developing this theme [29] can be seen as Epstein's partly satirical, symbolist interpretation of the sensuous imagery of Wilde's poem.[14] The winged figure is not the Sphinx herself but her imagined lover, the Egyptian god, Ammon,

> Whose wings like strange transparent talc, rose
> High above his hawk-faced head;
> Painted with silver and with red and ribbed
>   with rods of Oreichalch

The Sphinx whispering into the god's ear is a literal illustration of the line

> You whispered monstrous oracles into the
>   caverns of his ears

but the phallic form she takes and the frieze of lascivious vices below, though in keeping with the tenor of the poem, are also precisely the kind of visual jokes enjoyed by Epstein and Gill, whose interests at this period could justly be described as phallocentric!

In the final sculpture [Fig. 48] the main figure was substantially modified but its general conception — 'a flying demon-angel' with elaborate headdress and back-swept wings — is established. The world-weary face of the figure [Fig. 49*] also evokes the train of thought established in the poem as the poet speculates on the events the Sphinx may have witnessed in her 'thousand weary years', yet the suspended body is dominated by the irresistible flow of the wings, the reiterated parallels of their form reflecting the transcendancy they express.

The catalyst which metamorphosed the poetic image of the drawing [29] into the final carving was one of the man-headed, winged bull figures from the Palace of Sargon at Khorsabad, a treasured exhibit in the British Museum [Fig. 50]. Epstein later acquired a small alabaster standing figure of a male worshipper from Sumer, wearing a garment with a similar treatment [VI].[15] Characteristically, however, he was assimilating numerous sources and may well have examined Buddha

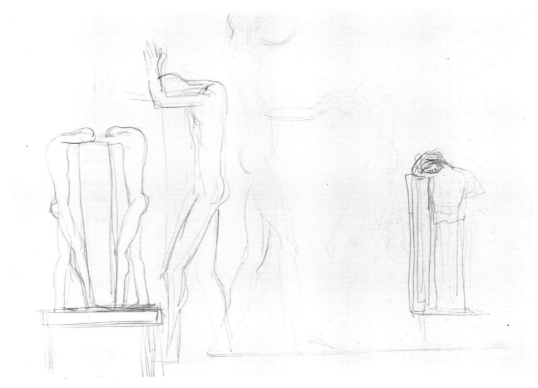

figures with elaborately figurative headdresses.[16] He transformed such statuettes of the Buddha into the crucified Christ in the drawing [29] and, this in turn, is superseded by the symbolic figures of Intellectual Pride, Luxury and Fame, on the finished sculpture.[17]

The design showing the tomb in its final form [30] may well be Charles Holden's working drawing, though it has usually been ascribed to Epstein himself.[18] The sculptor had gone back to him for the new plinth over which this figure would be dramatically suspended, but it would seem that after a disagreement, Holden handed over his working drawings to allow Epstein to supervise the rest of the project on his own.[19]

Having acquired a huge block of Hoptonwood stone, originally intended to be sliced up to face buildings, Epstein set to work, though not without a certain amount of preparation. On 6 January 1911 Gill wrote to William Rothenstein (who was then travelling in India) that Epstein was staying with him at Ditchling 'doing a large figure in stone' (possibly *Maternity* [37]). 'Epstein has decided to do the Wilde monument in stone and to carve it himself too — that is why he is down here — getting into the way of stone carving'.[20]

28
FOUR STUDIES FOR THE TOMB OF OSCAR
WILDE   1908–10
Pencil   50.8 × 35.6
Simon and Alessandra Wilson

Fig 46
TOMB OF OSCAR WILDE   Père Lachaise Cemetery,
Paris, 1909–12   (S40)
Hoptonwood stone

Fig 47
STUDY FOR THE TOMB OF OSCAR WILDE   c 1909
(verso of 28)
Pencil   50.8 × 35.6
Simon and Alessandra Wilson

Gill designed the inscription for the tomb, but he may also have assisted in the actual carving, since an eye witness recalled seeing him working on the wings.[21]

The work was finished and the tomb exhibited in Epstein's Chelsea studio in June 1912 to considerable acclaim for its unconventional power and direct carved technique.[22] *The Evening Standard*, which had led the attack on the BMA sculptures four years earlier, applauded Epstein's 'regard for his material, and its purpose. The work . . . is as reserved in execution as it is monumental in conception so that nothing destroyed the effect of a rectangular block of stone which has felt itself into expression'.[23] *The Pall Mall Gazette* enthused

Mr Epstein is a real sculptor — a carver not a modeller — but he is also a Sculptor in Revolt . . . This brooding, winged figure, born long ago in primitive passions, complex and yet incomplete, is a child of the marble, and not an enlarged copy, by some other hand, of a highly finished plaster model . . . This is Mr Epstein's commentary, serious and profound, unobscured by conventional formulas, and inspired by an acute necessity for utterance. "Go and see it at once", is my urgent advice to all who are interested in sculpture, and think of it, if you can, on a hilltop in Père Lachaise, dominating all those tawdry memorials of the easily-forgotten dead.[24]

Any tendency to exuberance the sculptor may have felt at these signs of critical and public understanding was soon dashed. First, the French customs demanded a huge payment of duty on the import of the stone, refusing to recognise it as a work of art, and then, in September 1912, once it had arrived in the cemetery and masons came to complete the installation, the authorities recoiled at its frankness and took immediate steps to protect the public.[25] A newly discovered letter[26] from the sculptor to Francis Dodd vividly evokes his agitation and fury at the ensuing impasse:

Dear Dodd

I received word that the monument was about to be finished and I have come here to see how things were and to give last instructions about the work; I had intended to rob you of 5 or 6 £ but as Mrs Dodd wouldn't hear of my seeking you out robbed her instead. I was sorry to leave the bust as I felt it getting on well but I will be back in a day or two and go at it like mad. Imagine my horror Dodd when arriving at the cemetery to find that the sex parts of the figure had been swaddled in plaster! and horribly. I went to see the keeper of the cemetery and he tells me that the Prefect of the Seine[27] and the Keeper of the Ecole des Beaux Arts were called in and decided that I must either castrate or fig leaf the monument! What am I to do? Here is the Strand business all over again. You cannot imagine how terrible the monument looks now. The work is nearing completion and the inscriptions will begin tomorrow. I am going to get of course Leon Bakst and any other influential people I know here to stop all this miserable business. I feel quite sick over it but ridicule will do the work I think. Imagine a bronze fig-leaf on the Oscar Wilde Tomb. For that is what the guardian of the cemetery suggested might be done . . .

This is a mad world.

Yours ever

Jacob Epstein

More rationally, on 14 September, Epstein wrote appealing for support to the painter–journalist H. P. Roché (later famous as the author of *Jules et Jim*):

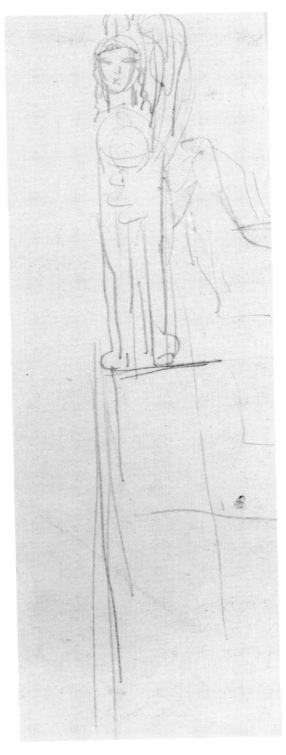

29 ▷

STUDY FOR THE TOMB OF OSCAR WILDE AND A FRIEZE c1910
Pencil 38.1 × 50.8
Anthony d'Offay Gallery, London

Fig 48 ▷▷

TOMB OF OSCAR WILDE, as reproduced in *The New Age*, 6 June 1912 (S40)

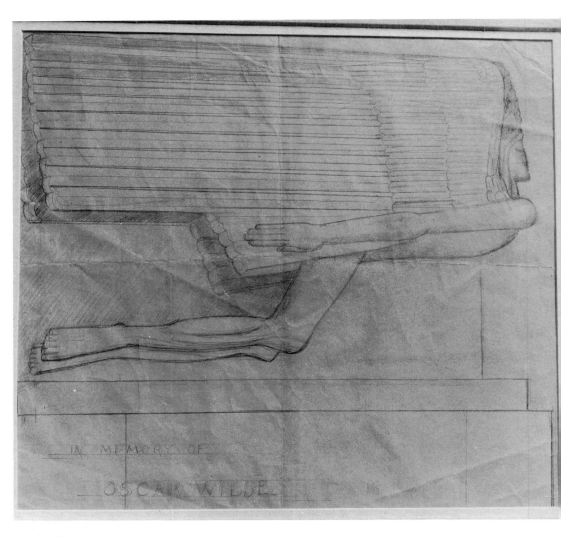

30
Jacob Epstein or Charles Holden (1875–1960)
STUDY FOR THE TOMB OF OSCAR WILDE   1909–10
Pencil   49 × 60
Walsall Museum and Art Gallery (Garman-Ryan
Collection)

Fig 50
MAN-HEADED WINGED BULL, from the Palace of
Sargon II, Khorsabad, *c*710 BC
Marble
The British Museum

The conservateur of the cemetery objects to the
work as it stands as immoral and wishes me to
modify it. It is not an immoral work and I
cannot modify it without destroying it or
rendering it ridiculous. I wish to bring this
matter to the attention of all artists and writers
who value the freedom of their conceptions and
who might wish to protest against the tyranny
of petty officials. Can you help me in this
matter?[28]

Despite letters of protest and periodic forays to
the cemetery during which Epstein, supported by
friends such as Brancusi, tried to remove the
tarpaulin which now covered the monument,
total success was not achieved. A bronze
fig-leaf-like plaque, made on Ross's instructions,
was attached to the figure. When this was
removed in a daring raid, and subsequently presented to Epstein one evening in the Café Royal, it
was succeeded by a tarpaulin which remained in
place until sometime during the Great War, when
it was removed 'without remark'.[29]

VI
STANDING FIGURE OF A MALE WORSHIPPER,
Sumer, Mesopotamia, c 2500 BC
Alabaster   29.2
The Trustees of the British Museum (formerly Jacob
Epstein collection)

5 · 1908–1912

EARLY CARVINGS

Judith Collins

When Epstein began work on the eighteen over-life-size figures for the British Medical Association in 1907, it is far from clear how much training he had received in carving. At the Art Students' League in New York during 1901 and 1902, he had attended George Grey Barnard's classes in mod-elling[1] and, as Epstein's own account makes clear, he had spent more time drawing and modelling than carving during the six months at the Ecole des Beaux Arts.

My mornings were spent in modelling from life, and I ate a hasty lunch which I brought with me, and then went into the carving class, and also drew from the Michelangelo casts, of which there was a room full. In carving there was practially no instruction, and we were left alone to do pretty well what we pleased.[2]

Working on the BMA figures alongside pro-fessional architectural carvers gave him a great deal of practice; looking at early photographs of *New-Born* [Fig. 38], one can observe his skilful use of a range of tools, especially the claw chisel, and his use of pointing devices since a number of drill holes are still visible.

In the spring of 1907, when Epstein received the commission for the British Medical Association Building in the Strand, he moved studios, from a tumbledown one — Stamford Bridge Studios in the Fulham Road — to a larger space at 72 Cheyne Walk, Chelsea.[3] Augustus John had a studio in the Kings Road and had become a friend of Epstein through New English Art Club connec-tions. Romilly John, the son of Augustus and Dorelia John, was born in 1905 and it seems that sometime in 1907 Augustus commissioned Epstein to make a portrait head of the young child [31]. The financial basis of the commission is not known; when Epstein was at a low ebb in the spring of 1908, with his BMA figures under attack, Augustus wrote a note to Dorelia about this and added, 'It is . . . monstrous . . . I sent him a fiver on account of Rom's portrait.'[4] John used to visit Epstein's studio in Cheyne Walk to watch his progress on the BMA figures and in 1907 noted how Epstein was working on the figure of *Maternity* [11], with his wife Margaret posing as the figure of the mother, holding a 'borrowed' baby. Epstein had already shown an interest in modelling babies' heads [6–7], indeed, they are the earliest sculptures of his which sur-vive. Romilly John is aged about two in the head, and Epstein has concentrated on his full cheeks and cap of hair which is smoothed to look like a helmet. In keeping with Epstein's method of working at that time, the portrait head would have been modelled in clay from life, cast in plaster and then cast into bronze. In several early casts the cap has been burnished to enhance its helmet-like appearance and contrast with the naturalism of the child's face [32].

This was a head Epstein was to use and reuse. Romilly is the child in the bronze *Standing Mother and Child* [Fig. 66] and was the starting-point for at least two carvings [33–34]. In both of the latter, he seems to continue the process of self-education in carving technique (just as he was improving his modelling technique in studies of *Euphemia* and *Nan* [14, 24]). Moreover, in 1909 and 1910 he carved two portrait busts in stone, *Mrs Emily Chadbourne* [Fig. 52], now lost,[5] and *Mrs Ambrose McEvoy* [Fig. 44]. Both Mary McEvoy, a painter like her husband, and Mrs Chadbourne, a wealthy collector of art, were friends of Augustus John and both were probably encouraged by him to commission a portrait bust from Epstein. Mary McEvoy sat to him and was modelled in clay for casting into plaster or bronze. Then for some reason Epstein copied the plaster or bronze bust in marble. The marble bust appears to be a most faithful copy of the head and hair, but the shoul-ders and dress are left unfinished. The marks of the claw chisel are still visible here because the area has been left unpolished, in contrast to the rest of the bust, which has a high finish. It seems reasonable to assume that the marble bust of *Mrs Chadbourne* was also not carved directly from a live sitter, but from the intermediate stage of a plaster or bronze version.

Epstein carved a life-size copy in limestone [33] of the bronze portrait of *Romilly John* [31] and this stayed in his possession all his life. Without a first-hand examination of the marble busts of *Mrs McEvoy* and *Mrs Chadbourne*, it is not possible to be definite about the pointing method of copying, but with the limestone copy of *Romilly John* this was obviously the method used, since the tell-tale exploratory depth marks are still visible. The limestone copy accurately reproduces the bun-ched features of the child's nose and mouth, and the empty eye-sockets, while it slightly alters the contour edge of the hair. The main impression is that the limestone head is unfinished, with a boss of stone left unremoved at the crown of the head and the striated marks of the claw chisel showing over the whole surface, thus revealing most clearly Epstein's working method of transferring directly from bronze using the traditional point-ing device. A possible date for this work is *c.* 1909–10, although it could be closer in date to the bronze 1907 version. By July 1910 Epstein had carved another stone version of the head of *Romilly John* [34], but this departs quite radically from the verisimilitude of the first stone version. Why did Epstein embark on a second stone carv-ing? Was it connected with a burgeoning pro-fessional friendship with the letter-cutter and stone-mason, Eric Gill?

According to Gill's diary, he and Epstein met socially for the first time on 12 April 1908.[6] Then on 23 June Gill, who was living in Ditchling in Sussex, travelled to London to look at Epstein's newly unveiled sculptures on the BMA building in the Strand. He wrote a letter in their support which was published in the *BMA Journal* for 4 July, describing Epstein as his friend and assert-ing that he was 'raising modern sculpture from the dead'. Gill's diaries for the second half of 1908 and the whole of 1909 are missing, so information about their relationship during that period is vague. By the spring of 1910, however, their friendship was ready to develop into a fruitful and close working relationship. William Rothenstein takes credit for this. Gill carved two small figures in stone at the end of 1909 on a sudden impulse, never having carved figures before. He took photographs of them to Rothenstein, who was impressed. Rothenstein then relates 'I sent Gill

31
ROMILLY JOHN   1907   (S8)
Bronze   H 20
Private collection

32
ROMILLY JOHN   1907   (S8)
Bronze   H 20
Private collection

Fig 53 △

Eric Gill (1882–1940)

ROMILLY JOHN   1910

Stone   H c 20 (studio photograph. HMCSS: Gill
Archive)

Whereabouts unknown

33

ROM (Romilly John, first version)   1909–10?   (S20)

Limestone   H 22.5

The Epstein Estate (on loan to Birmingham
Museums and Art Gallery)

---

down to Epstein, thinking he might work for him
for a time, and the two became friends. And truth
to tell, it was Gill who turned Epstein's attention
to stone-carving again, as is shown by Epstein's
Memorial to Oscar Wilde at Père-Lachaise; Gill
was no modeller, therefore was not likely to be
affected by Epstein's art.'[7]

To return to Gill's diaries, on 20 April 1910 he
had tea with Epstein in London, and a couple of
weeks later Mr and Mrs Epstein were invited to
spend the weekend of 4–5 June with the Gills at
Ditchling. After a further meeting with Epstein in
London on 16 June Gill spent much of his time (42
hours to be exact) from 25 June to 4 July carving a
stone head for Epstein; on 22 July Epstein paid
him £8, presumably for the head.[8] Gill's *Romilly
John* [Fig. 53] was also a copy of Epstein's bronze
head of the little boy [31]. Thus, by the summer of
1910, there were three stone variants on the
bronze. But why did Gill copy the bronze head in
stone, at the commission of Epstein, when Epstein himself had probably already carved two

stone versions of the same model? We know tha[t]
Epstein commissioned it from Gill because whe[n]
Gill decided to include his version in his first one[-]
man show at the Chenil Gallery in January 191[1]
the entry read 'Head of Romilly John, carved fro[m]
model by J. Epstein, lent by J. Epstein', and ther[e]
is also the evidence of Gill's diaries and work[-]
sheets. Presumably when Epstein lent his Gi[ll]
stone head in January 1911 for the show, he sti[ll]
had his own two stone versions; so at that date h[e]
owned all three. Gill's stone version was set on [a]
small rectangular stone base with an inscriptio[n]
carved by him — 'Romily John'. Epstein's so[-]
called first version of *Romilly John* had no base[,]
but his second version [34] was carved from th[e]
top section of a large rectangular piece of stone[,]
with the head taking up a third of the overa[ll]
dimensions. We know from records that Gill car[-]
ved the inscription on the front face of the ston[e]
base for this head. Unlike the full name on hi[s]
own carving, he only cut the letters ROM fo[r]
Epstein's version. Epstein first sent this work t[o]

34
ROM (Romilly John, second version)   1910   (S25)
Limestone   H 87
National Museum of Wales

the Allied Artists Association London Salon at the Albert Hall in July 1910, where in the mêlée of thousands of works it eluded press coverage. Then, in January 1911 he sent it, with two other portrait works — the plaster of *Fountain Figure* [Fig. 3] and *Mrs Chadbourne* [Fig. 52] to the first National Portrait Society Exhibition at the Grafton Galleries, where, not surprisingly, the press wrote about it at length. P. G. Konody (*The Observer*, 22 January 1911) reported that the show contained

> no synthetic abstractions, unless Mr Jacob Epstein's plastic joke Rom claims the distinction of being so described. What this rudely carved cross between a prehistoric Egyptian head and a caricatured and archaically simplified portrait of the laughing Japanese goddess Uzume or Okame can possibly have to do with Rome, may perhaps be explained by the sculptor. It certainly does not explain itself. One would almost think that the word 'Rom' graven on the basis is a mystical term borrowed from some Oriental language, and not merely the German spelling for the city of the Caesars and the Popes, if the character of the lettering did not remove every doubt in this respect.

C. Lewis Hind (*The Daily Chronicle*, 21 January 1911) found it quite powerful:

> Nor do I know what his Rom means. It starts to the eye, it rests there, and I am united with the beginnings of things in the dim majesty of Egypt. Epstein is never commonplace, nor is he ever smart . . . in his creations hovers and hides the interior knowledge of the immemorial, silently eloquent past.

In all probability the name Rom was a private joke between Epstein and Augustus John, since it is an abbreviation of Romany or gypsy. (John's love of gypsies and their way of life was well-known.) Lewis Hind was quite right in finding the beginnings of things in this stone *Rom*, since it seems quite likely that it is Epstein's first direct essay into stone. Before this his carvings had been careful copies of works originally modelled. With *Rom* that process was discarded, and it could be that Gill's practical influence as a stone-carver first and foremost lay behind this new step. Epstein carved his version without reference to a model, without turning to the bronze or the first stone version, instead paying attention to the nature of the material and letting that dictate the formal quality of the head.

Hind's book, *The Post Impressionists*, 1911, recorded his somewhat confused yet supportive response to the latest art manifestations that had been on show in London during the previous year. Chapter Ten concentrated on Post Impressionism in sculpture, which Hind found in the work of Gill and Epstein. Intrigued by Epstein's contribution to the National Portrait Society exhibition in January 1911, which included *Rom*, he sought an interview with the sculptor in his Chelsea studio, where he learnt that 'Rom . . . is . . . the Eternal Child, one of the flanking figures of a group apotheosising Man and Woman, around a central shrine, that the sculptor destines in his dreams for a great temple.'[9] Richard Buckle

relates how, when Epstein was a sculpture student in Paris in the years 1902–05, he dreamt of producing two monuments, one a *Temple of Love* and the other a *Temple of the Sun*.[10] Both were begun; the *Temple of Love* comprised a 'heroic-sized group' of a man and woman, while the *Temple of the Sun* started with 'a group of sun-worshippers'. Neither project survived in material form when Epstein moved from Paris to London, but the ideas remained to bear some fruit again in the years 1910–12. On 10 September 1910, Epstein went to stay with Gill at Ditchling in order to inspect a possible site on the Sussex Downs (Asheham House) for a projected Twentieth century Stonehenge which they had recently conceived together. They intended to carve a series of colossal figures in stone and set them in the landscape as an open air temple.[11] The symbolic nature of the temple was not stated by either sculptor, but on the evidence of their work in 1910–11, it would have celebrated the procreative nature of man, an interpretation strengthened by Augustus John's humorous retrospective account of the meeting in his studio between Gill, Epstein, Ambrose McEvoy and himself.[12]

There are a handful of sculptures and drawings by both Epstein and Gill which could relate to this temple project. Epstein produced four sculptures, the dates of which are still unresolved, all with titles referring to the sun. (The titles cannot positively be proved to be Epstein's own, however.) These works are *Crouching Sun Goddess* [35], *Sun God* [Fig. 57], *Sunworshipper*[13] and *Sunflower* [36]. *Crouching Sun Goddess* is the smallest of these works and represents a compact squatting female nude figure carved from a block of stone 14¾ inches high. During 1910, when Epstein was professionally closest to Gill, their shared sculptural interests focused strongly upon primitive African and Egyptian sculpture and the rock-cut temples of India.[14] Later in his life, as part of his superb collection of primitive sculpture, Epstein acquired more than one small Egyptian pottery figure of a crouching baboon [VII].[15] Such baboons were believed to have worshipped the sun, uttering cries at its rising. The subject matter and the formal content link Egyptian works like these with the *Crouching Sun Goddess*, but as well as these primitive sources, there were also a handful of crucial early Twentieth century precedents. In Paris, late in 1907, Brancusi, after a practice of modelling his sculptures, began to carve direct in stone. The first work was probably a limestone head, and this was followed by two small figural works, *Le Baiser* and *La Sagesse* [Fig. 54],[16] both of which consist of squatting figures carved so that they retain the cuboid nature of the stone block. Also in Paris in 1907, the painter André Derain showed a crudely carved squatting stone figure with its head bent over its knees and held there by tightly clasped hands.[17] The extent of Epstein's knowledge of these works by 1910 cannot be ascertained but it is more than likely that he was very well aware of *avant garde* sculptural activity in Paris at this time. The striated treatment of the backswept mane of hair in his *Crouching Sun Goddess* can be seen again in the Brancusi figures and in the Egyptian pottery baboons, and it indicates a shared primitive approach to the rendering of

hair. Two features of the *Crouching Sun Goddess* look as though they could have been observed from a model rather than having been inspired by working with the stone; these are the curvaceous, nipped-in waist, seen from the back view, and the way the thumbs are carved vertically, set away from the block of fingers.

Although this stone figure could well relate to the sculptural plans which Epstein and Gill were making in the autumn of 1910 concerning their outdoor temple (to the sun?), and news of which they related to their colleagues, Epstein appears never to have exhibited it. Gill, in contrast, carved what could almost serve as a companion figure, *St. Simeon Stylites* [Fig. 55], and he included this in a group of seven sculptures sent to Roger Fry's Second Post Impressionist Exhibition in the winter of 1912. Although Gill's squatting male figure, with its elbows poised on its knees, shares formal affinities with primitive wooden seated figures from the Philippines and Sierra Leone,[18] it is less

likely to have been initially inspired by primitive works than Epstein's *Crouching Sun Goddess*. The female figure is more elemental and raw in her appearance than Gill's somewhat doll-like, docile saint seated on top of his stone pillar. The pose of both figures has been arranged so that they display their genital organs, and here again Gill treats this feature much more decoratively than Epstein.[19] Since Gill saw this squatting male figure as a religious image, either a saint or the first man made by God, the mood of the sculpture would, thus, be less elemental and raw than Epstein's pagan goddess.

However, in 1910 both Epstein and Gill produced stone reliefs depicting a pagan sun god. Gill carved a chubby naked boy [Fig. 56] with legs splayed and arms crossed behind his back from the front face of a piece of stone 9 inches high and sent a photograph of this work to William Rothenstein. He replied enthusiastically on 10 August 1910: 'When, how and where did you

make the young sun god? He is a wonder — as witty as he is beautiful, as virile as he is short and tubby and I love his bad temper.'[20] Unprompted, Rothenstein named the young male figure *Sun God*, although Gill in his diary and worksheets referred to it as *Cupid* or *Cocky Kid*.[21] Epstein was just as enthusiastic as Rothenstein about the little figure and ordered another from Gill, who carved it for him during the autumn of 1910.[22] Epstein's *Sun God* relief [Fig. 57] bears several similarities, notably in the hieratic frontal pose with legs splayed, and in the way the striated hair radiates out from the face and merges into the background plane. Gill exhibited three of his *Cocky Kid* reliefs in his one-man exhibition at the Chenil Gallery in January 1911, while Epstein left his *Sun God* relief unfinished and unexhibited until 1932–33, when he completed it and carved another relief, *Primeval Gods*, on the reverse [Fig. 86].

It is not too difficult to see Epstein's *Sunflower* [36] as a direct descendant of his earlier *Sun God* relief, with the god's radiating halo of hair and the sun theme as the connecting links. The dating of this carving is not secure; it has long been assigned to 1910 but current opinion now favours a later date of 1912–13 on stylistic grounds.[23] Much has been written of its dependence upon African wooden heads [VIII], with their smoothed cabochon masks abutting halo-like forms. Alan Wilkinson draws attention to the similarities between the 'double halos of pointed, petallike forms surrounding the head' and tribal heads from both Africa and the Pacific Islands, from Yoruba, Baule, and the Gulf of Papua.[24] Since Epstein was poised to buy his first work of primitive art at a time possibly concurrent with the carving of *Sunflower*, it is not irrelevant to cite primitive source material. But much in his own sculptural development leads logically to the execution of this piece. An interest in a saw-toothed zig-zag edge to a plane appears in Epstein's treatment of the drapery of his stone fountain figure [Fig. 3] of 1908–10, a life-size female figure carved for Lady Ottoline Morrell. It appears again, not with sharp zig-zags but with softer undulations, at the ends of the pair of feathered wings which hold the angel aloft on the *Oscar Wilde Tomb* [Fig. 58].

Fig 56 △
Eric Gill (1882–1940)
COCKY KID   1910
Portland stone   H 22.9 (studio photograph.
HMCSS: Gill Archive)
Whereabouts unknown

Fig 57 ◁
SUN GOD   1910   (S26)
Hoptonwood stone relief   H 213.4
The Metropolitan Museum of Art, New York

VIII
DANCE MASK, Yauré, Ivory Coast
Wood   H 58.4
The Trustees of the British Museum (formerly Jacob Epstein collection)

Fig 58
TOMB OF OSCAR WILDE   Père Lachaise Cemetery, Paris 1909–12   (S40, detail)
Hoptonwood stone

6 · 1910–1917

LOVE AND BIRTH

Terry Friedman

Eric Gill described Epstein, whom he had met in 1908 in connection with the British Medical Association commission, as a sculptor 'mad about sex'.[1] Between working on the BMA figures in 1907–08 and 1917, when he became involved in the War, Epstein created fourteen sculptures, all but one stone carvings, and a number of drawings, on the themes of physical union, pregnancy and birth. He was not alone in this preoccupation. Around 1910 Gill carved two marble reliefs of passionately copulating couples inspired by Hindu erotic sculpture: *Ecstasy* [Fig. 60] and *Votes for Women* [Fig. 61], the latter acquired c 1910 by the economist, Maynard Keynes. Epstein's sculptures, however, represent a profoundly obsessional cycle concerned less with the physicality of intercourse than with the female mystery of fecundity.

The largest and most imposing of these sculptures, the one which incorporates many of his ideas on the subject, is the over life-size Hopton-wood stone *Maternity* [37], begun around 1910. The state of mind which is captured here is that described by Rodin in 1911:

> In true youth, that of virginal puberty, the body, full of brand-new vigor, awakens in its svelte pride and seems both to fear and to summon love. This moment hardly lasts more than a few months. Without even speaking about the deformations caused by child-bearing, the fatigue caused by desire and the fever caused by passion rapidly slackens the tissues and relax the lines. The girl becomes a woman. This is another type of beauty, still admirable, but less pure.[2]

Evelyn Silber has suggested that Epstein may have intended *Maternity* as one of the components of a 'great scheme of doing some colossal figures . . . a sort of twentieth century Stonehenge', as Gill, his collaborator, described the project in September 1910. This was planned for the grounds of an artistic commune at Asheham House, 'hidden away in a valley in the hills' near Lewes in Sussex, where they would be 'free to do all we wanted without the fear of hurting anybody's feelings [or having] our figures smashed up by some damned fools who didn't choose to like them'.[3] *Ecstacy* and Epstein's stone head of *Rom* [34], as well as the erotic drawing inscribed 'one of the hundred pillars of the Secret Temple' [41], and the unusual pencil and coloured wash drawing called *The Flame of Life* [42],[4] have

been associated with this mysterious project, which failed, from lack of funds.

Exactly when *Maternity* was conceived and executed is uncertain; a date as early as 1908 has been suggested.[5] The distinctive treatment of the hair as a smooth, helmet-shape recalls the bronze head of *Romilly John*, 1907 [31–32] and is also a feature of the four lesbian figures which form a frieze of unknown function in an early sketch, datable to the summer of 1910, for the *Oscar Wilde Tomb* [29]. A preliminary drawing for the full figure of *Maternity* [38], with the model wearing earrings, shows the position of the left arm and hand already resolved but the right arm swinging out from the body (in a manner close to the figure of *Nature*, 1907–08, one of the rejected BMA statues).[6] This gesture would have been physically possible since the figure sways to the left of the centre of the block, but technically difficult because of the unsupported arm. A second study [43] shows both arms turned inward towards each other, cradling the pregnant belly, with the tips of the fingers gently touching, as in the cosmic creative union of God and Adam on the Sistine Chapel ceiling. This drawing, which is identical in scale to the sculpture, may actually have been pinned to the block, but as he worked Epstein modified the gesture; the arms and hands are drawn apart to emphasise the hidden gestation of the child within the womb.

The emergence of the figure from the narrow block of Hoptonwood stone is recorded in a series of contemporary studio photographs [Fig. 62].[7] He worked from front to back. The front sections of the head, torso, belly, arms and hands emerged first from the roughly-cut block; the shape of the skirt is merely suggested. The upper part of the figure was then freed, except for some modest details, and work began in earnest on the skirt and feet. By 1912 almost the entire front of the figure was finished, as is evident by the delicate cutting of the face, nails and folds of flesh at the pit of the right arm; only the halter strap crossing between the breasts and the area between the arms are still unfinished. On the sides and back, however, many rough areas remain [40], and it is possible to see how the layers of fossilised limestone had been peeled away by the chisel from the smooth, flat outer face of the block as it was delivered from the quarry, through lesser grades of cutting to the extremely delicate, final surface. The sculpture, still unfinished, was first shown in public at the Allied Artists Association

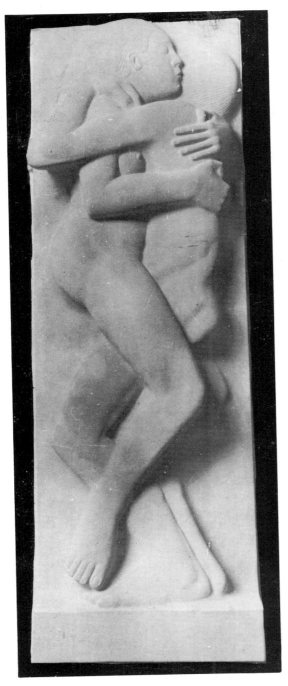

Fig 60
Eric Gill (1882–1940)
ECSTACY   1910–11
Stone   H 137.2 (studio photograph. HMCSS: Gill
Archive)
Tate Gallery, London

Fig 61
Eric Gill (1882–1940)
VOTES FOR WOMEN   1910
Stone (studio photograph. HMCSS: Gill Archive)
Whereabouts unknown

exhibition held at the Royal Albert Hall in July 1912. It was then returned to the studio and remained untouched (except perhaps for the removal of the hair bow). In this incomplete state, partly embedded in the unworked stone, *Maternity* is a rare and authoritative example surviving from the early modern period in British sculpture to demonstrate the newly-introduced 'direct carving' technique, otherwise recorded only in contemporary studio photographs or descriptions. Its 'rough-hewn areas gave viewers [in 1912] a startling raw idea of the passionate physical engagement which informed Epstein's chiselling of the stone'.[8] His only previous large-scale carvings, the eighteen BMA figures of 1907–08 and the *Fountain Figure*, 1908–10 [Fig. 3], involved making preparatory plaster models.[9] As far as is known, no maquettes or full-sized models and only two drawings preceded *Maternity*; prob-

ably only the general outline of the figure was sketched on the block of stone before carving began.[10] While the gentle, erotic sway of the figure could easily be accommodated within the width of the block, its restricted depth meant that the front and back of the body [Figs 39*–40] were forced to its very perimeter and started to flatten out (the antithesis of Rodin's approach to carving the human figure), giving it a rigid tenseness as, sometimes with uncomfortable results as, for instance, in the modelling of the left thumb. The extent of Epstein's compression of the monolithic form is evident when *Maternity* is compared to Gill's large, related carved figure, *Mulier*, 1914 [Fig. 63].

Maternity, like many of his major early carvings, is an amalgam of various sources of inspiration. Its distinctive interpretation of fecundity, a theme which captivated many *avant garde* sculptors

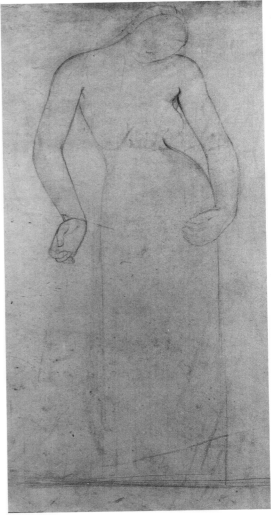

38
STUDY FOR MATERNITY   1910
Pencil   57.2 × 81.3
Leeds City Art Galleries (HMCSS)

40
MATERNITY   1910   (S23, detail)
Hoptonwood stone   H 206
Leeds City Art Galleries

during the years around the War, lies in its strong associations with the primitive. The figure has a claim to being the first sculpture made in Britain to display marked primitive and 'archaic' characteristics, and undoubtedly this is what separates it from the classically inspired BMA *Maternity* two or three years earlier [11]. It is still unclear what, if any, primitive sculpture Epstein may have owned at this early date or what specifically he looked at in public collections. The pose recalls Hindu erotic sculpture of a type he was later to acquire, most notably the superb eleven-century female figure in sandstone from Central India [IX], with her voluptuously provocative hips and formalised, globular breasts.[11] At this time there was considerable interest in the art of the sub-continent: E. B. Havell's *Indian Sculpture and Painting* and A. Coomaraswamy's *Medieval Sinhalese Art* were both published in 1908. In 1911, Gill wrote William Rothenstein (then on tour in India) that 'the best route to Heaven is via Elephanta, and Elura & Ajanta. They must be wonderful places indeed', and added, 'There has lately been appearing in our

37   ◁
MATERNITY   1910   (S23)
Hoptonwood stone   H 206
Leeds City Art Galleries

41
STUDY FOR 'ONE OF THE HUNDRED PILLARS OF
THE SECRET TEMPLE'   *c*1910
Pencil   42 × 25.5
Anthony d'Offay Gallery, London

42
THE FLAME OF LIFE   *c*1910
Pencil and coloured wash on panel   42 × 57.8
Private collection

---

midst a publication called the *Wonders of the World*
(7d. fort-nightly . . .) and, greatest of wonder of
all!, in it have been quite a large number of photographs of Indian sculptures.'[12] Such sources
probably account for *Maternity* as well as the
amorous couple in the 'one hundred pillars of the
Secret Temple' drawing [41].[13] The tender, con-
templative features of *Maternity* are akin to those
of the flying creature on the *Oscar Wilde Tomb*
[Fig. 49*], itself derived from Chinese bodhis-
attvas. Richard Cork has suggested that the
'jutting angularity of the arms reveals [Epstein's]

growing involvement with African carvings' and,
moreover, that the

whole figure is a testament to the wide range of
expressive possibilities opened up by [his]
pioneering audacity . . . Never before had a
British sculptor dared to present such an inescapably voluptuous image of fertility . . . In
this respect the theme of maternity could
hardly have been more appropriate. For this
flawed yet deeply impressive carving appears
poised for the birth not only of a child, but also

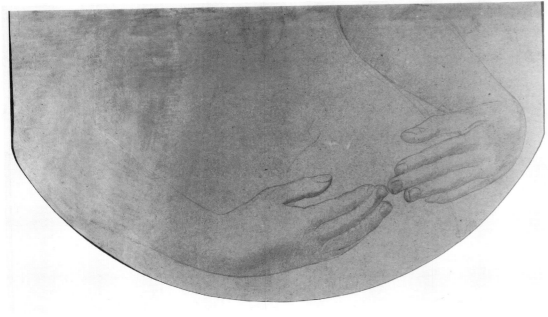

Fig 62
Epstein in his studio carving MATERNITY,
1910–12   (S23)

43
STUDY FOR THE ARMS AND HANDS OF
MATERNITY   1910
Pencil on cardboard   40.5 × 75.5
Leeds City Art Galleries (HMCSS)

Fig 63

Eric Gill (1882–1940)

MULIER   1914

Stone   H C 215 (studio photograph. HMCSS: Gill Archive)

Sculpture Garden, University of California, Los Angeles

IX

HEADLESS FEMALE FIGURE, Central India, 11th century AD (shown with the sculptor at 18 Hyde Park Gate, London, c 1959)

Sandstone   H 68.6

The Trustees of the British Museum (formerly Jacob Epstein collection)

of the revolutionary spirit which would provide twentieth-century sculpture with some of its most enduring achievements . . . a powerful new force had emerged in British . . . sculpture.[14]

Epstein found unexpected confirmation of his radically new approach in the summer of 1912 in Paris, where he saw in the studio of Amadeo Modigliani 'nine or ten of those long heads which were suggested by African masks, and one figure . . . carved in stone' [Fig. 64].[15] The two sculptors became friends and talked about sharing a studio,

and a souvenir of their friendship, which lasted until Modigliani's early death in 1920, is the magnificent pencil and blue crayon drawing of a *Caryatid* [44*].[16]

Although *Maternity* was exhibited briefly in public in 1912 and did not impress the critics (Roger Fry was particularly hostile),[17] the work made an impact on the character of emerging modernist sculpture in Britain. Gill saw it at the A A A Exhibition on 12 August 1912.[18] Both Henri Gaudier-Brzeska, who visited Epstein's studio in 1912, and Henry Moore, whom Epstein befriended in 1921, gleaned motifs from this figure.[19] It

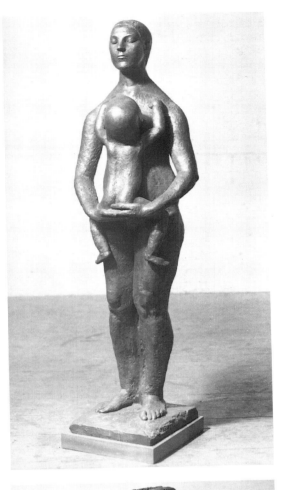

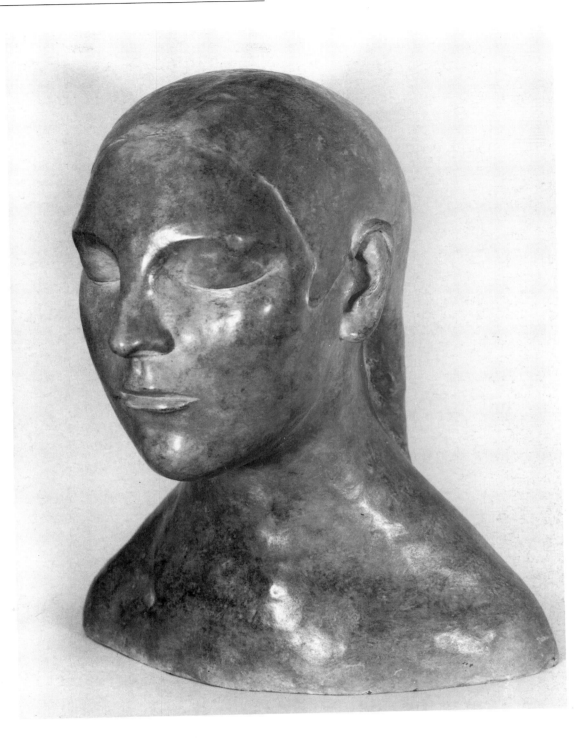

Fig 65
STANDING MOTHER AND CHILD   1911   (S34)
Bronze   H 167.6
Private collection

Fig 64 ◁
Amedeo Modigliani (1884–1920)
STANDING FIGURE   c 1909–12
Limestone   H 162.8
Australian National Gallery, Canberra

45
MARIE RANKIN (IRISH GIRL)   1910–11   (S29)
Bronze   H 29
Beth Lipkin

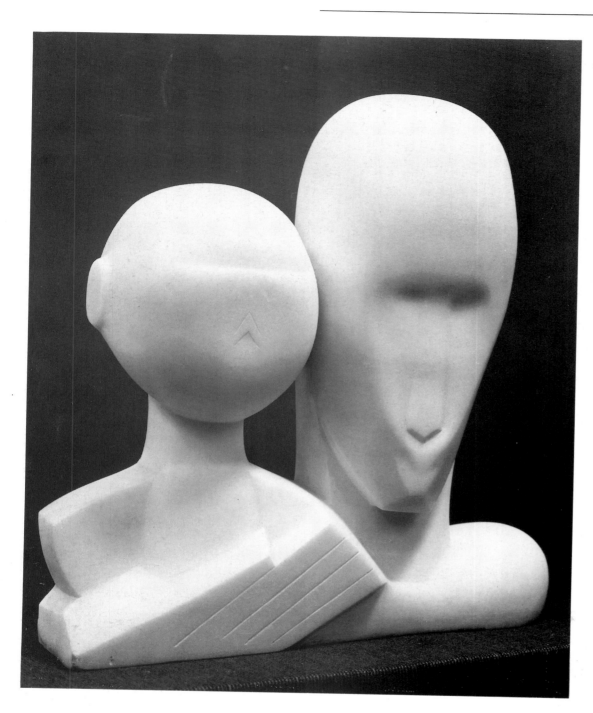

relative naturalism of *Maternity* to a more abstract and aggressive primitivism, which bound him to the concerns of the Vorticist group. Wyndham Lewis wrote in 1913 that Epstein found in 'the machinery of procreation a dynamo to work the deep atavism of his spirit'.[22] The nature of this stylistic change becomes clear in comparing the bronze *Mother and child* of 1911 [Fig. 65] with the marble *Mother and child* of 1913–14 [Fig. 66]. The former, reusing the helmeted baby *Romilly John*, 1907 [31] and the beatific bust of *Marie Rankin*, 1910–11 [45], looks back to the naturalism of the BMA figures, although it is true that the smooth surfaces and the elegantly stylised hair links this latter portrait to the simplified geometry of his more blatantly abstract sculpture. In contrast, the marble *Mother and Child*,[23] so characteristic of the post-Paris carvings, depends on specific modernist sources: Brancusi's marble *Prometheus*, 1911,[24] and the celebrated Fang *Reliquary head* (*bieri*) from Gabon [Fig. IV], which Epstein saw in Joseph Brummer's shop in Paris in 1913 and later (in 1935) acquired for his own collection.[25]

At Pett Level Epstein also carved his most austere and heroic sculptures on sexual themes: the pregnant female figures in flenite, the monumental *Venuses* and the three versions of copulating *Doves* in a wonderfully translucent white marble. The energy which he devoted to the bird groups may have been connected with a belief in them as fundamental expressions of procreation. When, in 1914, Quinn contemplated commissioning a third version [48] of the marbles carved in the previous year [46], Ezra Pound urged him to choose the version in which the doves are 'stuck together', that is, mating rather than preparing for the act.[26] The hesitancy and openness of the first group was replaced by larger but more compact versions, which Pound

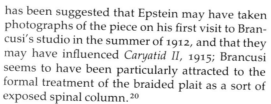

has been suggested that Epstein may have taken photographs of the piece on his first visit to Brancusi's studio in the summer of 1912, and that they may have influenced *Caryatid II*, 1915; Brancusi seems to have been particularly attracted to the formal treatment of the braided plait as a sort of exposed spinal column.[20]

Epstein's awareness of the sculpture of Brancusi and Modigliani, which he saw in 1912 and again during a second, briefer visit to Paris with David Bomberg in May and June of 1913,[21] had a startling effect on his own interpretation of the love and birth themes. In 1913, having already been stigmatised as a 'Sculptor in Revolt' (by *The Pall Mall Gazette*, 6 June 1912), he moved from London to a bungalow at Pett Level on the Sussex coast and entered a period of intense, isolated activity. His style changed dramatically from the

Fig 66
Mother and child 1913–14 (S52)
Marble H 43.1
The Museum of Modern Art, New York, Gift of
A. Conger Goodyear

47
Two studies for mating doves 1913
Pencil and grey wash 57 × 44.5
Walsall Museum and Art Gallery (Garman-Ryan
Collection)

46
Doves (second version) 1913 (S50)
Parian marble H 47
Collection of the Israel Museum, Jerusalem, Israel

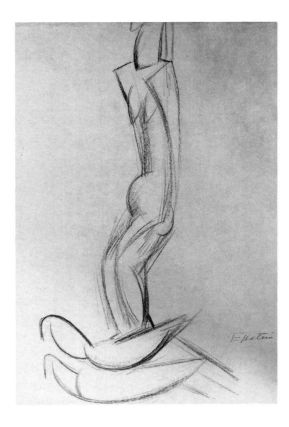

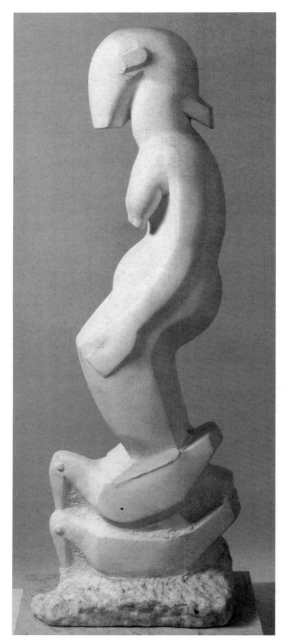

described in his review in *The Egoist* (16 March 1914) as 'placid with an eternal placidity [representing] the immutable, the calm thoroughness of unchanging relations'.[27] The transition to this more abstract interpretation is seen on a sheet of drawings, *c* 1913 [61] devoted mainly to the *Rock Drill* [60], a sculpture also concerned with the act of penetration, albeit metamorphosed into the mechanised vibration of a drill-head. In the second version [46] the doves are mating; the physical relationship between them is more intimate but at the same time more sexually tense: the necks and heads are erect, the tail rampant and imbricate. In the final version [48], commissioned by the American collector, John Quinn, on 12 April 1914 and finished by November of the following year,[28] the sexual act is unambiguous. The two birds are united into a single, primal ovoid, the male straddling his partner, his tail a stiff, downward-plunging phallic shape, his feet,

expressed as incipient incisions, as if gripping and pressing ecstatically into the female's yielding flanks.[29]

The idea for these sculptures seems to have originated during Epstein's visits to Brancusi's studio in 1912–13, where he may have seen the *Three Penguins*, 1912, in white marble.[30] A pair of mating turtles in wood from Papua New Guinea, acquired by The British Museum in 1886, may have inspired the tiered arrangement of Epstein's groups.[31] But he also kept birds at Pett Level and a sheet of sketches [47] includes a naturalistically rendered pair of cooing doves worked up into a formalised and more sexual composition which resembles the second marble version [46].

Just as the paired doves, in their cool, marmoreal sexuality, were intended to symbolise neither Noah's messenger of peace nor Christian gentleness, the two large contemporaneous carvings of *Venus*, the Roman goddess of love, each of which is portrayed surmounting mating doves, were not dependent on traditional ideas of classical beauty.[32] Epstein again turned for inspiration to African sculpture, in the case of the first version of *Venus*, 1913 [Fig. 67], probably to the famous De Miré Fang *Reliquary figure* from Gabon [Fig. 4:11], which he admired for its 'astounding attitude of being held spell-bound by sorcery', regarding it as equal to 'anything that has come out of Africa', and which he succeeded in adding to his collection in 1932.[33] Also among his treasures was a small, wood staff from Ibibo, Nigeria, in the form of a standing female figure surmounting a janiform head [X].[34] A blue crayon drawing [49], (its colouring reminiscent of Modigliani's studies [44*]) which combines the pendulous breasts and downward-looking birds of the first version of *Venus* [Fig. 67] and the austere, ascending pose of the larger, technically more challenging second version [Fig. 68], suggests that both marbles evolved at about the same time. Hubert Wellington, an early biographer, wrote of them as 'a remarkable positive achievement, and a key work of . . . the early twentieth century'.[35]

The complexities of the composition of the *Venuses* evolved from the smaller and simpler but no less potent female figures carved in serpentine, a highly polished, dark green and black-speckled stone, which Epstein renamed flenite (an amalgam of flint and granite). The earlier of the two sculptures [Fig. 69] was exhibited in July 1913 and the other [50*] was among several of the 'most extraordinary statues' Gaudier-Brzeska saw the artist carving on a visit to his studio a few months later, on 7 October, and which he described as 'absolute copies of Polynesian work with Brancusi-like noses'.[36] In fact, the flenite figures are not only more abstract concepts than the Leeds *Maternity* — an indication of the progress made in the three years towards this new vocabulary (which coincided with a radical change in drawing style, recognised by Epstein's friend, T. E. Hulme as 'extracting afresh [from] a traditional symbol . . . a new means of expression')[37] — but are more original than his previous work in the choice of models. Perhaps this happened as a result of meeting Brancusi, who counselled against *imitating* African sculpture.[38] In the flenite figures Epstein moved from motif to mood: the Vorticistic extroversion of their profiles contrasts with the compact, monolithic stillness of their fronts and backs, which seem to have been one of the lessons he learnt from a general study of Egyptian sculpture in the British Museum. Is this what Pound, writing in 1914, meant when he associated the 'permanent, inescaping' qualities which Epstein evoked in the flenite figures with the 'solemnity of Egypt'?[39]

The 'enigma of the germinal universe' which these two figures expressed for Pound was brilliantly achieved by making each of their aggressively pregnant bellies a pivot for vigorously contrasting curves of the upper and lower parts of the body, and then thrusting the head unnaturally forward in a protective gesture. Although serpentine stone has the physical qualities of 'almost impenetrable density',[40] the implication of a growing foetus within the womb is unambiguous. Indeed, in a preparatory study for the sculptures

49
STUDY FOR VENUS 1913–16
Blue crayon 41.3 × 62.8
Private collection, London

Fig 67
VENUS (first version) 1913 (S49)
Marble H 123.2
The Baltimore Museum of Art

Fig 68
VENUS (second version) 1914–16? (S56)
Marble H 244
Yale University Art Gallery, New Haven

X
STAFF IN THE FORM OF A FEMALE FIGURE SURMOUNTING A JANUS HEAD, Ibibio, Nigeria
Wood H 64.1
The Trustees of the British Museum (formerly Jacob Epstein collection)

the moment of birth'.[41] Two further drawings, one rendered in red crayon [52], reveal the upturned foetus sequestered in Vorticistic arcs and angles into which the phallic bit of a rock drill is penetrating. Hulme recognised in such drawings representing 'generation' ('the very essence of all the qualities' he defined as 'organic'), a paradox in the sculptor's 'desire to turn the organic into something hard and durable'.[42] Yet, herein lies the very extraordinary power of this group of works.

One of the generative drawings [53] shows the foetus uncurled, shoulders upraised with arms at right-angles. This pose was hinted at in the border reliefs of the drawing for 'one of the hundred pillars of the Secret Temple', 1910 [41], and now, in 1913–14, developed into a nearly four foot high figure of a howling baby (now lost) carved in wood, plastered and painted bright red, called Cursed Be the Day Wherein I was Born.[43] This savage pose, which was probably based on Kota ancestral figures of a type Epstein collected,[44] evolved further in a sketch [54] of a mother, her face contorted in a rictus of pain as her babe is forced from the womb and drops out in to a hostile world of universal strife; appropriately, the drawing was published in the first issue of the Vorticist journal BLAST, which appeared on 20 June 1914, a few months before the outbreak of the Great War.[45]

This idea was translated into two small stone reliefs datable to 1913–14. In one [55], which remained unfinished, the mother is represented only by her open legs, out of which the male child struggles urgently. The other, in flenite, is carved on both faces. On one side [56] is a female torso with crossed arms, recalling Brancusi's The Kiss on the Monument to Tania Rachevskaia, 1910 [Fig. 8], in Montparnasse Cemetery (which Epstein is likely to have seen on his visits to Paris in 1912–13), but with Epstein's characteristic emphasis on breasts and erect phallic forms. On the reverse [57] is a more developed version of the unfinished Birth [55]; the mother has been reduced to elemental forms flanking the splayed child, which appears to have just sprung from her womb. The pose and modelling is reminiscent of Maori Tiki [XI], of which Epstein owned many fine examples.[46] Richard Cork sees in this relief, which comes early in the cycle of love and birth carvings, the artist's return to fundamental principles on a technical as well as aesthetic level by identifying with the primitive 'beginnings of sculpture'.[47] Sometime between 1915 and 1917, towards the end of the cycle, Epstein attempted his most ambitious statement, an over life-size granite Mother and Child [Fig. 59], in which an enormous infant, posed like that in the flenite relief [57], is held in front of its mother as a totem of the ultimate fulfilment of physical union. Bernard van Dieren, Epstein's first biographer, saw the child, 'which seems to grow while one looks at it', as conveying 'with extreme clearness the underlying idea of the young generations making slaves of their mothers'.[48] The carving was shown unfinished at Epstein's Leicester Galleries exhibition in 1917, when it was bought by John Quinn. He, however, found difficulty in storing it in his New York apartment and it appears to have been destroyed around 1923.

[51], it has been observed that the mother looks down at her 'enormously swollen belly, exposing a sort of X-ray view of the child in the womb, with its head down ready for birth' (at the centre of what Wyndham Lewis defined as the vortex, the 'heart of the whirlpool . . . a great silent place where all the energy is concentrated'); moreover, that the dynamic arcs encircling the figure may be a 'symbolic representation of the open vagina at

Fig 69 ◁
FEMALE FIGURE IN FLENITE   1913   (S45)
Serpentine stone   H 45.7
The Tate Gallery, London

51
STUDY FOR FIGURE IN FLENITE   c 1913
Crayon   68.5 × 42.5
Anthony d'Offay Gallery, London

51a △
COMPOSITION   1913
Black and red crayon   45 × 60.3
Private collection, London

52
STUDY FOR BIRTH   1913
Red crayon   68.9 × 43.9
The Museum of Modern Art, New York, Gift of Mr
and Mrs Richard Deutsch
(Exhibited in Leeds only)

53 ◁
STUDY FOR BIRTH   *c* 1913
Pencil   62 × 51.5
Anthony d'Offay Gallery, London

54 △
STUDY FOR BIRTH, in BLAST, No. 1, 20 June 1914
(illustrated upside-down, facsimile)

55 △
BIRTH   1913?   (S43)
Stone   H 30.6
Art Gallery of Ontario, Toronto (Purchase 1983)

XI
PENDANT (TIKI), Maori, New Zealand
Greenstone   H 12.7
Walsall Museum and Art Gallery (Garman-Ryan
Collection, formerly Jacob Epstein collection)

56 ▷
FLENITE RELIEF: WOMAN CLASPING A PHALLUS
(recto)   1913   (S44)
Serpentine stone   H 30.5
Dr and Mrs Martin J. Evans, New York

57 ▷▷
FLENITE RELIEF: BIRTH (verso)   1913   (S44)
Serpentine stone   H 30.5
Dr and Mrs Martin J. Evans, New York

7 · 1913–1916

ROCK DRILL

Richard Cork

SELF-PORTRAIT IN A STORM-CAP   1917   (S88)
Bronze   H 50.8
Harris Museum and Art Gallery, Preston

Even if *Rock Drill* [60] remains the most mechanistic of all Epstein's major sculptures, its origins lie in his enthusiasm for 'primitivism' and the power of totemic structures.[1] A fascinating sheet of studies [61], probably drawn in the early months of 1913, shows how his imagination moved from the inspiration of tribal art towards a form-language more directly redolent of technological prowess. The centre of the drawing is occupied by a commanding angular presence, in which the hieratic body of a woman is pierced by a man inverted below her. The phallic tension in this amalgamation of male and female figures is clear enough, and a small sketch of two amorous doves elsewhere on the paper reinforces the theme of copulation. It dominated Epstein's vision during this period: the doves, after appearing in a separate carving,[2] then became the base of an ample marble *Venus* [Fig. 67] whose pendulous, African-inspired breasts and swollen belly made her into a symbol of fecundity. But in the rest of the drawing, Epstein revealed that he was also determined to explore the possibility of an even more monumental embodiment of masculinity. On the left of the sheet, the figure of a man appears, his thrusting and brusquely simplified limbs all embroiled in an activity of intense strain. It is bound up with the 'virility' which Epstein had first celebrated in his carving of *Man* for the British Medical Association building five years before, but now the classical anatomy of that early statue has given way to an altogether more schematic alternative. Half human and half automaton, the figure in this drawing appears to be the harbinger of a different, harsher and more disturbing world. On the right of the paper, Epstein has defined the jagged contours of a rocket-like form which explodes upwards, thereby revealing that he was already beginning to equate phallic power with the driving action of a machine.

Epstein's burgeoning friendship with the critic and philosopher T. E. Hulme [62] helps to account for this new involvement with mechanical metaphor. After all, Hulme had already discovered in the *Tomb of Oscar Wilde* [Fig. 48] elements which prompted him, as Epstein recalled, to 'put his own construction on my work — turned it into some theory of projectiles'.[3] As Hulme became more fascinated by the implications of *avant-garde* art, and Epstein's sculpture in particular, he came to believe that 'the new "tendency towards abstraction" will culminate, not so much in the simple geometrical forms found in archaic art, but in the more complicated ones associated in our minds with the idea of machinery'.[4] Hulme was bound to encourage his new friend to think about moving on from 'archaism' towards a mechanistic language, and Epstein's passionate concern with sexuality and the procreative force ensured that he would cast around for the mechanical equivalent of a penis. Two drawings of this period reveal his preoccupation with this theme [63–64]. Both the figurative form and sexual content rely strongly on precedents in primitive sculpture [II and XII].[5]

The idea of turning a phallus into a drill may have occurred to him during a visit to a stone quarry. Epstein remembered that 'it was in the experimental pre-war days of 1913 that I was fired to do the rock drill',[6] and his choice of the word 'fired' implies that it was a sudden, almost impulsive enthusiasm. Perhaps the sight of a drill boring into the rockface with deafening force came as a revelation to him, for there was no doubt about the formidable power of this mechanical tool. Mounted on a tripod, and capable of dislodging impressive quantities of rock in the mines where it was principally employed, the modern drill seemed an implement of prodigious strength and effectiveness. It revolutionised the mining industry, and Epstein decided that his *Rock Drill* would do its best to revolutionise twentieth-century sculpture as well.

The first drawings which outline his ideas for the work [65–66] stress the indomitable character of the machine, and place it in the charge of a driller with equally daunting powers. Framed by the gaunt, jutting sides of a cleft which seems to have been created by his mighty weapon, the driller stands on his tripod with legs as straight as pistons. He looks upward, as if to display his supreme confidence, and only in a subsequent back view of the ensemble [67] does his head bend down towards the task in hand. The locale, however, has now become even more awesome. Viewed from behind, the driller rides far above the ground and a cloud floats from the side of the drill as if to emphasise his airborne dimensions.

This cloud also signified a rush of steam from the machine, proving that it was in motion. As the drawing progressed, and the driller's legs curved into an arch which contrasted more strikingly with the pyramidal structure of the tripod, Epstein became more obsessed by the possibility of activating the drill. Doubtless aware of the kinetic experiments conducted by some Futurist sculptors, he thought at one stage 'of attaching pneumatic power to my rock drill, and setting it in motion, thus completing every potentiality of form and movement in one single work'.[7] The plan was subsequently abandoned, not so much because it was impractical but because Epstein shared the Vorticists' antipathy towards the blurred motion of Futurist art. Like Wyndham Lewis, who abhorred multiple movement in his work, Epstein preferred to enclose his forms in rigid outlines. His *Rock Drill* drawings show how much reliance he placed on the clean, hard clarity of defining contours, even when he focused on a particularly dynamic study of the drill's head biting into the rock [68]. The lines radiating from the point of impact may represent shattering vibration, but they are handled with a robust lucidity which leaves no room for excitable Futurist confusion. So a machine shuddering with movement was ultimately incompatible with Epstein's own stern imperatives as an artist.

He did, however, go ahead with the plan to incorporate a real machine in this extraordinary sculpture [60 and 69]. With a boldness which still seems astonishing today, he arranged 'the purchase of an actual drill, second-hand, and upon this I made and mounted a machine-like robot, visored, menacing, and carrying within itself its progeny, protectively ensconced' [70–72].[8] This foetal form, whose rounded masses could hardly be more opposed to the schematic harshness of the driller's torso, is the successor to the

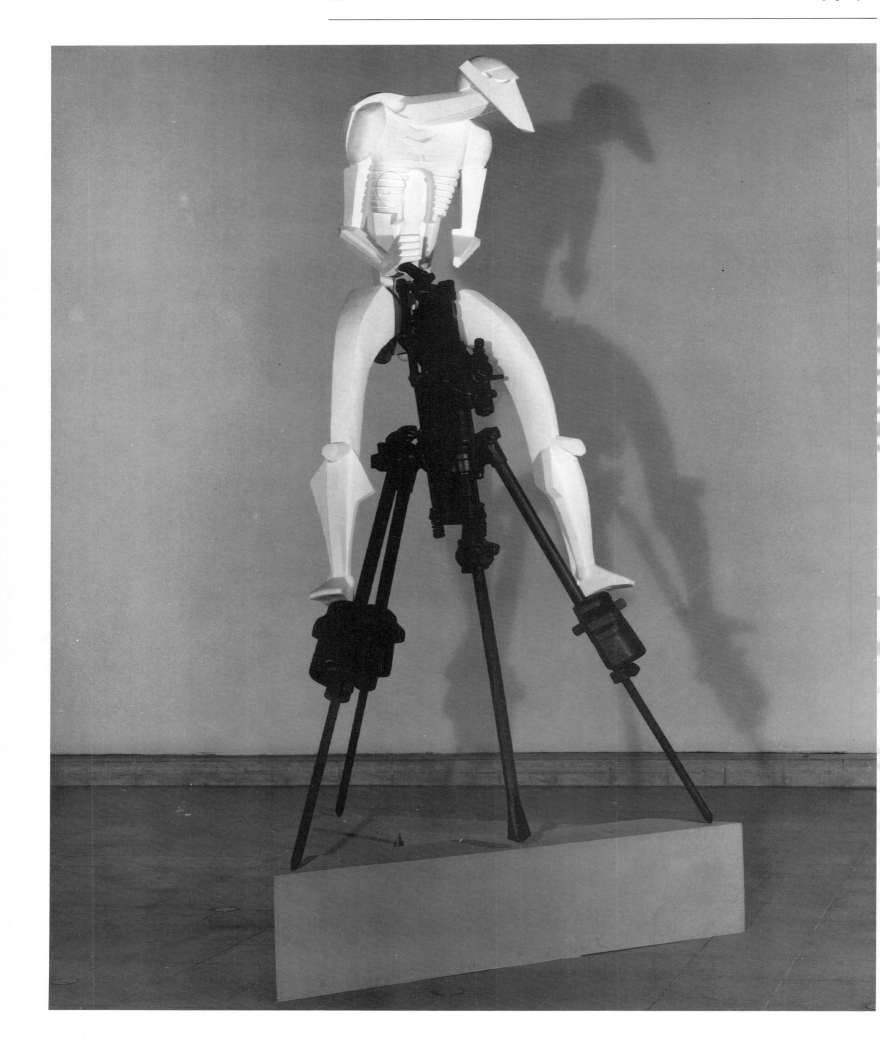

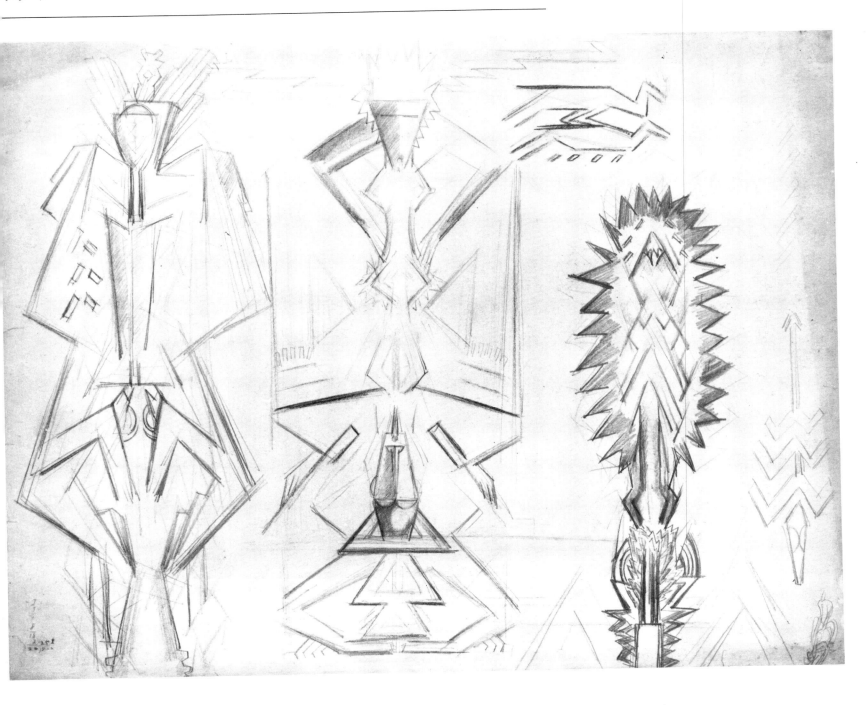

embryonic baby lodged within the rock carried by *Matter* [Fig. 7] on the BMA façade.[9] There, on the Strand frontage of Holden's building, it was exposed to view in the care of an ancient sage. Now, on the other hand, it is securely embedded in a cavity guarded by the armoured severity of the driller's rib-cage. But its presence in this strange assemblage still conveys a sense of apprehension. Turning the handle to operate the machine, the driller is unavoidably conscious of his responsibility towards the new life of the future. Epstein attached great importance to symbolism, even during this most innovative period when he came nearer to formalist purism than at any other time in his career. He seems to be asking whether the organic form of the foetus will be transformed, with the advent of maturity, into a robot as dehumanised as the driller himself.

When he was at work on the first, full-length version of *Rock Drill*, Epstein's self-confessed 'ardour for machinery'[10] probably prevented him from pondering too deeply on its more sinister implications. His admiration for the drill was, after all, great enough to convince him that it deserved to become an integral and, indeed, dominant part of a major sculpture. When the completed work was placed on view in the March 1915 London Group exhibition, its audacity astounded most of the viewers who examined it. For Epstein had gone almost as far towards the ultimate aesthetic heresy as Duchamp, who in 1913 nominated a *Bicycle Wheel* as a work of art. The ready-made drill was, admittedly, augmented by the man-made figure of a driller, cast in white plaster to distinguish it still more dramatically from the black, shining drill supported by the tripod. But Epstein was still challenging his audience to accept that a real machine could be recognised as a legitimate part of a sculpture. Most of the critics who wrote about it responded

60
ROCK DRILL: reconstruction 1973–74 by K. Cook and A. Christopher after the lost original, 1913–15   (S53)
Polyester resin, metal and wood   H 250.1
Birmingham Museums and Art Gallery

61
SIX STUDIES FOR ROCK DRILL AND DOVES   *c* 1913
Pencil and crayon   58.5 × 45.5
Anthony d'Offay Gallery, London

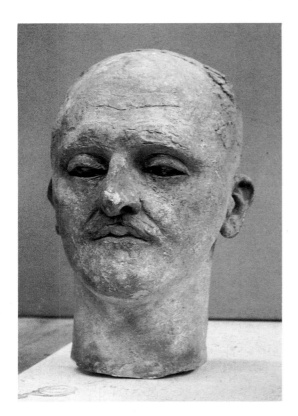

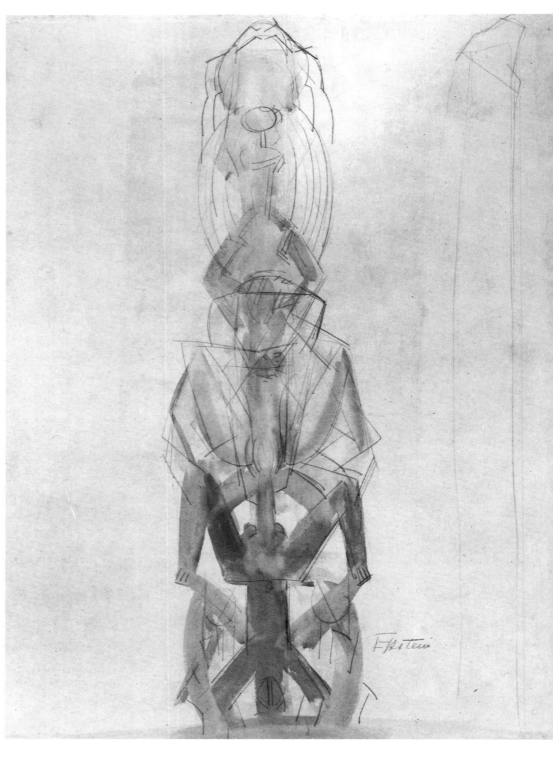

62
THOMAS ERNEST HULME   1916   (*S69*)
Bronze   H 35.6 (original plaster illustrated)
Private collection

63
TOTEM   *c*1913
Pencil and wash   41.9 × 57.8
The Trustees of the Tate Gallery

with predictable hostility, siding with P. G.
Konody, who declared in *The Observer* (14 March
1915) that 'the whole effect is unutterably loath-
some. Even leaving aside the nasty suggestive-
ness of the whole thing, there remains the
irreconcilable contradiction between the crude
realism of real machinery (of American make)
combined with an abstractly treated figure'.

Only one newspaper reviewer, the *Manchester
Guardian*'s (15 March 1915) correspondent, understood why Epstein had been tempted to place the
machine itself on view, and his excited reaction

vividly conveys the astonishment with which
Rock Drill must have been greeted by the London
Group's visitors. 'He has accepted it all, the actual
rock drill is here in this art gallery', wrote the
stunned *Guardian* critic.

Mr Epstein has accepted the rock drill, and says
frankly that if he could have invented anything
better he would have done it. But he could not.
One can see how it fascinated him; the three
long strong legs, the compact assembly of cylinder, screws and valve, with its control handles

decoratively at one side, and especially the long, straight cutting drill like a proboscis — it all seems the naked expression of a definite force.

although the reviewer acknowledged that pstein had 'found in a rock-drill machine the deal of all that is expressive in mobile, penetrat-ng, shattering force', he finally decided that the inclusion of a ready-made machine was too raw, lashing to an uncomfortable extent with the dril-er above. 'Even if the figure is to be cast in iron',

he concluded, 'the incongruity between an engine with every detail insistent and a synthetic man is too difficult for the mind to grasp'.

The criticism was understandable enough, for nothing like *Rock Drill* had ever been exhibited as sculpture in a British gallery before. Its reviewers failed to understand why Epstein had not taken as many liberties with the drill as he did with the driller, whose entire body was metamorphosed into a creature of the sculptor's own imagination. The visored helmet, attached to a neck as straight and sharp-edged as the shaft of some mighty

64
STUDY FOR MAN-WOMAN   c 1913
Pencil and watercolour   41.5 × 56.1
The Trustees of the British Museum

XII
STANDING MALE FIGURE, Fang, Gabon
Wood   H 56
The Trustees of the British Museum (formerly Jacob Epstein collection)

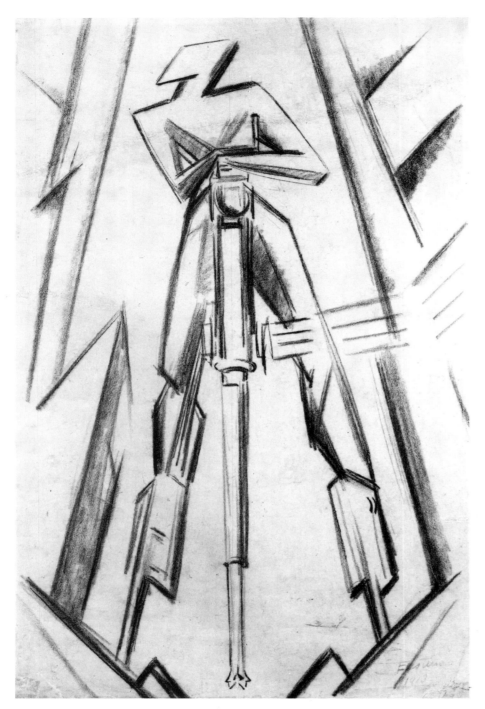

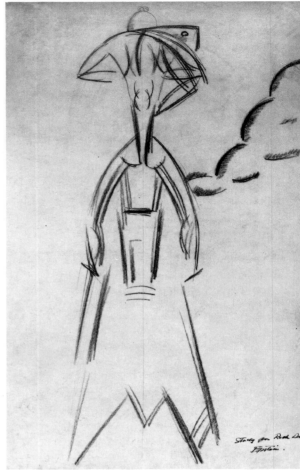

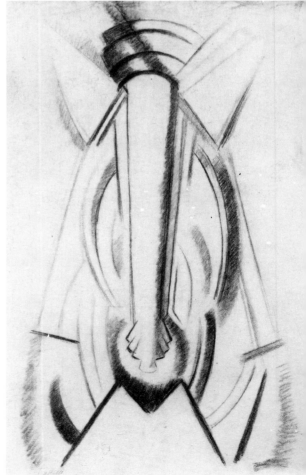

65 △
STUDY FOR ROCK DRILL   1913
Black crayon   53.3 × 64.1
The Trustees of the Tate Gallery

67
STUDY FOR ROCK DRILL, BACK   *c*1913
Crayon   40.6 × 67.5
Anthony d'Offay Gallery, London

68
STUDY FOR ROCK DRILL, DRILL HEAD   *c*1913
Crayon   40.5 × 68.5
Anthony d'Offay Gallery, London

66
STUDY FOR ROCK DRILL   c1913
Charcoal   42.5 × 67.5
Walsall Museum and Art Gallery
(Garman-Ryan Collection)

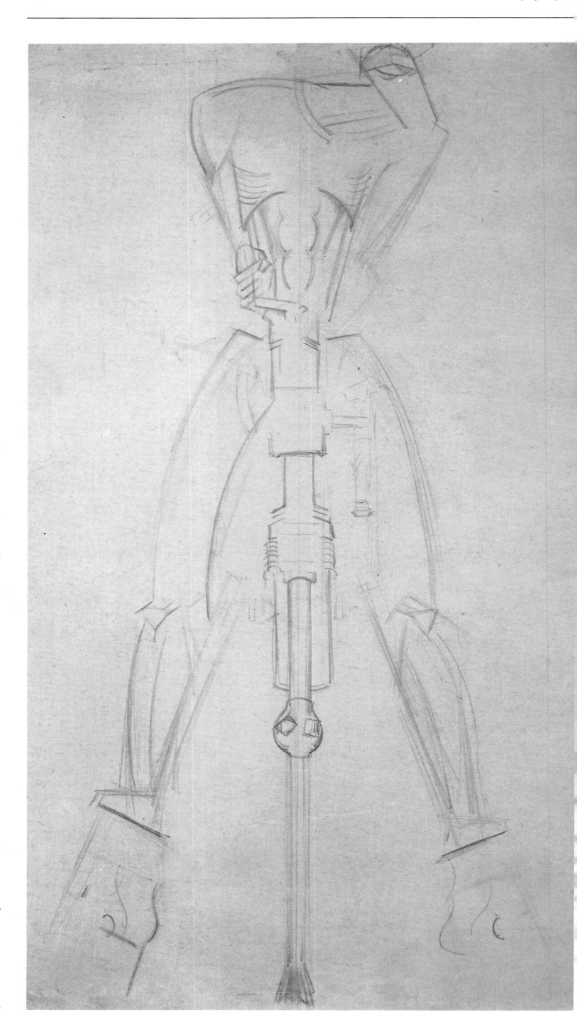

69
STUDY FOR ROCK DRILL   *c* 1913
Pencil   39.5 × 69
The Museum of Modern Art, New York. Gift of
Constance B. Cartwright

70
TORSO IN METAL FROM THE ROCK DRILL
1913–15   (S54)
Bronze   H 70.5
The Trustees of the Tate Gallery

71
TORSO IN METAL FROM THE ROCK DRILL
1913–15   (*S*54)
Bronze   H 70.5
The Trustees of the Tate Gallery

'machinery itself has used up so many of the fir
combinations of three-dimensional inorgan
forms that there is very little use in experimentir
with them in sculpture'.[11] How, Epstein mu
have thought, could he possibly improve on th
magnificence of the real rock drill? There was r
point; and besides, he doubtless wanted to mak
people appreciate the innate qualities of th
machine. Pound, who wrote admiringly abou
Epstein's work at this time, insisted in 1916 tha
'the forms of automobiles and engines . . . whe
they are truly expressive of various modes o
efficiency, can be and often are very beautiful i
themselves and in their combinations, though th
fact of this beauty is in itself offensive to the scho
of sentimental aesthetics'.[12] Epstein would hav
agreed with this argument when he installed th
first version of *Rock Drill* on its triangular plinth a
the London Group exhibition, where the impl
ment and its tripod challenged 'sentimentalists' t
deny that machinery deserved the respectfu
attention they normally reserved for more co
ventional works of art.

It was an amazingly provocative act. Eve
Wyndham Lewis, whose own figure drawing
had helped Epstein to develop the analogical la
guage employed in the driller's body, could n
accept *Rock Drill* without voicing some reserva
tions. 'The combination of the white figure an
the rock-drill is rather unfortunate and ghos
like', he wrote in the second issue of *Blast*, befor
going on to concede that 'its lack of logic has a
effectiveness of its own. I feel that a logical c
ordination was not intended. It should be take
rather as a monumental, bustling, and very pe
sonal whim'. Lewis was right to argue tha
Epstein had deliberately created an irration
apparition in *Rock Drill*. The dream-like amalga
of machine and worker certainly had the power t
haunt the imagination, and Lewis concluded th
it was 'one of the best things Epstein has don
The nerve-like figure perched on the machiner
with its straining to one purpose, is a vivid illu
tration of the greatest function of life'.[13]

When *Rock Drill* was first placed on view, fe
writers linked it with the First World War. Epste
had conceived the sculpture long before hostil
ties were declared, and only later did Davi
Bomberg realise that the assemblage he had fir
seen in Epstein's studio around December 191
contained 'a Prophetic Symbol . . . of the impen
ing war'.[14] As the carnage increased, howeve
and Britain began to understand just how man
lives were being sacrificed in a struggle whic
showed no sign of ending, so it affected Epstein
attitude towards the sculpture he had mad
Looking back on the work many years afterward
he maintained that *Rock Drill* possessed 'n
humanity, only the terrible Frankenstein's mon
ster we have made ourselves into'.[15] But th
verdict was delivered with the benefit of hin
sight, and bore little relation to the vision whic
had inspired the superhuman heroism of the orig
inal drawings. Only in the latter half of 191
when Epstein and everyone else left at hom
began to appreciate just how senselessly destru
tive the struggle in the trenches had become, di
his attitude towards the machine age really alte
The Great War was the first industrialised confli

engine, leads down towards a torso angular and
faceted enough to suggest mechanical components fit for inclusion in a rock drill itself. The
gothic arch described by the legs, as they sprout
so surprisingly from the driller's narrow waist,
introduces a more expansive note. But even here
the sense of dehumanisation remains as strong as
ever, reflecting Epstein's belief that the machine
age was transforming humanity into a race of
armoured and rigidly constructed figures.

Why, then, had he not subjected the drill to the
same schematic treatment? The most convincing
reason was voiced by his friend Henri Gaudier-
Brzeska, who told Ezra Pound in 1914 that

suffered by the world, and it claimed an obscene number of victims with the help of inventions like the rapid-fire machine gun. Once the devastating power of such weapons became widely understood, it was no longer possible to regard an object like the rock drill in a straightforwardly positive light. The menacing character of this aggressive implement became impossible to avoid, and Epstein came to the conclusion that it should be excluded from his sculpture. His widow Kathleen remembered him explaining, decades later, 'that he abandoned the drill because he hadn't made it himself, it was just a machine',[16] and so Epstein may have been impelled as well by misgivings about the controversial status of a ready-made in his own art. By 1916 he was beginning to reconsider the extremism of his work and contemplate returning to a more figurative approach. A growing preference for traditional materials and methods precluded any further dalliance with Duchampian experiments, and he decided that only the man-made part of his *Rock Drill* should be retained and cast in metal [70–72]. All the same, an examination of the final version of the sculpture, exhibited in the London Group show of summer 1916 under the title *Torso in Metal from the 'Rock Drill'*, proves that the discarding of the drill was not prompted simply by objections to the validity of a ready-made. For the truncated upper part of the driller is a figure far removed in meaning from the indomitable man who had once straddled his machine with such imperious confidence. The hand that previously held the drill's controls has been lopped off, too, along with the forearm and elbow. Although the other arm is left unchanged, it likewise lacks a hand and thrusts outwards only to hang uselessly in space. The driller's mask-like head takes on a more defensive and even hesitant air, peering forward as if to search for signs of imminent danger. But his amputated limbs hold out no hope of warding off an assault, and the embryonic form still nestling in his rib-cage appears far more vulnerable than it ever did when positioned above the drill.

Seen from behind, the driller's body looks frail rather than impregnable. His back is riven by a crooked fissure extending from the shoulders to the base of the spine. The left arm is similarly split by a gash savage enough to resemble a wound. In retrospect, Epstein declared that *Rock Drill* was 'a thing prophetic of much of the great war and as such within the experience of nearly all'.[17] He did not explain precisely what he meant, but his shattered *Torso* possesses the melancholy, stooping pathos of a soldier returning from the Front as a helpless invalid. This body will never recover from the damage inflicted on it by the horror of war; and it will certainly be unable to remount the drill and resume the triumphant battle against the primal rock-face. The struggle has been lost.

Epstein hated war, and this final tragic version of *Rock Drill* shows how determined he was to resist the propagandist view of the conflict still promoted by a government anxious to sustain the troops' flagging morale. But the *Torso* also goes a long way towards explaining why he would never again explore machine imagery in his sculpture. Two of his most valued friends, Gaudier and

Hulme, were killed during the war, and Epstein himself suffered a 'complete breakdown' in 1918.[18] He could not, in all conscience, return to the unqualified optimism which had produced his early *Rock Drill* drawings. The aggression both of the driller and his instrument were now anathema to a man who sought comfort in modelling an image of the *Risen Christ* [110]. Handled with a renewed respect for the gentle resilience of the figure who returns from death, this gaunt yet compassionate sculpture also announces the rebirth of a sculptor who wanted in the post-war world to put the machine age far behind him.

72
TORSO IN METAL FROM THE ROCK DRILL
1913–15   (S54)
Bronze   H 70.5
The Trustees of the Tate Gallery

PRIVATE CONCERNS: PORTRAITS

Evelyn Silber and Terry Friedman

Fig 70
Private Epstein of the Jewish 38th Battalion, Royal
Fusiliers, 1917–18

73
ADMIRAL LORD FISHER OF KILVERSTONE OM
(version with arms) 1916 (S63)
Plaster H 68.6
National Maritime Museum, Greenwich

In the midst of war, on the eve of modelling a
series of remarkable portraits in bronze which
were to establish him, in the words of Eric Gill, as
'the greatest portrait sculptor of our time',[1]
Epstein explained his approach in an article published in the *Weekly Dispatch* (24 December 1916)
entitled 'How I Sculptured Lord Fisher'.[2] The bust
[73] was commissioned for Nina, 15th Duchess of
Hamilton. In June 1916 Epstein's friend, Francis
Dodd, appeared unexpectedly at the Guildford
Street studio, bundled him into a taxi and took
him to a soirée at the Duchess's West End flat;
among the guests was John Arbuthnot, 1st Baron
Fisher of Kilverstone.[3]

Epstein had seen the seventy-five year old
Admiral of the Fleet in public and thought of 'all
living men I should like to do a bust' of him; he
has, the sculptor told the *Weekly Dispatch*,

> such a wonderful head . . . Here . . . is one of
> the greatest men of this age, one of the greatest
> figures of this war, and the head and features
> are a wonderful expression of this tremendous
> personality . . . His light eyes, with strange
> colours, were set in a face like parchment ivory,
> and his iron grey hair was cut short and bristled
> on his head. He was short, but had the appear-
> ance of combative sturdiness.

Fisher insisted on starting the sittings immediately; Epstein returned home for tools and clay
and was back within the hour, working very
rapidly for the first two hours, with the admiral
taking up different poses as the natural light in the
room shifted and talking incessantly. The subsequent five sittings, which took place within a
single week, lasted from 9 am to 7 pm, with breaks
only for meals, which Epstein considered exceptional.[4] The head was finished in four days, with
two further days devoted to the bust, with its
resplendent epaulettes, medals and decorations
(Fisher aptly referred to himself as a 'Christmas
Tree'). Epstein was diffident towards male sitters
— he found them on the whole more vain than
women[5] — but regarded this pugnacious head, in
which he strove to capture that 'grim, implacable
expression of determination' and to 'put life into
the inanimate metal and breathe into the graven
image the dynastic personality that for so long
was the soul of the British Navy', as the 'most
powerful I have ever done'.

Epstein was particularly struck by some of his
ruthless statements about war and by 'a look in
his eyes that was dangerous'. Later he told
Arnold Haskell that it is 'always necessary to

accentuate some particular trait that gives the
character to the face and distinguishes it from
other faces'.[6] When Fisher noted the prominence
given to his temples, Epstein told him this was a
trait characteristic of 'hunters and trappers' (the
Admiral had introduced Dreadnoughts into the
Navy). Equally distinctive are the leathery skin,
heavy-lidded eyes and firmly clamped mouth,
which have led one writer to liken the bust to an
old tortoise's head rising from its shell.[7] Fisher
declared Epstein a genius and urged the Duchess
of Hamilton to get her own portrait done at once.
She did.[8]

Shortly after the *Weekly Dispatch* interview,
twenty-six works by Epstein, including three
carvings, were revealed to the public in his first
one-man show at the Leicester Galleries.[9] Apart
from the study for the bust of *Lord Fisher*, an
armless version sharply cut off so that the head
rests on the arched shell of chest and back, there
were earlier works, including the figure studies
and bust of *Nan* [17–18, 24], the bust of *Euphemia
Lamb* [14], *Romilly John* [31] and *Baby asleep* [6]. The
recent work included an ordinary soldier, *The Tin
Hat* [74] and the head of *Muirhead Bone* [113]. The
latter was one of Epstein's closest friends and later
presented four bronzes, including both *Lord Fisher*
and *The Tin Hat*, to the Imperial War Museum. It
was important to Epstein that the Leicester Galleries exhibition should be a success since conscription had been introduced in 1916. As a
naturalised Briton since 1910, the sculptor was
liable to be called up unless he could obtain
exemption or special employment as a war artist,
following in the footsteps of Bone, Francis Dodd
and Augustus John.

The Tin Hat [74] had been undertaken specifically to demonstrate his potential as a war artist;
but far from being a jingoistic or self-consciously
heroic image, this portrait of an unknown soldier
emphasises his nondescript humanity. It contrasts his relaxed, weary features and the rakish
tilt of his helmet with the mechanistic and imper-
sonal dedication to war which the helmet
symbolises. Cast from a real trench helmet, the
geometrically streamlined shape is reminiscent of
the Futurist aesthetic of *Rock Drill* [70], but the
latter's glorification of creative force is tempered
by the cruel reality of war. Those realities were
only too clear.

Epstein's fellow sculptor, Henri Gaudier-
Brzeska, had been killed in 1915, aged only
twenty-three, and Epstein's closest friend, the
philosopher, T. E. Hulme [62] was killed in

September 1917. Epstein included a portrait of him wearing a tin hat, under the title *Officer*, in the Leicester Galleries show. Later in the same year he exhibited the portrait without the hat as *Lieutenant T. E. Hulme (killed in action)*.[10]

The portraits had, to some extent, the desired effect. D. S. MacColl, writing in the *Burlington Magazine*, hoped that 'Mr Epstein may model many more army types till the time comes for larger memorials', though he was unhappy about the sculptural propriety of juxtaposing the man with the helmet; Epstein's 'Man with Tin Hat was an admirable man, modelled with the force and keen character of many other portrait heads; it was also a tin hat, but the hat was merely an exterior object clapped on; it was not modelled *with the head*'.[11] Other critics were deeply impressed by the Leicester Galleries exhibition,

despite their reservations about carvings such as *Venus* [Fig. 68]. Frank Rutter applauded 'the rugged strength' of *Fisher*, the 'pensive romanticism' of *Mary McEvoy* [15*], the 'naive simplicity' of *Romilly John* [31] and the 'gentle delicacy and innocent wonderment' of the '*Babe's Head*' [6].[12] Already, however, some commentators were uneasy at the rough, unfinished surface of Epstein's more recent portraits. Laurence Binyon, in *The New Statesman*, hailed 'the hand of a master' and went into rhapsodies ('sheer beauty of form') over the portraits of *Nan* and *Euphemia Lamb* [14] but deplored 'the modern tendency to leave clay dabs, etc. directly showing in the bronze'.[13] During the Twenties it became habitual for Epstein not to obliterate the tool marks and snails of clay as he built up the image, though the degree of 'roughness' was varied. Critics continued to be

74
THE TIN HAT   1916   (*S*71)
Bronze   H 35.5
Imperial War Museum, London

75
GLADYS DEACON, LATER 9TH DUCHESS OF
MARLBOROUGH   1917   (*S*86)
Bronze   H 51.4
Victor Arwas, London

Fig 71
THE CHARIOTEER OF DELPHI (detail)   477 BC
Bronze, onyx inlay   H 180
Delphi Museum

76
CORPORAL HARRY KOSKY *c* 1918
Pencil 22.8 × 29.1
Birmingham Museums and Art Gallery

77
SARGEANT-MAJOR MITCHELL June 1918
Pencil 25.4 × 35
Mr and Mrs Peter Retey

78
STUDY OF MARGARET (MRS JACOB) EPSTEIN
Pencil 47.4 × 44.5
Beth Lipkin

79
MARGARET (MRS JACOB) EPSTEIN
(second portrait: mask with earrings) 1916 (*S70*)
Bronze H 21.5
Manchester City Art Galleries

divided about whether this technique aided the expressive effect or was simply a 'mud-pie' effect of wilful distortion.

Epstein, shifting around from the abstracted purity of the early, smooth heads, told Haskell

It is the rough surface which gives both character and likeness to the face, not just the rough surface as such, but the particular individual treatment. No face is entirely round and smooth. The face is made up of numberless small planes and it is a study of where those planes begin and end, their direction, that makes the individual head.[14]

The Leicester Galleries show and the work exhibited at annual exhibitions of the National Portrait Society between 1911 and 1918, established Epstein as a major portrait sculptor, capable of doing justice to anonymous soldier and admiral alike. His major client was still the American collector, John Quinn, but he had in England a devoted following amongst his fellow artists and a small but growing côterie of society patrons.

Prominent among the latter was Gladys Deacon, an American of wit and culture, whom Epstein, even twenty years later, recalled as 'a woman of great discrimination in Art [who] owned works by Rodin and Degas, and had known both these artists, and thoroughly understood what an artist was aiming at'.[15] At that time she was mistress to the 9th Duke of Marlborough;

when she subsequently became his Duchess she was instrumental in getting Epstein to do his portrait too! She met the sculptor early in 1917 and was delighted to recognise 'un génie qui est jeune'. In April she paid him £150 for a marble clock, which she assuredly never expected to receive from him, and sat for her portrait [75]. Miss Deacon's beauty was celebrated and she was especially proud of her 'Grecian' profile, even going so far as to perfect it with the aid of plastic surgery.[16] Epstein's elegantly poised portrait, with its emphasis on the sitter's extraordinarily profile, large, widely spaced eyes, necklace and short, permed hair, pays homage to her taste and looks even though, as he later bitterly recalled, 'this bust . . . was the cause of great uneasiness amongst English patronesses . . . who expect a work to be entirely lacking in any character and would rather have a portrait lacking all distinction than one which possessed psychological or plastic qualities!'.[17]

Contemporary critics recognised the 'archaic' strain underlying its naturalism. Hubert Wellington suggested Polynesian sources and observed that the 'study of archaic work, which so often shows the paradox of an overwhelming sense of life given to forms so simplified as to be superficially unlike life, has liberated creative forces in the artist and suggested fresh experiments aiming at both formal beauty and character'.[18] Later, Richard Buckle, organiser of Epstein's Memorial

Exhibition in 1961, compared it with the celebrated bronze *Charioteer of Delphi* [Fig. 71].[19]

Gladys Deacon, together with John Quinn and
Mrs Epstein, were in the forefront of the campaign to obtain Epstein's exemption from military
service or at least keep him away from active
duty.[20] Despite their efforts Epstein was conscrip-
ted into the Jewish Battalion of Royal Fusiliers in
September 1917 and sent for training to barracks
at Crownhill, Plymouth [Fig. 70]. Though
deprived, unjustly as he saw it, of his liberty,
Epstein without clay and stone was not entirely a
fish out of water. He soon armed himself with a
sketch pad and began to draw his fellow soldiers,
such as *Corporal Kosky* [76].[21] Perhaps such rapid
portraits were undertaken to entertain his companions in misfortune, many of whom were dis-
paraged by their officers as 'types of whom

soldiers and soldiering were anathema and were
to be evaded at almost any cost'[22] but they also
demonstrated that the 'forces that have worked
against me' had been unsuccessful in 'achieving
their object: my decease as an active artist'.[23]

In spite of his enforced service, Epstein still
hoped (following the success of *The Tin Hat*) to be
appointed an official war artist. He had the
dependable support of Robert Ross (for whom he
had produced the *Tomb of Oscar Wilde* and who
was Art Advisor to the newly founded Imperial
War Museum) and Muirhead Bone, both of whom
were members of the British War Memorials
Committee. Their efforts were all unavailing,
partly because of a damning letter written to the
Committee by Sir George Frampton, the sculptor
of *Peter Pan* (1912) in Kensington Gardens.[24] The
contents are unrecorded but their caustic nature is

80
MARGARET (MRS JACOB) EPSTEIN
(fifth portrait: in a mantilla)   1918   (S94)
Bronze   H 38.1
Laing Art Gallery, Newcastle Upon Tyne, Tyne and
Wear Museums Service

81
MEUM (Mrs Lindsell-Stewart)   1916–18
Pencil   23.7 × 30.2 (from a sketchbook)
Beth Lipkin

nted at in a contemporary letter to a fellow
oyal Academician, Sir Hamo Thornycroft,
hich refers to 'your shirking confrère Epstein'.[25]
Whether because of his determined refusal to
rve abroad or through a nervous breakdown,
pstein remained in England. When the regiment
iled for Egypt, Epstein was found wandering on
artmoor and, following a period of detention
nd medical observation, was transferred to a
ilitary hospital at Mount Tovy, Plymouth. There
e drew portraits of a nurse and of fellow
atients, including *Sargeant-Major Mitchell* [77].[26]
he draughtsmanship, perhaps surprisingly
nder the circumstances, is self-assured; Eps-
in's usual inclination to work on life-size scale is
ident in the way the design overflows the
aper, though there is a noticeable tension in the
rawing which may reflect both his and his
tter's anguish.

Before, after and even during leave periods
om the army, Epstein was busy modelling por-
aits as well as completing the *Risen Christ* [110].[27]
wo women dominated this period — Margaret
unlop, Epstein's first wife since 1906, and a
retty blond typist much in the social swing, Mrs
eum Lindsell-Stewart.

Margaret ('Peggy') was a resilient Scotswoman
f pronounced left wing views, whom Epstein
ad met in Paris. She was then nine years his
nior and married to someone else. Gertrude
tein, who knew her in the Paris days, recalled
er 'very remarkable brown eyes, of a shade of
rown I have never before seen in eyes'.[28] Little
se is known about her. She remained something
f an enigma, even to Peggy Jean, Epstein's eldest
aughter (born in Paris in 1918), whom Peggy
rought up lovingly despite the fact that she was
he child of Epstein's union with Meum.

Epstein studied Peggy at about this time [78]
nd her character, with its pervasive impression
f endurance, determination and quiet thought-
ulness, dominate the five portraits modelled
etween 1912 and 1918.[29] The second portrait, of
916 [79], is a mask with earrings, patinated to a
oft green which emphasises its kinship with
ntique sculpture. But the most haunting and
rofound of the series is the last, executed in 1918,
howing *Mrs Epstein in a mantilla*, a *mater dolorosa*
o]. Of the 1916 portrait the sculptor later recalled
hat 'I worked at this mask without effort,
chieving it happily'; but the last 'was unhurried
nd brooded over, and the drapery worked with
reat care' to get the downward flow 'like the rills
f a fountain'.[30] Epstein himself placed this piece
mongst his finest portraits and an early com-
entator praised its 'great monumental
ignity'.[31]

A parallel series of five portraits was made of
eum, who was also the subject of an oil painting
y Epstein showing her in a soft green dress. It
ung in Epstein's home until about 1947 but its
resent whereabouts is unknown.[32] He made a
umber of sketches [81] in preparation for the first
nd second portraits, which date from 1916.[33]
wo far more unconventional portraits followed;
ask of Meum [82-83] has a mysterious exoticism
early derived from non-European art, though
pinions differ on the nature of his sources.
ineton Parkes in 1921 called her 'a lady of the

82   ◁
MEUM (Mrs Lindsell-Stewart, third portrait:
mask)   1918   (S89)
Bronze   H 19.2 (another cast illustrated)
Victor Arwas, London

83
MEUM (Mrs Lindsell-Stewart, third portrait:
mask)   1918   (S89)
Bronze   H 19.2 (another cast illustrated)
Victor Arwas, London

so-called Aztek type'.[34] Wellington suggested that her 'elegance of line and silhouette' recalled Indian sculpture and the 'fruits of many walks in the museums'.[35]

Unusually strong contemporary references abound in the splendidly vibrant portrait of *Meum with a fan* [84], not only to her hair, but also to her clinging evening dress and fan. Nevertheless, Epstein's image signifies not merely a fashionable young woman at a soirée but a latter-day Venus whose gestures serve to emphasise her sexuality. This was Epstein's second attack on the Western ideal of Venus; just as the carved *Venuses* of a few years earlier [Figs. 67–68] had subverted the classical model, *Meum* wittily updates it [Fig. 72].

The related yet contrasting character of the portraits of Mrs Epstein and Meum, and of the sculptor's relationship with the two women, was observed by the journalist, Ashley Gibson, who had known Epstein since about 1909. While on leave Gibson, meeting 'Miss M', invited her to lunch but found she had an assignation with Epstein. Together they went to the studio and while Mrs Epstein 'gravely sat and stitched, the sweet silhouette of Miss M, enthroned where the light made cunning play with the folds of her green velvet, wavered nebulously. Epstein was quietly busy with his clay. His movements had the stealthy quick precision of a tiger's'.[36]

The most innovatory aspect of *Meum with a fan* is its extension of a female portrait to include the torso, arms and hands, though Epstein had included arms in his first portrait of his wife in 1912. It is just conceivable that he may have been influenced in this break with English and French sculptural tradition by some contact with the work of the German sculptor, Wilhelm Lehmbruck [Fig. 73], who was living in Paris between 1910 and 1914, and, like Epstein, was associated with Brancusi and Modigliani. Epstein later thought his attenuated nudes 'sensitive [but] frail' and of 'no great interest sculpturally'.[37] What he attempted in *Meum with a fan* is extrovert and artfully contrived, emphasising the plastic qualities of the figure by contrasting the elongated arms and fingers, so apt to embrace, with the cylinder formed by the clinging dress.

84 ◁ ◁

MEUM (Mrs Lindsell-Stewart, fourth portrait: with a fan) 1916–18 (S90)
Bronze H 87.6
The Burrell Collection, Glasgow Museum and Art Gallery

Fig 72
THE CAPITOLINE VENUS (Roman copy of original 300–250 BC)
Marble H 187
Musei Capitolini, Rome

Fig 73
Wilhelm Lehmbruck (1881–1919)
PRAYING WOMAN 1918
Bronze H 84
Lehmbruck Estate

PORTRAITS

Evelyn Silber and Terry Friedman

During the Twenties and after, Epstein's critics were divided on the merits of the impressionistically modelled surface he had made his trade mark. In 1924 Frank Rutter reported that the current show at the Leicester Galleries (which included *Dolores* [123], *Girl from Senegal* [87], *Old Pinager* [92] and *Cunninghame Graham* [112]) enhanced his reputation as 'the greatest modeller since Rodin'.[1] R. H. Wilenski, in *The Meaning of Modern Sculpture*, published in 1932, suggested that students of sculpture approved Epstein's surface treatment because they had already accepted it in Rodin. Wilenski recognised a difference between the French master, who was 'deliberately emotive in the Romantic tradition', and Epstein, whose 'romantic-emotive' treatment derived from his 'conscious desire to stress the minor forms that give character to a face [and] from a feeling that the surface is aesthetically intriguing in itself'.[2] These observations were based on Epstein's conversations with Arnold Haskell, *The Sculptor Speaks*, published in the previous year, in which Epstein firmly connected his modelling with both physiological and psychological aspects of portraiture: physiologically with 'the numberless small planes' which make up the face, and psychologically with the way in which the rough texture breaks up the light and accentuates character. This was not merely a surface effect, such as could be observed in artists who tried to imitate his technique; 'the texture is a definite and inseparable part of the whole; it comes from inside so to speak; it grows with the work'. This was a fundamental change of attitude from the smoother, geometric forms of his pre-War portraits like *Romilly John* [31–32]. Epstein now believed that it

> would be an easy mechanical matter to polish and sandpaper until the material was entirely smooth, but to do that would be really to produce a grave distortion. The reflection of the light would play havoc with the sculptor's effects, while the rough surface breaks up the light, and accentuates the characteristics, giving life to the work.[3]

Rather than smoothing and regularising the features as Frank Dobson, for instance, did with his sleek *Osbert Sitwell* [Fig. 75],[4] Epstein harnessed the inherent structure and mobility of the face. In 1920, a reviewer noted: 'One device employed by Mr Epstein, which resembles that employed by Rodin in figure subjects, is to represent different parts of the same face in different phases of movement [producing] a varied effect of mobility of feature.'[5]

Epstein claimed that he started work with no preconceived idea about his subject's character but allowed his observations over the period of the sittings (usually three weeks) to guide his interpretation, though he might emphasise salient features, just as he had with *Lord Fisher* [73]. He told Haskell

> I do not observe the sitter for a long time first, but commence work right away and the likeness already exists in the first stages. There is no question of making first a head, and then putting in the features and getting a likeness

with a few finishing touches, though the finishing touches accentuate the already existing likeness. The basis of the likeness lies in the shape of the skull and in the bony structure of the face, which I accentuate at times. In order to gain the first impression of the character of a head it is often necessary to view it at an unusual angle, from up above or from down below . . . Both profiles must be carefully studied.[6]

This approach can be compared to Rodin's as described by his secretary, the German poet, Rainer Maria Rilke, who witnessed the modelling of a bust of George Bernard Shaw in 1906. Rodin began working spontaneously

> with the model standing quite close, to shape four profiles, then eight, then sixteen, making the model turn every three minutes [beginning] with the front view and the two profiles [then the head is viewed] from above in roughly the same position as the model sitting at arm's length below him . . . The Master works quickly, compressing hours into minutes . . . carrying out strokes and touches after short pauses in which he assimilates tremendously, filling himself with form.[7]

Apparently Epstein worked with the same sort of romantic fervour. Clare Sheridan, who sat for him in 1918, described him as 'a being transformed . . . his stooping and bending, his leaping back, poised then rushing forward, his trick of passing clay from one hand to the other over the top of his head while he scrutinised his work from all angles, was the equivalent of a dance'.[8] However, Epstein's intuitive, almost recklessly direct approach to sitter and material were anathema to Roger Fry and those who supported his assertion that abstract relationships of form were the prime aesthetic criteria in the judgement of a work of art. It was precisely the dramatic character of Epstein's portraits which Fry reacted against, calling them brilliant but 'rather crude representations in the round'. He was reluctantly compelled to admit that 'By frankly accepting the nature of clay modelling, he gets a strangely vivid and exhilarating surface quality . . . one sees how the head has grown centrifugally, how the prominences have gradually pushed outwards to receive the light.'[9] However, these were personal mannerisms and distortions, to use Fry's own terminology. Epstein might 'make bronze reveal to us . . . human beings, more definite, more emphatically personal, more incisive . . . more invasive . . . of our own consciousness that the individuals of actual life', but for Fry his modelled sculpture lacked the 'harmonic sequence of planes [and] complete equilibrium, established through the interplay of diverse movements' for the full appreciation of which 'a perfect subordination of surface and handling' were necessary. Such views make it clear why Fry supported Frank Dobson as the standard bearer for 'pure sculpture' during the Twenties, and saw in Aristide Maillol the outstanding French sculptor.

Fry's views were followed by Stanley Casson, whose *Some Modern Sculptors*, 1928, attacked Epstein's technique.

Fig 74
Epstein with MADONNA AND CHILD, 1926–27 (S175), and the third portrait of KATHLEEN GARMAN, 1931 (S213) at the Leicester Galleries, London, 25 April 1933.

Fig 75
Frank Dobson (1886–1963)
SIR OSBERT SITWELL 1923
Polished brass H 31.8
The Tate Gallery, London

Epstein has brought rough-cast bronzes to a mud-pie perfection; nearly all his bronzes are smeared with countless finger-marks, in such a way that the bronze is little more than metallic clay. This seems to me a dire misuse of a splendid medium, whose very beauty rests in a fine surface and a smooth texture . . . To leave it knobbed and corrugated in the manner adopted by Epstein and to cover this uneven surface with a chemically-made patina seems little short of sacrilege.[10]

For Casson and other contemporary critics,[11] stone rather than clay or terracotta was the proper medium for pure sculpture. Epstein's awareness of the arguments on the rival merits of modelling versus carving inform many of his comments about his own work. Haskell broached the issue directly: 'You are both modeller and carver'.

I am a sculptor. The distinction is purely an imaginary one, except to the artist in the actual execution of his work . . . There is apparently something romantic about the idea of the statue imprisoned in the block of stone, man wrestling with nature . . . According to the modern view Rodin stands nowhere . . . Personally I find the whole discussion entirely futile and beside the point. [Nevertheless, he believed modelling the] most genuinely creative. It is the creating of something out of nothing . . . In carving the suggestion for the form of the work often comes from the shape of the block [and concluded that sculpture] must not be rigid . . . It must quiver with life.[12]

Nowhere is this more brilliantly demonstrated than in the bust of *Jacob Kramer* [85]. Epstein wrote to the Leeds painter on 29 November 1920:

Are you thinking of coming to London soon? I have been lately pondering a new large work & if you are still in the mood to sit for me, I wish you would. You could be of immense use to me & I hope you will give me an opportunity to make a study of you. I would want to do your head torso & arms. In return I will sit to you & you can make drawings or an oil study . . . I hope you will come soon because I feel full of my idea & am eager to get at it.[13]

The large new work was a *Deposition* group, never completed, although he modelled two busts in preparation, a mourning St Mary Magdalene (the celebrated *Weeping Woman*),[14] based on an elderly artist's model, and St John, for which Kramer (who had already posed for part of the *Risen Christ* in 1917) was the model. Epstein recalled that the painter 'seemed to be on fire. He was extraordinarily nervous. Energy seemed to leap into his hair as he sat, and sometimes he would be shaken by queer tremblings like ague. I would try to calm him'.[15] Kramer's high-strung nervous energy is suggested by the unkempt springing of his hair and the tension, even pain in his face. This might have led to an exaggerated portrait, but Hubert Wellington pointed out, regarding the *Weeping Woman*, that the sculptor 'pushes the expression of a dramatic movement to the verge of caricature, but is saved by its convincing truth of gesture, which has the intensity and purpose always

found in strong natural passion, unhampered by self-consciousness',[16] and this is also true of the *Kramer*. When the Contemporary Art Society presented a cast to the Tate in 1921, the press proclaimed it 'one of the most remarkable pieces of sculpture recently produced, the head being specially notable for the dramatic beauty of its modelling'.[17] How Epstein would have completed the figure may be indicated in a drawing [86] of a biblically-clad male stepping forward, hands locked in a gesture of rejection. This would have complemented the weeping figure of the Magdalene, wringing her hands over the dead Christ's body. For whatever reason the group was never carried out, but four years later Epstein revised the gesture almost unaltered in his Donatellesque *Visitation*.[18]

If the emphasis Epstein placed on naturalism, character and expression was a traditional one, going back to Rodin, Donatello and the great portraitists of the Ancient World — the Egyptians and Sumerians — the portraits themselves broke new ground. During the Twenties most were not commissioned; they were friends, casual aquaintances and people stopped in the street and asked if they were willing to come to the studio. Amongst them were many non-Europeans — American blacks, Africans, Indians, Asians and people of mixed race — people who, if depicted at all, were treated as 'picturesque' or exotic.[19] From his childhood in New York, when he was able to move freely in Black, Chinese, Italian and other ethnic communities, as well as his own, Epstein had recognised 'the plastic quality of coloured people'.[20]

One of the first such sitters was the daughter of a French officer and an African slave, Madeleine Béchet, the *Girl from Senegal* [87], whom Epstein modelled in 1921. Her portrait was acclaimed by *The Times* (19 January 1924) reviewer, A. Clutton-Brock, as 'a great piece of sculpture'. L. B. Powell, the critic of the *Birmingham Post and Mail* and a lifelong admirer of Epstein's work, commented on the tonality of the bronze: 'the brighter, harsher surface, the bold manner which light is reflected, help as much as the wonderful poise of the head, to emphasise the impression of a young life full of boundless vigour and pride'.[21]

Epstein's most important model during the Twenties was a Kashmiri woman, Amina Peerbhoy, nearly six feet tall and uncommonly magnificent.[22] He met Amina and her sister Miriam Patel, nicknaming them Sunita and Anita, in 1924 at the British Empire Exhibition at Wembley, where they kept a stall of exotic artefacts. The two women and Sunita's young son, Enver, moved in with the Epsteins and between 1925 and 1931 he drew them many times and made several portraits in bronze; Sunita and Enver also posed for the *Madonna and Child* group of 1926–27, now at Riverside Church, New York [Fig. 74].[23] The overwhelming impression of Sunita from the sculptures is her melancholy gravity as she gazes into the unfathomable distance [88]. The symmetry of her features is dramatically set off by her asymmetric pose and the thin, snake-like necklace; the eyes and mouth are drawn with a simplicity and directness which intentionally recalls classical Indian sculpture. Yet the sensuality, at

85
JACOB KRAMER 1921 (S119)
Bronze H 64
Leeds City Art Galleries (Leeds Art Collections Fund)

86
STUDY FOR ST JOHN FOR A DEPOSITION GROUP 1920
Pencil 27.5 × 44.1
Leeds City Art Galleries (HMCSS)

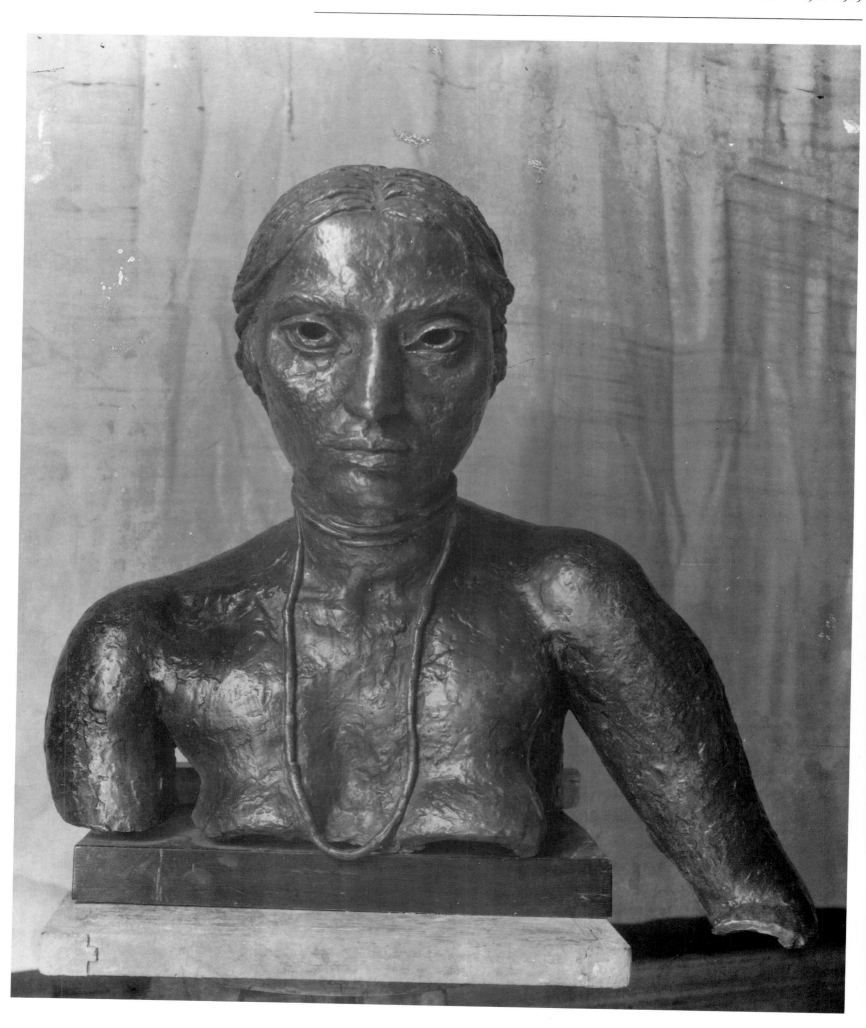

which the necklace hints, and an unsuspected humour emerge in the far more informal context of the many drawings Epstein did, either of Sunita alone [100], of the two sisters or of Sunita and her son [89].

Several portraits of Sunita, as well as one of Anita, were shown at the Leicester Galleries in 1926 with other portraits and the life-size *Visitation* amidst considerable publicity. The extent to which seeing the latest Epsteins had become a social duty among the culturally minded can be gauged from the diary entry of the society portrait sculptor, Kathleen Lady Kennet. On 15 July she noted 'Lunch with Bernard Shaw. We went on to see the Epstein dollies!'[24]

Two years later, a further exhibition, which included many drawings of Sunita, was held at

Godfrey Phillips' gallery at 44 Duke Street, St James's.[25] Although nude studies predominated, there were a handful of bronze portraits, among which that of *Mrs Phillips* was outstanding [90]. Her striking beauty and fashionable haircut seems to have prompted Epstein to model the flesh more smoothly, in a manner which recalls his earlier portraits and emphasises the regularity of her features. The stiff collar, unique in his portraits, and the chic green patination add a flamboyant accent to what might have become a conventional 'society portrait'.

Another Indian sitter, this time for a commissioned portrait, was the Hindu poet and mystic, *Rabindranath Tagore* [91]. This bronze, like that of *Sunita*, is 'a rather sombre, warm earthy colour'; patinated a brown so deep as to be almost black,

87 △
MADELEINE BÉCHET: GIRL FROM
SENEGAL 1921 (S122)
Bronze H 55.9
Whitworth Art Gallery, University of Manchester

88
AMINA PEERBHOY, CALLED SUNITA (third portrait: with necklace) 1926 (S166)
Bronze H 55.2 (another cast with extended left arm illustrated)
Marcus Wickham-Boynton

89

SUNITA AND HER SON ENVER   c1925
Pencil   56.5 × 52
Birmingham Museums and Art Gallery

90

DOROTHY (MRS GODFREY) PHILLIPS
1928   (S185)
Bronze   H 47 (another cast illustrated)
The Phillips Family

---

which seemed paradoxical in works so full of vitality. Wellington put this down not only to Epstein's 'instinctive feeling [for] the mysterious beauty of dark bronze', but also to 'the necessity of transposing natural forms into another key of colour to escape the awful commoness of the *trompe l'œil* and the wax work, and the wish to concentrate on form for its own sake'.[26] Here the effect is to deepen the preternatural gravity and 'commanding presence' of the poet who, despite his humble creed, displayed an autocratic manner towards his entourage. The head appears to be over-life-size, partly because of the beard and ridge of shoulder upon which the large mask rests. It is hard to tell where Epstein's purely sculptural interest in Tagore ends and his distaste for his proud manner begins. 'It has been remarked that my bust of him rests upon the beard, an unconscious piece of symbolism.'[27]

Epstein's sympathy, political and personal, was extended less to the powerful, or to those who pretended to be something other than they really were ('impossible sitters', he told Haskell) than to the humble and powerless.[28] *Old Pinager* [92] was a matchseller who lived in a dosshouse and who sat every evening on the doorstep of a shop labelled 'Old Masters'. He accepted himself as 'a natural failure'.[29] His patient resignation in the face of hardship makes him the descendant of the East Side garment workers [96] and unwordly Jewish mystics Epstein had drawn in his youth. This head, with its experimental use of the old man's gnarled hands as a natural plinth for the

bent head, was an instant success when it was exhibited in 1924. Wellington, who found it a *tour de force*, even feared that in its 'vivid life-likeness' Epstein was in danger of 'transgressing the bounds proper to sculpture and to a material like bronze'.[30] The unease to which such overt emotions give rise emerges still more clearly in the comments of Stanley Casson, who associated the emotive characer of this 'bent and beaten old man, calm and peaceful, but broken in spirit', with the sculptor's origin as a member of 'an oppressed race'.[31] It was the calibre of pieces such as *Old Pinager* which prompted P. G. Konody's observation in 1924 that Epstein had broken through the usual British indifference to sculpture; people were flocking to an

exhibition exclusively devoted to sculpture, and not even idealistic statuary, but just bronze busts — busts, with one or two exceptions, not of celebrities, but of unknown people which have to be admired and judged purely on aesthetic grounds and whose merit cannot be considered from the point of view of a more or less obvious resemblance to the sitter.[32]

In Spring 1924, Muirhead Bone, a long-standing friend of Epstein's, arranged for him to model *Joseph Conrad* [93*]. Such was Epstein's admiration for the Polish-born writer that he had tried, without success, to arrange sittings ten years earlier.[33] Now, at Conrad's home, Oswald's near Canterbury, the author sat each day for three weeks, Epstein encouraging him to talk about his

art as well as the work of others — Melville, Lawrence and Henry James. Conrad 'was crippled with rheumatism, crochety, nervous and ill' and gave Epstein 'a feeling of defeat; but defeat met with courage'.[34] Not withstanding his irascibility and initial unwillingness to sit, the two men established a good rapport. An eye-witness recalled 'Conrad sitting on a pedestal, trying to keep still while waves of expression passed over his face; and Mr Epstein working at the clay and looking every few seconds from it to Conrad with his appraising glance.'[35] The sculptor discovered 'a demon expression in the left eye, while the right eye was smothered by a drooping lid, but the eyes glowed with a great intensity of feeling. The drooping, weary lids intensified the impression of brooding thought. The whole head revealed the man who had suffered much'.[36]

In conversation with Arnold Haskell, Epstein insisted that the 'fierce, almost demoniac, energy' which was apparent in the bust stemmed not from his interpretation of Conrad's psychology but solely from unbiased observation.[37] This disingenuous remark was a blow at those critics like Fry and Casson who deprecated the subjectivity and emotional pitch of his portraiture. Epstein was an extremely perceptive observer who related observations about posture, dress and expression to the inner logic of his portrayal. He himself was notoriously bohemian about how he dressed, but he repeatedly stressed the importance of Conrad's formality:

> Another sculptor made a highly romanticised bust of him, and tried to depict him as the Conrad of the sea, with an open collar and a set dramatic expression. Nothing could be more in error . . . I never once saw him without those high collar points which dug so deeply into his chin that I wondered how he could endure them. There is nothing shaggy or bohemian about him.[38]

On the completion of the portrait, the arrival from London (by taxi lest they got drunk on the way) of Epstein's Italian plaster moulders brought chaos to the quiet household and a heightened state of tension between the two irritable masters — Epstein restlessly pacing up and down, Conrad fuming at the upheaval. Mrs Conrad never forgot it!

> The bust in clay was in a big room over the kitchen, and the fun began when the Italians began to fling the wet plaster at it in order to make the cast. Water poured into the kitchen between the floor planks . . . and no amount of old newspapers spread on the floor around the effigy were efficient in keeping the floor above dry. It was impossible to stop the work of making the cast because the wretched stuff dried too quickly . . . The final touches and the packing of the bust were concluded during the afternoon of that never-to-be-forgotten Sunday . . . Epstein and his helpers occupied the room with the bust, my husband and his secretary locked themselves in the study, Madame Epstein went to sleep in the drawing room all the afternoon, and I was left to the tender mercies of Peggy Jean . . . Then a little after six we watched the overloaded taxi negotiate the

drive, piled up with steps, stage, buckets of clay, and the precious cast packed into it. Then the Epstein family, five men and one woman and child, and the personal luggage made up the load.[39]

Nevertheless, Conrad thought it 'a really magnificent piece of work. It is nice to be passed to posterity in this monumental and impressive rendering'.[40]

91 ◁
RABINDRANATH TAGORE 1926 (S172)
Bronze   H 52 (another cast illustrated)
Bernard Lyons

92
OLD PINAGER 1923 (S138)
Bronze   H 42
Aberdeen Art Gallery and Museums

EPSTEIN AS A BOOK ILLUSTRATOR

Frank Felsenstein

Fig 76

Epstein with studies for C. Baudelaire's LES FLEURS DU MAL at Tooth's Gallery, London, 29 November 1938.

It is not as a sculptor but as an illustrator that Epstein began his artistic career, yet although he later befriended such accomplished etchers as Muirhead Bone and Francis Dodd, he never himself practised, perhaps never even learned, conventional graphic techniques like wood engraving or etching. The number of books he illustrated is actually surprisingly few, although he told Arnold Haskell in 1931: 'You mustn't make the mistake of thinking that I despise illustration. I don't at all. Most of the great artists have been illustrators'.[1]

Epstein found his earliest artistic inspiration in the teeming world of the Hester Street pushcart market outside his window on the Lower East Side of New York. 'I could look down', he wrote many years later,

> upon the moving mass below and watch them making purchases, bartering, and gossiping. Opposite stood carpenters, washerwomen, and day-workers, gathered with their tools in readiness to be hired. Every type could be found here, and for the purpose of drawing, I would follow a character until his appearance was sufficiently impressed on my mind for me to make a drawing.[2]

An early visitor to Epstein's first studio described climbing the 'pestiferous and dingy' stairs to a garret hung with sketches and paintings of Ghetto types, 'of old Jewish applewomen . . . of poverty-stricken old . . . rabbis and philosophers in the cafés, of anaemic feverish writers on the Yiddish newspapers, sweatshop workers, girls and young men'. The visitor was struck by 'the intense vitality' of these charcoal sketches and by the artist's enthusiasm for sympathetic and realistic representation rather than the crude caricature of immigrant Jewish types sometimes found in contemporary American magazine illustration. Epstein 'tells the truth about the Ghetto,' says this early witness, 'but into the dark reality of the external life he puts frequently a melancholy beauty of spirit'.[3] Of the many sketches done during this seminal period only a small number survive; most were destroyed when his garret burnt to the ground, the artist returning to find only 'charred drawings (hundreds of them) floating about in water with dead cats'.[4]

His early visitor was the journalist and miscellaneous writer, Hutchins Hapgood, who was the first to bring Epstein's illustrative talent to public attention. As a reporter on the New York *Commercial Advertiser*, Hapgood had come into contact with the Yiddish author, Abraham Cahan, who encouraged him to write for various journals a series of articles on the Jews of the Lower East Side. In researching these pieces, he would linger in the Russian Jewish cafés in Canal and Grand Streets,[5] and on one of these visits, probably in 1899, he made the acquaintance of young Epstein.

The first of Hapgood's articles, 'Four Poets of the Ghetto', appeared in *The Critic* in March 1900 and was illustrated by five drawings, each 'Sketched from life by Jacob Epstein'.[6] One of them, 'A Ghetto Café', admirably captures the Canal Street ambiance, where, according to the author, the 'chosen crowd of intellectuals . . . get together and talk by the hour, over their coffee and cakes, about politics and society, poetry and ethics, literature and life'.[7] A splendidly prophetic note added by the editor states: 'This interesting article is most appropriately illustrated by an artist of the Ghetto . . . This, we believe, is the first time any of his work has been published, but we do not think it will be the last'. Another article by Hapgood, 'The Foreign Stage in New York', published a few months later in *The Bookman*, contains four further drawings by Epstein.[8]

In, or shortly before, 1900 Epstein helped to organise his first exhibition at New York's Hebrew Institute. He showed paintings considered by Hapgood as 'very crude as far as the technique of colour is concerned', and charcoal sketches that appeared 'rough and showing comparatively slight mastery of the craft'.[9] It is probable that a selection of drawings noted by Hapgood constitutes a partial list of the work Epstein exhibited:

> Portraits of old pedlers . . . an old Jew in the synagogue . . . sweat-shop scenes, gaunt figures half-dressed, with enormously long arms and bony figures; mothers working in the shops with babies in their arms; one woman, tired, watching for a moment her lean husband working the machine . . . a woman with her head leaning heavily on her hands; Hester Street market scenes, with dreary tenement-houses — a kind of prison wall — as background.[10]

1. THE SPIRIT OF THE GHETTO, 1902

After the conflagration that destroyed his studio, Epstein found himself another room in a tenement building occupied by clothing workers.[11] A crayon drawing, 'New York Garment Worker', is one of the few known original studies to survive from this time.[12] Meanwhile, Hapgood was persuaded to collect together his articles into a book,

hich he entitled *The Spirit of the Ghetto*, its inten-
on being to capture the contact of Old and New
orld cultures before the traditions and customs
immigrant Russian Jewry were transformed
at of recognition by American ways. His chap-
rs provide snapshots of a Ghetto life precari-
usly intact. The choice of title is a deliberate nod
the successful dramatisation of Israel Zang-
ill's novel, *The Children of the Ghetto*, which had
cently been performed in New York.
apgood's stance is that of the sympathetic
porter fascinated by a rich and vibrant culture
therto submerged from view to the average
ew Yorker, not that of the social reformer intent
on actively improving the lot of those less
ivileged than himself. In his autobiography,
ritten many years later, he recounts the initial
fficulty of finding a publisher before the book
as finally accepted by Funk & Wagnalls, who,
ecognising the picturesque character of the
aterial, desired to have it profusely illustrated,
d asked me about people to do it'.[13] He not only
commended Epstein but also devoted a large
rt of the chapter on ghetto artists to a considera-
n of his young protégé.

The charcoal sketches prepared for the edition
nearly fifty were reproduced — are boldly
fective in their ability to make significant the
emingly trivial details of every day life. In style,
ey are indebted to the vivid social realism asso-
ated with the drawings of the Parisian poor by
e Swiss-French artist, Théophile-Alexandre
einlen, whose work, as well as that of Forain
d Toulouse-Lautrec, Epstein could have seen in
blications and perhaps also at the Durand-Ruel
llery on Fifth Avenue.[14] As well as depicting
e anonymous street people of the ghetto — a
rpenter with his saw and bag of tools pausing at
e street corner [94], a chassidic father and his
ung son on their way to synagogue — Epstein
so provided portraits of the poets, scholars,
tors and playwrights of the quarter.

Even before the illustrations were complete,
ving been paid the 'enormous' sum of $400,
stein set out for Paris, entrusting the comple-
n of the commission to his friend, the artist
rnard Gussow.[15] Not long after this, in Novem-
r 1902, *The Spirit of the Ghetto* was published, at
.35 in a cloth-bound edition of 1800 copies,[16]
d was generally well received by a number of
wspapers and journals. The unfamiliarity of
e subject matter prompted one reviewer to
scribe the work as 'a voyage of discovery into
arkest New York'; another saw it as 'a volume of
ide and extraordinary interest'.[17] Only a few of
ese reviews make mention of the artist.[18] In
e, Epstein is called 'one of the most prominent
the Ghetto artists' and elsewhere praised for
ustrations that 'are firmly and informally done,
in a pocket sketchbook [by] a Yiddish artist who
aws nothing but Ghetto types'.[19] As much for
apgood's intimate knowledge of the ghetto as
so for Epstein's illustrations, *The Spirit of the
hetto* has achieved the status of a minor Amer-
an classic that has been occasionally, though
nsistently, reprinted. In 1939, the plates of the
iginal edition were sold by Funk & Wagnalls to
apgood for $25.[20] Their present whereabouts is
known.

Russian is more constantly
able to apply a decisive test.
    The Russian Jew of culture
when he comes to New York
carries with him Russian ideals
of literature. The best Yiddish work produced in America is Russian in principle.
Many of the writers who publish literary sketches in the
newspapers of the Ghetto have
written originally in the Rus-
sian language, and know the Russian Jewish life
better than the life of the Yiddish east side ; and
even now they write mainly about conditions in
Russia. Moreover, those who know their New

A TYPE
OF
LABORING
MAN

200

Before his departure for Europe, Epstein also
sold 'a considerable number' of his drawings to
Richard Watson Gilder, the editor of *The Century
Magazine*. Gilder, in turn, asked Hapgood 'to
write an article to go with the drawings' and he
obliged by penning a short piece entitled 'The
Picturesque Ghetto', which, however, was not
published until 1917, with eight further ghetto
illustrations by Epstein.[21] Two of these drawings

94
'A Type of Laboring Man' in H. Hapgood, *The
Spirit of the Ghetto*, 1902, p. 200
Frank Felsenstein

re now in the Garman-Ryan Collection at Walsall
Iuseum and Art Gallery. 'Street Market, New
ork: Man with Mice and Birds' appeared in *The*
entury Magazine in an engraved version by C. W.
hadwick, with the title 'Telling Fortunes with
ats' [95]. 'Lunch in the Shop' [96*], in the
ngraving by S. Davis, belongs to the same series
s 'A Sweat-Shop in Birmingham Place', also pub-
shed in the same magazine, and 'New York
arment Worker'. A third drawing is the original
or the head-piece to 'The Picturesque Ghetto',
here the engraving by J. W. Evans is entitled 'A
lester Street Crowd' [97].[22]

CALAMUS, *c*1902

ittle seems to have survived from Epstein's three
ears in Paris (1902–05). He had gone there to
ain as a sculptor and most of his draughtsman-
hip was directed to that end. However, one
roup of about a dozen drawings, that has its
rigin in New York but may have been executed
uring the Paris sojourn, is the strange illustra-
ons to Walt Whitman's *Calamus*, which are tradi-
onally dated *c*1902. According to Lady Epstein,
ho wrote notes to the illustrations after her
usband's death, he first fell under the spell of
Vhitman at about the age of sixteen, when he
tended classes run by James Kirk Paulding, a
iend of Abraham Cahan, at a centre in New York
nown as the Community Guild. On a Sunday
iorning, Paulding would gather together a
roup of four or five boys to read to them a major
terary work. Through him, Epstein was first
itroduced to the novels of Turgenev and Con-
d, the writings of John Ruskin and of Whitman.
pstein himself recalled finding 'a secluded place
n Central Park] far away from crowds and
oise', where he read *Leaves of Grass* 'out of doors,
mong the rocks and lakes', and then wandering
. the docks area, amid 'the shrieks and yells of
rens and the loud cries of overseers'. New York
ecame in the young artist's mind 'the city of
iips of which Whitman wrote'.[23] In particular,
Vhitman's vision of America, the prophetic strain
iat runs through his poetry and his manliness,
rofoundly affected Epstein throughout his life.
Calamus, first published in the third edition of
eaves of Grass, 1860, is a sequence of poems
iterpreted by some as 'an allegory of democratic
rotherhood', by others as an open celebration of
omosexual love.[24] Epstein's interpretations
.8*] are unlike any other work by him either in
yle or technique. They do not necessarily relate
) specific poems, although several depict the
nbrace of male lovers, perhaps illustrating the
)em 'We Two Boys Together Clinging':

Power enjoying, elbows stretching, fingers
    clutching,
    Arm'd and fearless, eating, drinking, sleeping,
    loving

has been suggested that their attenuated,
ed-like delicacy has affinities with the nude
rawings of Puvis de Chavannes, whose work
as particularly fashionable at the turn of the
ntury.[25] It is also possible that they may have
een influenced by the remarkable series of draw-
gs of lesbian lovers by Rodin, which Epstein

could have seen when he visited the master's
studio during 1902–05.[26]

Given contemporary views on homosexuality,
it is unlikely that Epstein intended the drawings
for publication, but had prepared them in antici-
pation of his departure from Paris to London,
where he hoped to get them exhibited. As soon as
he arrived there in 1905, he took them, with a
letter of introduction from Rodin, to George Bernard Shaw (who was to sit for Rodin in the following year).[27] In a letter dated 13 March 1905 to
Robert Ross, the director of the Carfax Gallery and
Oscar Wilde's literary executor, Shaw introduced

a young American sculptor named Jacob
Epstein . . . who has come to London with
amazing drawings of human creatures like
withered trees embracing. He wants to exhibit
them at the Carfax, which is to him the centre of
real art in London . . . when I advised him to
get commissions for busts of railway directors,

95
'TELLING FORTUNES WITH RATS'   1900–02
Black Chalk   41 × 59.5
Walsall Museum and Art Gallery (Garman-Ryan
Collection)

97
'A HESTER STREET CROWD'   1900–02
Black chalk   50.8 × 58.4
The Jewish Museum, New York. Gift of Karl Nathan

99
STUDY OF A NEGRESS   *c* 1929
Pencil   43.2 × 34
Leeds City Art Galleries

he repudiated me with such utter scorn that I relented & promised to ask you to look at his portfolio. It is a bad case of helpless genius in the first blaze of youth; and the drawings are queer and Rodinesque enough to be presentable at this particular moment. [28]

Shaw wrote another letter along the same lines to the painter, William Rothenstein, a friend of Rodin since the 1880s, [29] describing the *Calamus* drawings as 'mad, like burnt furze-bushes'. Rothenstein found them 'intense in feeling, if somewhat thin and tenuous' and suggested that they would probably be more acceptable in Paris or Berlin. [30] In fact, none of them were ever seen in public in Epstein's lifetime, but they served to bring him to the attention of Ross, who was later responsible for giving him the commission to carve the *Tomb of Oscar Wilde* [Fig. 46], and to Rothenstein, who managed to solicit financial support for the sculptor during his early years in London. Epstein's admiration for Whitman never

abated and, many years later, he accepted a commission from a member of the Whitman Society Detroit to model a bronze of the poet for Westminster Abbey, though permission for the placi of the bust was refused and the sculpture nev made. [31]

3. SEVENTY-FIVE DRAWINGS, 1929

During the fifty-five years that Epstein lived Britain, he produced illustrations for only thr published works: *Seventy-Five Drawings*, 1929, T *Book of Affinity*, 1933, and *Les Fleurs du Mal*, 194 the latter commissioned by a prestigious Ne York private press aimed primarily at collectors fine printing in the United States. He had made conscious decision to turn from book illustratic to sculpture:

What turned me from drawing to sculpture [told Arnold Haskell] was the great desire to s things in the round, and to study form in different aspects from varying angles, and also the love of the purely physical side of sculpture. I felt here a full outlet for my energy, both physical and mental, that was far more satisfying to me than drawing.[32]

He later wrote: 'I could have remained in America and become one of the band, already too numerous, of illustrators, but that was not my ambition.'[33] In fact, he remained a compulsive sketcher whose drawings were far from exclusively preliminary studies for sculpture. In order to supplement what was frequently only a meagre income, he would often resort to selling watercolours and drawings of Epping Forest landscapes [116*], flowers and *Old Testament* themes [101]. Despite the quantity of *Old Testament* illustrations, done mainly during the Thirties, no publication materialised.

By 1929, when *Seventy-Five Drawings* appeared in a limited edition of 220 signed copies (of which 200 were for sale),[34] he was already well established as the *bête noire* of British sculpture. Hubert Wellington, then a lecturer at the Royal College of Art, who had already written a monograph on Epstein in 1925, supplied the Introduction. The volume, he writes, was intended as a 'permanent record' of an exhibition held at the Godfrey Phillips Gallery, 44 Duke Street, London, between July and October 1928. The drawings are mainly nude studies of the beautiful Indian sisters, Sunita [100] and Anita, who often modelled for Epstein, and of an unidentified negress, who was the subject of further unpublished drawings [99]. The first twenty-four works in the book, a group entitled 'Drawings for an Odalisque', are studies of Sunita. One critic, Herbert Furst, who reported the exhibition for *Apollo* (December 1928) was particularly struck by the way that Epstein was able to 'make his lines "tell" superbly; even an unshaded contour drawing such as "Odalisque" . . . suggests a fully modelled solidity and resiliency with astounding skill'. He remarked upon the artist's ability to capture 'the psychological significance of the head and its features, with profound meaning and truth', though he found fault with what he called 'a strange habit of misdrawing arms and hands'. Furst also alluded to Epstein's preference for 'Oriental — Jewish, Indian and exotic — negroid femininity, *chacun à son goût*. That surely is his affair'.[35]

4. OLD TESTAMENT DRAWINGS, 1932

When, in 1932, Epstein exhibited fifty-four *Illustrations to the Old Testament* at the Redfern Gallery, it was this racial aspect that created most controversy and scandalised the critics. William Gaunt, for instance, writing in *The Studio*, began his review by recognising that Epstein was being made 'the scapegoat of the whole modern movement', and that there was danger of relating his sculpture and drawings 'to a multiform prejudice, racial, religious and even political'. Yet, for Gaunt, Epstein's interest in biblical illustration was specifically to depict 'the racial epic of the Jews as it emerges from the historical and legendary books of the Old Testament'.[36] *The Times* (23 February) critic stated even more bluntly

that where Epstein's 'work differs from that of other Bible illustrators is in its strongly racial flavour'. In his autobiography, written eight years later, Epstein still smarted at the 'countless jibes' that the exhibition produced, but added with dignity that he was happy the 'retrograde element' of Nazis and Fascists 'does not make much headway' in England.[37]

Epstein's interpretation of the *Old Testament* is essentially visionary. In *Let There Be Sculpture*, he describes how, working from his studio on the edge of Epping Forest, he became completely

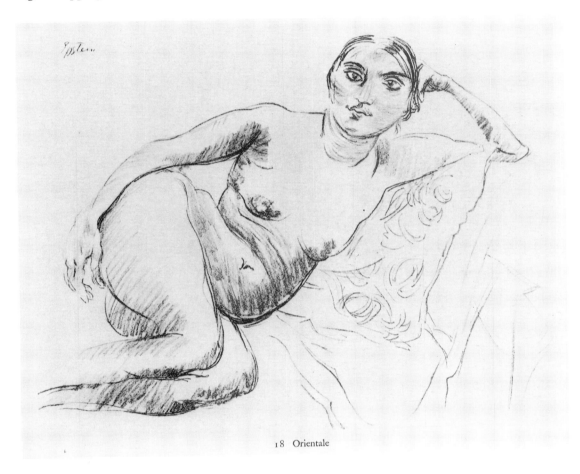

18 Orientale

absorbed in the text of the Bible until 'in the countless images evoked by my readings, a whole new world passed in vision before me. I lost no time in putting this upon paper'.[38] What distinguishes the illustrations is what Cyril Connolly praised as 'their sureness and simplicity, the power of the line, the extraordinary sense of drama the artist brings out in them' [101]. The patriarchal figure of Noah, supported by two of his sons going forth from the ark, God's covenantal rainbow overhead, seems to bear the weight of generations to come, of 'the whole earth overspread' (Genesis 9:19). The vision is shared by both artist and patriarch. It is as if, says Connolly, 'we see them as Blake would have drawn them had Blake been a Jew'.[39]

When these extraordinary watercolours were exhibited in 1932, priced at twenty guineas each, the catalogue stated that all copyrights were reserved to the artist, implying perhaps that Epstein intended to publish them. However, according to Lady Epstein, they were all 'sold immediately and became so dispersed that when

100
AMINA PEERBHOY, CALLED SUNITA, AS AN 'ORIENTALE',
in *Epstein. Seventy-Five Drawings*, 1929, plate 18
Leeds City Art Galleries (HMCSS)

101

NOAH AND TWO OF HIS SONS   1932

Pencil and watercolour   43.8 × 57.2

The Trustees of the Victoria and Albert Museum, London

The Book of Affinity is a quasi-scriptural work ○ prophecy, intended by its author as 'a Defence ○ Judaism and an Appeal for Zion'.[43] Utilising mixture of free verse and poetical prose, Oyve● creates a somewhat tendentious allegory in whicl he envisages the Jews as God's 'World People linking together nation to nation [through] a mes sage of Creative Harmony'. He himself is th loosely disguised prophet 'to whom the Lor● entrusted the Jewel of Love'.[44] An anonymou reviewer in *The Times Literary Supplement* (1 Marcl 1934) considered the work 'extremely esoteric an● obscure', 'a book . . . written in a particular stat of mind for those who are in the same state ○ mind'. Epstein's drawings, similar in style t● those for the *Old Testament*, are diminished onl by the minor quality of the text they illuminate The frontispiece [102] shows the author's drear vision, capturing what Epstein calls elsewhere th 'fluttering and naive . . . expression [of his] sensi tive, nervous features'.[45]

6. FLOWERS OF EVIL, 1940

In 1936, during a visit to Paris, while quietl drinking in the Café des Deux Magots in th● Boulevard Saint-Germain, Epstein was by chanc introduced to George Macy, the founder of th● Limited Editions Club of New York. This led to a● invitation to illustrate a book. After initially sug gesting Ovid and then rejecting the idea becaus of the difficulty of settling on a particular work Epstein 'with a flash of inspiration' proposed a● edition of Baudelaire's poetry.[46] (As early as 190 he had owned a French edition of *Les Fleurs d● Mal*).[47] The contract was signed in London o● 13 September 1936, with the artist receiving £30● half in advance and 'half when he delivers th● illustrations to the Publisher'. By it, the Limite● Editions Club purchased the reproduction rights whereas the original drawings and the right to se● them remained Epstein's property. Howeve● unlike the other artists who contributed to Macy' series, Epstein insisted that a clause stipulatin● that he sign every printed copy of the book wa● deleted from the contract.[48]

Macy was quick to appreciate the appropriate ness of the choice of Baudelaire, 'the darling ○ Paris when Jacob Epstein was a student' there,[49] time when the reputation of the great nineteenth century poet was beginning to enjoy a posthu mous revival. As Epstein wrote in 1938, 'Thi● Bible of the modern man has long called t● me . . . For long I have been haunted by th● images of revolt, anguish and despair — disgus with the world and self — expressed in *Les Fleur du Mal*.'[50] In Paris again in the spring of 1938, h● 'walked for hours in daylight & by night' absorb ing the atmosphere of the *quartiers* where th● poems had been written and making 'in the bye ways of Montparnasse' a large number of preli minary sketches. Several of these have survived including studies of 'grotesque heads on the Pon● Neuf which Baudelaire would cross on his dail● walks when he doubtless often lingered lookin● down on the Seine' [103].[51] Memories of his ow● early sojourn in Paris seem also to have infuse● Epstein's nightmarish vision of a Satanic city o● 'splendid and maleficent entities'.[52] He was late

later on someone wanted to publish them with the text it was thought to be too great a task to trace all the owners and collect them again for reproduction, so the idea fell through'.[40]

5. THE BOOK OF AFFINITY, 1933

Epstein's penchant for the prophetic led him, in 1933, to contribute seven pencil and watercolour illustrations to Moysheh Oyved's *The Book of Affinity*.[41] Each of the 525 copies was numbered and signed by the author. Oyved (the *nom de plume* of Edward Good) was a London jeweller and minor writer who had befriended Epstein during the Twenties and had sat to the sculptor in 1926; he praised him as 'the mighty sculptor of our heroic time'.[42]

o recall that on his very first walk in 1902, passing
ver one of the bridges leading to the Ile de la Cité
o see Nôtre Dame, he had chanced to enter 'a
mall building, the morgue, and I had to regret
he curiosity that took me into that tragic build-
ng'. On another occasion, he attended the ana-
omy class at the Ecole des Beaux Arts with a
orpse as a model until squeamishness got the
etter of him 'when a green arm was handed
round for inspection [and he] nearly fainted',
eaving the class never to return. He also recalled
aving joined the 'strange company of revellers
n the] uproarious and blasting saturnalia' of the
al des Quatres Arts 'with nude girls astride the
ab horses'.[53] The recollection of these events is
ot lost in the Baudelaire drawings.

On his return to London, Epstein brooded over
he poems, many of which he had got to know by
eart, and at the same time prepared a series of
ighly-finished pencil drawings. The technical
ffect that he was seeking was to produce 'a result
omewhat like lithography', which he felt was
ustified by the austere and measured form of the
oems'.[54] Instead of the comparatively small
umber of illustrations that were needed for the
imited Editions Club volume, Epstein took the
ommission perhaps too seriously and, to Macy's
onsternation, produced about sixty final draw-
ngs. Of these, thirty-seven were included in *An
xhibition of Drawings by Jacob Epstein for 'Les Fleurs
u Mal' of Charles Baudelaire* at Tooth's Gallery in
Iew Bond Street in December 1938 [Fig. 76]. The
xhibition was immediately vilified by the critics.
n his autobiography, Epstein quotes from a
tring of negative reviews, accusing him of 'hor-
or and near-obscenity, with no aesthetic value'
The Daily Mail), of a result 'so dynamically forc-
le to crudity that he is in danger of obliterating
nuch of what Baudelaire may mean to us' (*The
bserver*), of impertinently diminishing 'a great
lassical poet, at once marmoreal and exquisitely
ine' with drawings that 'are hardly more sig-
ificant than graffiti' (*The New Statesman*).[55] Only
few critics, notably L. B. Powell in *The Birming-
am Mail*, who remarked upon Epstein's essential
umanism and directness of inspiration, had any-
ning favourable to say.[56] In disgust more than in
rustration, and following a quarrel with the gal-
ry directors, Epstein withdrew the exhibition
fter a fortnight in which only fifteen works had
een sold.

Of the total series, twenty-four drawings,
most all of which appeared at Tooth's, had been
elected for inclusion in the Limited Editions Club
olume. When he received the drawings, Macy
ecided to embark on a double publication, since
e was aware of the existence of an edition of
audelaire privately printed in Paris by Gallimard
1898, a copy of which contained drawings in
ne margin by Rodin.[57] It came into his mind to
ring out his Baudelaire in two volumes, one in
rench with Rodin's illustrations, the other in an
nglish translation with those of Epstein. It is
oubtful whether Epstein realised, when he sub-
itted his drawings, that they would embellish
n English version rather than Baudelaire's origi-
al.[58]

To design and print the volume, Macy turned to
rnest Ingham at the Fanfare Press in London, the

same printer who had been responsible several
years earlier for the printing of *Seventy-Five Drawings*. Even before the exhibition at Tooth's, the
Baudelaire drawings selected for publication had
been redrawn on lithographic stone and pulled by
the firm of Fernand Mourlot in Paris. By 1940, the
volume, bound in full red buckram, gold stam-
ped, was ready and, in September of that year,
published to members of the Limited Editions
Club as *Flowers of Evil Translated into English verse
by various hands*. At the same time, in Paris, its
twin, *Les Fleurs du Mal* with Rodin's pen and ink
drawings, hand coloured for the edition by
Maurice Beaufumé, was being printed by
J. Dumoulin. Barely had this been completed but
the German army marched into Paris and the
edition was seemingly lost. However, at the close
of the War, the sheets were discovered intact in a
cellar and the book was finally distributed to
members in April 1947. The two volumes boxed
together constitute the 117th publication of the
Club.[59]

A few years after the War, a series of books
designed, printed or illustrated in Britain for
Macy, including the Epstein Baudelaire, were
exhibited in the King's Library and later presented to the British Museum. It was the first time
that the Museum had accorded an exhibition to
the work of a living publisher. In his Introduction
to the catalogue, Sir Francis Meynell wrote that

> Mr. Macy's own interest and style in book
> design is more after the French than the English
> fashion. . . . It shows in the emphasis on illus-
> tration; it shows in . . . an amplification of
> attitude, whether it be in picture or in binding,
> which on rare occasion we may find over-
> abundant but which not infrequently reveals by
> a contrast a certain timidity of our native atti-
> tude to limited edition designing.[60]

Epstein considered the series of drawings
'amongst my best work and my greatest failure
when exhibited . . . in the ugly parlance of to-day,
"a flop"'. In an attempt to explain the significance
of the drawings, he said that he had tried 'to
represent the spiritual, religious, and ecstatic
sense of the poems with their tragic and sombre
shades, avoiding for the most part those cheap
sensual interpretations in illustrations so com-
monly found in volumes of the *Fleurs du Mal*'.[61] It
is this emphasis that led him to describe the
poems as a 'Bible of the *modern* man', in the
political climate of the late Thirties a frightening
antithesis to his own earlier conception of the *Old
Testament*. Baudelaire had created a vision of evil
challenging conventional orthodoxies by forcing
us to feel uncomfortable with our accepted
notions of good and evil.

Epstein's long 'brooding upon [Baudelaire's]
powerful and subtle images' was stimulated by
his comprehension that the poet had conceived
just such 'an adventure wholly of the soul, [of
man] caught in the snare of sinful existence
seek[ing] to escape "la conscience dans le
MAL"'.[62] In attempting to capture this spirit,
Epstein made illustrations that are distinct from
anything else in twentieth-century drawing. The
incomprehension of the critics derives in large
measure from their inability to come to terms with

102
'AT LENGTH IN THE MIDST OF HIS DESPAIR HIS
SOUL MIGHTILY AWOKE AGAIN', in M. Oyved,
The Book of Affinity, frontispiece, 1933
Evelyn Silber

103
THE PONT NEUF, PARIS   1936
Pencil   14 × 18
Beth Lipkin

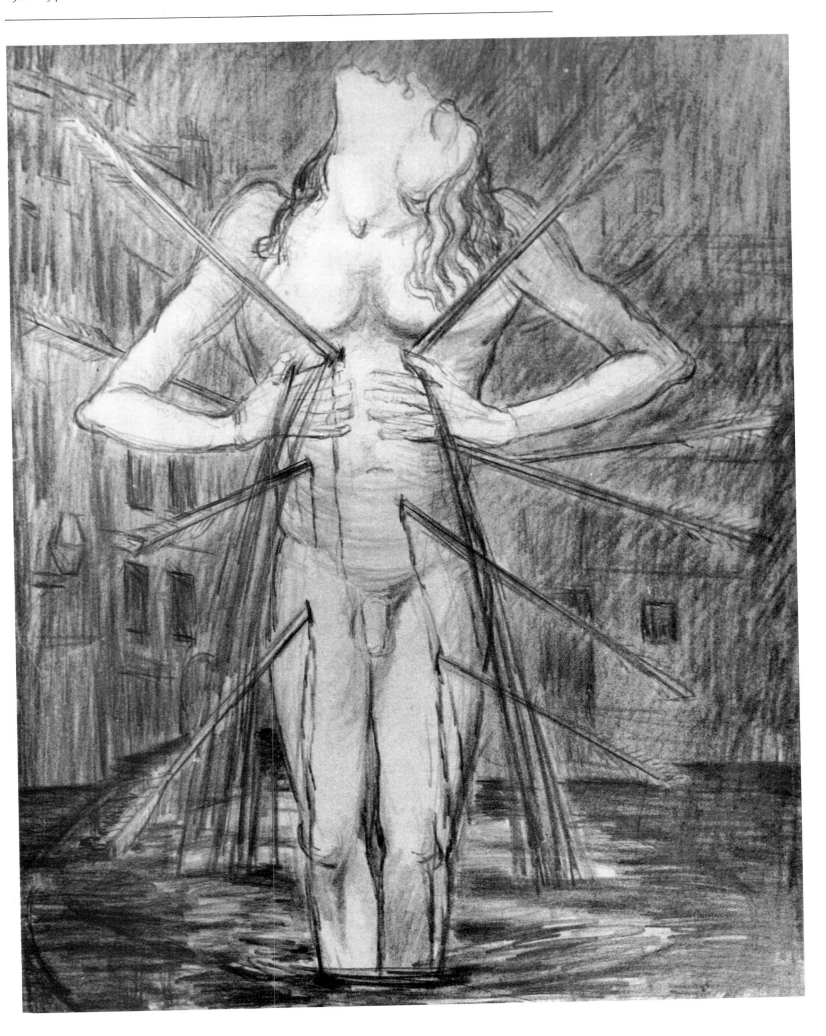

106
Study for 'JE SUIS COMME LE ROI
D'UN PAYS PLUVIEUX' | 'THE KING OF
A RAINY COUNTRY'   1936–38
Pencil   44.5 × 56.7
Leeds City Art Galleries

104 ◁◁
'LE CREPUSCULE DU SOIR' | 'EVENING
TWILIGHT'   1936–38
Pencil   44.4 × 57.2
Dr and Mrs Jeffrey Sherwin

105 ◁
'LA FONTAINE DE SANG' | 'THE FOUNTAIN OF
BLOOD'   1936–38
Pencil   43.2 × 55.9
Private collection

the imaginative daring of Epstein's stark vision.
(Many years earlier, T. E. Hulme wrote in an
essay on Epstein that the critics 'seem unable to
understand that an artist who has something to
say will continually "extract" from reality new
methods of expression, and that these being personally felt will inevitably lack prettiness and will
differ from traditional clichés').[63]

Les Fleurs du Mal drawings are disturbingly
powerful in their immediacy and visually haunting in their expression of the images of revolt,
anguish and despair that infuse Baudelaire's
poetry and its portrayal of Paris. For 'Le Crepus-
cule du Soir' | 'Evening Twilight' [104], Baude-
laire's description of the metempsychosis of
criminal man into wild animal, Epstein dramatically captures, in purely physical terms, the hor-
rible moment of transformation, the man sharing
the legs and hind quarters of the fanged beast that
now controls him. (The metamorphic aspect may
perhaps be seen as a lingering reflection of his
earlier proposal to illustrate Ovid). The destruction of the soul is set in a sombre city of destruction, the haunt of the criminal and the prostitute.
In 'La Fontaine de Sang' | 'The Fountain of Blood'
[105],[64] Epstein brilliantly depicts the horrid ecstacy of a bleeding St Sebastian transfixed with
arrows, a very free interpretation of lines describing the effect of a morbid terror. In his own
imagination, the poet's fears have become physical wounds from which his blood flows like wine
inundating yet invigorating the city:

Il me semble parfois que mon sang coule à flots,
    Ainsi qu'une fontaine aux rhythmiques
      sanglots.
Je l'entends bien qui coule avec un long
    murmure,
Mais je me tâte en vain pour trouver la blessure.
A travers la cité, comme dans un champ clos,
Il s'en va, transformant les pavés en îlots,
Désaltérant la soif de chaque créature,
Et partout colorant en rouge la nature.

It seems to me sometimes my blood is bubbling out
As fountains do, in rhythmic sobs; I feel it spout
And lapse; I hear it plainly; it makes a murmuring
*   sound;*
But from what wound it wells, so far I have not
*   found.*
As blood runs in the lists, round tumbled armoured
*   bones,*
It soaks the city, islanding the paving-stones;
Everything thirsty leans to lap it, with stretched
*   head;*
Trees suck it up; it stains their trunks and branches
*   red.*

Translated by Edna St Vincent Millay

'Je suis comme le roi d'un pays pluvieux' | 'The
King of a Rainy Country' [106], from *Spleen et
Idéal*, reflects the *ennui* of the poet represented by
the king of a fairy-tale country, rich but impotent,
bored by hangers-on — the jester, the alchemist,
beauteous ladies of the court and pet spaniels —
all unable to revive his spirits which ebb away like
the green waters of the river of Hell.[65]

The imaginative freedom with which Epstein
interprets Baudelaire means that his drawings are
never merely glosses to the poetry. As a result,

some of the illustrations remain difficult to ascribe to particular poems.[66] An unpublished study [107], with its dominant figure of a primordial horned idol in an underworld of lost souls, has no specific attribution but may be intended to illustrate the poem 'Hymne à la Beauté', a drawing for which was exhibited at Tooth's (no. 37):

> Que tu viennes du ciel, ou de l'enfer, qu'importe,
> O Beauté! monstre énorme, effrayant, ingénu!
>
> *Comest thou from highest heaven or from the abyss,*
> *O Beauty? For thy look, hellish, divine,*
> *Is fraught with mingled misery and bliss . . .*
>
> Translated by Sir John Squire

Epstein's imagination gives further dimension to the verse and engenders a vision of violent power, ritualistic and nightmarish, that depends only incidentally upon the poem. If only for the shocking violence of the expression, perhaps also for their technical austerity, Epstein's illustrations to Baudelaire find a singular contemporary parallel in the *Guernica* drawings of his friend Picasso that were exhibited in London earlier in the same year.

In their lithographic effect, extraordinary depth and chiaroscuro, and imaginative impact, Epstein's drawings reject the cheap sensuality of portrayals 'of seductive mulattos, exotic negresses and nostalgic eldorados'[67] that the artist found so unsatisfactory in earlier attempts to illustrate the poems. With this series, which pays homage to yet ultimately reinterprets its inspirational source, Epstein had at last achieved his full potential as a graphic artist [108]. Ironically, the drawings are his swan-song as a book illustrator.

107
'HYMNE À LA BEAUTÉ' | 'HYMN TO BEAUTY'
1936–38
Pencil   44.4 × 57.2
Dr and Mrs Jeffrey Sherwin

108
PORTRAIT OF BAUDELAIRE
title-page of C. Baudelaire, *Flowers of Evil*, 1940
Lithography   16.5 × 23
Dr and Mrs Jeffrey Sherwin

11 · 1935–1936

EPSTEIN AND THE THEATRE

Terry Friedman

In an interview given to *The Daily Telegraph* on 18 November 1935 devoted to his design for the drop curtain for the Markova-Dolin Company production of a new ballet, *David*, Epstein remarked that it represented 'a new departure for me, the first work of this kind I have done, although I executed some Biblical drawings three or four years ago' [101]. Written by Poppoea Wanda, with music composed by Maurice Jacobson, imaginative neo-archaic sets and costumes by Bernard Meninsky[1] and choreography by Keith Lester, with the title role danced by Anton Dolin, the ballet received its première at The Duke of York's Theatre on 13 January 1936.

The curtain was in progress by November of the previous year, when Epstein told *The Daily Telegraph*, 'I am doing all the work myself, including the original designs of the 75 figures that appear and all the actual painting of the curtain [which] I find . . . an extraordinarily interesting and stimulating experience', adding that a feature of the scheme was the 'brilliance of the colouring', which he described as being 'like a Russian ikon'. A preliminary watercolour for part of the central panel [109*] reveals the use of scintillating reds, yellows, oranges and blues. A 'large water-colour of dazzling hue' [Fig. 77] exhibited at The Redfern Gallery in January 1936, had the effect of 'shimmering movement, already partaking of the triumphant rhythm of the dance it preludes'.[2]

The completed curtain, 30 by 25 feet, (which has not survived) was shown privately to the press on 7 January 1936. *The Dancing Times* (February issue) likened it to the 'title-pages of books of a bygone age, in which, by means of engraved panels, the artist delineated the most exciting events that were to follow in the reading.' Like the ballet itself, the nine panels depicted scenes from David's life.[3] The large central section showed the King enthroned before a huge Star of David flanked by the Lions of Judah and various biblical persons. *The Dancing Times* associated this with the 'antiquities of Egypt and Assyria', and there is good reason to believe that for the pair of powerful guardian beasts, Epstein had looked at the seventh-century BC bas-reliefs depicting King Ashurnasirpal hunting lions, from the Throne Room of the Palace at Nimrud (in the British Museum),[4] just as he had turned to Assyrian sources for the *Oscar Wilde Tomb* [Figs 48–50]. Above the enthroned David, a concourse of angels is arranged like the apsidal decoration of a Byzantine church. An almost identical motif was used by Epstein in an illustration to Moysheh

Oyved's *The Book of Affinity*, published in 1933 [102].

To the top-left in the curtain is a smaller scene showing the Prophet Samuel annointing young David (I Samuel 16:20).[5] Below is a group of voluptuous women, which might refer to the famous episode with Bathsheba (II Samuel 11). To top-right the near-naked David dances before the Lord 'with all his might' (II Samuel 6:14), his extrovert pose recalling Epstein's flenite figure of 1913 [Fig. 69]; this was, perhaps, the feature which suggested to *The Observer* (19 January 1936) a 'tribal note' in the design. Below is what appears to be the story of David's confrontation with Goliath the Philistine (I Samuel 17). Epstein had earlier rejected this episode,[6] but it was subsequently reinstated and became a poignant image for the years which saw the Nazi promulgation of the Nuremberg Laws and the rise of Mosley's fascistic brand of anti-semitism. The two bottom flanking panels depict priests praying before the Seven Branched Candlestick (*menorah*). Between them are the episodes of David playing the harp for Saul (I Samuel 16:23) and of the young virgin chosen to cherish and lie in the bosom of the old, stricken David (I Kings 1:1–2).

Epstein's friend, Arnold Haskell, who was then *The Daily Telegraph* ballet critic, considered the curtain the 'most striking feature of the production'. *The Dancing Times* commented that from the

> decorative standpoint, probably no ballet of recent years has been so eagerly anticipated as this, for it brought into the theatre for the first time two artists of great repute [Epstein and Meninsky], one even of internationally accepted genius. [The] curtain sent hopes soaring . . . it is a fine thing to have brought a sculptor of this calibre into the theatre.

Haskell expressed the hope that 'One day [Epstein] will have the time to devise a complete *decor*', although the sculptor, in fact, was never to return to this genre.[7]

Fig 77
STUDY FOR THE DROP-CURTAIN FOR THE BALLET
DAVID   1935
from *The Sketch*, 15 January 1936, p. 105
Whereabouts unknown

EPSTEIN IN THE PUBLIC EYE

Evelyn Silber and Terry Friedman

Fig 78
Epstein and Kathleen Garman visiting the W. H. HUDSON MEMORIAL (S147), Hyde Park, London, from *The Sphere*, 30 May 1925.

110
RISEN CHRIST 1917–19 (S97)
Bronze H 218.5
The Scottish National Gallery of Modern Art, Edinburgh
(Exhibited in Leeds only)

111
STUDY FOR RISEN CHRIST 1917
Pencil 26.5 × 37
Birmingham Museums and Art Gallery

'Their virility is not to be denied; there are always some who like their meat raw!', so Epstein's 'crudities [which] seem nevertheless to have a considerable vogue in London' were dismissed by the American critic, Lorado Taft in his ultra-conservative Scammon Lectures for 1917, published four years later as *Modern Tendencies in Sculpture*.[1] During the Twenties the public was offered opportunities to sample five of Epstein's most controversial works: *Risen Christ*, exhibited in 1920 at the first of a series of important one-man shows held after the War at the Leicester Galleries, the *W. H. Hudson Memorial*, unveiled in Hyde Park in 1925, *Visitation*, shown at the Leicester Galleries in 1926, and the pair of huge figure groups of *Day* and *Night* of 1928–29 on the London Underground Electric Railways Building in Westminster.

1. RISEN CHRIST, 1917–19

Epstein began working on the over-lifesize bronze of *Risen Christ* [110] in 1917 and completed all but the feet before being called-up in September that year. On his discharge from the Royal Fusiliers in July 1918 he returned to it with considerable excitement. For the previous six or seven years he had devoted himself almost exclusively to carving (the exceptions being a few portraits) and his only previous life-size bronze had been the *Standing Mother and Child*, 1911 [Fig. 65].

This majestic figure, 'a modern living Christ', was his private memorial to the Great War: 'It stands and accuses the world for its grossness, inhumanity, cruelty and beastliness.'[2] The Leeds artist, Jacob Kramer [85], and the musician, Cecil Gray, had posed for the figure, while the head was based on the Dutch composer, Bernard van Dieren, a friend since 1915 and already the subject of a hard, brooding portrait in 1916.[3] Things were very different now. Dieren was lying ill with kidney stones: 'Watching his head, so spiritual and worn with suffering, I thought I would like to make a mask of him. I hurried home and returned with clay and made a mask which I immediately recognised as the Christ head, with its short beard, its pitying accusing eyes, and the lofty and broad brow, denoting great intellectual strength.'[4] Epstein likened the realisation that what he had made was far more than a portrait to the kind of 'accident' that revealed Christ to his two companions at Emmaus; such moments of visionary insight were to recur in later works, enabling him to see an Indian woman and her son

as the Madonna and Child [Fig. 74],[5] and Kramer as a potential St John in a planned *Deposition* group.

In the sculptor's own retrospective account, the overall composition of *Risen Christ* came instantly to mind:

> I saw the whole figure . . . in the mask. With haste I began to add the torso and the arms and hand with the accusing finger . . . I then set up this bust with an armature for the body. I established the length of the whole figure down to the feet . . . The statue rose swathed in clothes. A pillar firmly set on two naked feet — Christ risen supernatural, a portent for all time.[6]

The image did not refer to any specific incident, but was symbolic of the Christ who had suffered at the hands of men and returned to life as an eternal examplar. The preparatory drawing supports this account [111]: the columnar stillness of the figure and the position of the hands are clearly indicated though the details of the drapery and feet have not yet been fixed. It is significant that this, like several of Epstein's early drawings for sculpture, shows the figure in profile. There is a conscious archaicism in his choice of profile views which recalls the figures on Greek funeral reliefs; it is possible that he was still influenced by memories of E. Loewy's *Die Naturwiedergabe in der älteren griechischen Kunst*, 1900, published in 1907 in an English translation as *The Rendering of Nature in Early Greek Art* by John Fothergill, one of Epstein's very first contacts in England.[7] Loewy had stressed the importance of profile and frontal views of the human figure in both archaic relief and free-standing figures. Throughout Epstein's career his preference was for hieratic figures best viewed from the front or in profile, irrespective of the medium of which he was working. Here he may also have been influenced by other sources. The *Christ's* spare, demonstrative gesture, calm gaze and slender, upright form recall nothing in Western art so much as Romanesque jamb figures, likewise intended to impart an eternal lesson to sinful humanity. So close is Epstein's figure in several respects to the mid-twelfth century central doorway of the West Portal at Chartres [Fig. 79] that it is tempting to see this as a direct source of inspiration.

Epstein's respect for tradition was considerable. He had read the *New Testament* closely during his boyhood and, when his sculpture was

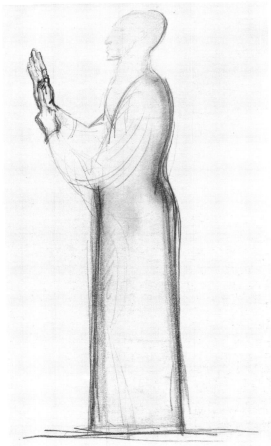

Fig 79 ◁
OLD TESTAMENT FIGURES, Chartres Cathedral,
West Portal, central door, left jamb, 1145–55

Fig 80
W. H. HUDSON MEMORIAL   Hyde Park, London
(contemporary photograph), 1923–25   (S147)

vehemently attacked for the supposedly blasphemous misrepresentation of Christ, he was able to reply

> You have only to read the Gospels to see that the sweet, lovable Christ is but one of many aspects of that wondrous Personality. There was intellect as well as sentiment; power and a rare sense of justice as well as compassion and forgiveness. The passivity and weakness have been too much emphasised. The sterner elements are repressed or lost sight of . . . He inspired fear as well as devotion. He drove the moneychangers out of the Temple. He could blaze out in righteous wrath, and voice justifiable indignation. [It] is this complex Christ that I have endeavoured to body forth.[8]

Beyond an underlying resentment that a Jewish artist should have represented a Christian subject, public and critical wrath focused on the supposed savagery of the figure, unlike the dulcet Pre-Raphaelite type of Christ now fixed in the Anglo-Saxon canon of religious images. Comments ranged from the hysterical and ignorant racialism of Father Bernard Vaughan in *The*

Graphic and the incomprehension of Frank Rutter, A. Clutton-Brock and P. G. Konody, who reviewed for the heavyweight press, to the suspicions (voiced by a senior British sculptor, Frederick Pomeroy) that Epstein's work was being hyped into prominence by the dealers. Vaughan's diatribe, describing the impression made upon him by the sculpture as 'some degraded Chaldean or African . . . some Asiatic, American or Hun-Jew . . . some emaciated Hindu or badly grown Egyptian',[9] was knowledgeably and wittily put-down by George Bernard Shaw the following week.[10] Pomeroy, in a letter to a distinguished sculptor, Sir Hamo Thornycroft, related

> I saw the so called 'Christ' at the Bronze Founders [Parlanti] & a more scrofulous, unhealthy looking thing I never set eyes on. I was told that Epstein got very little pay for these works but his natural inclination is towards filth, and this is a gratuitous insult to Christianity. I expect we shall have it recommended for purchase by some of the Tate people. Well we must be loyal to your institution and defy such adventurers.[11]

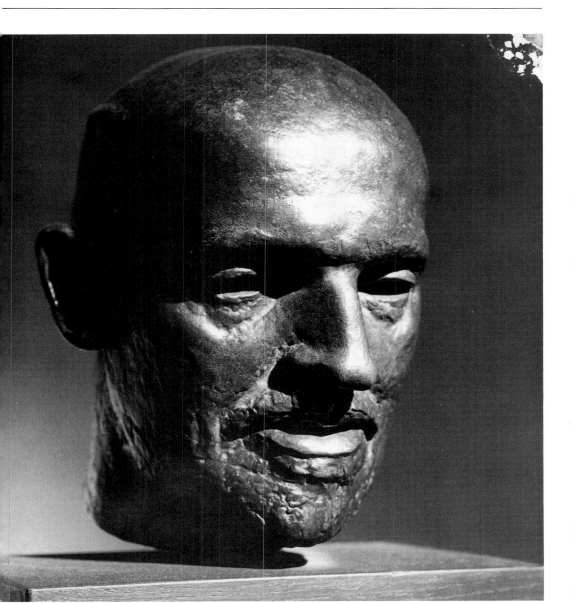

In fact, the *Christ* was purchased for the consider-
ble sum of £2,000 by the explorer Apsley Cherry-
arrard, who already owned a cast of Rodin's
Walking Man. The other works in the Leicester
alleries show — portraits — were widely
raised. The result was a huge public attendance:
he proprietor, Oliver Brown, recalled 1,000 visi-
ors on many days and as many as 1,500 on one or
vo occasions.[12]

The W. H. Hudson Memorial, 1923–25

No sooner had the ragings surrounding *Risen
hrist* died down than another controversy, by far
he worst Epstein was ever to sustain — indeed, a
ontroversy unparallelled in the annals of modern
rt in Britain — descended on the sculptor. On
9 May 1925, Stanley Baldwin unveiled the *W. H.
Hudson Memorial* [Figs 80–81*], with its vigorously
arved Portland stone relief of Rima, in the Bird
anctuary at Hyde Park, to 'dead silence followed
y a gasp of horror' — more than one member of
he congregation saw a shiver run down the
rime Minister's spine. The ensuing public 'hulla-
aloo', incited by the conservative press, was,

according to Epstein, 'unequalled for venom and
spite'.[13] No work by him caused more dissent
among members of the art establishment and the
public alike: 'Mr. Epstein's amorphous miscar-
riage in marble'. The President of the Royal
Academy feared a 'Danger That the World
Will be Made Hideous' by its presence. Epstein
later spoke of the Nation suffering from
'Rimaphobia'.[14]

The *Memorial* is the most comprehensively
documented of the sculptor's works.[15] The
famous naturalist and author, William Henry
Hudson, died on 18 August 1922. At the end of
November the idea of a memorial, to be funded by
public subscription and erected somewhere in
London, was launched by a committee of friends
and admirers, who included John Galsworthy,
J. M. Dent, Muirhead Bone and R. B. Cunninghame Graham. A rugged, flamboyant bronze of
Cunninghame Graham [112], a close friend of Hudson who had lived in the Argentine, was modelled in April 1923, as Epstein was working on the
Memorial.[16] He found the sitter a Quixotic figure,
debonair, courteous and agile; the portrait head
'seems to sniff the air, blowing from the
Sierras . . . his hair . . . swept by a breeze'.[17]

112 △
Robert Bontine Cunninghame
Graham 1923 (*S*145)
Bronze H 35
Manchester City Art Galleries

113
James Muirhead Bone 1916 (*S*75)
Bronze H 26.7
Dundee Art Galleries and Museums

114
STUDY FOR THE W. H. HUDSON
MEMORIAL   Hyde Park, London, 1922–23
Pencil   48.3 × 38
Leeds City Art Galleries (HMCSS)

115
MAQUETTE FOR THE W. H. HUDSON
MEMORIAL   Hyde Park, London, 1922–23   (S146)
Bronze   43.2 × 33
P. Henriques

XIII
STANDING FEMALE FIGURE, Baga, Guiné
Wood   H 63.5
The Trustees of the British Museum (formerly Jacob
Epstein collection)

.. B. Powell, an early biographer of the sculptor, classed it, with the busts of *Joseph Conrad* [93*] and *Jacob Kramer* [85], as among the portraits of the 'twenties noted for their 'acute observation and sympathetic awareness'.[18] The earlier, more delicately modelled and introspective portrait of *Muirhead Bone* [113] is reminiscent of some ancient Egyptian Black basalt head. He was one of Epstein's staunchest champions, defending the British Medical Association figures in 1908, as he was soon obliged to do with the *Hudson Memorial*. On 6 December 1922 the Memorial Committee directed Bone to approach Epstein regarding this commission, and on 10 January they approved his 'clay model', later cast in bronze [115], based on a lively sketch [114] in which a life-size figure of Hudson reclines in a wood 'in an attitude of watching the birds drinking and bathing, in the runnels, & channels, & pools of water hewn from the stone below the figure'.[19]

However, representations of actual persons were not permitted in the Royal Parks and early in February, 'anxious as ever to get something really strikingly imaginative and beautiful from Epstein', Bone suggested the alternative idea of a stone relief representing Rima, the 'wonderful woman spirit' in Hudson's novel *Green Mansions: A Romance of the Tropical Forest*, first published in 1904.[20] Epstein's next design, again prepared (during February and March 1923) as a model and showing Rima in a setting of trees and birds, was also rejected (in June) because the government feared it would 'evoke wide and even bitter controversy'.[21] Despite opposition from within in the Memorial Committee, in July Epstein was invited to prepare a revised scheme based on the novel. The special appeal of *Green Mansions*, which he had read and re-read and which he himself may have suggested to Bone in the first place as an appropriate subject, was its daring tale of primitive life in the Venezuelan forests, a story whose authentic atmosphere was closer to Darwin than to Edgar Rice Burroughs (whose *Tarzan of the Apes* appeared in 1914). Rima, the 'imaginary person, half human, half spirit . . . so akin to wild Nature', could with impunity (or so Epstein believed) be interpreted not as a conventional European beauty but as a ferine primitive force of a type he had come greatly to admire in African and Oceanic sculpture [XIII]. He retreated to the seclusion of his studio at Baldwyn's Hill, Loughton, on the edge of Epping Forest [116*], to ponder the problem in a stunning series of eighty-seven large drawings forming a sketchbook, now at Leeds.[22] The variety of compositions and drawing styles indicates that he worked, throughout the late Summer and Autumn of 1923, with a sustained explosion of energy. The broad, bright washes in red, blue, green and mauve watercolour, unique to these drawings, were Epstein's method at this preliminary stage, of calculating the ultimate effect of bold relief against a shadowed ground which could only be viewed frontally and from a considerable distance [Fig. 82], as specified in the scheme designed by Bone's friend, Lionel Pearson, of the architectural firm of Adams, Holden and Pearson.

The sketchbook drawings follow Hudson's narrative closely. The hero of the novel, Abel, has

117
STUDY FOR THE RIMA RELIEF FOR THE
W. H. HUDSON MEMORIAL Hyde Park, London,
1923 (catalogue nos. 117–22, 124–26 from a
sketchbook of 87 drawings on 56 sheets)
Pencil and watercolour 58.7 × 45.1
Leeds City Art Galleries (HMCSS)

Fig 82
James Muirhead Bone (1876–1953)
PROPOSED LAYOUT BY LIONEL PEARSON FOR THE
W. H. HUDSON MEMORIAL Hyde Park, London,
in *Country Life*, 22 March 1924, p. 425

THE W·H·HUDSON BIRD SANCTUARY · HYDE PARK

finally succeeded in penetrating the sacred forest and first espies Rima [117]

reclining on the moss among the ferns and herbage, near the roots of a small tree. One arm was doubled behind her neck . . . the other . . . held extended before her, the hand raised towards a small brown bird . . . She appeared to be playing with the bird, possibly amusing herself by trying to entice it on to her hand [118]; and the hand appeared to tempt it greatly, for it persistently hopped up and down, turning rapidly about this way and that, flirting its wings and tail [119] . . . I could make out that she was small . . . in figure slim, with delicately shaped little hands and feet. Her feet were bare, and her only garment was a slight chemise-shaped dress reaching below her knees, of a whitish-grey colour, with a faint lustre as of a silky material [120] . . . I had not been watching her more than three seconds

before the bird, with a sharp, creaking little chirp, flew up and away in sudden alarm; at the same moment she turned and saw me through the light leafy screen. But although catching sight of me . . . suddenly, she did not exhibit alarm like the bird; only her eyes, wide open, with a surprised look in them, remained immovably fixed on my face [121].[23]

Epstein's concern with the formal aspect of Rima's face, represented by a number of single and group studies, was certainly linked to his passion for collecting African masks, of which he was to gather many fine examples. Several of these sketches, however, are rendered naturalistically [122] and the head, particularly in profile, bears a striking resemblance to Epstein's model, Dolores, his 'High Priestess of Beauty' [123]. She had appeared as a singer and dancer at Madame Frida Strindberg's Cabaret Theatre Club (also known as The Cave of the

118
STUDY FOR THE RIMA RELIEF   1923
Pencil   58.7 × 45.1
Leeds City Art Galleries (HMCSS)

119
STUDY FOR THE RIMA RELIEF   1923
Pencil and watercolour   58.7 × 45.1
Leeds City Art Galleries (HMCSS)

120
STUDY FOR THE RIMA RELIEF   1923
Pencil   58.7 × 45.1
Leeds City Art Galleries (HMCSS)

Golden Calf) in Heddon Street, Piccadilly, which Epstein had decorated in 1912 with elaborately carved, brilliantly coloured plaster columns (destroyed in 1914).[24] During 1922–23 Dolores sat for four portraits; the sculptor described the third as 'tragic and magnificent' and it was, therefore, ideally suited as a model for Rima.[25] In November 1925, at the height of the public furore over the *Memorial*, Dolores and Anita (another Epstein model) were arrested for throwing tomatoes at a caricature of Rima mounted on the stage of The Aldwych Theatre.[26]

A number of the Leeds drawings are devoted to resolving the relationship between Rima and her bird companions (a theme which had long interested Epstein [9]), ranging from rigidly symmetrical, hieratic compositions [124*] to vigorously primitive ones [125], where the treatment of the human body recalls great sculptures in the British Museum, such as the crouching *Hawaiian Deity* [Fig. 83] which, perhaps not coincidentally, Henry Moore had noted and sketched around 1923.[27]

Epstein concentrated on the climactic episode of the novel, when the superstitious natives guarding the sacred forest turn against Rima and burn her alive in a tree:

> the flames went up higher and higher with a great noise; and at last from the top of the tree, out of the green leaves, came a great cry, like the cry of a bird, 'Abel! Abel!' and then looking we saw something fall; through leaves and smoke and flame it fell like a great white bird killed with an arrow and falling to the earth, and fell into the flames beneath'[28]

The seven studies on the penultimate sheet [126], which come close to the finished sculpture [Fig. 80] appear to be Rima's apotheosis.

The final design was approved by the Office of Works in February 1924 and the Committee promptly launched a further public appeal to raise the £2,000 needed to execute the project.[29] A Portland stone block was ordered in May (costing £282 10s) and two months later Epstein constructed a felt-lined shed at Epping. In September 1924

121 ◁◁
STUDY FOR THE RIMA RELIEF   1923
Pencil and watercolour   58.7 × 45.1
Leeds City Art Galleries (HMCSS)

122 ◁
STUDY FOR THE RIMA RELIEF   1923
Pencil   58.7 × 45.1
Leeds City Art Galleries (HMCSS)

123
DOLORES (third portrait: with crossed arms)   1923   (S134)
Bronze   H 55.9
Private collection

125
STUDY FOR THE RIMA RELIEF   1923
Pencil and watercolour   58.7 × 45.1
Leeds City Art Galleries (HMCSS)

Fig 83
DEITY, Hawaiian
Wood, shell, teeth, hair tufts   L 67
The Trustees of the British Museum

Cunninghame Graham reported that he was 'starting work with great enthusiasm'.[30] Epstein, in a Whitmanian mood, recalled working for seven months 'through the winter, solitary, surrounded by silent and often fog-laden forest'.[31] The carving was finished by the end of April 1925 and unveiled the following month.

Unlike Epstein's previous controversial work, the *Hudson Memorial* was condemned on a variety of charges by the public, the press and some Members of Parliament. *Rima* was 'hideous, unnatural, un-English, and essentially unhealthy' (*The Morning Post*, 24 November 1925); 'Sheer Bolshevism' (*The Daily News*, 25 May). Some criticism was directed to specific misdemeanors: the old chestnut of 'violating the canons of academic draughtsmanship' in favour of an abstract interpretation of beauty[32] which was 'A Travesty of Nature' (*The Daily Mail*, 21 May); a crude, ugly, primitive thing 'carved even less artlessly than [the] aborigines in Sarawak their

hornbills'.[33] Particular attention was directed to the 'deformed female figure with elephantiasis of the hands', 'soup-plate hands' (*The Times*, 26 and 25 May), a 'goddess wearing boxing gloves' (*The Daily News*, 25 May). A strong element of anti-semitism was also present: 'It is significant that nearly all the support for violence rather than beauty . . . should come from Socialists, foreigners, and Jews . . . Epstein's name proclaims his nationality' (*The Morning Post*, 28 December 1925) and later, in 1935, the Independent Fascist League defiled the relief with Swastikas and graffiti: 'God Save Our King and Britain from the Cancer of Judah'.[34] Epstein had many supporters — Muirhead Bone's letter to *The Times* (23 September 1925) was signed by fifty-one prominent people from all walks of life, including Arnold Bennett, Frank Dobson, Ramsay McDonald, Sir Michael Sadler and George Bernard Shaw, and another letter signed by 255 students of the Royal College of Art and the Slade was also widely publicised. Nevertheless, it

126
STUDY FOR THE RIMA RELIEF   1923
Pencil   58.7 × 45.1
Leeds City Art Galleries (HMCSS)

METROPOLITAN DISTRICT RAILWAY · NEW OFFICE BUILDING · BROADWAY · WESTMINSTER · ADAMS HOLDEN & PEARSON ARCHITECTS

127

Charles Holden (1875–1960)
PERSPECTIVE DRAWING FOR THE LONDON
UNDERGROUND ELECTRIC RAILWAYS
HEADQUARTERS 1928
Pencil and wash   47 × 43.5
British Architectural Library, Royal Institute
of British Architects, London

Fig 84

DAY and NIGHT   London Underground Electric
Railways Headquarters, Westminster, 1928   (S189)
From W. Aumonier, *Modern Architectural Sculpture*,
1930, p. 126

was suggested that *Rima* be camouflaged with plantings or even with reinforced concrete, and there was widespread clamour for its expulsion from the site altogether: 'The Hyde Park Atrocity | Nightmare in Stone | Public Demand for its Removal' (*The Daily Mail*, 20 May).

3. DAY AND NIGHT, 1928–29

The *Hudson Memorial* remained newsworthy for several years as a byword for the most despicable aspects of modernist sculpture. When Epstein's colossal figure groups of *Day* and *Night* [Fig. 84] were unveiled in 1929, *The Morning Post* (13 April) referred to them as the 'monstrous Rima in one of its recurrent epileptic fits'.[35] The artistic, if not critical, success of the *Memorial*, and the earlier figures on the British Medical Association Building and the *Oscar Wilde Tomb*, all set within architectural setting designed by the firm of Adams, Holden and Pearson, encouraged Charles Holden again to entrust Epstein, early in 1928, with the sculpture for his new office block for the London Underground Electric Railways (now London Transport) at 55 Broadway, Westminster.

Holden's severely unadorned, modernist, cruciform tower of Portland stone, rising 174 ft above the St James's Underground station, was the most progressive attempt of the decade to experiment with the alliance of architecture and sculpture [127].[36] The upper walls of the building are embellished with reliefs of the four winds, images perhaps suggested by the flying figure on the *Wilde Tomb* [Fig. 46],[37] which were carved by what *The Times* (5 April 1929) identified as the 'full range of contemporary young talent': Eric Aumonier, A. H. Gerrard, Eric Gill, Henry Moore, Frank Rabinovitch (the painter, Sam Rabin) and Allan Wyon.[38] Epstein's *Day* and *Night* occupy more prominent positions, sixteen feet above the pavement, directly over the two main entrances.

Although the building design, begun in 1926, was finalised before either the sculptors or the positions for the groups and reliefs were selected, Epstein conceived his carvings as integral with the architecture. He told Haskell in 1931: 'My groups . . . are not meant to be seen apart from the whole mass of the building [yet] However much [they] are part of the building, they have their own separate existence as carvings'.[39] The

conditions of Holden's brief were unusual in that the figures were to be 'carved direct in the stone without the use of mechanical means of reproduction' in order to 'preserve all the virility and adventure brought into play with every cut of the chisel, even at the expense of some degree of accuracy of form'.[40] He told *The Christian Science Monitor* (15 July 1929) that this method retained the 'imaginative conception and growth and development of the sculptor's ideas fresh from his own hands' so that the finished carvings formed an integral part of the building rather than irrelevant excrescence. This unconventional approach, which naturally appealed greatly to Epstein, is reflected in his preparatory drawings and the Portland stone carvings themselves.

Day was begun first, while the building was still an unclad steel skeleton, and carved *in situ* on the south-east elevation, facing the morning sun. Epstein explored several different ideas. An early sheet of sketches [128] shows a seated figure holding a model of the building; to the right another, more blatantly female figure is clothed in flowing drapery flanked by foliated branches, emphasising the notion of budding life inherent in the concept of *Day* (or *Morning*, as the group was also referred to at the time).[41] Another sheet [129] has a standing nude woman, her arms embracing a child. She recalls the Leeds *Maternity* [37] and her mesmeric features were perhaps inspired by African masks in Epstein's collection. In a further study [130], the figure is again seated, with the child standing within the enclave of her legs, arms uplifted, a composition which Epstein had used to powerful effect in the life-size bronze *Mother and Child* of 1926–27 [Fig. 74].[42] In the final sculpture [Fig. 84], which he conceived as 'a kind of cult-image' and described as a figure of 'the father in nature [with a] man-child',[43] the masculine connotations are strong, like Michelangelo's figure of *Day* on the Medici tomb. However, the composition, regarded at the time by both James Bone and L. B. Powell as one of Epstein's most inventive,[44] avoids the European tradition. The simplified, rigidly upright pairs of legs, echoing the vertical emphasis of the architecture of the doorway directly below, returns to the *Birth* relief in flenite of 1913 [57] and perhaps ultimately to Brancusi's *The Kiss* in Montparnasse Cemetery [Fig. 8].[45]

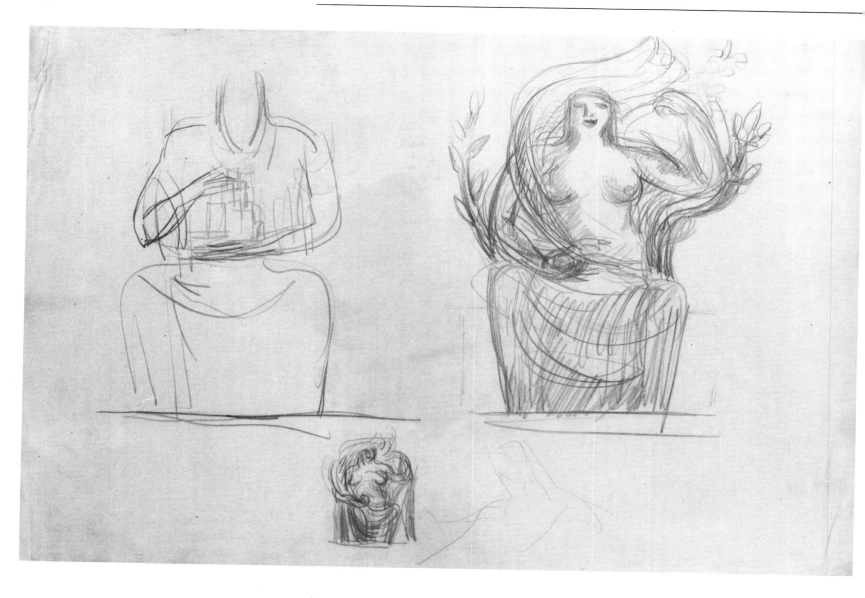

128 △
THREE STUDIES FOR DAY   1928
Pencil   58.1 × 44.5
Leeds City Art Galleries (HMCSS)

129 ▷▷
TWO STUDIES FOR DAY   1928
Pencil   37.8 × 55.8
Leeds City Art Galleries (HMCSS)

130 ▷
STUDY FOR DAY   1928–29
Pencil   45.8 × 55.6
Birmingham Museums and Art Gallery

131
MAQUETTE FOR NIGHT   1928   (S188)
Bronze   H 35.5
Dr and Mrs Jeffrey Sherwin

132
STUDY FOR NIGHT   1928–29
Pencil   43 × 56
Beth Lipkin

Night [Fig. 84] underwent a more subtle transformation in terms of both composition and carving. Its origin is a plaster maquette, later cast in bronze with a dark brown patina [131], for a *Pietà* group Epstein was working on around 1928.[46] This may have been the 'small model' Holden showed Frank Pick, the Underground Railways's Publicity Manager, during a preliminary visit to the studio in an attempt to reverse Pick's decision not to employ Epstein on the scheme. Epstein did not want to portray a 'pretty lady with a sad face all dressed in flowing black drapery', and stressed that the 'touch of the inhuman' in the main figure was necessary since the subject 'must inspire awe'.[47] One commentator aptly described the effect as that of an 'elementary conception of might, ponderable and remote, making strange calls to our consciousness'.[48] While the basic composition of the *Pietà* was retained, there is no longer a suggestion of lamentation. The image has become more mysterious. In the preliminary sketches [132–33] two embracing figures lie asleep in the mourner's lap. The composition of the finished sculpture [Fig. 84] is tightened-up, the limbs treated with what one critic described as a 'hard square expressiveness',[49] particularly the mother-figure's mighty arm hovering in benediction over the now single figure 'exhausted and asleep under her protection'.[50] Some critics complained that her stony, mask-like features were Mongolian, but Epstein insisted that he had 'no particular race . . . in mind'.[51] The drapery is treated as a series of dramatically rhythmic incisions of 'beautiful fulness',[52] reminding Wilenski of the surface of Chinese bronzes.[53] Because the group was sited on the north-west face of the building, which catches no sun and, therefore, produces no harsh shadows, the carving is sharper and deeper than on *Day*.[54]

The two groups were executed under unusual circumstances. Since the carving had to be done *in situ*, a shed was erected to enclose the work area from the inquisitive eyes of the public and press [Fig. 85] — Holden wisely withheld the sculptor's identity because 'Dark forces might upset things', and Epstein recalled 'I had to be smuggled in'.[55] *Night*, which was the second of the groups to be started, was completed first — the scaffolding was removed on 24 May 1929; then Epstein returned to complete *Day*, which was unveiled on 1 July.[56]

Both groups attracted the usual vituperative comments. Reginal Blomfield wrote in *The Manchester Guardian* of 'The Cult of Ugliness',[57] while *the Daily Express* proclaimed *Night* a 'prehistoric, blood-sodden cannibal intoning a horrid ritual over a dead victim'.[58] But there was also some enthusiastic support from Augustus John, William Orpen, Frank Rutter, Bernard Shaw and H. G. Wells. Wilenski, writing in *The Evening Standard* (1 July 1929), regarded them as the 'best things that Epstein has yet done' and Charles Aitken, Director of The Tate, as 'a great achievement', while Edgar Wallace observed that if *Day* and *Night* were 'dug up by some archaeologist they would immediately he hailed as masterpieces'.[59] Nevertheless, Epstein received no further public commission until 1949.[60]

133
STUDY FOR NIGHT   1928–29
Pencil   38.2 × 56
Birmingham Museums and Art Gallery

Fig 85 ▷
Epstein carving NIGHT, 1928–29   (S189)

Isolation and Defiance

Evelyn Silber and Terry Friedman

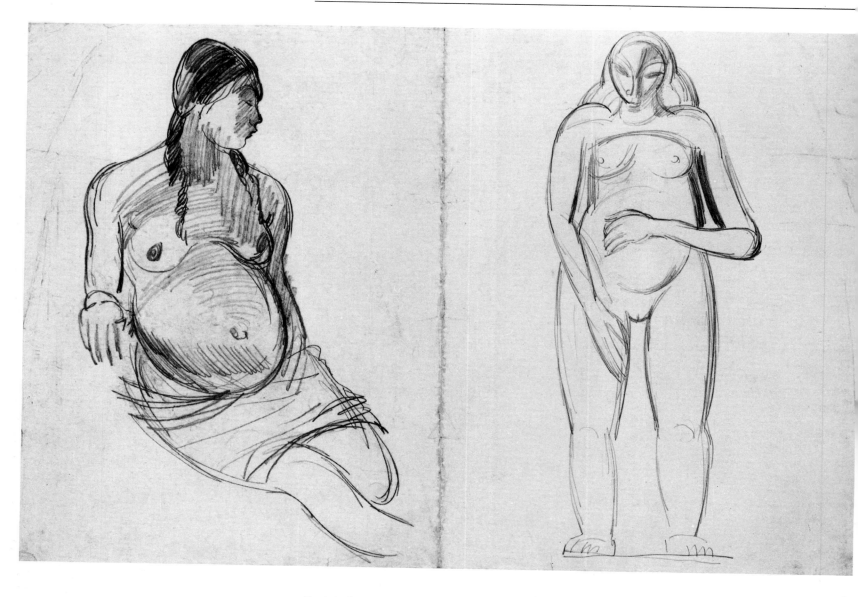

Epstein began carving the five-foot high, three-ton, white Seravezza marble *Genesis* [134*] later in 1929, at Deerhurst on the edge of Epping Forest, not far from where, a few years earlier, he had worked on *Rima* [Fig. 80], which this figure somewhat resembles. He completed it in 1930 in the more elegant surroundings of the former ballroom of the new family residence at 18 Hyde Park Gate in Knightsbridge. It was unveiled at the Leicester Galleries in the following year. He later provided a memorable recollection of his conception of the figure, which shared with the life-size stone *Maternity* of 1910 [37] and *Visitation* of 1926 a

necessity for giving expression to the profoundly elemental in motherhood, the deep down instinctive female, without the trappings and charm of what is known as feminine; *my feminine would be the eternal primeval feminine*, the mother of the race. The figure from the base upward, beginning just under the knees, seems to rise from the earth itself. From that the broad thighs and buttocks ascend, base solid and permanent for her who is to be the bearer of man. She feels within herself the child moving, her hand instinctively and soothingly placed where it can feel this enclosed new life so closely bound with herself. The expression of the head is one of calm, mindless wonder.

This boulder, massive yet delicate, with transparent shadows of the light marble goes deep, deep down in human half-animal consciousness. The forms are realistic, the treatment grave. There is a luminous aura about it as if it partook of light and air. Complete in herself, now that there is that consummated within her, for which she was created. She is serene and majestic, an elemental force of nature. How a figure like this contrasts with our coquetries and fanciful erotic nudes of modern sculpture. At one blow, whole generations of sculptors and sculpture are shattered and sent flying into the limbo of triviality, and my 'Genesis', with her fruitful womb, confronts our enfeebled generation. Within her man takes on new hope for the future.[1]

Epstein was reacting to the tradition in both ancient and modern art that pregnancy could only be depicted with the 'delicacy and reverence proper to the theme'. *Genesis* was found wanting in that 'finesse . . . elegance [and] lyrical quality invariably present in a first-rate creation'[2] (that is, something like Frank Dobson's *Cornucopia*, 1925–27, hailed by the critics as a masterpiece).[3] This was utterly to misinterpret Epstein's intention. *Genesis* is no more a conventional evocation

of motherhood than is the many-breasted, antique cult statue of *Diana of Ephesus*.[4] The better
equipped critics noted the combination of naturalistic and abstract traits in *Genesis* [135], that
above all it was to be understood as an intensely
imaginative and symbolic work rather than an
academically accurate rendering of a female nude,
and they compared it to Rodin's monumental
figure of *Balzac*, which was more than a mere
portrait of the great writer. *Genesis*, therefore, was
neither conventionally realistic nor wholly abstract.[5] This explains Epstein's interpretation of
the figure and the manner of its carving.

He told Arnold Haskell in 1931 that he intended
expressing 'the feeling of "In the Beginning," the
commencement of things'.[6] A preliminary sheet
of sketches [136] reveals how a life drawing of a
heavy-breasted, pregnant Indian model was
transformed into a more formal, abstract standing
figure. The treatment of the head shows the influence of Picasso, whose progress in the Twenties
towards a monumental femaleness in his art was
not unappreciated by some British sculptors.
During 1922–24 Henry Moore sketched a standing
nude which he annotated 'Picasso', and on the
same sheet is a similar but partial-figure 'cut off
below the knees'.[7] In the finished sculpture by
Epstein, the massive Mother of Mankind is similarly rooted to the earth by a pair of huge columnar thighs, like tree-trunks, as a means of expressing her enduring generative role. This approach
again links the figure to Moore's mother and child
groups of the Twenties and early Thirties, an
example of which Epstein acquired in 1931
[Fig. 16]. Sander Pierron, in his sympathetic
review of *Genesis* published in *Neptune* in 1931,
rightly observed that in this

> awesome image . . . the disproportions . . . are
> justified because they are called for by the
> imperious necessity of the symbol striven after
> . . . the disproportions and deformities are the
> essential qualities, since it is they that express
> the supreme idea to which Epstein has been
> obedient . . . Everything about this figure, so
> full of clarity and mystery, is expressive.[8]

Not surprisingly, Epstein turned, as he had done
in his earlier carvings on the same theme —
Maternity [37], the two flenite figures [50* and Fig.
69] and the *Venuses* [Figs 67–68] — to sources in
primitive sculpture. However, these were not, as
the critic of *The Daily Telegraph* unflatteringly suggested, 'a face like an ape's . . . breasts like pump-
kins . . . hands twice as large and gross as those of
a navvy [and] hair like a ship's hawser'.[9] By
1929–30 Epstein owned several hundred African,
Oceanic, Oriental and ancient American sculptures, perhaps already among them the *Seated
woman with child* from Nigeria [XIV], in which the
lower limbs are cropped and the pose is similiarly
assertive.[10] The bust of a black model named *Lydia*
[137], a cast of which was displayed near *Genesis*
in the 1931 Leicester Galleries exhibition, seems to
have served as a springboard from which the
naturalistic elements, as well as a sense of passive
expectation, were transformed into a simplified
and universal image under the influence of African masks, of which Epstein owned a number of
fine examples.[11]

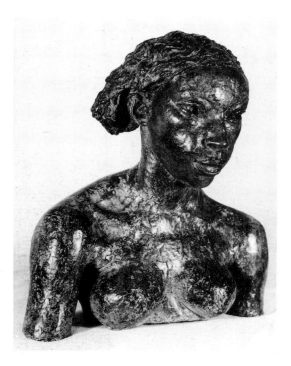

137

LYDIA (first portrait) 1929–30 (S193)
Bronze H 52
Marcus Wickham-Boynton

XIV

SEATED WOMAN WITH CHILD, Idoma, Nigeria
Wood H 64.8
The Trustees of the British Museum (formerly Jacob
Epstein collection)

Genesis assumed almost mystical properties, for
Haskell recalled seeing it in the studio one evening as it grew dark and the white marble figure
'seemed to hold all the light, casting everything in
the shade. It was living and gigantic'.[12] Although
L. B. Powell, in his 1932 biography of the sculptor,
proclaimed the carving a masterpiece and
devoted two chapters to extolling its virtues,[13]
and Geoffrey Grigson ended his review (*The Yorkshire Post*, 27 July 1932) of R. H. Wilenski's *The
Meaning of Modern Sculpture*, published in the
same year, by warning those who criticised the
figure to 'check their tongues from vulgarity or
nonsense', it was not appreciated by some of
Epstein's other *avant garde* colleagues[14] and, of
course, the press had its usual field day.
'COARSE AND REPELLENT', 'EPSTEIN'S
BAD JOKE IN STONE | MONGOLIAN
MORON THAT IS OBSCENE' (*The Daily Telegraph* and *The Daily Express*, 7 February 1931).[15]
Indeed, *Genesis* suffered an ignominious fate.
Alfred Bossom, MP, purchased it from the Leicester Galleries and arranged a provincial tour to
raise funds for charity. When the sculpture was

offered to Manchester, concern was expressed
that it would result in a 'besmirching of various
fair names',[16] while in Liverpool, The Sandor
Studio Society, wishing to show it at The
Bluecoat, was warned against expecting to clear
expenses; in the event, the month-long exhibition
attracted 49,687 amazed visitors and £1,000 was
raised for the building fund.[17] Paul Fierens illustrated it in his important anthology *Sculpteurs
D'Aujourd'hui*, 1933, where he associated it with
Lady Chatterley's Lover, implying that Lawrence's
readers, who prided themselves on being
advanced, were akin to those who dared to
admire the frankness of *Genesis*.[18]

Epstein plunged deeper into his defiance of
academic complacency and the art establishment
by embarking on a series of sensational figure
carvings, cousins of those radical sculptures of his
youth but bolder and more aggressive in concept
and often bigger in scale: the Thirties, after
all, was the decade of the carving of Mount
Rushmore, the Empire State Building, Warner
Brothers' *Gold Diggers of 1933* ('The Biggest Show
on Earth') and *King Kong*! Almost yearly from
1931 to the outbreak of the War a major carving
was put on show: *Chimera*, *Primeval Gods* [Fig. 86]
and *Woman Possessed* [140*] in 1933, *Behold the
Man* (*Ecce Homo*) [Fig. 6] in 1935, *Consummatum Est*
[Fig. 9] in 1937 and *Adam* [Fig. 88] in 1939 (of this
series, only the 1932 *Elemental* [138*] was not
exhibited). All were personal commitments, none
were commissions. Epstein was out to show that
he could still be as daring and controversial as
ever. The actor, Emlyn Williams, who sat for his
portrait bust in 1932 [149], described Epstein's
studio as

> crammed with sculpture. Mixed up with heaps
> of wood, piles of clay, stacks of old newspapers
> and the dust of years [was] every sort of head
> and limb at every height and angle, from the
> ruthless stares of statesmen to the writhing
> thighs of agonized Titians and the swollen
> hungry lips of giantesses with corrugated
> wings of hair caught in mid stream and in
> between the wings, fierce caverns for eyes. It
> was hard to reconcile the gentle caretaker figure
> with the welter of frozen power around him.[19]

Elemental [138*–39], with the chisel and file
marks still plain to see on its unpolished,
veined-alabaster surface, is the foetus which the
year before had been gestating in the pregnant
womb of *Genesis*. Evelyn Silber has written that it
contains

> a multiplicity of possible meanings; by adapt-
> ing the foetal posture, which Epstein believed,
> erroneously, to be a Gabon burial posture, he
> created an ambiguous tension expressive of the
> latent dynamism of unborn life, or of the frozen
> tension of terror, or of the impersonal grip of
> death.[20]

Its compact, ovoid shape had interested the
sculptor as early as 1910 [35*].

In contrast, the contemporary *Woman Possessed*
[140*] is recumbent and expansive, a form
unusual in Epstein's *oeuvre* (although not unique,
since it anticipates *Consummatum Est*, 1936) and
closer in spirit to Moore's reclining figures of

1929–32 [Fig. 18]. Yet, whereas those figures are quiescent, Epstein's female unfurls in orgasmic ecstacy. It has been suggested that he was inspired by the sacrificial scene of Massine's recent Covent Garden production of Stravinsky's *The Rite of Spring*.[21] Two drawings, which can probably be dated to this period, are linked to the ballet [Fig. 87].[22]

Direct carving on a monumental scale assumed a special poignancy for Epstein in 1937 as he witnessed the mutilation of his early architectonic masterpiece, the group of eighteen Portland stone figures on the British Medical Association Building of 1907–08 [Fig. 41]. In 1935 the premises had passed into the ownership of the Southern Rhodesian Government, which immediately announced its intention to remove the sculptures because of their inappropriate subject matter. Epstein told *The Observer* that this would be 'a victory of the Philistines from the outposts of the Empire'. The debate continued on and off for two years, with many distinguished artists and museum curators vociferous on both sides. Epstein was particularly irked by a letter to *The Daily Telegraph* in which the architect, Sir Edwin Lutyens, suggested that the statues' loss was not so serious since their creator was still alive, in the 'full vigour of work and imagination' and possessing the knowledge that he can 'yet achieve better than he did years ago'.[23] Two years later, Epstein offered the defiant and uncompromisingly barbaric statue of *Adam* [Fig. 88].

He had, in fact, been working towards this image for some time. The upturned head and clenched fists come from *Elemental* and *Woman Possessed*, perhaps by way of Moore's monumental, untitled and unfinished carving of *c* 1925–27 which, in the early Thirties, seems to have belonged to the sculptor, Gertrude Hermes [Fig. 20].[24] Then, in 1934–35, as nations slid further into the abyss, Epstein carved the eleven foot high Subiaco marble *Behold the Man (Ecce Homo)*, now at Coventry Cathedral [Fig. 6], as a 'symbol of man, bound, crowned with thorns and facing with a relentless and over-mastering gaze of pity and prescience our unhappy world'.[25] Although a few critics understood Epstein's aims — Anthony Blunt writing in *The Spectator*, T. W. Earp in *The Daily Telegraph*, James Bone in *The Manchester Guardian* ('the sense of crushing agony bearing upon the squat enduring figure', a 'stark, enigmatic [figure having a] kinship with the rock carvings at Easter Island') — conservative sensibility was outraged by 'one of the greatest insults to religion' (G. K. Chesterton in *The Daily Mirror*), this 'grotesque' (a Salvation Army official), with the 'debased, sensuous, flat features of an Asiatic monstrosity' (*The Catholic Times*). The 'charges of blasphemy' reminded the sculptor of 'the days of witchcraft and the *auto-da-fé*'.[26]

By this time the myth of Epstein as the ageing, radical maker of disgusting travesties was firmly entrenched in the popular consciousness. His name had become a household word. In 1935, the brother of the writer, Vera Brittain, unkindly described to her the body of their recently deceased father as 'tremendously swollen, like an Epstein figure'[27] and the crime writer, Ngaio Marsh, in *Death in Ecstasy*, 1936, characterised the

robust, helmeted and booted figures of Nordic gods and goddesses in the House of the Sacred Flame as looking as 'though they had been begun by Epstein and finished by a frantic bricklayer'.

Then, in 1939, came the biggest shock of all: the seven foot high, three ton, Derbyshire alabaster figure of *Adam* [Fig. 88]. Blunt's 1935 article in *The Spectator* dealing with *Ecce Homo*, recognised that the sculptor's aim was to revitalise European religious art by creating a twentieth-century imagery which was modern in style yet had the power to kindle orthodox emotions, an aim he achieved, Blunt suggested, by an 'infusion of dark blood, itself not pure but drawn from the African, the Aztec and many other races'.[28] This application of savage principles to a Christian theme was, of course, precisely what disturbed and shocked the public about the Thirties carvings. (Among major British artists of the time perhaps only the painter, Stanley Spencer was treading a comparably unorthodox path.) Towards the end of the decade, as the political situation in Europe worsened, Epstein's attitude towards these sculptures grew more sombre. Like Moore, he aligned himself

139
ELEMENTAL 1932 (S225, detail)
Alabaster H 81
Private collection

141
WOMAN POSSESSED   1932   (S226)
Hoptonwood stone   L 101.6
Austrialian National Gallery, Canberra

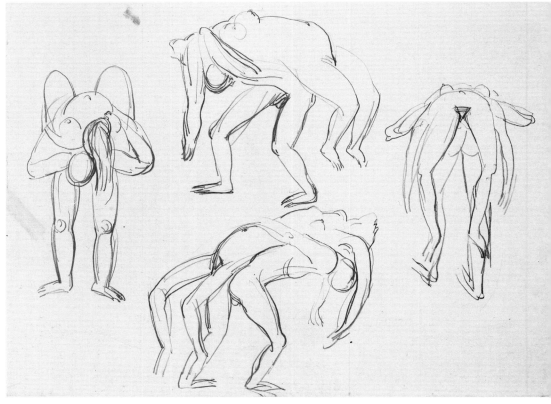

Fig 87
FOUR STUDIES FOR LE SACRE DU PRINTEMPS
Pencil   76.2 × 51
Birmingham Museums and Art Gallery

Fig 88
ADAM (S288), 1938–39, albaster, H 218.5, on
exhibition at the Leicester Galleries, London, 7 June
1939 (now collection Lord Harewood, Harewood
House, Yorkshire)

144
ADAM AND EVE   1938   (*S292*)
Bronze   H 11.4
Watford Museum

145
BURIAL OF ABEL   1938   (*S291*)
Bronze   H 17.8
Watford Museum

with the anti-fascist cause and wrote of imagining a waste world [in which] argosies from the air have bombed the humans out of existence, and perished themselves, so that no human thing is left alive'.[29] Biblical subjects, particularly those drawn from the *Old Testament*, were now interpreted with a feeling of great emotional conflict, reaching its climax in the titanic struggle between *Jacob and the Angel* [143*].

Two preliminary studies for this over-life-size alabaster group [142] reveal how, by dramatic pictorial means — swift, frantic strokes of the crayon unrelated either to the formal or the technical problems of carving a large block of stone — he laboured to impart the story of his biblical namesake: 'And Jacob was left alone; and there wrestled a man with him until the breaking of the day' (Genesis 32:24). In the finished sculpture, the spiritual and carnal wrestling match is depicted as a highly-charged embrace of unprecedented power, made more intense by the reddish-brown

veins shooting through the alabaster. Although Epstein left no explanation of the work, a late biographer, Richard Buckle, has written:

> When God came to Jacob as he meditated, prayed or slept . . . he came to change his life . . . and He decided to make the revelation or conversion a terrible, wonderful and unforgettable experience . . . The struggle, which was of course a struggle in Jacob's mind, culminated in a sudden blinding vision of God and a momentary understanding of the whole purpose and order of creation; and this the sculptor has represented by showing Jacob at the pinnacle of sexual fulfilment.[30]

During the same period that he was working on *Adam* [Fig. 88], Epstein was also considering other sculptures based on the *Book of Genesis*. Unlike *Adam* or any of his earlier monumental works, these were to be narrative groups or tableaux rather than single symbolic figures and were to

142

TWO STUDIES FOR JACOB AND THE ANGEL
1939–40
Pencil   56 × 43
University of Liverpool: on permanent loan from Granada Television Ltd

146
STUDY FOR LUCIFER AND HIS ANGELS   c1943
Pencil and watercolour   57.8 × 44.1
Christopher Bunting

relate to the *Old Testament* watercolours he had been doing since about 1931 [101]. *Adam and Eve* [144] was a favourite theme, three watercolours, whose appearance is unknown, having been included in the Redfern Gallery exhibition in 1932.[31] One project, preserved only in a preparatory drawing, was for a bas-relief showing the *Expulsion of Adam and Eve from Paradise*.[32]

Perhaps out of a desire to escape the banality of the actual scene of the Expulsion, Epstein chose the still more poignant moment of the *denouement* which followed the eating of the forbidden fruit, when Adam says to God: 'I heard thy voice in the garden, and I was afraid because I was naked; and I hid myself' (Genesis 3:10). Both *Adam and Eve* and its companion piece, *The Burial of Abel* [145] have an expressive poise and fluency which was often lacking in Epstein's monumental bronzes. The sculptor evokes a whole world of experience with extreme economy, condensing into a single flow of closed and open movement, flight, stillness, fear, isolation and questioning. Huddled together, the enclosed ovoid form of Eve, so close to *Elemental* [138*], is enveloped by that of Adam, whose outstretched leg and upraised hand create an arabesque of suspended flight. Echoing lines of arm and legs create a choreographic fall, yet both heads are sharply twisted back as if irresistably drawn towards the voice of God as it seeks them out.

The Burial of Abel is conceived as a tableau, cast with an integral plinth that fixes the relationship of the figures. The aged Adam, bearing before him the limply trailing corpse of his son, is a free interpretation into a plastic medium of the hieratic

figure of *Night* [Fig. 85], while Eve, bent in bitte grief, walks behind.

According to Lady Epstein, the sculptor ofte modelled ideas for sculptural groups rapidly i plasticine. These are the earliest such studies t have survived. They were cast and exhibitec together with other maquettes, nude studies ar portraits, at the Leicester Galleries in 1947.[33] The may have been made in the faint hope of receivin a commission to translate one into monument form, but their spontaneous brevity and intuitiv unity of form and feeling were no more transfe able to monumental scale than were Rodin's lat studies of dancers. The flow of movement in bot is expressed not by anatomical precision but by kinaesthetic impetus carried in the malleab material through the reflexive action of the sculp tor's fingertips.

During the latter part of the War, after th completion of *Jacob and the Angel* [143*], Epstei turned once again to modelling and bronze as vehicle for his monumental, abstract themes. Th drawing *Lucifer and his Angels* [146] and th maquette *Lucifer, Belial and Beelzebub* [147] wer preparatory studies for Epstein's only majc bronze sculpture on a poetic theme, *Lucife* [Fig. 89], from Milton's epic poem, *Paradise Los* Not for the first time, what began as a project for sculptural group, ended up as a singl over-life-size figure. The particular approac embodied by the maquette stems from th watercolour interpretation of *Old Testament* epi sodes which Epstein had produced during th Thirties. One drawing, dateable to about 193c depicted Shadrack, Meshack and Abednego a

nude figures fleeing from the fiery furnace. Though Epstein's hopes of turning this subject into a sculpture never materialised, the broad, frontal grouping with the central figure leading, recurs little changed in the maquette.

The preparatory drawing [146], showing the three figures half-length, already typifies two of the angels as wide-eyed, long-haired figures who at once recall the idealised bronze portrait of Sunita, done in 1930 and called *Israfel*, an alternative Hebraic title for the Archangel Raphael.[34] The short-haired, wingless Lucifer, however, seems closer to a self-portrait.

The figure of Rodin looms large behind this project. In contemporary terms a large, naturalistically modelled bronze of a literary subject appeared a belated Romantic gesture. It recalled Rodin's *Gates of Hell*, based on Dante's *Inferno*, and his *Monument to Balzac*. Epstein was a lifelong admirer of the Frenchman's work, calling him 'without dispute the greatest master of modern times', and recognising in the *Balzac* his masterpiece.[35] However, he was critical of the *Gates of Hell*:

Rodin did not possess a sense of the architectural, and that is why his Porte D'Enfer is such a failure architecturally. From even a little distance it has all the appearance of an ant-hill in commotion. Rodin concentrated on the individual groups and figures, and the Porte D'Enfer, to be appreciated, must be studied close to, when the tragic and splendid qualities of the groups reveal themselves.[36]

The maquette [147] has an architectural clarity of structure. That only a single, monumental figure finally resulted was probably due to the excessive demands on the sculptor's resources which modelling three such pieces on a large scale would have entailed. However, during this period, he was looking again at the dimunitive, writhing female nudes on the *Gates of Hell* and perhaps also at the larger nude bronze called *The Martyr*, 1884, which he reinterpreted in an extensive series of small reclining nude studies in bronze of Betty Peters, Marie Tracey and other women models [148], a type which developed from *Nan the Dreamer* [18] and the studies of *Dolores*, 1923, and *Sunita*, 1931.[37]

147
LUCIFER, BELIAL AND BEELZEBUB   1943   (S338)
Bronze   H 25.1
Private collection

Fig 89
LUCIFER 1944–45 (S362)
Bronze H 315
Birmingham Museums and Art Gallery

148
NUDE STUDY 1943–45 (S352)
Bronze L 63.5
Private collection

14 · 1932–1959

THE GREAT PORTRAITIST

Evelyn Silber and Terry Friedman

At Number 18, a large respectable house, the front door was opened by a coatless caretaker with sleeves rolled up who seemed to be engaged on some job in the shabby hall. He smiled and bowed. 'Please come in.' It was Epstein: a burly man with curly dark thinning hair, teeth ragged and discoloured, and a manner as diffident as his voice. I followed him down a couple of steps into a large high studio crammed with sculpture . . . He then took me gently by the elbow as if I were a breakable object and led me to a gnawed high stool in the middle of the studio. I climbed on to it and sat immobile, determined not to look at him. Straight in front of me, a criss-cross contraption had been knocked together from raw wood mixed with a shapeless grey mass pitted with holes: tiny snails of clay rolled and pressed together between finger and thumb. He did as he had said, he walked round me. I could not resist quick sidelong looks and saw the shy host give way to a cool detached professional with narrowed eyes. He proceeded in his continuous circle on feet suddenly light; abruptly he would stop, squint, then dip his knees to scrutinise a new plane of my face from another angle. He took up a palette filthy with the stains of old clay and slapped fresh stuff on to it which he rolled briskly into more snails and slapped on to the mess on the stand. 'Relax, please.' After studying my face with the cold absent stare of an adversary, he set to work with lightning dexterity; no sound but the rapid breathing which I was to hear for nine more mornings, alternating with the sharp unconscious grunts of creation. As the end approached, the hammer-gossamer hands took to hovering stealthily above the work, as if about to pounce and destroy it, while the eyes bored into my face and then into the clay, darting with increasing speed from one to the other. Then two fingers would slowly descend, stubby and yet feather-light and flick the clay with the last vital touches. They would press it a thousandth of a millimetre to left or right: a stroking which, if it had not been professional, would have been a caress. The rhythm of his movements — of the fanatical jerks of the head as he stared from me to the clay and back, of the airy touches — began to accelerate; the grunts grew sharper, the breathing more frantic, as if this were a sex ritual and an act of consummation were taking place. After the very last brush of a finger-tip coaxing a lost edge of clay-flesh

one hair's breadth into perfection, the hands rose slowly together from the work and turned back into the peasant hammers. Then came the long expulsion of breath, as final as the end of life. It was done. He broke a packet of cigarettes and gently, over the head he had created, draped a frayed dishcloth with a cigarette-burn on it. 'I think that's all,' he said.

In 1933, the young actor and playwright *Emlyn Williams* sat for a portrait [149] commissioned by Miss Cook, the schoolteacher who had fostered his talent.[1] The two men had never met and Williams approached the Hyde Park Gate studio with some trepidation. His account of a memorable ten days, which opens this section, accurately reflects the experience of other sitters, notably John Gielgud, who recalls: 'he had beautiful manners and spoke with an extraordinary half-American foreign accent'.[2] After finishing Williams's bust, Epstein did let drop what he regarded as one of his sitters's most interesting characteristics: 'I have always found that the face of every male sitter has one profile masculine and the other feminine. I've rarely seen it so marked as in this one.'[3] Even with goodwill on both sides, however, not all Epstein's portraits were so successful. Gielgud recalls,

> I sat to Epstein in 1932 or 33, when I was acting in Richard of Bordeaux in London. We got on very well, but I think he was less interested in me after seeing the play, which he thought sentimental and uninteresting. Also he had just received a commission to do a head of Einstein, who was living in Suffolk somewhere, and dashed off my bust, rather brutally spoiling the likeness I thought in the last four sittings . . . The most characteristic view was from the back — the set of the neck and shoulders.[4]

It is not clear from whom the commission for a head of *Albert Einstein* [150] came. The physicist had recently arrived in England and was being looked after at an army camp near Cromer, 'a secluded and wild spot very near the sea', where Epstein arrived for the sittings. The place may well have reminded him of his beloved Pett Level, where he had worked so well from 1913–15.

Einstein appeared dressed very comfortably in a pullover with his wild hair floating in the wind. His glance contained a mixture of the humane, the humorous, and the profound. This was a combination that delighted me. He resembled the ageing Rembrandt.[5]

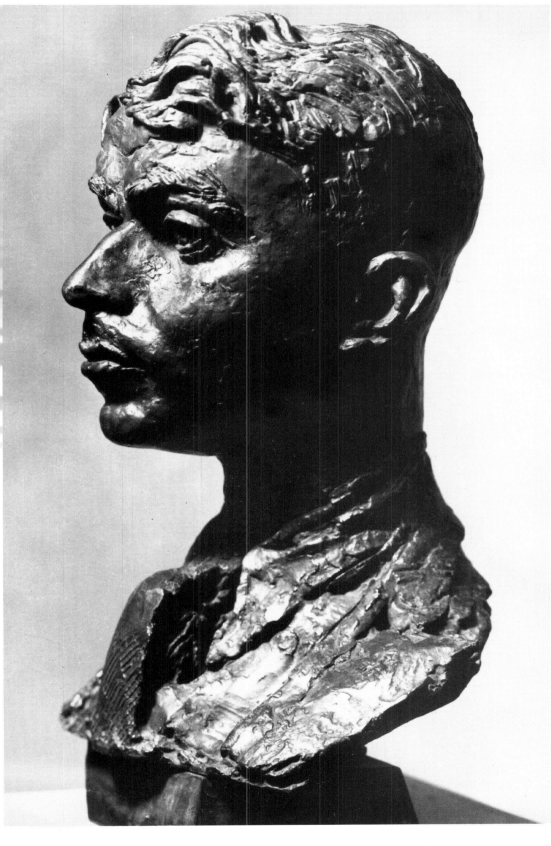

Despite the army camp atmosphere and the cramped conditions in which the sittings took place ('a small hut filled with a piano — I could hardly turn round'), the two men established an immediate rapport. In less than fourteen hours (two hours every morning for only a week), an extraordinarily direct and spontaneous portrait emerged. The sculptor himself felt that it was incomplete, and this is possibly why the back of the head is

prefunctorily handled, but its very breadth and dash lend it an air of Rembrandtesque impasto, especially as the light plays over the dark brown surface of the bronze.[6]

Yet another technique, more raucous, with staccato incisions enriching the brow and areas around the eyes, was applied to the head of *Ralph Vaughan Williams* [151]. On 9 February 1949, Epstein wrote to his daughter, Peggy Jean: 'I have

150 ▷
ALBERT EINSTEIN 1933 (*S*234)
Bronze H 45.3
The Syndics of the Fitzwilliam Museum, Cambridge

151 ▷▷
RALPH VAUGHAN WILLIAMS OM 1949 (*S*416)
Bronze H 38.4
Birmingham Museums and Art Gallery

begun a head of Dr Vaughan Williams the great composer. He is a *very* old man, 75, but he poses with a will and as he has a fine head I hope to make something of it.'[7] In fact, Epstein gives him the alert, vigorous look of a considerably younger man and suggests the decisive manner which he recalled at their sittings: 'Here was a master with whom no-one would venture to dispute. He reminded me in appearance of some eighteenth-century admiral whose word was law. Notwithstanding, he was the epitomy of courtesy and consideration. . . .' When the bust was complete, opinions within the composer's circle differed as to its accuracy, but Vaughan Williams merely remarked 'Well it's very strange, my boy, I can't see myself there, but I see my father and I see my grandfather there.'[8]

Even on those frequent occasions when undertaking commissioned portraits of less famous clients, Epstein's sympathetic rapport with the sitter and understanding of his or her character could produce a commanding image, as in the case of the bust of *George Black*, a Leeds ophthalmic surgeon [152]. Mr Black had already purchased a cast of the *Study for Resurrection*[9] at the Leicester Galleries in 1941 when, in the summer of the following year, he visited the sculptor's retrospective (sixty-seven bronzes and eighteen drawings) at Temple Newsam House. Epstein shared the Leeds exhibition with his old friend, the Yorkshire-born painter, Matthew Smith. A number of sensuously coloured oils once owned by the sculptor, such as *Lilies*, *c* 1913 [153], were included. It was organised by the Director, Philip Hendy, who wrote in the catalogue of Epstein's

'amazing faculty for catching a likeness' and of his increasing reliance on pictorial methods, which endowed his 'forms with the equivalent of colour by making the light and shade play with great intensity over skilfully broken surfaces'. Black contacted the sculptor and sat about twelve times over a three month period during the winter of 1942. Epstein suggested lifting the strong portrait head on a torso with arms in which he set aside the conventional suit with lapels in favour of the more austere surgeon's gown;[10] it is this feature, together with the deeply drilled eyes, which gives it a majestic authority.

It had been observed as early as 1931 that Epstein's forté lay in his ability to portray strong psychological and expressive character, the art critic of *The Times* (13 November) contrasting his portraits with those of Frank Dobson, 'the English Maillol'. The latter's celebrated bronze bust with arms of the actress *Margaret Rawlings*, 1936 [Fig. 91],[11] is as demure and classically non-committal as Epstein's portrait of *Isobel Nicholas* [154], an art student [Fig. 90] who was later to marry the composers, Constant Lambert and Alan Rawsthorne, is aggressively sexual, 'a picture of savage sophistication'.[12] Her slender waist and torpedo-like breasts exposed above a clinging shawl, recalls statuettes of Cretan goddesses. What gives the portrait its punch is the exaggerated contrast between the geometric solids of the head, arms and breasts and the amazing, flimsy, corkscrew earrings.

In 1931 Epstein spoke of seeing 'sculpture everywhere. People may bore me when they talk, but everyone interests me as a possible problem in

152
GEORGE BLACK   1942   (S323)
Bronze   H 62
George Black

153
Matthew Smith (1879–1959)
LILIES   *c* 1913
Oil on canvas   53.2 × 73.6
Leeds City Art Galleries (formerly Jacob Epstein collection)

Fig 91
Frank Dobson (1886–1963)
MARGARET RAWLINGS   1936
Bronze   H 57.8
Leeds City Art Galleries

154 ▷
ISOBEL NICHOLAS (second portrait)   1932   (S232)
Bronze   H 72.4 (another cast illustrated)
Ferens Art Gallery: Hull City Museums and Art Galleries

155 ▷▷
LYDIA (third portrait: laughing)   1933–34   (S245)
Bronze   H 35.5
Leeds City Art Galleries

156 △
POLA GIVENCHY   1937   (S278)
Bronze   H 53.3
Mr and Mrs Victor Sandelson

158
MARION (MARION ABRAHAMS)   1950   (S425)
Bronze   H 43.2
Private collection

159 ▷
KATHLEEN GARMAN (fifth portrait)   1935   (S262●
Bronze   H 75
City of Bristol Museum and Art Gallery

161
THEODORE (THEO) GARMAN   1930
Pencil   38 × 50.2
Walsall Museum and Art Gallery (Garman-Ryan
Collection)

sculpture', and he particularly mentioned the 'great beauty' he discovered in women other people may call ugly.[13] A fine example of this is the head of *Lydia* [155], a coloured girl he first modelled in 1929 [137], who is here caught in a mirthful, toothy grin which is hardly becoming yet communicates a spontaneous warmth which no other sculptor at the time was able to capture. The premeditated sexuality of *Isobel* [154] is transmuted in the portraits of the Polish model, *Pola Givenchy* [156] and the Russian *Girl from Baku* [157*], into a haughty self-containment, as they look down with half-closed eyes. They have a feline quality and the sultry beauty of the *Girl from*

Baku is enhanced by its lustrous, silvery patination.

Towards the end of Epstein's career, when he was overburdened with commissions ranging from portraits of the rich and famous to large architectural projects, he shied away from further commitments. The entertaining circumstances surrounding one of his outstanding late portraits, *Marion Abrahams* [158], which has only recently come to light, suggest that a bohemian spontaneity still lingered about the Epstein household in the Fifties. Dr Abrahams was convinced that only Epstein could no justice to his wife's unusual beauty and wrote asking if he would undertake a

portrait of her. He got no reply. Undeterred, they drove to London and, while Mrs Abrahams waited in the car, the good doctor knocked at 18 Hyde Park Gate. After some delay Epstein himself appeared on the doorstep; he was in the middle of shaving, his face still covered in soap, and apologetically remarked, 'I am very ill-served'. He could only decide whether to do the portrait if he could have a look at the sitter, so 'the first thing I saw', recalls Mrs Abrahams, 'was this soapy face at the car window!' They were promptly invited in and sittings were arranged. She was completely terrified at first and sat bolt upright in a chair in the studio. 'You are not in a

dentist's chair!' she was told and soon relaxed as they began to talk about 'everything under the sun'.[14] Epstein decided to include her earrings in the portrait and borrowed them to make a cast (this had been a frequent practice since early portraits like the *Bust of Nan* [24], from which such embellishment has sadly been lost, and the second portrait of *Isobel* [154]). Often Moyshe Oyved, who ran Cameo Corner near the British Museum, and who was an old friend and patron of Epstein's work [102], lent antique jewellery.

Epstein believed that the 'model who just sits and leaves the artist to his own thoughts is the most helpful one, not the model who imagines

160
PEGGY JEAN EPSTEIN (twelfth portrait: THE SICK CHILD) 1928 (S186)
Bronze H 36.2
Whitworth Art Gallery, University of Manchester

she is inspiring the artist'.[15] However, for thirty years no one was more important to him than Kathleen Garman, the daughter of a Midland doctor. They met in August 1921, when she was a twenty-year-old music student. They fell in love, set up house (although Jacob was still living happily with Margaret) and had three children — Theo [161], Kitty [162] and Esther [165]. They eventually married in June 1955, some years after the death of Mrs Epstein in 1947. The first portrait of Kathleen was begun the day after they met. Seven others followed: in 1922 (a bust which has 'the divine fire [and] dominates by emotional intensity and terrific vitality', according to *The Liverpool Echo* (19 September 1930), 1931, 1932, 1935, 1941, 1943 (the lyrical, full-length figure carrying gardenias) and 1948.[16] Epstein's account of working on the fifth portrait of *Kathleen* in 1935 [159] makes it clear that both formal analysis and a degree of emotional commitment were essential to achieve the 'strange metamorphosis, incarnation and consummation'.[17] According to Richard Buckle, who knew Lady Epstein well, this was the 'Portrait of a Lady' whose creation is described in detail in *Let There Be Sculpture*, 1940.[18] There the artist tried to convey to the public, who all too readily dismisses portraiture as somehow easier than other forms of sculpture, 'an impression of how the sculptor works, the state of mind, and the moods by which successive stages are reached'.

To the exclusion of all else his vision is concentrated on the model . . . His searching and loving eye roams over the soft contours of the face and is caught by the edges of the brow enclosing the eyes, and so to the cheek-bones, and then downwards past the mouth and nose. The mask is lightly fixed and the salient points established. This mask is arrested by the twin points of the ears. Behind the mass of hair from above, the brow and falling to the shoulders is then indicated, by broad and sketchy additions of clay, without particular definition, merely a note to be taken up later. Return to the mask, the expression of the eyes, and the shape and droop of the upper eyelid, the exact curve of the under-lid is drawn . . . [with] hair-breath exactness. The nostrils are defined, and for this a surgeon's sharp eye [is] necessary; a trembling sensitiveness, for the nostrils breathe; and from thence to the contours of the lips and the partition of the lips. Then the contours of the cheeks, the faintest indication of cheek-bones, and the oval of the head never exactly symmetrical . . . and when so much is achieved — a halt . . . The movement of the head is finally resolved on, and by ceaseless turnings of the stand, the planes are modelled and related. The subtle connections between plane and plane knit the form together. The forms catch the light, emphasis is placed, now here, now there . . . Now the shoulders are formed, they are related to the cheeks, the back is studied, the arms and hands come into being, the hands flutter from the wrists, like flames, a trembling eagerness of life pulsates throughout the work . . . a quartet of harmonies . . . Head, shoulders, body, and hands, like music.[19]

162
KITTY GARMAN   1937
Pencil   43.2 × 55.3
Walsall Museum and Art Gallery (Garman-Ryan Collection)

163
JACKIE EPSTEIN (third portrait: RAGAMUFFIN) 1939 (S309)
Bronze H 22.8
Private collection

This portrait, more than any other, sums up what Kathleen the Muse meant to the sculptor — femininity, intelligence, responsiveness, physical grace and a certain visionary quality. Unlike many of his younger *avant garde* contemporaries, who were wedded to 'primitive' cultures, Epstein never abandoned the more pictorial and dramatic subtleties of the main European tradition.[20] Fifteenth-century Italian sculpture had been a frequent source, especially for his early female portraits, and he again turned to this period for inspiration in his drawn and sculpted studies of children.

He felt that, apart from the fifteenth-century Florentines ('Donatello's mad incarnations of robust vitality, to graceful Verrocchio's, to the waywardness of a Desiderio da Settignano'), 'the life of children has hardly been touched upon in sculpture'. Technically they were the most difficult sitters and the sculptor required 'endless patience'; 'At the end of an hour or two the nerves of an artist are torn to shreds'.[21]

Naturally, Epstein's own children and grandchildren were his prime models. Peggy Jean, his eldest daughter, born in October 1918, was an unending source of inspiration. 'I never tired of watching her, and to watch her was, for me, to work from her. To make clay studies of all her moods; and when she tired and fell asleep, there was something new to do, charming and complete'. Just such a study of *Peggy Jean Asleep*, aged about two (the fourth of the twelve portraits made during her childhood)[22] anticipates, in its incorporation of the child's arms and hands, the twelfth portrait, *The Sick Child* [160]. This was modelled in 1928, when Peggy Jean was ten and ill

165
ESTHER GARMAN (first portrait: with long hair) 1944 (*S*355)
Bronze H 45
Walsall Museum and Art Gallery (Garman-Ryan Collection)

XV
HEAD OF AN OFFICIAL, Egypt (Thebes), XVIIIth Dynasty, *c* 1375 BC
Limestone relief H 26.7
Beth Lipkin (formerly Jacob Epstein collection)

166
ANN FREUD 1949–50 (S418)
Bronze H 21.5
Private collection

with measles, itchy and bored. Epstein stated that he tried to capture 'the pathetic droop of the child when she is feeling weak and downcast' (*The Woman's Journal*, March 1930).[23] The portrait has the appearance of an unpremeditated study but was, in fact, posed in the studio, with the child enjoying it immensely as her mother read to her all morning or sang, with Epstein joining in.[24] Notwithstanding its classic qualities of repose and balance, it exemplified what Epstein meant when he insisted that modelled sculpture 'must not be rigid [but] must quiver with life'. 'Twenty years ago I would have simplified the hair of the child into what critics call "true sculptural form" while today I find a rhythm in the hair of each individual head that I must capture.'[25]

Curiously, Theo Garman, alone of Epstein's children, was never modelled, though a number of drawn portraits survive, such as this one from 1930 [161], when he was six. He probably looked much as Epstein himself did at the same age and, like his father, showed great artistic promise, painting in a robust, colourful style akin to Matthew Smith, whose paintings he could study daily in his own home.[26] Kitty [162] was not sculpted until 1944, but this drawing dates from 1937, when she was ten.[27] Densely worked with powerful rhythmic strokes, both the technique and the sitter's rather concentrated expression suggest a kinship with the illustrations for Baudelaire's *Les Fleurs du Mal* [104–07], upon which Epstein was working in the following year.

Epstein's youngest son, Jackie, born in 1935, was also the subject of numerous drawings during the late Thirties. He was a strikingly active boy, who subsequently developed a passion for cars which led him to a career in motor racing. He was an irresistible but infuriating subject.

It is the life, free, careless, and apprehensive at the same time, of the little boy with his lively intelligence and quick ways, especially his eyes, and also his expressive hands in their infinite and unconscious gestures, that I wish to capture.

By making numerous drawings, most of which he rejected, 'I seem to gain in swiftness and assurance'.[28] *Ragamuffin* [163] is the culmination of these studies and seems to capture one of the moments described by his father:

I have him read to, and that fixes his attention. The stories with pictures hold him, especially drawings of animals. Rabier's graphic accounts, above all, and stories about snakes fascinate him. At the adventures of the monkey, the rabbit, the hedgehog, and the ducks, he roars with delight, and I then work with devoted fury and attention.[29]

Peggy Jean had married a Scots doctor, Norman Hornstein in 1937, and their first child, Leda, was born in 1939. Her poignant expression, especially in *Leda with Coxcomb* [164], is irresistible, although unsentimentally, Epstein also depicted her, aged six or seven months, with arms outstretched, demanding instant attention, and again, as a pretty but cross five-year-old, pouting.[30]

Epstein made three portraits of his youngest daughter, Esther, whose sympathetic, gentle temperament made her a great favourite: 'Everyone loved Essie', her sister recalled. The first portrait of *Esther* [165] dates from 1944, when it was exhibited under the title *Esther Amaryllis*.[31] She was sixteen and the loving accuracy with which Epstein evokes the still unfocused beauty of adolescence is touching. Yet, the portrait also employs elements taken from the sophisticated Egyptian conventions of portraiture [XV]. The elongated neck and the eager poise of the head recalls the famous head of Nefertiti in Berlin, of which Epstein owned a plaster mask which he judged superior to it.[32]

In the small, exquisite heads of his grandchildren, *Ann* [166] and *Annabel* [167], the daughters of Kitty and Lucien Freud, youthful innocence is expressed by treating the eye-sockets as deep, dark voids. Epstein believed that in this way the child 'confronts time and [its] destiny . . . boldly and trustingly [looking out] upon a world newly born of [its] vision'.[33] *Annabel*, *Ian* (the son of Norman and Peggy Jean Hornstein), *Isobel Hughes* (the daughter of Mr and Mrs Peter Hughes, who had been introduced to Epstein by the painter, Matthew Smith) and a little boy named *Peter*, each of whom had posed for portraits in bronze, were the starting points for a set of bronze door handles [168]. These were commissioned by the architect, Louis Osman and made in 1952 for the Convent of the Holy Child Jesus in Cavendish Square, London, for which Epstein had just completed the magnificent *Madonna and Child* [Fig. 93]. Their delightfully cherubic faces were ideally suited and Epstein may well have felt that this modest decorative embellishment perpetuated one of the main preoccupations of Renaissance sculptors.

Epstein's rapport with children extended beyond his family. *Roland Joffe* [169], born in 1943, became a member of the household during the period after his mother had disappeared and his father, Mark Joffe, the author and publisher, was living abroad. He was looked after by Esther [Fig. 2] but following her tragic death by suicide, was adopted into the Epstein household (calling the sculptor his 'step-father'). This traumatic childhood is hinted at in the head.[34] The head of *Victor* [170], the son of the Epstein's West African cook, demonstrates the care taken in balancing the child's most pronounced ethnic characteristics, the flat nose and full lips, with the overall structure, which is treated as a series of simple, interlocking geometric shapes; a balance between naturalism and the abstract, informed by an unsentimental approach. He admired Donatello, who 'saw the child's awkward walk', rather than Della Robbia, who 'sentimentalised it',[35] and wrote:

I should be quite content . . . to do only children . . . to fill my studio with . . . children . . . just born . . . Children growing up. Children nude. Children in fantastic costumes *en prince*, with pets of all kinds, and toys. Dark children, Piccaninnies, Chinese, Mongolian-eyed children.[36]

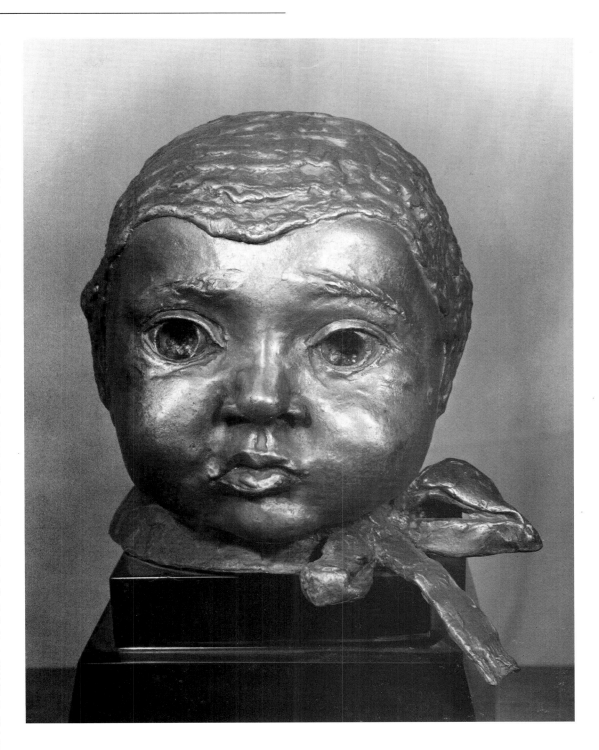

167
ANNABEL FREUD (first portrait: with bonnet)
1952 (S452)
Bronze   H 18 (another cast illustrated)
Beth Lipkin

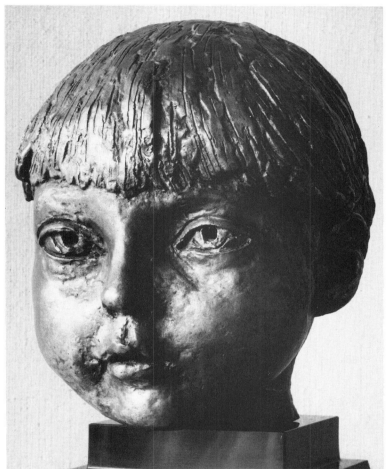

168
FOUR DOOR HANDLES FOR THE CONVENT OF THE
HOLY CHILD JESUS, Cavendish Square, London,
1952   (S454)
ANNABEL FREUD (top left), IAN HORNSTEIN (top
right), PETER (bottom left), ISOBEL HUGHES
(bottom right)
Plaster   H 10.2 (each)
Beth Lipkin

ICTOR   1949   (S414)
ronze   H 17.5
eeds City Art Galleries

169
ROLAND JOFFE   1949–50   (S419)
Bronze   H 20.3
Vane Ivanović

15 · 1950–1959

THE BURDEN OF FAME

Evelyn Silber and Terry Friedman

1. THE CAVENDISH SQUARE MADONNA AND CHILD, 1950–52

Epstein had received no commission for architectural sculpture since *Day* and *Night* in 1928 [Fig. 84] and, apart from the lifesize bronze *Youth Advancing* commissioned in 1949 for the Festival of Britain, none for large, modelled figures either. Regardless of the fact that there was no guarantee of money to carry out the project, let alone to pay him, in 1950 he leapt at the opportunity offered him by the architect, Louis Osman to produce a 13 foot high sculpture for the north side of Cavendish Square [Fig. 93]. Osman was restoring four Palladian houses damaged during the War and had designed a bridge to link and buttress the two central blocks on either side of Dean's Mews, occupied by the Convent of the Holy Child Jesus. In his view the bridge wall demanded sculpture. Quite apart from its structural and functional role, the bridge would round off the vista which runs north from St George's, Hanover Square, across Oxford Street to Dean's Mews on the north side of Cavendish Square. Osman held strong views on the partnership between architect and sculptor, and in a lecture to the Royal Society of Arts in 1957 declared:

> One cannot just apply a great work of art to a building and expect a happy marriage. If the sculpture is important it must be given its head, like the role of a soloist in a concerto; the orchestra being like the architecture, with the solo instrument speaking its poetry; related but clear and independent.[1]

For him, Henry Moore, John Skeaping and Epstein were the only possible candidates and 'he was convinced that only Epstein of all contemporary sculptors could fulfil the many diverse requirements and produce a work of the scale required and one in scale and harmony with the Palladian buildings'.[2] Without waiting for approval or agreement about fees, Epstein produced within a week a maquette of the *Madonna and Child* [171], a subject apparently independently selected by him, although the nuns had already discussed with Osman their intention of commissioning from a Catholic sculptor a figure of the Madonna and Child, when they could afford it. Epstein's design clearly looks back to his work in the Twenties — to Sunita and Enver in the *Mother and Child* of 1926 [Fig. 74], to the beautifully draped and reticent *Visitation*[3] and, finally, to the nude boy in *Day* [Fig. 84]. Though at first taken aback by the rapid appearance of the maquette for a sculpture they had not commis-

sioned, the nuns were greatly impressed. In what must have been an extraordinary ceremony, Epstein, accompanied by Osman and Sir Kenneth Clark, was catechised on his approach to the subject by the assembled community. Later, several members studied the final work in progress in Epstein's studio and the depth of their response, related in a letter of January 1952 to the Reverend Mother Provincial, conveys the extent to which the sculptor had arrived at an intuitive interpretation of the symbolic requirements of the theme:

> The group presents Our Lady not standing, but poised between heaven and earth . . . [Her] outward gazing is inexpressibly compelling because the sculptor has succeeded in conveying that it is essentially an inward look, unfathomable in its utter serenity . . . Our Lady's arms are stretched downwards in a gesture of giving and support, directed Godwards and manwards . . . The support is delicately yet powerfully indicated by the fact that her hands appear just beneath the outstretched hands of the Holy Child who is poised immediately in front of her, looking straight out over the world facing His Vocation: 'Behold I come'. The Child is more difficult to describe because the artist has subtly conveyed inherence of the divine in the immaturity of a child's body. The Mother stands completed as human person. The Child poignantly reveals that as a man He has still to grow, to experience, to suffer. The foreknowledge of the face pertain to the divine, as does the strength in the poise of the head, the courage of the arms outstretched, the directness of the gaze, the vitality of the hair. Yet the whole visage asks the very human question . . . What will it avail? And because it is the face of a child, it looks uncertain of the answer. Yet the hands of the sculptor have made this very poignancy into a challenge, and the outcome of the challenge for past, present and future is expressed in the feet of both Mother and Child; they proclaim the reality of the world of the spirit transcending the world of sense, the peace that comes when desire is at rest, the 'Consummatum Est' of the task accomplished. One might justly call them the artist's signature.[4]

When the figure was almost completed, Epstein agreed to the community's request for a more meditative Madonna, in place of the outward-looking one which he had based on

Fig 93
MADONNA AND CHILD   Covent of the Holy Child
Jesus, Cavendish Square, London, 1950–52   (S438)
Lead   H 390

171
MAQUETTE FOR MADONNA AND CHILD
1950   (S437)
Lead and bronze   H 33 (another cast illustrated)
Louis Osman

Kathleen Garman. Epstein modelled a new head from a friend, the pianist *Marcella Barzetti*, of whom he had made a study in 1950 [172]. In the finished work, with her head covered in a mantle, she recalls the subtle reticence of *Mrs Epstein in a Mantilla* [80], modelled more than thirty years before.

Cast in lead by A. Gaskin of the Fine Art Bronze Foundry and mounted on a bronze armature, the sculpture group was put into place in May 1953. When it was unveiled by R. A. Butler, on Ascension Thursday, 14 May, the sculpture was, for once in Epstein's turbulent career, acclaimed not only by the religious community but by critics and public alike. Epstein was delighted to be hailed by a bus driver and told 'Hi, Governor, You've made a good job of it!'[5]

By a curious coincidence the *Madonna and Child* was one of three public sculptures unveiled at that time, the others being Henry Moore's carvings on the Time and Life Building in Bond Street, and Charles Wheeler's two female figures on the Office of Works in Whitehall. Robert Furneaux Jordan and John Berger hastened to review recent public sculpture and were unanimous in praising Epstein's group above the rest. For Jordan, the partnership between Osman and Epstein was 'less sophisticated bút more noble' than that between Rosenauer and Moore, and he judged the sculpture as a whole and in detail 'beautifully conceived for its position'. It was, he concluded, 'with perhaps Le Sueur's *Charles I* [in Trafalgar Square] — London's finest post Reformation figure'.[6] Berger concurred:

> Epstein's Madonna and Child . . . is one of the most successful pieces of modern public sculpture now to be seen in London . . . The elongated distortion of their limbs is considered in relation to the perspective from which one views the group. The spread-eagled poise of the figures, a little like that of a bird momentarily held against the wind, aptly expresses the transience of childhood security. Their placing on the wall is so careful that even the sculpturally unsatisfying corrugated-iron treatment of the Madonna's dress seems architecturally justified. In fact, . . . Epstein has *accepted* the sculptural 'expectations' of the site and then rightly fulfilled them in an unexpected way.[7]

2. SOCIAL CONSCIOUSNESS, 1951–53

The work with the somewhat baffling title of *Social Consciousness* was Epstein's only major project for his native country. He modelled the five massive figures, which now stand on a terrace outside the Philadelphia Museum of Art [Fig. 94], in under two years, from November 1951 to September 1953.[8] However, the group was not originally intended either for that site or for an independent role, since it was commissioned by the Fairmount Park Association as part of the Ellen Phillips Samuel Memorial, a project of megalomaniac proportions to set symbolic bronzes and carvings 'emblematical of the history of America' on terraces fronting the Schuylkill River. It had been begun in 1914 and two-thirds of the sculptures were in place by 1949, when the Fairmount Park Committee commissioned six sculptors to com-

plete the scheme along predetermined lines.] was only when Gerhard Marcks's proposal fo *Social Consciousness* was rejected that Epstein wa invited to replace him.[9] Epstein's bronze grou was to be flanked by the single carved figure of th *Poet* and the *Preacher* already being produced b José de Creeft and William Raemisch, respec tively. It was also to complement a bronze grou entitled *Constructive Enterprise* by Jacques Lips chitz with flanking carvings of the *Inventor* an the *Labourer*.

In 1914, the grandiloquent symbolism of th project, which also included works called *Welcon ing to Freedom* and *Birth of a Nation*, resonated wit the earnest social and democratic idealism of th young nation-continent. Marcks was certainl baffled by what the Committee expected of sculpture called *Social Consciousness* and pro duced a maquette for two standing figures — man with his arm over his female companion' shoulders — which was deemed inadequate t express 'the practical Christianity' of the theme Epstein, however, was not at a loss. His formativ years had been spent in the heady atmosphere c café debate on the Lower East Side and he ha been profoundly moved by the poetry of Whi man, the journalist turned poet and sage, whos work epitomised the whole-heartedly practic: idealism the Memorial implied.

It is not clear precisely when the maquette [173] were made, probably between June, whe the contract was signed, and November 195: when Epstein began work on the ten foot hig figure of the *Seated Mother*, which he described a 'a figure of judgement — seated in eternity'.[10] Th wording clearly refers to Whitman's *Americ* which Epstein again quoted in describing th central figure as 'seated in the adamant of time'.' The full (and correct) quotation was eventuall placed on the plinth in 1972:

> A grand, sane, towering Seated Mother
> Chair'd in the adamant of time.

Only this central maternal figure and th tableau-like placing of the group which was inter ded to be seen frontally remains unchanged fro maquette to final composition. The emphaticall archaic character of the two flanking figures, *Warrior with Sword* and a *Mourner* [173], was app rently abandoned before work began on th full-scale figures. Neither seems especiall appropriate to the theme, nor are they linked i any way to the central figure. However, the angu lar shapes of arms and sword do create an abstra pattern of projections against the planar masses c the figures.

The Warrior was succeeded by a pair comprisin a Samaritan figure Epstein called *The Consol* succouring a fallen man. *The Mourner* was ever tually superseded by another funerary imag which he described in Whitmanesque terms as ' figure supporting man who turns with confidenc towards the great supporting mother as the so turns finally with utmost surrender to thos powers that guide and support us'.[12] In Octobe 1953, Henri Marceau, Director of the Philadelphi Museum and a member of the Fairmount Par Committee, saw the finished plasters in Epstein studio and reported:

172

MARCELLA BARZETTI   1950   (S436)
Bronze   H 26.7 (another cast illustrated)
Private collection

SOCIAL CONSCIOUSNESS

JACOB EPSTEIN
SCULPTOR

Fig 94
SOCIAL CONSCIOUSNESS   Fairmount Park,
Philadelphia, 1951–53   (S451)
Bronze   H 371

173
MAQUETTE FOR SOCIAL CONSCIOUSNESS   1951–
52   (S450)
Bronze   H 35.5 (another cast illustrated: MOURNER,
right-hand figure, H 32.5, only exhibited)
Birmingham Museums and Art Gallery

You will be delighted to hear that Epstein's
Social Consciousness is magnificent — a really
great and impressive, deeply moving work . . .
I was completely overwhelmed by its impressive scale, its dignity and power and by a quiet
tenderness I had not expected to find. To my
mind it completely tells the story of a rather
difficult and abstract theme.

The scale and expansiveness of Epstein's group
was clearly not going to balance Lipschitz's still
unfinished but far more compact sculpture.
Accordingly, it was eventually unveiled on a
temporary site which became permanent in
Fairmount Park on the terrace outside the
Philadelphia Museum of Art. The sculptor regretted the loss of rocks, trees and grass against which
it would have been placed but approved the new
site, silhouetted against the sky.[13]

3. CHRIST IN MAJESTY, 1953

The partial destruction of two great medieval
religious buildings provided Epstein with his next
public commissions and confirmed him as the
most serious and able British sculptor of the day
dealing with Christian subject matter. In 1941 a
landmine reduced the cathedral at Llandaff,
Glamorgan, to a ruin. A restoration programme
begun soon after the end of the War and completed in 1960 under the direction of the York
architect, George Pace, incorporated a lofty para-
bolic arch of reinforced concrete positioned at the
junction of the nave and choir, in place of the
medieval pulpitum removed in the nineteenth
century, to carry the organ case and a fifteen-foot
high figure of *Christ in Majesty* [Fig. 95]. This was
commissioned in October 1953 (only a few
months after and as a direct consequence of the
unveiling of the Cavendish Square *Madonna and*

Child),[14] when Epstein was seventy-three, and unveiled on 10 April 1957. His concept was an immensely elongated Christ suspended high above the nave floor, its flattened cylindrical robe recalling the *Risen Christ* [110] of thirty years earlier, but now with both arms outstretched, like the Cavendish Square *Madonna* [Fig. 93]. The entire body is concealed in a simple garment with the seam running dramatically off-centre from neckline to hem; in contrast, the head and hands are treated with a grave naturalism. All this had been worked out in a lead maquette [174]. The full-size figure was modelled first in the Hyde Park Gate studio and then moved to the larger facilities provided at the Royal College of Art in nearby Kensington [Fig. 92], and was cast by Morris Singer between April 1955 and Spring 1956. Aluminium rather than bronze was preferred for its light, durable qualities, as well as its soft, luminous, silvery patina, which shone in the dim cathedral light. The magnificent presence of the *Christ* increases dramatically as the spectator moves eastward down the nave and the angle of vision become more acute until he is confronted by the great monolithic figure looming like some Byzantine Pantocrator.

4. St MICHAEL AND THE DEVIL, 1955–58

Whereas the Llandaff site dictated a columnar-shape, reminiscent of Romanesque door jambs [Fig. 79], the lofty, unembellished, red sandstone wall of Basil Spence's new cathedral at Coventry, replacing the fifteenth century fabric destroyed by German bombs in 1940, allowed Epstein to create an independent and expansive sculpture group [Fig. 96]. Spence had won the competition in 1950 and envisaged his new building (consecrated in 1962) housing a series of works of religious art by distinguished British artists: Elizabeth Frink, John

XVI ▷

STANDING MALE FIGURE, probably Lake Sentani, Papua New Guinea
Wood   H 160.5
The Trustees of the British Museum (formerly Jacob Epstein exhibition)

174 ▷▷

MAQUETTE FOR CHRIST IN MAJESTY
1953   (S474)
Lead   H 66 (another cast illustrated)
Mr and Mrs Victor Sandelson

Fig 95 ▷▷▷

CHRIST IN MAJESTY   Llandaff Cathedral, Wales, 1954–55   (S475)
Aluminium   H 430

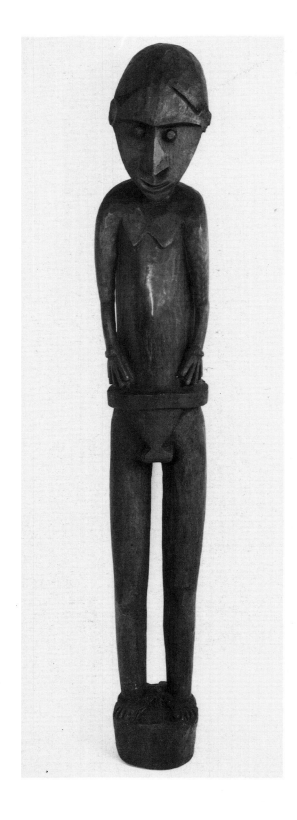

Fig 96
ST MICHAEL AND THE DEVIL   Coventry
Cathedral, 1956–58   (S503)
Bronze   H 1066

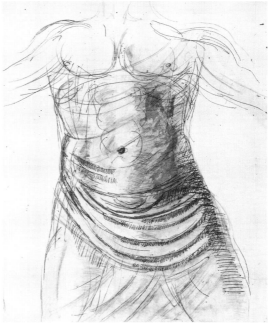

175
THE HON. WYNNE GODLEY   1956   (S501)
Bronze   H 50
Private collection

176
STUDY FOR THE TORSO OF ST MICHAEL   1956–57
Pen and biro   41.3 × 53.3
Birmingham Museums and Art Gallery

Fig 97
MAQUETTE FOR ST MICHAEL AND THE DEVIL
1956   (S502)
Plasticine   H 53.5
Whereabouts unknown

Piper, Graham Sutherland and others. He relates in *Phoenix at Coventry* how Bishop Gorton, taken in 1954 to see the Cavendish Square *Madonna and Child*, 'oblivious of the traffic, stood looking up at this masterpiece' and proclaimed 'Epstein is the man for us'.[15] Spence went to see the sculptor, then at work on the Llandaff *Christ* at the Royal College of Art, and he accepted the commission at once (November 1955). The Reconstruction Committee, although concerned that Epstein was both controversial and a Jew, had acquiesced on condition that he submit a maquette for approval [Fig. 97]. The group, representing *St Michael and the Devil*, is an appropriate symbol for the resurgent cathedral: the victory of the spiritual over the brute instincts of man. The warrior saint, arms, legs and wings triumphantly outspread, stands over the prone, enchained figure of the Devil. Michael's features were based on a contemporary portrait bust of Epstein's son-in-law, *The Hon Wynne Godley* [175], whose features are transformed, by simplifying the planes and emphasising the deep shadows of the eyes and cheeks, into an heroic and divine image. There was at least one preparatory drawing for the torso of the saint [176]; it develops the very sketchily suggested tunic in the maquette by structuring the drapery over the muscular body.

The *Devil* was modelled by Gordon Bagnall-Godfrey, a chartered surveyor. Epstein radically altered this figure. In the maquette it is emaciated and cowers as it is forced under Michael's feet; in the finished sculpture, it is separated from the saint, divested of wings and posed like the muscular figure of *Raving Madness*, *c* 1676, originally made for the gate of Bedlam Hospital, and in Epstein's day displayed in the London Guildhall.[16] During 1957–58, the full-size plaster of the two figures was prepared[17] and cast from April 1958 by Morris Singer. The group was unveiled on 24 June 1960 by Lady Epstein. The sculptor had hoped it would be his masterpiece[18] but the transfer from maquette to a thirty-five-foot high bronze posed difficulties, and Evelyn Silber has observed:

> There is a pictorial and theatrical element in Epstein's large bronzes which is least successful when it is most physically dynamic. [His] grasp of anatomy, so brilliant in his portraiture, frequently failed when it came to articulating the whole body . . . [its] stylised rigidity can, all too easily, appear mere rhetoric.[19]

5. THE TUC WAR MEMORIAL, 1955–56

In the stone group for the *Trades Union Congress War Memorial* [Fig. 98] in the new Great Russell Street headquarters, Epstein returned to the compact, static *Pietà* composition of *Night* [Fig. 85]. He had declined to participate in the two-part open competition for the memorial launched in December 1954 (the Main Entrance group was won by Bernard Meadows) but accepted a direct invitation in March the following year for the courtyard group, which was to cost £16,000, the sculptor receiving £5,000. The competition had specified that the 'Promoters do not wish to have groups of a purely abstract character, and such designs will not be considered. Apart from this complete freedom is given in the conception of the group [which] should be in stone, is to commemorate the trade unionists . . . who lost their lives in the two world wars in defence of freedom and democracy.'[20] The site was very dramatic [Fig. 98]. The TUC's original idea of a viewing gallery was abandoned in favour of the group being seen from across the internal courtyard and elevated on a tall stone plinth set against a lofty, pyramidal precipice of green marble. A powerful maquette [177*] was produced between March and May 1955. Epstein was formally commissioned in August and a contract was drawn up on 7 November. He began carving in March 1956, immediately after the block of Roman stone (300 × 150 × 120 centimeters) was in position, working on a narrow plank on the wall face,[21] employing an assistant for the first time in his career. He wrote to his daughter:

> I have let myself in for some devilish hard work as this particular block is as hard as granite and tools just break on it . . . I find myself tired out at about 1.30 and go back and have lunch and rest. I am making good progress and if it weren't for the terrible noise of building going on all about me I would feel all right.[22]

Nevertheless, the group is a hard-hitting concept free of patriotic sentiment (a feature which renders so many war memorials impotent) boldly executed in Epstein's characteristically austere naturalism. The horrified mother, rising directly from the plinth, cradles her dead son, 'a fearful indictment of the pitiless indifference of war'.[23] The group was completed by Christmas 1956, some time before the building itself; at the time of the formal opening in March 1958 Epstein was seriously ill in hospital.

6. THE BOWATER GROUP, 1958–59

A few months earlier, Epstein had begun work on an ambitious multi-figure composition for the new Bowater House headquarters in Knightsbridge, the so-called 'Pan Group' [Fig. 99]. This was to be positioned on the north side of the building, on an axis with the Edinburgh Gate. His idea was to make a family group — father, mother and child, all nude, and accompanied by a pet dog — driven by the figure of Pan and surging forward across The Carriage Road into Hyde Park; a sort of symbolic Bacchic rout from the city into the country. Epstein had explored the possibilities of single striding figures — the portrait of *Kathleen Garman with Gardenias*, *Youth Advancing* and the *Liverpool Giant*[24] — but never in such a complex arrangement. It is interesting, therefore, that in 1931 he told Arnold Haskell that he regarded François Rude's masterpiece, *The Marseillaise* (*Le départ des Voluntaires en 1792*), 1836 [Fig. 100] as an outstanding example of how to achieve 'violent action and drama . . . together with perfect unity [of] composition'.[25] Epstein calculated precisely the dimensions of his figures [178] in order to achieve the degree of exaggeration, particularly in the straining limbs, necessary to create a dramatic impression of accelerated, diagonal movement. The design was then further developed in a lively

Fig 98
TRADES UNION CONGRESS WAR MEMORIAL
Congress House, Great Russell Street, London,
1956–57   (S490)
Roman stone   H 300

bronze maquette [179]. Although conceived fully in the round, with Pan as the pivot of a fan-like composition, the sculpture is seen most effectively on its two long sides [Fig. 99] as a frieze, like Rude's group. The ambitious solution is adventurous and inventive, but Epstein was all too well aware that he was engaged in a race against time. He had written to his daughter, Peggy Jean in 1956:

> I am inundated with requests for work on buildings, large works which I don't know I will ever be able to accomplish. I was for so long without any commissions, I don't feel like turning down anything that comes my way: but it is all coming too late I'm afraid. [26]

Epstein finished preparing the *Bowater Group* full-size model for casting on the day he died, 19 August 1959.

Fig 99 △
BOWATER HOUSE GROUP   Edinburgh Gate,
Knightsbridge, London, 1958–59   (S522)
Bronze

Fig 100
François Rude (1784–1855)
LE DÉPART DES VOLUNTAIRES EN 1792 | THE
MARSEILLAISE   Arc de Triomphe de l'Etoile,
Paris   1833–36
Limestone   H c 42 feet

178
STUDY FOR BOWATER HOUSE GROUP   1958
Pencil   25.6 × 15 (detail)
Beth Lipkin

179
MAQUETTE FOR BOWATER HOUSE GROUP
1958   (S521)
Bronze   H 28
Bowater Industries plc

Notes

Abbreviations

BML
E. Bassani and M. D. McLeod, *Jacob Epstein Collector*, 1987

Buckle
R. Buckle, *Jacob Epstein Sculptor*, 1963

Cork 1976
R. Cork, *Vorticism and Abstract Art in the First Machine Age*, 1976

Cork 1985
R. Cork, *Art Beyond The Gallery in Early 20th Century England*, 1985

Epstein 1940
J. Epstein, *Let There Be Sculpture*, 1940

Epstein Drawings
Lady Epstein and R. Buckle, *Epstein Drawings*, 1962

FPAA
Fairmount Park Association Archive, The Historical Society of Pennsylvania, Philadelphia

Geist
S. Geist, *Constantin Brancusi, 1876–1957: A Retrospective Exhibition*, New York, 1969

Gill Diaries
Unpublished diaries of Eric Gill: William Andrews Clark Memorial Library, University of California, Los Angeles

Hapgood
H. Hapgood, *The Spirit of the Ghetto*, 1902

Haskell
The Sculptor Speaks: Jacob Epstein to Arnold L. Haskell: A series of conversations on Art, 1931

HMCSS
The Henry Moore Centre for the Study of Sculpture, Leeds City Art Galleries

Hopper
R. Hopper, *true and pure sculpture: Frank Dobson 1886–1963*, 1981

James
P. James, ed., *Henry Moore on Sculpture*, 1966

LEC
Limited Editions Club (The Harry Ransom Humanities Research Centre, University of Texas at Austin)

LH
D. Sylvester, ed., *Henry Moore: Sculpture and Drawings 1921–1948* (fourth edition) 1957

Powell
L. B. Powell, *Jacob Epstein*, 1932

Reid
B. L. Reid, *The Man from New York: John Quinn and His Friends*, 1968

RSPB
The Royal Society for the Protection of Birds, Sandy, Bedfordshire

Rubin
W. Rubin, ed., *'Primitivism' in 20th Century Art: Affinity of the Tribal and the Modern*, 1984

S
Denoting catalogue number in E. Silber, *The Sculpture of Epstein*, 1986, pp. 119–227

Schinman
E. P. and B. A. Schinman, eds, *Jacob Epstein. A Catalogue of the Collection of Edward P. Schinman*, 1970

Shewring
W. Shewring, ed., *Letters of Eric Gill*, 1947

Silber
E. Silber, *The Sculpture of Epstein*, 1986

Vigurs
P. F. Vigurs, *The Garman-Ryan Collection: Walsall Museum and Art Gallery*, 1976

Wellington
H. Wellington, *Jacob Epstein*, 1925

Wilenski
R. H. Wilenski, *The Meaning of Modern Sculpture*, 1932

Zilczer
J. Zilczer, *'the Noble Buyer': John Quinn Patron of the Avant Garde*, 1978

Epstein in Person

1 J. Gordon and H. M. Bateman, *Art ain't all Paint*, 1944, p. 63.

2 Aural communication from Mrs S. Parsons to Evelyn Silber, 1982.

3 'Sir Jacob Epstein Sculptor and Humanist', Radio 3, 1 August 1960. The London Group was founded in 1914; Brodzky may have meant the Allied Artists' Show of 1912.

4 Quoted in *Autobiography* (comprising *Chiaroscuro* and *Finishing Touches*), 1975, pp. 87–88.

5 D. D. Paige, ed., *The Letters of Ezra Pound 1907–1941*, 1950, p. 63.

6 p. 59.

7 Quoted in *Haskell*, p. xii.

8 BBC talk on Epstein, 16 October 1961.

9 Adams, Holden and Pearson, London.

10 p. 55.

11 *James*, pp. 194, 197.

Epstein and his Patrons

1 Miss H. Campbell in conversation with Evelyn Silber, 1982 and 1986. Her portrait, of *Joan Greenwood* (*S* 397), was purchased *c* 1948–49.

2 J. B. Manson to E. E. Lowe, 28 January 1924, referring to *S* 126 (Leicester Museum and Art Gallery files). Dundee, Newport and Bradford had all received Epstein sculpture before 1920 but as gifts rather than purchases.

3 *Epstein 1940*, p. 249.

4 An instance of Epstein repenting of his hasty temper is told by A. Haskell, *Balletomane at Large*, 1972, p. 60.

5 No. 9. On that occassion the Jury Committee included Bone, Dodd, John, McEvoy and Rothenstein.

6 When Shaw sat for his portrait in 1934 it was commissioned by Mrs Blanche Grant, and Shaw declined a cast as his wife did not like it. Later he said it made him look like 'an Irish navvy'. See *S* 252–53.

7 Shaw was prominent in Epstein's defence over the BMA Building, the *Tomb of Oscar Wilde, Risen Christ* and *Rima*.

8 *Epstein. Arts Council Memorial Exhibition*, Tate Gallery, 1961, no. 94, for Rothenstein's drawing.

9 M. Holroyd, *Augustus John*, 1976, pp. 228–29.

10 R. Speight, *William Rothenstein*, 1962, p. 186.

11 W. Rothenstein, *Men and Memories 1900–1922*, 1932, pp. 87, 128–29.

12 M. Pennington, forthcoming publication on the *Tomb of Oscar Wilde* (Whiteknights Press, Reading).

13 M. Holroyd, *Augustus John*, 1976, p. 228.

14 R. Speight, *William Rothenstein*, 1962, p. 312.

15 H. Brodzky, *Henri Gaudier-Brzeska*, 1933. For Gaudier's portraits of both men, see R. Cole, *Burning to speak*, 1978, nos 21–22.

16 They also owned Gaudier-Brzeska's lost *Amour* (R. Cole, *Burning to speak*, 1978, no. 029, p. 128).

17 Tate Gallery Archives, 721.38–40.

18 Epstein to Wolmark, 30 April 1915 (Tate Gallery Archives, 721.38–40). There are also references to Coria in two undated letters (datable to mid- and late-1917) from Epstein to Bernard van Dieren (Humanities Research Center, University of Texas, Austin). Epstein went on a walking tour with Coria in 1921.

19 A. John to R. Ross, undated letter (? June 1908), quoted in M. Holroyd, *Augustus John*, 1976, pp. 268–69.

20 Epstein to Lady Morrell, 22 October 1908 (Humanities Research Center, University of Texas, Austin).

21 Payment recorded in Mrs Epstein's bank book, 12 January 1911 (Private collection).

22 Holden's firm was also involved with the *Tomb of Oscar Wilde*, the plinth for which Holden began designing at Epstein's request, though he later handed over all the working drawings to avoid an argument. Lionel Pearson, Holden's partner, designed the setting for the *W. H. Hudson Memorial* at the request of the Memorial Committee.

23 *S* 32, there dated 1911. However, the newly discovered letter to Dodd about the reception of the *Wilde Tomb* (p. 127), includes instructions to Dodd on how to keep moist an unfinished portrait Epstein abandoned in his haste. If this was the portrait of *Mrs. Francis Dodd*, it dates from 1912 (*S* 32).

24 *Cork 1985*, chapter 4.

25 K. Lechmere interview with R. Cork, quoted in *Cork 1976*, p. 125.

26 L. Binyon, 'The Art of Jacob Epstein', *The New Statesman*, 17 March 1917; P. G. Konody, 'Mr Epstein's Sculpture', *The Observer*, 18 February 1917.

27 Both these sculptures are listed as lent by Mrs G. E. Rogers at the Leicester Galleries in 1933, but details of this owner (if not fictitious) are unknown.

28 Epstein had this article, originally published in *The New Age*, 25 December 1913, reprinted both in *Haskell* and in all editions of his autobiography; Tate Gallery Archives 8135.35.

29 *Zilczer*.

30 *Schinman*; *Sculpture of Jacob Epstein: The Eisenberg-Robbins Collection*, Corcoran Gallery of Art, Washington, 1973–74.

31 *Reid*, p. 100.

32 *Reid*, p. 111.

33 *Reid*, pp. 129–30.

34 *Reid*, p. 160.

35 International Exhibition of Modern Art, 69th Regiment Armory, Lexington Avenue, New York, 1913; *Reid*, p. 144.

36 *Reid*, pp. 203–04. *S* 65.

37 *Reid*, p. 259. *S* 60.

38 *Reid*, p. 261.

39 *Zilczer*, pp. 27, 34.

40 *Reid*, pp. 202–03.

41 *Zilczer*, pp. 158 and 40, note 15, citing a letter from Epstein to Quinn, 24 November 1915, stating that he thought the second version of *Doves* superior to the first. Quinn had paid for *Doves* in June 1915.

42 *Reid*, p. 203.

43 Letter quoted in *Reid*, p. 203.

44 *Vanity Fair*, October 1917.

45 *Reid*, p. 373.

46 *Reid*, p. 374.

47 16 June 1919, quoted in *Reid*, p. 397.

48 *Reid*, p. 461.

49 *Reid*, p. 560.

50 *Reid*, p. 616.

51 *Reid*, p. 617.

52 One of the proprietors of Scott & Fowles, who retained the portrait of *Gabrielle Soene* (*S* 101), which entered the Chicago Art Institute in 1933.

53 28 March 1917, quoted in *Reid*, p. 298.

54 A full history of the Rutherston Collection has yet to be written; see J. Farrington, 'Wyndham Lewis and a Prescient Collector', *Apollo*, Vol. 111, 1980, pp. 46–49.

55 *HMCSS*: Moore to Jocelyn Horner, 1923.

56 Epstein to C. Rutherston, 24 May 1923 (Tate Gallery Archives TAM 49/2).

57 M. and S. Harries, *The War Artists*, 1983, chapter 3.

58 M. and S. Harries, *The War Artists*, 1983, pp. 127–28. *S* 100.

59 *Epstein 1940*, pp. 176–77. A press note accompanying the photograph illustrated in Fig. 9 states that 'the photograph was taken from a viewpoint specially selected by the sculptor.'

60 *Epstein Memorial Exhibition*, Edinburgh, 1961, no. 99.

61 J. Epstein, *Epstein: An Autobiography*, 1955, p. 232.

62 An extraordinary number of small to medium-sized collections of Epstein bronzes grew up during the Thirties and Forties (*Loan Collection of Works by Jacob Epstein*, 1948, Laing Art Gallery, Newcastle upon Tyne).

63 *The Daily Mail*, 25 November 1932.

64 *S* 255; *Epstein 1940*, p. 89. It is interesting to note that Bone was the intermediary in setting up this commission; Epstein wrote, 13 September 1933?: 'Dear Mr Walpole, Muirhead Bone writes to me that you would like me to do a head and neck of you in bronze'; they agreed a price of £200 (Humanities Research Center, University of Texas, Austin).

65 *S* 271; *Epstein 1940*, p. 103.

66 J. Epstein, *Epstein: An Autobiography*, 1955, p. 235.

67 *Epstein 1940*, p. 13.

68 *Hapgood*, p. 257.

THE PASSIONATE COLLECTOR

1 E. Bassani and M. McLeod, *Jacob Epstein Collector*, 1987.

2 The term is deeply unsatisfactory. It is used in this essay because during Epstein's lifetime, and since, it was a common way of designating a range of materials from pre-literate and pre-industrial societies. It is, however, inaccurate and has unpleasantly derogatory undertones; there is nothing primitive about any of these items. For Epstein's similar belief, see *Haskell*, pp. 107–08.

3 *The Epstein Collection of Tribal and Exotic Sculpture*, 1960.

4 Christie's, 15 December 1961, with more than 300 items in 276 lots. In 1963, 358 pieces from the collection were bought privately from Lady Epstein by a single collector; the majority of these are still in that collection.

5 Pieces are now in the British Museum; Metropolitan Museum and Brooklyn Museum, New York; Australian National Museum, Canberra; Dapper Foundation, Paris; Musée Barbier Muller, Geneva; Musée des Arts Africains et Océaniens, Paris; Nigerian Museum, Lagos.

6 By the photographer, Geoffrey Ireland, then on the staff of the Royal College of Art.

7 *BML* 259.

8 *Negerplastik*, 1915, pls 7–11. *BML* 349.

9 *BML* 517.

10 *BML* 420.

11 *Haskell*, p. 87.

12 See the derogatory remarks by Sir Herbert Samuel quoted in *Epstein 1940*, p. 58.

13 Goldwater discussed Epstein's collection in his pioneering book, *Primitivism in Modern Art*, 1938.

14 Introduction to *The Epstein Collection of Tribal and Exotic Sculpture*, 1960.

15 *BML* 267.

16 *BML* 1, 3.

17 *BML* 38.

18 *BML* 349.

19 *BML* 323.

20 *BML* 281.

21 *BML* 151A and B.

22 *BML* 186–87.

23 *BML* 451.

24 *BML* 585.

25 *BML* 969.

26 J. Herman in conversation with E. Bassani, 1984.

27 *Buckle*, p. 216. *S* 247.

28 *Epstein 1940*, p. 218.

29 *Haskell*, p. 88.

30 *Buckle*, p. 42. Epstein's passport, no. 62069 (Beth Lipkin Collection), dated 10 September 1902, is annotated on the verso 'Musee Guimet near Trocodero'; the Guimet contains important examples of Near Eastern and Indian sculpture.

31 *Epstein 1940*, p. 215.

32 Holme to Robert Ross, 19 February 1912, quoted in *Silber*, p. 25.

33 *Reid*, p. 160.

34 Information from William Fagg.

35 *Haskell*, p. 87.

36 S. Hooper, ed., forthcoming complete catalogue of the Sainsbury Collection.

37 *Epstein 1940*, p. 215.

38 G. Apollinaire and P. Guillaume, *Sculptures Nègres*, 1917.

39 'Il y a un mouvement melanophile en Angleterre et le sculpteur Jacob Epstein semble en avoir promoteur' ('Une Esthetique Nouvelle-L'Art Nègre', *Les Arts à Paris*, No. 4, Mai 1919, p. 2).

40 *Epstein 1940*, p. 152.

41 *Rubin*, pp. 143–48.

42 *BML* 349, 281.

43 *BML* 280.

44 *BML* 259.

45 *Collection, André Breton and Paul Eluard*, Hôtel Drouot, Paris, 2–3 Juillet 1931.

46 *Epstein 1940*, p. 217.

47 *BML* 260.

48 *BML* 261.

49 *BML* 38.

50 *BML* 1.

51 J. J. Sweeney, *African Negro Art*, 1935.

52 *BML* 281.

53 *BML* 256.

54 *Epstein 1940*, p. 216.

55 *BML* 257.

56 *BML* 420 (S. Kooijman, *The Art of Lake Sentani*, 1959).

57 *An Important Collection of Oceanic, African and American Art*, 30 April 1930, lots 22, 42, 49, 54, 55, 57, 76, 88, 92.

58 *BML 686. The Important Collection of Antiquities*, Sotheby's, 11 July 1939, lot 382.

59 J. Hewett in conversation with E. Bassani, 1984. *BML 663*, formerly owned by the collector Ken Webster.

60 *BML 663*.

61 Philip Goldman in conversation with M. D. McLeod, 1985.

62 *Haskell*, pp. 88–89.

63 *Epstein 1940*, p. 215.

64 *Epstein 1940*, p. 216.

65 *Epstein 1940*, p. 220. *BML 832; The Epstein Collection of Tribal and Exotic Sculpture*, 1960, pl. xv. Epstein also owned a cast of the Berlin head, which can be seen in Fig. 5.

66 *Haskell*, p. 89.

67 *Haskell*, p. 90.

68 *Epstein 1940*, p. 216.

69 *Haskell*, p. 90.

Image from Stone

1 *Epstein 1940*, p. 168.

2 H. Moore, 'Jacob Epstein', *The Sunday Times*, 23 August 1959, reprinted in *James*, p. 197.

3 See note 2.

4 *Silber*, p. 43, rightly emphasises that 'it is primarily as a portrait sculptor that Epstein was and is celebrated'.

5 *Epstein 1940*, p. 221.

6 *Epstein 1940*, p. 22.

7 *Epstein 1940*, p. 11.

8 *Epstein 1940*, p. 12.

9 *Epstein 1940*, p. 16.

10 *Epstein 1940*, p. 21.

11 *Epstein 1940*, p. 22.

12 *Epstein 1940*, p. 23.

13 *Epstein 1940*, p. 23.

14 *Epstein 1940*, p. 25.

15 *Epstein 1940*, p. 249.

16 *Epstein 1940*, p. 247.

17 *Epstein 1940*, p. 249.

18 *S 1–2*.

19 For a detailed account of Epstein's sources in the BMA scheme, see *Cork 1985*, chapter 1.

20 C. Holden, memoir dated 3 December 1940, unpublished, preserved in the archives of Adams, Holden & Pearson, London.

21 C. Holden, speech delivered at Epstein exhibition opening in Bolton, unpublished, Adams, Holden & Pearson, London.

22 A. Mola to J. Stern, 25 October 1942 (?), quoted by *Silber*, p. 123.

23 See note 20.

24 J. Epstein, 'The Artist's Description of His Work', *British Medical Journal*, 4 July 1908.

25 See note 24.

26 Gill to W. Rothenstein, 25 September 1910 (*Shewring*, p. 32).

27 C. L. Hind, *The Post Impressionists*, 1911, p. 67.

28 He finished deepening the relief in 1933, when he exhibited it at the Leicester Galleries (*S 26*).

29 No. 1179 at the Allied Artists' Salon, Albert Hall, summer, 1912.

30 *Silber*, p. 21.

31 On the reverse of a study for Fry's garden statue, Gill wrote: 'The statue should echo the slope of the hill and "appreciate" the view'. *Eric Gill 1882–1940. Drawings & Carvings. A Centenary Exhibition*, Anthony d'Offay, London, May–June 1982, p. 24, no. 7. The carving is now in Holland Park, London.

32 *Diaries*, 9 December 1913.

33 *Silber*, p. 131.

34 *Epstein 1940*, p. 65.

35 See note 20.

36 *Epstein 1940*, p. 65.

37 *The New Age*, 21 January 1915.

38 *Reid*, p. 130.

39 *Epstein 1940*, pp. 60–62.

40 Modigliani's *Head* was lent to the Whitechapel Art Gallery's *Twentieth Century Art* exhibition, May–June 1914, by Edward Roworth; it subsequently entered the Tate Gallery via the Victoria & Albert Museum.

41 *Epstein 1940*, p. 64.

42 *Epstein 1940*, p. 63.

43 *Epstein 1940*, p. 64.

44 Information from Evelyn Silber.

45 Quoted in T. E. Hulme, 'Mr Epstein and The Critics', *The New Age*, 25 December 1913.

46 The date of Brancusi's *Three Penguins* (Philadelphia Museum of Art) is disputed, but *Geist*, p. 61, attributes its execution to *c* 1912.

47 Epstein to Bernard van Dieren, 8 March 1917, quoted in *Silber*, p. 34.

48 B. van Dieren, *The New Age*, 7 March 1917.

49 *Reid*, p. 299 (11 February 1917?).

50 See note 49.

51 *S 111* and *Silber*, pp. 35–37.

52 *S 136*.

53 *Silber*, p. 44, pl. 21.

54 *Epstein 1940*, p. 128.

55 *Epstein 1940*, p. 64.

56 Dobson's *Pigeon Boy* was executed in 1920 (*Hopper*, no. 27) and Gaudier's *Boy with a Rabbit*, 1914, is in the Rachewiltz Collection, Brunnenburg (R. Cole, *Burning to speak*, 1978, no. 53).

57 See *Cork 1985*, pl. 304.

58 *Haskell*, p. 47.

59 *Epstein 1940*, p. 159.

60 'Mr. Epstein Replies', interview with J. Bone, *The Manchester Guardian*, 3 August 1929. *Night*, he explained, 'had to be deeply cut, for there is not the same weight of shadow as on the sunny side where "Day" is'.

61 See note 60.

62 *Epstein 1940*, p. 163. At least two preliminary studies [136] are known.

63 *Epstein 1940*, p. 162.

64 *Epstein 1940*, p. 217.

65 *Epstein 1940*, p. 168.

66 *The Spectator*, 15 March 1935.

67 See note 66.

68 *Epstein 1940*, pp. 168–69.

69 *Epstein 1940*, p. 177; *S 275*.

70 *Epstein 1940*, p. 176.

71 *Epstein 1940*, p. 178.

72 *Epstein 1940*, p. 195.

73 *Epstein 1940*, p. 195.

74 J. Epstein, 'The Artist's Description of His Work', *British Medical Journal*, 4 July 1908.

75 J. Lipchitz, *My Life in Sculpture*, 1972, p. 120.

76 *Silber*, p. 201.

77 Epstein to Quinn, March 1912 (*Reid*, p. 130).

78 Contract, 7 November 1955 (*Silber*, p. 221).

79 *Epstein. A Camera Study of the Sculptor at Work by Geoffrey Ireland*, 1956, last two plates.

80 Epstein to his daughter, 1 March 1956 (*Silber*, p. 221).

81 *Epstein 1940*, p. 257.

'Epsteinism'

1 *James*, p. 194. Moore recalled a man 'dogged . . . all his life [by] Insults and misunderstandings [which] hurt him [but which] he shrugged off' (p. 197) and told Evelyn Silber: 'One can be defeated by strength as well as weakness. Epstein retaliated with too much strength' (interview, 17 November 1980). Moore's friend, the painter, Raymond Coxon, observed that if 'the victim is a sculptor of the kidney of Mr. Epstein, the mere name is used as a bogey, and each new work which a bold client commissions him to do be hailed with a delirium of execration' (*Art: An Introduction to Appreciation*, 1932, p. 194). Epstein was fond of publishing press attacks (see *Haskell* and *Epstein 1940*); from the mid-Twenties Moore, too, collected press clippings concerning his work (The Henry Moore Foundation).

2 Recollection of the painter, Raymond Coxon, who accompanied Moore on that occasion (*HMCSS*: letter dated 19 October 1986).

3 E. Williams, *Emlyn: An Early Autobiography 1927–1935*, 1976, p. 263.

4 Evelyn Silber interview with Moore, 17 November 1980. Moore later wrote: 'In the 1920s the only practising sculptor in England for whom I had any respect was Epstein' (*Henry Moore at the British Museum*, 1981, p. 10).

5 *James*, p. 194.

6 *HMCSS*: Thornycroft Papers *c* 335, letter dated 7 June 1917, referring to 'your shirking confrere Epstein'.

7 *HMCSS*: Thornycroft Papers *c* 62, letter dated 19 June 1919.

8 *Henry Moore: Early Carvings 1920–1940*, Leeds City Art Galleries, 1982, p. 23.

9 *HMCSS*: letter to Jocelyn Horner, Autumn 1921.

10 H. Moore, *Henry Moore at the British Museum*, 1981, p. 10. See also *James*, p. 201.

11 *S 9:12–13. Henry Moore: Early Carvings 1920–1940*, Leeds City Art Galleries, 1982, p. 25, fig. 17.

12 *Epstein*, 1920, pl. xi.

13 *HMCSS*: letter to Jocelyn Horner, dated August 1923. Moore also mentions seeing sculpture by Dobson and Gill, and a forthcoming Epstein exhibition in London. These bronzes (*S 3, 70, 73, 105, 145*) were presented by Rutherston to Manchester City Art Gallery in 1923–25.

14 *LH 26*.

15 *LH 8, 48*.

16 *Geist*, p. 150.

17 Undated article by Claire Price.

18 *Epstein 1940*, p. 158.

19 *Epstein 1940*, p. 155.

20 A. T. Spear, *Brancusi's Birds*, 1969, no. 15.iv, pl. 20.

21 *LH* 42. *James*, p. 44; Moore's wording suggests Epstein also purchased drawings, although these cannot be identified.

22 W. Packer, *Henry Moore: An Illustrated Biography*, 1985, pp. 73–75.

23 *Cork 1985*, Chapter 6.

24 *Haskell*, p. 47.

25 The *1920 Notebook*, entitled 'History of Sculpture Notes' (*HMCSS*), signed 'H.S. Moore 1920', includes notes on Mesopotamian, Greek and Italian Renaissance art, with drawings.

26 *The Bulletin and Scots Pictorial*, 8 March 1929, mentions only Epstein and Moore as the contributing sculptors.

27 *Cork 1985*, p. 2, sees *West Wind* as an 'overt act of homage to the magisterial precedent Epstein had created for the Tomb' and his 'paternal friendship with Moore'.

28 *Standing Woman* (*LH* 33) was shown at the Warren Gallery in 1928 (*The Times*, 26 January) and featured in *The Yorkshire Observer* article (5 February 1929) about the Underground commission.

29 *Wilenski*, p. 133.

30 *The Evening Standard*, 4 May 1929. Wilenski published appreciations on Epstein in *Woman's Journal*, March 1930 (in the series 'People You Would Like to Know') and on Moore in *Apollo*, December 1930 ('Ruminations on Sculpture and the Work of Henry Moore'). Geoffrey Grigson's review (*The Yorkshire Post*, 27 July 1932) of *The Meaning of Modern Sculpture* is entitled 'Epstein to Henry Moore'.

31 *LH* 92, 59.

32 Epstein wrote: 'I never saw the abstract as an end in itself, and I do not agree with the people who would divorce art entirely from human interest' (*Haskell*, p. 44); Moore wrote in 1934: 'The human figure is what interests me most deeply' (*James*, p. 70).

33 *James*, p. 37; *Epstein 1940*, p. 135.

34 p. 61.

35 Moore was photographed for *The Bulletin and Scots Pictorial*, 19 March 1930, carving the Green Hornton stone *Reclining Woman* (*LH* 84), described as 'Epstein-like'. Both sculptors were represented at the International Biennial Exhibition in Venice and the new Zwemmer Gallery in London in 1930 (*The Evening Standard*, 26 November) and in *L'Art Vivant* at the Palais des Beaux-Arts in Brussels in April 1931 (*The Daily Mail*, 28 February).

36 *LH* 42 (whereabouts unknown) and 105 (The Hirshhorn Museum, Washington DC) respectively; nos 1 and 10 in the 1931 exhibition catalogue. *The Birmingham Evening Despatch*, 13 April, commented that *Mother and Child* 'so much impressed Epstein that he has bought it'.

37 *The Observer*, 12 April 1931.

38 D. Mitchinson, *70 Years of Henry Moore*, 1968, under 1931. The partisan *Yorkshire Post*, 14 April 1931, echoed these sentiments: Moore was coupled with that 'happy band of sculptors [which included Hepworth and Skeaping] to whom the future belongs'. Skeaping illustrated work by Moore, Hepworth, Dobson, Zadkine, Epstein and himself in his address on the subject of a 'general survey of the modern look in sculpture' to Polytechnic School of Art students (*The Kentish Independent*, 27 February 1931). See *The Times*, 13 April 1931, on Epstein's misinterpretation of Moore's feeling for sculptural mass and material.

39 pp. 135–36.

40 pp. 148–53 and 143–44 respectively; Epstein is also mentioned briefly on p. 31.

41 W. Packer, *Henry Moore: An Illustrated Biography*, 1985, p. 84.

42 *Henry Moore: Early Carvings 1920–1940*, Leeds City Art Galleries, 1982, p. 31.

43 *LH* 91.

44 *James*, p. 194.

45 Epstein and Moore were both well represented in W. Aumonier, *Modern Architectural Sculpture*, 1930, pp. 126–29, 137, 141.

46 *The Sunday Dispatch*, 12 April 1931, described the work as 'very similar in subject and treatment to that of Epstein in his Genesis mood'.

47 *The Yorkshire Post*, 28 November 1932, coupled them with Gill, Hepworth and Skeaping as those who were 'bringing about the present movement in sculpture'; all, except Gill, had been chosen to show in an exhibition of British art in Moscow, Leningrad and Magnetogorsk (*The Yorkshire Post*, 21 April 1932), although this event never took place.

48 Epstein by the *Female Figure in Flenite* [Fig. 69], *Genesis* [134] and *Night* [Fig. 85], Moore by *Reclining Figure*, 1930 (*LH* 90), which appeared on the cover, and *Reclining Woman* of 1930 (*LH* 84); *Girl* (*LH* 109), *Composition* (*LH* 102) and *Composition* (*LH* 132) of 1931.

49 *The Daily Mail*, 6 June 1932; *The Yorkshire Post*, 15 July 1932.

50 pp. 153–54, where Epstein is described as 'primarily a modeller'.

51 *James*, p. 194.

52 '"Freak Potato" Art' (*The Morning Post*, 16 April 1931), 'Nightmares in Stone' (*The Western Morning News & Mercury*, 7 May 1931) as well.

53 *The Evening News*, 1 January 1931. Moore resigned from the RCA in 1931 and in the following year established a sculpture department at Chelsea.

54 Quoted in *Silber*, p. 38.

55 This carving also appeared in the press (*The Record and Mail*, 11 June 1935) described as belonging to the 'same school as Epstein', and with a misleading but pertinent caption: 'Controversy Rages round Epstein. Are his Sculptings the ravings of a disordered imagination . . . Most People . . . dismiss his work as unnatural rubbish'.

56 J. Clapp, *Art Censorship: A Chronology of Proscribed and Prescribed Art*, 1972, p. 242.

57 *Cork 1985*, pp. 293–96.

58 *S* 224.

59 See *Shewring*, pp. 291–92.

60 The book caused 'a great deal of comment' (*The Yorkshire Post*, 28 June 1934).

61 Epstein is listed as the lender in the catalogue of Moore's November 1933 Leicester Galleries exhibition (no. 11). *The Yorkshire Weekly Post*, 28 July 1934, pointed out that 'Moore's reputation is now second only to that of Epstein', and that Epstein 'owns many works by his most serious rival'.

62 See *Konkretion*, November 1935, published in Stockholm, and *XXe Siècle*, March 1938 (D. Mitchinson, *70 Years of Henry Moore*, 1968).

63 K. Parkes, *The Art of Carved Sculpture*, 1931, vol. I, pp. 24–25, described Epstein's work as non-glyptic.

64 *James*, p. 197. The verdict was shared by Stanley Casson (*Some Modern Sculptors*, 1928, p. 115): Epstein 'seems to have fixed his style definitely and finally. His experimental stage belongs to the remote past and he will bow to no new influence. The hopeful years of 1913 and 1914 are gone' (p. 117).

65 *Balletomane at Large*, 1972, p. 54. Epstein later sold all four of his Moore carvings.

66 *LH* 171 (now in Leeds City Art Galleries). R. Penrose, *Penrose Scrap-Book 1900–1981*, 1981, p. 102; *Angels of Anarchy and Machines for Making Clouds: Surrealism in Britain in the Thirties*, Leeds City Art Galleries, 1986, no. 108.

67 *Cork 1985*, p. 60.

68 Percy Horton to Walter Strachan, 2 January 1936 (C. Hewett, ed., *The Living Curve: Letters to W. J. Strachan 1929–1979*, 1984, p. 14; see also p. 23, n. 1); *The Daily Independent*, 24 October 1935 ('In Revolt Against War and Fascism').

69 In various newspapers, including *The Daily Worker*, 15 October 1937 (W. Packer, *Henry Moore: An Illustrated Biography*, 1985, p. 108).

70 University of Leeds, Brotherton Collection: Kramer correspondence, Bomberg to Kramer, 18 January 1938.

71 *The Times*, 15 February 1939.

72 *LH* 212; *Henry Moore: Early Carvings 1920–1940*, 1982, no. 43.

73 Vol. 5, no. 2, issue no. 26, pp. 132–33. *Lilliput*, vol. 8, 1941, juxtaposed *Adam*, 'One of Epstein's Primitives', with a deformed potato, 'One of Nature's Abstracts' (courtesy of Adrian Budge). See *The Manchester Daily Dispatch*, 8 July 1939.

74 See also *The Daily Sketch*, 8 June 1939, *The Times*, 8 June 1939, *Picture Post*, 24 June 1939, pp. 28–32, *Epstein 1940*, pp. 198–201, 327–30.

75 The carving is uncatalogued and its present whereabout is unknown. The head and torso, separated at the waist from the unfinished body, appears in a *c* 1930 photograph taken in the sculptor, Gertrude Hermes's garden (courtesy of James Hamilton).

76 *Sculpture Inside and Out*, 1939, p. 29; see also p. 49. Interestingly, Moore but not Epstein is represented in A. T. Broadbent's anthology, *Sculpture Today in Great Britain 1940–1943*, 1944 but see A. Wragg, 'Moore and Epstein', *Modern Woman*, July 1947, pp. 66–71.

'THE PRIMITIVE WITHIN'

1 D. Grafly, 'Gill and Epstein', *The American Magazine of Art*, June 1934, pp. 325–34.

2 'Atavism in Art', *The English Review*, December 1925, vol. 41, p. 175.

3 pp. 153–54.

4 p. 113.

5 *The Meaning of Art*, 1933, p. 200. Read discussed 'The Racial Factor in Art' after a review of the 'Jewish expression' in Chagall's painting.

6 See C. Holmes, 'The Myth of Fairness: Racial Violence in Britain 1911–19', *History Today*, October 1985, vol. 35, pp. 41–46, and *Anti-Semitism and British Society 1876–1939*, 1979.

7 The restricted scope of this essay prevents discussion of this complex issue, but an analysis of Epstein's use of the primitive as a way of mediating between various cultural traditions forms part of the author's current research, to be published in the forthcoming book, *The Black Presence in English Art*, ed. by D. Dabydeen. The image of Jewish immigrants as a mediator between 'inside' and 'outside', the forces of modernity and tradition, Western and non-Western races, was not merely a feature of anti-Semitic stereotyping but found corresponding forms in Jewish historiography and literature of the period. Georg Simmel characterised the Jewish intellectuals of Europe as 'prototypical strangers'; their strangeness consisting of a paradoxical unity of nearness and remoteness, and because of this inevitable marginality they gained a

unique and critical perspective on their host culture (P. R. Mendes, 'The Study of the Jewish Intellectual: Some Methodological Proposals' in *Essays in Modern Jewish History. A Tribute to Ben Halpern*, eds, F. Malino and P. C. Albert, 1982, p. 151, discusses Simmel's concept of the 'stranger' in *Soziologie Untersuchung Ueber die Formen der Vergesellschaftung*, 1908).

8 Epstein became convinced of conspiracies against him during the War when, following a vitriolic press campaign and questions in Parliament, his military exemption was rescinded. Furthermore, he was denied any official patronage as a War Artist, the only offer of a commission by the War Trophies committee to sculpt the heads of 'different racial types . . . Jews, Turks, infidels, heretics and all the rest', who were employed in the War, was withdrawn after the receipt of a mysterious letter from Sir George Frampton. In his autobiography Epstein remarked on the analogies which were drawn during the War years between his alien status and artistic primitivism: 'One of the sticks which was used to hit me during the war was the saying that my work smacked more of Dürer than of Leonardo — that I was really like a Boche . . . They thought also, when they said my work was more like Easter Island work, that they had accused me of barbarities unspeakable' (*Epstein 1940*, pp. 136–37).

9 Epstein to John Quinn, 19 January 1917 (New York Public Library Archives: The Quinn Collection). On his inclusion of the bronzes about which Quinn had been critical, Epstein declared: 'This part of the show will interest the many. I feel in any case that these solid statues give me the right to launch out on work of a different character and establish myself solidly as a sculptor. They give the lie to any attempt to label me a charlatan'.

10 'Epstein', *The New Statesman*, February 1917.

11 'Epstein: Tamed and Untamed', February 1917 (untitled press clipping in the Epstein folder, Tate Gallery Archives).

12 'Some Impressions of A Layman', *The Jewish Chronicle*, 27 April 1917.

13 *Haskell*, p. 56. See *Epstein Lampooned* in the present catalogue.

14 Quoted in G. C. Lebzelter, *Political Anti-Semitism in England 1918–39*, 1978, pp. 17, 19.

15 C. Holmes, *Anti-Semitism and British Society 1876–1939*, 1979 (part III: 'The Protocols and The Britons').

16 'The Protocols Plan at Work In The Sphere of Art', *The Hidden Hand*, 12 June 1925. *The Britons* related Epstein's *Risen Christ* and *Hudson Memorial* to an 'evil' Jewish control of the arts which was exploiting Epstein himself as a vehicle for their conspiracy to undermine the moral fabric of Western civilisation: 'How much longer are we going to tolerate this bestiality, this attack upon the Christian culture which we have inherited?'. See also 'Bolshevist Art and Jew Art Control', *The Hidden Hand*, April 1924, in which *The Britons* listed examples of Jewish control in the sphere of modern art. For a discussion of this in relation to Henry Moore, see T. Friedman's essay 'Epsteinism' in the present catalogue.

17 D. Goldring (*The Nineteen-Twenties: A General Survey and Some Personal Memories*, 1945, p. 91) commented that the British public objected to the 'strongly racial art of Jacob Epstein'; this reputation for 'racial art' was not provoked by any of Epstein's overtly primitivist works but by the vividly modelled portraits and religious bronzes of the period.

18 Epstein's own discussions of his statue were ambivalent. On the one hand, he condemned the racial interpretations of the figure, attempting to justify his conception of Christ within a Christian tradition (*Haskell*, Chapter 4, and *Silber*, pp. 35–38,

no. 97), but, on the other hand, he asserted its Jewish identity when he claimed: 'The Jew — the Galilean — condemns our wars, and warns us that "Shalom, Shalom", must be still the watchword between man and man' (*Epstein 1940*, p. 123).

19 'The face is Asiatic in type, with thick sensual lips; cheeks which are markedly different in shape, a gaunt thin body . . . If Mr Epstein were to cut off the head and give it another trunk it would not be an inappropriate face for Satan' ('Chamber of Horrors By Epstein', *The Evening Standard*, 8 February 1920).

20 *The Graphic*, 14 February 1920 (quoted in *Epstein 1940*, pp. 123–25).

21 3 March 1920.

22 *The Nation*, 14 February 1920 (quoted in *Epstein 1940*, pp. 287–91).

23 *The Jewish World*, 11 February 1920, and *The Jewish Guardian*, 13 February 1920.

24 B. Falk, 'The Sculptor at Bay or The Strange Case of Jacob Epstein', *The Daily Mail*, 29 May 1930.

25 *The New Age*, 14 February 1924 (quoted in *Epstein 1949*, pp. 223–25).

26 *Haskell*, pp. 93–94.

27 *Epstein 1940*, pp. 222–23.

28 *The New Age*, 14 February 1924 (quoted in *Epstein 1940*, pp. 223–25).

29 *The Hidden Hand*, Februray 1924, p. 22.

30 'The Hudson Memorial', *The Dial*, LXXIX, 1925, pp. 370–73. Fry defended the *Memorial* during the public furor which followed its unveiling in 1925. However, he acknowledged that he had no personal liking for Epstein's work and one can detect his antipathy in the descriptions of *Rima's* 'haggard shyness' and the 'strangeness of wild things' which he detected in the panel.

31 R. Fry, 'Mr Epstein's Sculpture', *The Dial*, February 1924, p. 505.

32 *Wilenski*, pp. 104, 147.

33 *The Manchester Guardian*, 27 July 1929 (quoted in *Epstein 1940*, pp. 303–04).

Epstein Lampooned

1 A rhyme of the Twenties, quoted in R. J. Sontag, *A Broken World 1919–39*, 1972, p. 182 (courtesy of Elizabeth Barker).

2 An anonymous versifier, quoted in *Cork 1985*, p. 250. An alternative to this verse is in J. Clapp, *Art Censorship: A Chronology of Proscribed and Prescribed Art*, 1972, p. 276. *Haskell*, p. 56, refers to the *Children's Magazine*, 15 June 1929, where Epstein and Einstein are confused: 'I know they both misuse figures'.

3 *Cork 1976*, p. 146.

4 A version of this drawing appeared in *Colour*, November 1914, p. 142 (illustrated in *Cork 1976*, p. 458). See also E. X. Kapp's portrait caricature, 1914 (*Cork 1976*, p. 161).

5 Epstein with *Venus* (second version), 1914–16, (*S* 56). Sold Christie's, 2–3 March 1978, lot 242 (National Portrait Gallery, London, neg 28550).

6 Christie's, 14 December 1973, lot 114. 'I was caricatured as depicting Napoleon with a moustache, but the parallel cannot hold good' (*Haskell*, p. 41).

7 p. 603. The *W. H. Hudson Memorial*, Hyde Park, London (*S* 147), unveiled in 1925.

8 *Punch*, 3 June 1925, p. 595. 'Ordinary folk with an interest in sculpture turned this week-end from

Epstein in Hyde Park to Gilbert in Temple Gardens, for Eros alighted on the Thames Embankment on Saturday' (*Yorkshire Observer*, May 1925).

9 p. 714.

10 p. 725. A variant cartoon by Frank Reynolds, entitled *Another Tribute. Proposed Memorial to a Cricketer Who Has No Interest in Ducks*, appeared in *Punch*, 24 June 1925, p. 686.

11 *Sun God*, begun 1910 (left) and *Primeval Gods*, 1931–33 (*S* 26 and 218).

12 *Genesis*, 1929–30, *Rima*, 1923–25, and *Primeval Gods*, 1931–33 (*S* 194, 147 and 218) meeting to discuss the proposed mutilation of the BMA figures.

13 p. 529.

14 Vol. 5, no. 2, issue no. 26, p. 133.

1 'CE SAUVAGE AMÉRICAIN'

1 *Epstein 1940*, p. 27.

2 *Epstein Drawings*, p. 13, pl. 1.

3 *Hapgood*, pp. 255–57.

4 *Epstein Drawings*, pp. 13–14, pls 7–8.

5 When it was exhibited in Epstein's first one-man show in 1913. The original wax and plaster (The Epstein Estate) are shown in the present exhibition as uncatalogued items.

6 *Silber*, pp. 14–15.

7 *Epstein 1940*, pp. 27–28.

8 *S* 1–2.

9 *Epstein 1940*, p. 16.

10 *Silber*, pp. 14, 16, fig. 2. Both Epstein's and Dalou's bronzes were cast in Paris by A. A. Hebrard. Dalou's was exhibited in the Salle Dalou in late 1905, after Epstein had left Paris.

11 *Geist*, pp. 36–37.

12 B. A. Bennett and D. G. Wilkins, *Donatello*, 1984, fig. 76.

2 THE BMA BUILDING

1 *S* 1–2, datable 1902–04.

2 *Epstein 1940*, pp. 28–29.

3 *S* 6. The BMA commission is discussed in detail in *Cork 1985*, chapter 1; *Silber*, pp. 16–19 and *S* 9–12; *Epstein 1940*, pp. 33–55, 259–75.

4 C. Holden, 'Thoughts for the Strong', *Architectural Review*, July 1905, p. 27.

5 C. Holden, speech delivered at opening of Epstein exhibition in Bolton, unpublished, courtesy Adams, Holden and Pearson, London.

6 See note 4.

7 C. Holden, memoir dated 3 December 1940, unpublished, courtesy Adams, Holden and Pearson, London.

8 *Epstein 1940*, p. 34.

9 See note 5.

10 J. Epstein, 'The Artist's Description of His Work', *British Medical Journal*, 4 July 1908.

11 See note 10.

12 See note 10.

13 See note 10.

14 *The Evening Standard* headline ran: 'BOLD SCULPTURE. AMAZING FIGURES ON A STRAND BUILDING. IS IT ART?'.

15 'The Scribe and the Sculptor', *British Medical Journal*, 11 July 1908.

16 *The Evening Standard*, 20 June 1908.

17 *The Evening Standard*, 23 June 1908.

18 Evelyn Silber has recently suggested that Epstein may have used this photograph, published in *The Studio*, vol. 37, 1906, p. 166, as the starting-point for the two *Dancing Girls* (*S* 9: 12–13). I find the link convincing, particularly with the figure on the right of *The Studio* photograph, and the debt helps to explain why Epstein's dancing figure belongs to a more attenuated Viennese world than the other BMA statues. Lüksch is discussed in K. Parkes, *The Art of Carved Sculpture*, 1931, vol. II, pp. 86–89.

19 P. Vaughan, *Doctors' Commons. A short history of the British Medical Association*, 1959, p. 174.

20 *The Evening Standard*, 10 May 1935.

21 *Epstein 1940*, p. 55.

22 *Silber*, p. 14.

23 *Epstein 1940*, p. 33.

3 EARLY PORTRAITS

1 *S* 9: 12–13.

2 *S* 362.

3 *Epstein 1940*, p. 56.

4 *Haskell*, p. 10.

5 *S* 33.

6 H. S. Ede, *Savage Messiah*, 1931, pp. 206–07.

7 J. Lewison, ed., *Henri Gaudier-Brzeska, sculptor 1891–1915*, 1983, no. 41.

8 R. Speight, *William Rothenstein*, 1962, p. 186, quoting a letter, datable *c* 1908, referring to the BMA figures.

9 *Epstein 1940*, pp. 56–57.

10 Lady Gregory, *Hugh Lane*, 1973, pp. 83, 266.

4 TOMB OF OSCAR WILDE

1 *Silber*, p. 14.

2 I am indebted to Michael Pennington, whose research on the *Oscar Wilde Tomb* will form a part of his MA dissertation (Edinburgh University).

3 Epstein became a naturalised British subject on 22 December 1910. The certificate (no. 19830, Home Office no. 197970) describes him as 'a Sculptor', gives his address as 72 Cheyne Walk, Chelsea, and is signed by Winston Churchill (whose portrait he was later to model, *S* 371), with the oath of allegiance sworn on 4 January 1911 and registered on 9 January (Beth Lipkin Collection).

4 J. P. Raymond and C. Ricketts, *Oscar Wilde Recollections*, 1932.

5 Exhibited at the International Society, 1906, no. 52 and illustrated in *The Studio*, vol. 37, 1906, p. 237 (sold Sotheby's, 17 March 1954, lot 64, as a design for the *Wilde Tomb*); information courtesy of David Fraser Jenkins.

6 *Epstein 1940*, p. 65.

7 *Haskell*, p. 19.

8 A. E. Elsen, *Rodin*, 1963, p. 56. See also Albert Bartholomé's *Monument aux Morts*, 1889–99, in Père Lachaise Cemetery, Paris (*La Sculpture Française au XIXe Siecle*, Galeries nationales du Grand Palais, Paris, 1986, fig. 339).

9 The details of the commission are discussed in *Silber*, pp. 22–23, *S* 40.

10 *Epstein 1940*, p. 65.

11 Holden, unpublished notes on sculpture, Adams, Holden and Pearson, London.

12 J. P. Raymond and C. Ricketts, *Oscar Wilde Recollections*, 1932, p. 38.

13 R. Goldwater, *Symbolism*, 1979, pp. 53–55.

14 Compare with Felicien Rops, *Pornocrates*, 1889, reproduced in R. Goldwater, *Symbolism*, 1979, p. 56.

15 *BML* 953.

16 A number of examples are illustrated in H. Mori, *Sculpture of the Kamakura Period*, 1974. See particularly the *Fuku Kenjyaku Kannon*, 8th century, in the Hokke-do at Todai-ji.

17 *The Evening Standard*, 3 June 1912, quoted in *Epstein 1940*, p. 277.

18 *Vigurs*, p. 43.

19 See note 11.

20 *Shewring*, pp. 36–37.

21 *S* 40, where the reference is quoted.

22 Henri Gaudier-Brzeska saw and sketched it there on 18 June 1912 (A. G. Wilkinson, *Gauguin to Moore: Primitivism in Modern Sculpture*, 1982, p. 183, illustration).

23 3 June 1912, reproduced in *Epstein 1940*, pp. 276–77.

24 6 June 1912, reproduced in *Epstein 1940*, pp. 277–78.

25 Similar objections were raised by the US Customs in 1927, when they sought to charge duty on the import of Brancusi's *Bird in Space* as a manufacture rather than a work of art; Epstein testified in Brancusi's defence (*Epstein 1940*, pp. 155–58 and L. Adams, *Art on Trial from Whistler to Rothko*, 1976, pp. 48–52).

26 Since Joseph Cribb carved the inscription on the *Tomb* between 24 September and 8 October 1912, the letter (reproduced by courtesy of Mrs J. Sanso) may date from late September, after the more composed letter to Roché (see note 28).

27 Jean Paul Laurens, a committee member of the Prefecture of the Seine, was the very person who had earlier stigmatised young Epstein as 'ce sauvage Américain'! (*Epstein 1940*, p. 27).

28 Epstein to Roché, written from London, 14 September 1912 (Humanities Research Center, University of Texas, Austin); *S* 40.

29 *Epstein 1940*, p. 68.

5 EARLY CARVINGS

1 *Epstein 1940*, p. 21.

2 *Epstein 1940*, p. 25. French studio practice *c* 1900 is described in *La Sculpture Française au XIXe Siecle*, Galeries nationales du Grand Palais, Paris, 1986, pp. 4–41, 60–159.

3 A. Crawford, *C. R. Ashbee: Architect, Designer and Romantic Socialist*, 1985, p. 448, n. 89.

4 The edition size and the name and place of casting of *Romilly John* are not known; Augustus John and Epstein both had a cast (M. Holroyd, *Augustus John*, 1974, vol. I, p. 221 n), and from the evidence of Epstein's December 1913 Twenty-One Gallery exhibition catalogue, where further copies are offered for sale, the edition must have numbered about six at least (*S* 8).

5 *S* 22.

6 *Gill Diaries*.

7 *Men and Memories 1900–1922*, 1932, vol. II, p. 195.

8 *Silber*, p. 20, note 7.

9 p. 67.

10 *S* 1–2.

11 *Silber*, p. 21.

12 See *Epstein in Person*, in the present catalogue.

13 *S* 27.

14 See section 6, note 13, in the present catalogue.

15 *BML* 855, 861, 883.

16 *Geist*, pp. 41–42.

17 *Rubin*, vol. I, p. 215.

18 *BML* 14–27.

19 Gill returned to the pose in 1923 in an engraving of a figure entitled *Adam* (*The Engravings of Eric Gill*, 1983, p. 265).

20 R. Speight, *The Life of Eric Gill*, 1966, p. 41.

21 See note 6.

22 See note 6.

23 *S* 42.

24 *Gauguin to Moore: Primitivism in Modern Sculpture*, 1981, pp. 168–69.

6 LOVE AND BIRTH

1 *Gill Diaries*, 9 December 1913, quoted in *Silber*, p. 29. For a similiar view in 1914, see N. Carrington, ed., *Mark Gertler: Selected Letters*, 1965, pp. 71–72.

2 *L'Art: Entretiens Réunis par Paul Gsell*, 1911 (English translation, 1984, pp. 49–50).

3 Letter to William Rothenstein, 25 September 1910 (*Shewring*, pp. 32–33). See *Silber*, p. 21 and the earlier, Paris-period plaster called the *Temple of Love* (*S* 1).

4 *Epstein Drawings*, pp. 16–17, pl. 26.

5 R. Black, *The Art of Jacob Epstein*, 1942, p. 227, no. 7, pl. 93; *Buckle*, p. 424, dates it to 1909.

6 *S* 10. See also the drawing (private collection, London) originally on the verso of [38]; *Schinman*, p. 108.

7 See also *Cork 1976*, p. 117; B. Van Dieren, *Epstein*, 1920, pl. VI.

8 R. Cork, 'Epstein's "Maternity"', *National Art-Collections Fund Review*, 1984, pp. 137–38.

9 *S* 9:14–15.

10 Later evidence of this practice is offered in fig. 9 of the present catalogue: a press photograph of 21 October 1937 showing Epstein in his studio with the completed *Consummatum Est* and a large stone block on the side of which is sketched the outline of an unidentified reclining figure.

11 *BML* 972.

12 *Shewring*, pp. 36–37.

13 Gill was also inspired by such Indian sculpture (M. Yorke, *Eric Gill: Man of Flesh and Stone*, 1981, pp. 198–99).

14 See note 8.

15 *Epstein 1940*, p. 61. A. Werner, *Modigliani The Sculptor*, 1962, pl. 1. Epstein mentions Modigliani in *Haskell*, pp. 88–92, and one of the painter's models, Gabrielle Soene, sat for Epstein in 1918–19 (*S* 101).

16 *Vigurs*, p. 86, no. 170. The drawing can be seen hanging in Epstein's house in *Sculpture of Jacob Epstein: the Eisenberg-Robbins Collection*, Corcoran Gallery of Art, Washington DC, 1973–74.

17 See note 8.

18 *Gill Diaries*.

19 For Gaudier-Brzeska, see R. Cole, *Burning to speak*, 1978, pp. 21–22, and a design for a vase (Anthony d'Offay Gallery, London); for Moore, see the present catalogue, p. 36, fig. 13.

20 S. Geist, *Brancusi: A Study of the Sculpture*, 1968, pp. 149, 198. *Epstein 1940*, pp. 63–64.

21 *Cork 1976*, p. 82.

22 W. Michel and C. J. Fox, *Wyndham Lewis on Art*, 1969, p. 57, quoted in *Silber*, p. 30.

23 *Zilczer*, pp. 94–95, 158.

24 *Geist*, p. 47.

25 *BML* 256.

26 D. D. Paige, ed., *The Selected Letters of Ezra Pound 1907–1941*, 1950, p. 52. The first group of *Doves* (*S* 48) is in the Hirshhorn Museum, Washington DC.

27 *Epstein 1940*, pp. 71–72.

28 *Zilczer*, p. 40, n. 15.

29 Gaudier-Brzeska toyed with a similiarly simple geometry in a drawing of a *Swan*, 1914 (*Cork 1976*, p. 432).

30 *Geist*, pp. 60–61.

31 *Rubin*, vol. II, p. 435.

32 Epstein's un-Greek interpretation of this subject is discussed by Ivan Ivor in an unnamed press clipping dated February 1917 (Tate Gallery Archives, Epstein file).

33 *Epstein 1940*, pp. 216–17; *BML* 260.

34 *BML* 237.

35 *Wellington*, p. 20.

36 H. S. Ede, *Savage Messiah*, 1931, p. 247.

37 *The New Age*, 25 December 1913, quoted in *Epstein 1940*, p. 81.

38 *Epstein 1940*, pp. 63, 218.

39 *The Egoist*, 16 March 1914, quoted in *Epstein 1940*, p. 72, adding 'There is in [Epstein's] work an austerity, a metaphysics, like that of Egypt' (p. 72). In July 1912, Epstein introduced an enthusiastic Gertler to Egyptian art in the British Museum (N. Carrington, ed., *Mark Gertler: Selected Letters*, 1965, p. 43).

40 *Silber*, p. 27.

41 *Rubin*, vol. II, p. 434. A variant (lost) drawing was published in BLAST, no. 1, June 20, 1914, pl. xv. T. E. Hulme (*The New Age*, 25 December 1913, quoted in *Epstein 1940*, p. 81) described a lost drawing entitled *Creation* as showing 'a baby seen inside many folds'.

42 *Speculations*, 1924, p. 107.

43 *S* 51; *Cork 1976*, pp. 462–63.

44 *BML* 271–73.

45 *Cork 1976*, pp. 460–61.

46 *BML* 550–79.

47 *Cork 1976*, p. 119. One critic condemned the work as 'rude savagery [having] vague memories of dark ages' (*Epstein 1940*, p. 65).

48 Quoted in *S* 67.

7 ROCK DRILL

1 *Rock Drill* is discussed in detail in R. Cork, *Jacob Epstein: The Rock Drill Period*, 1973; *Cork 1976*, pp. 464–82; *Epstein 1940*, chapter 7; *Silber*, pp. 31–33 and *S* 53.

2 *S* 48.

3 Epstein's foreword to T. E. Hulme, *Speculations*, 1924 (H. Read, ed.).

4 T. E. Hulme, 'Modern Art and its Philosophy', *Speculations*, 1924, p. 104.

5 A. G. Wilkinson, *Gauguin to Moore: Primitivism in Modern Sculpture*, 1982, pp. 178–79; *Rubin*, vol. II, pp. 433–34, 439–41.

6 *Epstein 1940*, p. 70.

7 *Epstein 1940*, p. 70.

8 *Epstein 1940*, p. 70.

9 *S* 9:2.

10 *Epstein 1940*, p. 70.

11 E. Pound, *Gaudier-Brzeska. A Memoir*, 1916 (revised edn., 1960, p. 17).

12 See note 11.

13 *BLAST No. 2*, 1915, p. 78.

14 D. Bomberg, draft of unsent letter to W. Roberts, 1957 (collection of the artist's family; *Cork 1976*, p. 467).

15 *Epstein 1940*, p. 70.

16 Lady Epstein interview with R. Cork (*Cork 1976*, p. 479).

17 *Epstein 1940*, p. 56.

18 *Silber*, p. 36.

8 PRIVATE CONCERNS

1 *Shewring*, p. 323 (letter dated 28 February 1935).

2 Tate Gallery Archives. A different version, also quoted here, is given in *Epstein 1940*, pp. 105–06.

3 In the interview, Epstein stated that he modelled Fisher's bust during the week of Lord Kitchener's death (5 June 1916).

4 *Epstein 1940*, p. 88.

5 *Epstein 1940*, p. 87.

6 *Haskell*, p. 67.

7 *Silber*, p. 33.

8 *Silber*, p. 33, nos 63–64, dating both portraits to 1915. The Duchess's portrait followed that of Lord Fisher, but the *Weekly Dispatch* article indicates that both date from 1916.

9 *The Sculpture of Jacob Epstein*, Leicester Galleries, exhibition no. 238, February–March 1917.

10 *S* 69, citing a photograph in the possession of Kate Lechmere. *An Exhibition of Watercolours and Drawings by a group of artists serving with His Majesty's Forces including recent sculpture by Jacob Epstein*, Leicester Galleries, exhibition no. 246, October 1917, no. 4.

11 'Uncommissioned Art', *Burlington Magazine*, vol. 32, 1918. pp. 29–30. See also *S* 84.

12 F. Rutter, *Sunday Times*, 25 February 1917.

13 'The Art of Jacob Epstein', *The New Statesman*, 17 March 1917, pp. 567–68.

14 *Haskell*, p. 78.

15 *Epstein 1940*, p. 115.

16 H. Vickers, *Gladys Duchess of Marlborough*, 1979, pp. 152–53. *S* 142.

17 *Epstein 1940*, p. 115.

18 *Wellington*, p. 24.

19 *Epstein Memorial Exhibition*, 1961, no. 56.

20 H. Vickers, *Gladys Duchess of Marlborough*, 1979, p. 153.

21 *British Jewry Book of Honour*, p. 280, no. 8522.

22 H. D. Myer, *Soldiering of Sorts* (unpublished memoir, Royal Fusiliers Museum), p. 89.

23 Epstein to Bernard van Dieren, quoted in full in *Silber*, p. 36.

24 *Silber*, p. 36.

25 HMCSS: Thornycroft Papers *c* 335, letter from Walter Horsley, 7 June 1917.

26 *Epstein Drawings*, p. 18, pls 35–36.

27 *S* 57–108.

28 *The Autobiography of Alice B. Toklas*, 1933, quoted in *Buckle*, p. 85.

29 *S* 41, 70, 92–94.

30 *Epstein 1940*, p. 116.

31 *Wellington*, p. 25. S. Casson described the fifth bust as having a 'calm beauty . . . quite perfect examples of the pure and almost unemotional style' (*Some Modern Sculptors*, 1928, p. 114).

32 Mrs P. Lewis in conversation with Evelyn Silber, October 1986.

33 *S* 73, 76.

4 *Sculpture To-day*, 1921, vol. I, p. 119.

5 *Wellington*, p. 23.

6 A. Gibson, *Postscript to Adventure*, 1930, pp. 150–51.

7 *Epstein 1940*, p. 253. See particularly *Kneeling Woman*, 1911, and *Praying Woman*, 1918 (S. Salzmann, *Wilhelm Lehmbruck 1881–1919*, 1979, nos 9, 32).

PORTRAITS

1 *Sunday Times*, 20 February 1924.

2 pp. 27–28.

3 pp. 78–79.

4 E. H. Ramsden (*Twentieth Century Sculpture*, 1949, pls 5–6) contrasted the Sitwell bust with Epstein's *Rabindranath Tagore*, 1926 (S 172).

5 'Recent sculpture by Jacob Epstein', *Burlington Magazine*, 3 June 1920, p. 146.

6 *Haskell*, pp. 68–69.

7 From a letter postmarked 19 April 1906 (R. F. C. Hull, trans., *Selected Letters of Rainer Maria Rilke 1902–1926*, 1946, p. 87).

8 *Silber*, p. 39.

9 R. Fry, *New Statesman*, 26 January 1924, p. 450, quoted in S. Casson, *Some Modern Sculptors*, 1928, pp. 115–16, and *Silber*, p. 41.

10 S. Casson, *Some Modern Sculptors*, 1928, p. 11.

11 For example, K. Parkes, *The Art of Carved Sculpture*, 1931.

12 *Haskell*, pp. 62, 60–61 respectively. 'There is an ancient myth about the image asleep in the block of marble until it is carefully disengaged by the sculptor. The sculptor must himself feel that he is not so much inventing or shaping the curve of breast or shoulder as delivering the image from its prison.' (A. de Saint-Exupéry, *Wind, Sand and Stars*, 1939; 1983 ed., p. 37).

13 University of Leeds, Brotherton Collection: Kramer Correspondence. A letter, in the same collection, from Julian Huxley to Kramer, 17 November 1931, mentions 'the other drawing you kindly left of Epstein'. A lithographic portrait of Epstein is in the National Portrait Gallery (neg. 9531).

14 S 126 (dated 1922).

15 *Epstein 1940*, p. 113.

16 *Wellington*, p. 26.

17 Tate Gallery Archives: Epstein file.

18 S 162.

19 Epstein was often marked out for his 'Oriental' taste, but his relative success is apparent from a comparison with work such as Christine Gregory's *Rhythm* (RBS, *Modern British Sculpture*, nd, p. 41). See Elizabeth Barker's essay on this matter in the present catalogue.

20 *Epstein 1940*, p. 15.

21 pp. 90–91.

22 A. Haskell, *Balletomane at Large*, 1972, p. 60.

23 S 159, 160, 163, 166, 176, 199, 206.

24 *Self Portrait of an Artist*, 1949, p. 247.

25 These were later published as *Epstein. Seventy Five Drawings*, 1929 [present exhibition cat. no. 100].

26 *Wellington*, p. 24.

27 *Epstein 1940*, pp. 111–12.

28 *Haskell*, p. 66.

29 *Epstein 1940*, pp. 112–13.

30 *Wellington*, pp. 26–27.

31 *Some Modern Sculptors*, 1928, pp. 113–14.

32 *The Observer*, 27 January 1924.

33 *Epstein 1940*, pp. 89–94. J. Conrad, *Joseph Conrad and his Circle*, 1935, p. 236.

34 See note 33.

35 R. Curle, *The Last Years of Joseph Conrad*, 1928, pp. 129–30.

36 *Epstein 1940*, p. 92.

37 *Haskell*, p. 69.

38 *Haskell*, p. 69 and *Epstein 1940*, pp. 89–94.

39 J. Conrad, *Joseph Conrad and his Circle*, 1935, pp. 237–38.

40 J. Baines, *Joseph Conrad: A Critical Biography*, 1960, p. 435.

10   EPSTEIN AS A BOOK ILLUSTRATOR

1 *Haskell*, p. 29.

2 *Epstein 1940*, p. 12.

3 H. Hapgood, *A Victorian in the Modern World*, 1939 (reprinted 1972), p. 142; *Hapgood*, pp. 256, 259–60.

4 *Epstein 1940*, p. 13.

5 *Hapgood*, p. 255.

6 vol. XXVI, pp. 250–61: 'A Ghetto Café' (p. 251), 'Zunser in his Printing-Office' (p. 253), 'Dolitzki' (p. 255), 'Rosenfeld' (p. 257) and 'Wald' (p. 259).

7 p. 250.

8 vol. XI, August 1900, pp. 348–58. 'Sketch Writers of the Ghetto', *The Bookman*, vol. XIV, 1901, pp. 263–75, includes illustrations by Epstein's friend, Bernard Gussow.

9 *Hapgood*, p. 259.

10 *Hapgood*, pp. 259–60.

11 *Epstein 1940*, p. 13.

12 *100 American Drawings from the J. D. Hatch Collection*, Heim Gallery, London, October–November 1976, no. 95, pl. 99.

13 *A Victorian in the Modern World*, 1939, p. 142. The contract for the book, dated 3 March 1902, is in the archives of Harper & Row, Publishers, Inc, New York.

14 *Epstein Drawings*, p. 13; *Haskell*, p. 113.

15 *A Victorian in the Modern World*, 1939, p. 142. Three drawings published in *The Spirit of the Ghetto* are by Gussow.

16 M. Rischin, ed., H. Hapgood, *The Spirit of the Ghetto*, 1967, p. vii n.

17 *The Bookman*, March 1903, vol. XVII, p. 97; *The World*, 8 November 1902, vol. XLIII, no. 15, 054, p. 8.

18 *The Literary Digest*, 22 November 1902, vol. XXV, no. 21, p. 684, with an advertisement for the book with one of Epstein's illustrations on its inside back cover.

19 *The New York Evening Post*, 6 December 1902, p. 21; *The New York Daily Tribune*, 15 November 1902, p. 10.

20 Correspondence between Hapgood and Funk & Wagnalls (Harper & Row, Publishers, Inc. archive).

21 vol. XCIV, pp. 469–73. See *Haskell*, p. 13; *Epstein 1940*, p. 19, H. Hapgood, *A Victorian in the Modern World*, 1939, p. 143.

22 Another drawing, 'A Political Discussion at the "Independent Cafe" on Grand Street' (not as quoted in *Silber*, p. 11, n. 8) was almost certainly one of those published in the *Century Magazine*.

23 *Epstein Drawings*, p. 13; *Epstein 1940*, pp. 15–16, 19–20.

24 G. W. Allen, *The New Walt Whitman Handbook*, 1975, pp. 99–100. Whitman's allusion to the implied

phallic symbolism of the calamus plant ('the biggest & hardiest kind of spears of grass') appeared in a private letter unknown to Epstein (E. H. Miller, ed., *Walt Whitman Correspondence*, 1961, vol. I, p. 347).

25 *Silber*, p. 14.

26 C. Judrin, *Rodin Drawings and Watercolours*, 1983, pls. 32–38; *Epstein 1940*, p. 249.

27 *Rodin: Sculpture and Drawings*, 1970, nos 118–19.

28 D. H. Laurence, ed., G. B. Shaw, *Collected Letters 1898–1910*, 1972, p. 521.

29 C. Lampert, *Rodin: Sculpture & Drawings*, 1986, no. 103, pl. 55. Rothenstein had organised the Rodin exhibition at the Carfax Gallery in January 1900.

30 *Men and Memories 1900–1922*, 1932, vol. II, p. 87.

31 *Epstein Drawings*, p. 13.

32 *Haskell*, p. 13.

33 *Epstein 1940*, p. 19.

34 Printed in a series of phototype plates by the Fanfare Press and published by J. Saville & Co. Ltd.

35 vol. 8, pp. 376–77. See also T. W. Earp, *The Studio*, vol. 96, 1928, pp. 441–42.

36 'Jacob Epstein and the Old Testament', *The Studio*, vol. 103, 1932, pp. 290–91.

37 *Epstein 1940*, p. 166.

38 *Epstein 1940*, p. 166.

39 'The Sculptor Paints', *The Architectural Review*, vol. LXXI, 1932, p. 101.

40 *Epstein Drawings*, p. 20. At least 35 other uncatalogued biblical illustrations were sold at the Redfern Gallery exhibition. Two (*Joash*, no. 21, and *Moses on Mount Sinai*, no. 28) were bought by Epstein for Matthew Smith (information from the Redfern Gallery).

41 Collotype reproductions printed by Donald Macbeth, text set at the Windmill Press and published by William Heinemann; reprinted by Coward-McCann Inc, New York, 1935. See I. Roth, *Cecil Roth: Historian without Tears*, 1982, p. 36.

42 *Gems and Life*, 1927, pp. 13–17 (reprinted in *Visions and Jewels*, 1952); *Epstein 1940*, pp. 110–11; S 164.

43 p. 5 (1935 edition).

44 pp. 107, 3 respectively (1935 edition).

45 *Epstein 1940*, p. 111.

46 [G. Macy] *The Monthly Letter of the Limited Editions Club*, September 1940, no. 126 (quoted by courtesy of S. Shiff).

47 The title-page is missing but the edition includes an introduction by Théophile Gautier dated 20 February 1868 and is inscribed 'Jacob Epstein . . . December 1904' and 'Jacob Epstein 5. Rue Campagne Première', with a pencil sketch on p. 91 for 'Élévation' from *Spleen et Idéal* (Beth Lipkin Collection).

48 *LEC* Archives (by kind permission of the Librarian).

49 See note 46.

50 Introduction to *An Exhibition of Drawings by Jacob Epstein for 'Les Fleurs du Mal' of Charles Baudelaire*, Arthur Tooth & Son, London, 1938. A grangerised copy, with photographic reproductions and lithographic proofs of some of the illustrations, is in the Beth Lipkin Collection.

51 Lady Epstein, MS notes on '14 Epstein Pencil Sketches', 1978 (Pennyslvania State University Library).

52 See note 50.

53 *Epstein 1940*, pp. 23, 25, 27.

54 See note 50.

55 *Epstein 1940*, pp. 190–92.

56 *Epstein 1940*, pp. 193–94.

57 A. E. Elsen, *Rodin*, 1963, p. 209. The original drawings of 1886–89 are in the Musée Rodin, Paris.

58 The translations were edited by James Laver, then Keeper of the Department of Engravings at the Victoria and Albert Museum (J. Laver, *Museum Piece*, 1963, p. 199).

59 *Quarto-Millenary: the First 250 Publications and the First 25 Years 1929–1954 of the Limited Editions Club*, 1959, pp. 14, 28, 254; J. Laver, *Museum Piece*, 1963, pp. 198–99; P. Petro, 'The Limited Editions Club: The Macy Years, 1929–1956', *The Private Library*, vol. 8, 3rd series, 1985, pp. 48–61.

60 *An Exhibition of Books Designed, Illustrated or Printed in Great Britain for Mr George Macy of New York*, July–September 1952, p. 3.

61 *Epstein 1940*, pp. 188–89.

62 See note 50.

63 *The New Age*, 25 December 1913, reprinted in *Epstein 1940*, p. 81.

64 This was illustrated in Tooth's 1938 exhibition catalogue but not in the *Limited Editions Club* volume. A heated correspondence between Macy and Epstein during 1939 is in the *LEC* Archive.

65 A version of the drawing is at Walsall (*Vigurs*, no. 58, illustrated).

66 The drawing Epstein prepared for 'La Servante au Grand Coeur' (Tooth's no. 9) had been placed to illustrate 'Alchimie de la Douleur' (the original, now in the Victoria and Albert Museum, has the correct title). See Ingham to Macy, 22 December 1939 (*LEC* Archive).

67 See note 50. A reviewer in *Time* magazine, 19 December 1938, p. 30, concurred with Epstein's view that *Les Fleurs du Mal* 'has been abundantly profaned by illustrators who interpreted it as high-class pornography'.

11   EPSTEIN AND THE THEATRE

1 Meninsky had served along side Epstein in the Jewish Battalion of the Royal Fusiliers in 1917–18. His designs for *David* are illustrated in *The Morning Post*, 14 January 1936, *Illustrated Sporting and Dramatic*, 31 January 1936 and elsewhere (courtesy of The Duke of York's Theatre file: The Museum of the Theatre, Victoria and Albert Museum).

2 T. W. Earp in *The Daily Telegraph*, 19 January 1936. This drawing (whereabouts unknown) was shown in a Redfern Gallery exhibition, 17 June– 25 September 1964, no. 171.

3 Described in *The Times*, 14 January 1936.

4 Particularly BM no. 124534 (R. D. Barnett, *Assyrian Palace Reliefs and Their Influence on the Sculpture of Babylonia and Persia*, 1960, pl. 26; also *Sculptures from the North Palace of Ashurbanipal at Nineveh (668–627 BC, 1976)*.

5 For a similar but earlier (1930) composition, see *Epstein Drawings*, p. 19, pl. 44.

6 'My original scheme included the famous Goliath encounter, but for various reasons this has now been discarded' (*The Daily Telegraph*, 18 November 1935).

7 14 January 1936. *The Sphere*, 18 January 1936, published a photograph of Epstein standing before the curtain; see also *The Sketch*, 15 January 1936, p. 105, and G. Ashton, *History of the Duke of York's Theatre*, 1980, pl. 49.

12   EPSTEIN IN THE PUBLIC EYE

1 p. 80.

2 *Epstein 1940*, p. 122.

3 *S 74*.

4 *Epstein 1940*, p. 122.

5 *S 175* (a bronze group dated 1926–27, using Sunita and her son Enver as models).

6 *Epstein 1940*, p. 122.

7 J. Fothergill, *Innkeepers Diary*, 1931, frontispiece illustration.

8 Epstein interviewed in *The Sunday Evening Telegraph*, 15 February 1920.

9 *Epstein 1940*, p. 123–25.

10 *The Graphic*, 14 and 21 February 1920 respectively, reprinted in *Epstein 1940*, pp. 123–27.

11 *HMCSS*: Thornycroft Papers c. 486, letter dated 19 February 1920.

12 O. Brown, *Exhibition: The Memoirs of Oliver Brown*, 1968, pp. 70–71.

13. *The Worthing Herald*, 29 July 1977, *Epstein 1940*, p. 129.

14 *Haskell*, p. 3.

15 *Minute Book* of the Hudson Memorial Committee, lists of subscribers, specifications, contracts, letters and press cuttings 1922–26 (*RSPB*); Parliamentary Debates, police reports and press cuttings (Public Record Office, Kew); sketchbook and letters (*HMCSS*); architect's drawings (Royal Institute of British Architects, London); press cuttings (The Henry Moore Foundation and Tate Gallery Archives); *Epstein 1940*, chapter x, Appendix 4; *Silber*, pp. 43–45, *S 146–47*; *Haskell*, pp. 24–35.

16 Graham wrote to Mrs Frank Lemon, 18 April 1923: 'I have just come from Epstein's. I am sitting for my bust' (*RSPB*: letters).

17 *Epstein 1940*, p. 107.

18 *Powell*, p. 117.

19 *RSPB*: *Minute Book*, pp. 11–17.

20 *HMCSS*: Bone to Graham, 2 February 1923.

21 *RSPB*: Earle to Lemon, 26 June 1923.

22 *HMCSS*: inscribed 'Jacob Epstein 49 Baldwin's Hill Loughton Essex. 1923'. See T. Friedman, 'Rodin is Dead' in T. Knipe, ed., *Drawing in Air: An Exhibition of Sculptor's Drawings 1882–1982*, 1983, pp. 22–23.

23 *Green Mansions* (1937 edition, pp. 65–66).

24 *S 39*; *Cork 1985*, pp. 92–96; *Epstein 1940*, pp. 108–09.

25 *Epstein 1940*, p. 109; *S 131–32, 134–35*; *Buckle*, pls 180–90.

26 *The Evening Standard*, 20 November 1925.

27 The Henry Moore Foundation: *No 3 Notebook*, 1922–24, p. 91; *Henry Moore: Early Carvings 1920–1940*, Leeds City Art Galleries, 1982, pl. XI, fig. 46).

28 p. 270.

29 *RSPB*: *Minute Book*, p. 40.

30 *RSPB*: *Minute Book*, p. 45.

31 *Epstein 1940*, p. 128. 'Here by myself away from the clank of the world' (from 'In Paths Untrodden', the opening of *Calamus* in *Leaves of Grass*).

32 *Powell*, p. 81.

33 *RSPB*: H. M. Ranee Margaret of Sarawak to Mrs Frank Lemon, 22 May 1925.

34 Public Record Office, Kew: Metropolitan Police Report, 8 October 1935.

35 Epstein believed the attacks were the result of the same prejudices and misconceptions surrounding *Rima*, now repeated *ad infinitum* (*Haskell*, p. 43).

36 J. Lever, ed., *Catalogue of the Drawings Collection of the Royal Institute of British Architects*, 1973, vol. G–K, pp. 133–34.

37 *Cork 1985*, pp. 256–57, noting Holden's involvement with the *Tomb*.

38 *S 189*. R. Cork, 'Overhead Sculpture for the Underground Railway', in S. Nairne and N. Serota, eds, *British Sculpture in the Twentieth Century*, 1981, pp. 90–101; *Cork 1985*, chapter 6; *Epstein 1940*, chapter 14 and appendix 5.

39 *Haskell*, pp. 47–48. This aspect was stressed by *The Evening News*, 16 January 1929.

40 *The Manchester Guardian*, 3 August 1929 (*Cork 1985*, p. 258).

41 *The Evening News*, 16 January 1929.

42 *Cork 1985*, pl. 365, illustrates an intermediary stage drawing. What is the relationship between *Day* and the stone carving *Man and child*, c 1910, attributed to Epstein and/or Gill by Evelyn Silber (*Silber*, fig. 8)?

43 'Mr Epstein Replies', *The Evening Standard*, 31 January 1929.

44 *Powell*, pp. 82–83, *Epstein 1940*, p. 306.

45 S. Geist, *Bancusi: The Sculpture and Drawings*, 1975, pp. 55, 177, no. 68.

46 *S 188*.

47 *Haskell*, p. 46.

48 James Bone in *The Manchester Guardian* in 1929 (*Epstein 1940*, p. 306).

49 See note 48. *Wilenski*, p. 132, likened them to the 'cubic form' of Egyptian sculpture.

50 Epstein in *The Manchester Guardian*, 3 August 1929.

51 *Haskell*, p. 46.

52 *Powell*, p. 85.

53 *Wilenski*, p. 132.

54 Epstein in *The Evening Standard*, 31 January 1929.

55 *Epstein 1940*, p. 159.

56 *The Daily Telegraph*, 24 May 1929.

57 *Epstein 1940*, pp. 303–07; see also *Haskell*, p. 55.

58 *Cork 1985*, p. 290.

59 *Haskell*, pp. 52–54, 58.

60 *Youth Advancing* (*S 423*), commissioned for the Festival of Britain.

13   ISOLATION AND DEFIANCE

1 *Epstein 1940*, p. 162; *S 194*.

2 *The Daily Telegraph*, 7 February 1931, reprinted in *Epstein 1940*, p. 310.

3 *Hopper*, no. 41.

4 G. M. A. Hanfmann, *Classical Sculpture*, 1967, pl. 305.

5 *Powell*, p. 48; *Haskell*, pp. 63–64.

6 *Haskell*, p. 73. See also R. Black, *The Art of Jacob Epstein*, 1942, p. 20.

7 The Henry Moore Foundation: *No 3 Notebook*, 1922–24, p. 137 recto (D. Mitchinson, *Henry Moore: Unpublished Drawings*, 1971, pl. 24).

8 26 February 1931, reprinted in *Epstein 1940*, p. 317. Epstein, who was in New York City briefly in 1927, may have seen Lachaise's *Standing Woman*, bronze, 177.8 cm high, begun in 1912 and completed in 1927 (H. Kramer and others, *The Sculpture of Gaston Lachaise*, 1967, pls 12–14).

9 7 February 1931, reprinted in *Epstein 1940*, pp. 309–11.

10 *BML 229*; see also 241 (p. 59, fig. 87).

BML. Wilenski, p. 145, noted the similarity between the negroid character of *Genesis* and the concave treatment of the cheeks of some African masks, although he saw 'nothing here of the negro principle of form revolving round an axis'.

2 *Haskell*, p. 12.

3 *Powell*, p. 46, chapters VIII–IX.

4 *Regenesis*, 1930, was carved in reaction to what Underwood considered Epstein's misinterpretation of the subject (C. Neve, *Leon Underwood*, 1974, pp. 139–42, pl. 97).

5 See also *Haskell*, pp. 80–84.

6 *The Yorkshire Post*, 16 April 1931.

7 R. F. Bisson, *The Sandon Studios Society and the Arts*, 1965, p. 174 (courtesy of Alan Swerdlow).

8 p. 20, pl. 5.

9 *Emlyn: An Early Autobiography (1927–1935)*, 1976, p. 263.

10 *Silber*, p. 51.

11 *Buckle*, p. 192.

12 A second drawing (Birmingham Museums and Art Gallery, 1985. P. 21) is inscribed by Epstein 'Sacre du printemps'.

13 *Epstein 1940*, pp. 42–55; *Cork 1985*, p. 60.

14 See the discussion in 'Epsteinism' in the present catalogue.

25 *Epstein 1940*, p. 168; *S 246*.

26 *Epstein 1940*, p. 174. Nevertheless, *Ecce Homo* had its imitators, as in A. J. J. Ayers's *Head of Christ*, 1938 (*Art and Artists*, June 1986, p. 4).

27 A. Bishop, ed., *Vera Brittain, Diary of the Thirties 1932–1939: Chronicle of Friendship*, 1986, p. 174, entry dated 5 August 1935.

28 *Epstein 1940*, pp. 172–74, entitled 'Epstein and Religious Art'.

29 *Epstein 1940*, p. 178.

30 *Buckle*, pp. 263–64.

31 *Illustrations to the Old Testament by Epstein*, Redfern Gallery, London, 23 February–19 March 1932, comprised 54 pencil and wash drawings priced at 20 guineas each.

32 Birmingham Museums and Art Gallery, 1985. P. 18.

33 *Epstein Drawings*, p. 21, no. 58.

34 *S 199*.

35 *Haskell*, pp. 125–27.

36 *Epstein 1940*, p. 248. See *The Fall of Lucifer* relief (*S 362*).

37 *S 133, 206, 341–53*. C. Lampert, *Rodin: Sculpture and Drawings*, 1986, pp. 42–99. A statuette of this type appears in Matthew Smith's *Still-Life with clay figure*, c 1939, Southampton Art Gallery (R. Shone, *The Century of Change: British Painting since 1900*, 1977, pl. 89).

14 THE GREAT PORTRAITIST

1 The bust cost £200 (E. Williams, *Emlyn: An Early Autobiography 1927–1935*, 1973, pp. 238–41).

2 Gielgud to Evelyn Silber, 9 November 1983.

3 E. Williams, *Emlyn: An Early Autobiography 1927–1935*, 1973, p. 240.

4 See note 2.

5 *Epstein 1940*, p. 94.

6 *Epstein 1940*, p. 95.

7 Reproduced courtesy of Mrs Lewis.

8 *Epstein 1940*, p. 234.

9 *S 317*.

10 Interview with T. Friedman, Winter 1986.

11 *Hopper*, no. 68.

12 *Buckle*, p. 209. Isobel Nicholas (Rawsthorne) also modelled for Francis Bacon.

13 *Haskell*, p. 25.

14 Interview with Evelyn Silber.

15 *Epstein 1940*, p. 87.

16 *S 123, 130, 213, 222, 265, 316, 336, 399*; see also 528.

17 *Epstein 1940*, pp. 117–18.

18 *Buckle*, p. 222.

19 *Epstein 1940*, pp. 117–18.

20 The fifth portrait of *Kathleen* is closely based on Verrocchio's *Portrait of a Lady*, Museo Nazionale, Florence (*Silber*, p. 40).

21 *Epstein 1940*, p. 202, in chapter XXI, entitled 'Studies of Children'.

22 *S 98, 107, 108, 110, 114, 115, 117, 118, 125, 167, 186*.

23 P. G. Konody, *The Observer*, 27 January 1924, thought it 'a wonderful plastic interpretation of childish helplessness . . . modelled with a sensibility and a feeling for the quality of flesh and bone that is truly astounding'.

24 Oral communication by Mrs Lewis to Evelyn Silber, 1 November 1986.

25 *Haskell*, pp. 60–61. See, for example, *Romilly John* [31–32].

26 Theodore Garman (born 1924) developed schizophrenia and died tragically in 1954 (*Vigurs*, nos 107–21).

27 *Epstein Drawings*, pl. 60.

28 *Epstein 1940*, pp. 204–05.

29 See note 28.

30 *S 305, 357*.

31 Leicester Galleries, exhibition no. 794, 1944, no. 10.

32 *Epstein 1940*, p. 220.

33 *Epstein 1940*, p. 203.

34 T. Grove, 'Joffe's Mission', *The Observer Colour Magazine*, 19 October 1986, p. 18.

35 *Haskell*, p. 124.

36 *Epstein 1940*, p. 203.

15 THE BURDEN OF FAME

1 'Cavendish Square — Past and Present', 20 February 1957 (*The Journal of the London Society*, p. 23).

2 'Architect, Sculptor and Client', *The Builder*, 25 June 1964, p. 1099, an account of a discussion at the Architectural Association, 28 April 1954.

3 *S 162*.

4 Courtesy of the Convent of the Holy Child Jesus. See *Epstein 1940*, p. 235.

5 *Epstein 1940*, p. 236.

6 'Sculpture in the Streets', *The Observer*, 7 June 1953.

7 'Public Sculpture', *The New Statesman*, 4 July 1953.

8 *Silber*, p. 59; *S 450–51*, for full details and sources of the conversation.

9 Ingersoll to Epstein, 16 February 1951 (*FPAA*).

10 Epstein to Noble, 18 April 1952 (*FPAA*).

11 *Epstein 1940*, p. 237.

12 Epstein to Ingersoll, 16 April 1953 (*FPAA*).

13 Marceau to Ingersoll, 22 October 1953 (*FPAA*).

14 James Laver published an appreciation, 'A Sculptor in Hot Water!' (*Everybody's*, 7 February 1953), when the commission became known.

15 Quoted in *S 502*.

16 H. Faber, *Caius Gabriel Cibber 1630–1700: His Life and Work*, 1926, chapter VIII; illustrated in *Apollo*, March 1938, p. 119. The figure, and its companion, *Melancholy Madness*, are now in the Victoria and Albert Museum, London.

17 *Buckle*, pls 626, 647.

18 *Buckle*, p. 395.

19 *Silber*, pp. 57–58.

20 *Trades Union Congress Memorial Building Sculpture Competition General Conditions and Instructions*, 1954, items 21–22.

21 *Buckle*, pl. 607.

22 Quoted in *S 489*.

23 *Silber*, p. 48.

24 *S 336, 423, 476*.

25 *Haskell*, pp. 102–03. A photograph of a lost drawing by Epstein for the torso and legs of the mother figure is in the Beth Lipkin Collection.

26 Letter dated 30 April 1956, quoted in *Silber*, p. 56.

Addendum

180

LAZARUS   1947–48   (S391)
Hoptonwood stone   H 254
New College Chapel, Oxford
(Exhibited at Whitechapel Art Gallery only)

Epstein was approaching his seventieth year when he worked on his last, and arguably his greatest, free-standing carving [Fig. 10]. As usual he worked without a commission and it was only two years after *Lazarus* was first exhibited in 1950 that A. H. Smith, Warden of New College, Oxford, was so impressed by it (as he sat for his own portrait in the Hyde Park Gate studio, *S449*) that he arranged its purchase and eventual placing in the nave of New College Chapel. Epstein described this as 'one of the happiest issues of my working life' since the sculpture might have been designed for the site; 'the lofty soaring arches seemed to continue the upward thrust of my figure' (*Epstein: An Autobiography*, 1955, p. 232).

It is carved from a tall, shallow block of Hoptonwood stone, a material which the sculptor had favoured for early carvings such as *Maternity* [37] and the *Tomb of Oscar Wilde* [Fig. 49], but which he had largely abandoned in favour of the translucency of alabaster and marble during the Thirties. The sole exception is *Woman Possessed* [140* and 141] and this, like the earlier pieces, is highly finished and smooth, quite unlike the rough grandeur of *Lazarus*. The subject is ostensibly traditional; the raising of Lazarus was a common narrative theme in medieval and Renaissance art and an archtype of the Christian belief in Resurrection and the doctrine of salvation through Christ, but it is almost unprecedented as a single sculpture. Epstein, who despite his close reading of Old and New Testaments, was disdainful of the minutiae of doctrine and the trappings of religious observance, recorded that 'the work, suggested by the gospel account of Lazarus being raised from the dead, was the outcome of an idea that had haunted me for many years' (*Epstein: An Autobiography*, 1955, p. 231). Thus, *Lazarus* grew out of a deepseated, personal preoccupation and has a private as well as a public meaning.

Indeed, despite the traditional subject, medium and technique, *Lazarus* is a surprising work. It is hard to say whether it startles more because of or despite its numerous resonances from the history of sculpture and from within Epstein's *œuvre*. Its main viewpoints, dictated by the acute angle of the upturned head, are from the figure's back and side. Though foreshadowed in the titanic struggle of his *Jacob and the Angel*, 1940–41 [143*], it acquires an added force in the single, monolithic figure through the diagonals of head and cerecloth which encourage movement around the stone, and bring about the gradual revelation of its unassertive, almost architectural, strength, the impact of the whole being so much greater than the sum of its parts. That head, slewed round upon its shoulders, the face peacefully uplifted to catch the light of the sky after its tenancy of the dark earth,

barely hints at consciousness but rather at the severance of body from spirit.

As a whole the piece evokes memories of Epstein's columnar, stately figures — *Risen Christ* [110] and *Visitation* (S162), while the head also reminds us of his most naturalistic work — the studies of babies sleeping [4, 5, 6 and Fig. 33] and *Peggy Jean asleep*, 1920 (S110). At the same time, is a synthesis of Epstein's allegiance to both western and non-western traditions of sculpture. The cerements in which *Lazarus* is swathed, a motif he used as early as 1910 [40], have European precedents but Epstein was also familiar with the ultimate source, which he had studied in the Egyptian collection at the British Museum. The acutely turned head may have been inspired by the very similar motif in a child strapped to its mother's back in an Nigerian carving in his own collection, as much as by his own observation from life (as suggested by W. Fagg, *The Tribal Image*, 1970, no. 27). The looming presence of the piece has a quality perhaps less monolithic than megalithic, an enduring presence as final as Stonehenge or the patriarchs and prophets who guard cathedral portals. Perhaps because the work was a statement of personal philosophy this is also the most Michelangelesque of Epstein's carvings: the deep, muscular chest, powerful yet helpless limbs and unawakened languor invite numerous comparisons — with the sculpture of the Julian Tomb and the *Rondanini Pieta* – just as the juxtaposed areas of smoothly finished and roughly chiselled stone seem a muted echo of the Florentine master.

Epstein's philosophy of life was shaped not by Christianity or even by orthodox Judaism, except in so far as he relished life in all its diversity. From his youth Whitman's *Leaves of Grass* had been a sort of Bible to him and throughout *Song of Myself* there are numerous concordances with the sculptor's enormously positive acceptance of the elemental rhythms of life from conception to death. In old age, Epstein replaced the fecund mother and child with the rebirth implicit in mortality and the renewal of the life cycle in man reunited with the earth and sky. The equivalence here between virgin substance and created form between the sleeping child and the severance of body and spirit in death, yields a masterpiece in which *Lazarus*, resiliently upright in death as in life, firmly anchored in the earth from which he came, faces with tranquility the immensity of the sky.

My foothold is tendon'd and mortis'd
   in granite,
I laugh at what you call dissolution,
And I know the amplitude of time.

WALT WHITMAN
Song of Myself

181

FROG *c* 1912–15
Red sandstone H 20.3
Private collection

This sculpture appears nowhere in the published sources and has not been exhibited until now. Its attribution to Epstein depends on both its provenance (it remained at Deerhurst, where the sculptor worked from 1928, and passed to successive owners of the house before entering the present private collection) and its style, which is entirely consistent with the geometrically abstracted naturalism of his work between 1912 and 1915.

Animal themes are usually considered the special preserve of Henri Gaudier-Brzeska, for whom the zoo was a more important source than the British Museum and who, until his death in 1915, drew and sculpted birds and animals with enormous verve (S. Fauchereau, 'Gaudier-Brzeska: animalist artist', in J. Lewison, ed., *Henri Gaudier-Brzeska, sculptor 1891–1915*, 1983, pp. 7–20). Such subjects were rarely treated by Epstein — his only early carvings of this type are the three pairs of marble *Doves*, 1913–15 [46, 48* and S48]. *Frog* is less closely related to these than to the *Crouching Sun Goddess*, *c* 1910 [35*], and like it *Frog* grows out of the integral, rectangular shape of its block,

though the unity of material and image is more strongly underlined by the low relief of the animal's limbs along the side and front surfaces of the block-base. The scarab-like form of this sculpture and *Crouching Sun Goddess* are further related in sharing common sources of inspiration in ancient Egyptian art.

The idea of exploring the broad, squat form, globular eyes and delicate limbs of the frog as sculpture, however, may have occurred to Epstein quite naturally as he worked on drawings and carvings of new-born children, whose splayed forms and stylised limbs have a distinctly amphibian character [52–57]. Indeed, the sheet of studies for *Rock Drill and Doves*, *c* 1913 [61] shows him experimenting, on the far right, with a lizard-like form. In keeping with these studies, *Frog* is more geometric than organic, though animate elements remain in the rounded, uneven ridges, resembling the skeletal bones of a hand, along the back. Everything else — flanks, eyes and limbs — are reduced to angular folds, simple solids and lines in a manner closely comparable with *Birth, Flenite relief* and their related drawings.

Given the paucity of early carvings from this vital, experimental phase of Epstein's career, *Frog* allows us new insight into the sculptor's preoccupations with geometric design applied to natural forms.

Evelyn Silber

Photographic Acknowledgments

The exhibition organisers would like to thank the following for making photographs available.
Abbreviations: HW (Hans Wild), JJ (James Jarché), PL (Paul Laib)

Aberdeen Art Gallery and Museums   [92]

Anthony d'Offay Gallery   [29, 41, 49, 51, 52, 53, 61, 63, 64, 65, 67, 68]

Victor Arwas   [22]

Dennis Assinder Photography, Birmingham   [3, 44, 96, XI]

BBC Hulton Picture Library   Fig. 2

Birmingham Museums and Art Gallery   [25, 33, 45, 76, 89, 91, 93, 111, 130, 133, 136, 151, 176].   Figs 87, 89 (Helmut Gernsheim)

Bolton Museum and Art Gallery   [164, 177]

Bristol Museum and Art Gallery   [159]

British Architectural Library   [127]

The British Museum   [VIII, IX, X, XII, XIII, XIV, XVI].   Figs 50, 83

Bruton Gallery   [31, 32]

Richard Buckle   [110]

Burrell Collection   [84]

Fitzwilliam Museum, Cambridge   [19, 150]

Australian National Gallery, Canberra   [140].   Fig. 64

Centre for the Study of Cartoons and Caricature, University of Kent, Canterbury   Figs 28, 29

Judith Collins   Fig. 58

John Cope   [102, 181]

Richard Cork   [11]   (reproduced by permission of the National Gallery of Victoria, Melbourne)

Courtauld Institute of Art   [60]

The Fine Art Society, London   [2].   Fig. 31

Terry Friedman   Figs 8, 49, 81

National Maritime Museum, Greenwich   [73]

Jerry Harman-Jones   [6, 85, 152]

The Henry Moore Foundation   Figs 11, 13 (Gordon Bishop Associated Ltd), 14, 18

University of Hull Art Collection   [12]

Geoffrey Ireland   [I, II, III, IV, V, VI].   Figs 4, 5, 65 and p. ii

Larkfield Photography, Brighouse   [15, 18, 20, 23, 27, 39, 43, 78, 81, 98, 99, 100, 103, 104, 106, 107, 108, 109, 114, 131, 132, 148, 157, 163, 168, 178].   Figs 25, 26, 27, 40, 82

Leeds City Art Galleries   [1] (frontispiece). Fig. 100.   The Henry Moore Centre for the Study of Sculpture: Gill Archive: Figs 53, 55, 56, 60, 61, 63

Leeds University Photographic Department   [21, 42, 54, 94, 146].   Figs 16, 17, 19, 20, 21, 22, 32, 33, 35, 36, 54, 72, 84

Leicester Galleries   [75 (James Mortimer), 95, 123, 155, 166, 167 (Ida Kar), 173, 174 (James Mortimer)]

Lehmbruck Estate   Fig. 73

Beth Lipkin   [8(HW), 9, 17(HW), 37(HW), 46(HW), 80(PL), 113(HW), 154(PL), 165(HW), 175].   Figs 3, 7, 48 (Walter Benington), 51, 52(HW), 57, 59, 68, p. iii

University of Liverpool   [142, 143]

London Transport Picture Library, London   Fig. 15

National Monuments Record, London   Fig. 37

National Portrait Gallery, London   Figs 23, 24, 30, 42, 70

Manchester City Art Galleries   [79, 112]

Whitworth Art Gallery, University of Manchester   [87]

National Gallery of Victoria, Melbourne   [36]

Minneapolis Institute of Arts   [50]

James Mortimer   [169]

Carlo Monzino   [VII]

Jewish Museum, New York   [97]

Museum of Modern Art, New York   [96]

R. Parker   [137]

Phaidon Press Ltd   [56 (Susan Evans), 57 (Susan Evans), 58 (HW), 74, 88 (PL), 135, 139, 141, 149 (PL), 172, 179].   Figs 6, 10, 38 (HW), 39 (HW), 43 (HW), 44, 46 (Jacqueline Hyde), 62, 66, 67, 69, 71 (Hirmer Fotoarchiv), 79 (Bildarchiv Foto Marburg) 80 (PL), 92 (Geoffrey Ireland), 93, 94, 95 (Stanley Travers & Partners, Photographers), 96, 97 (Geoffrey Ireland), 99

Photo Sources Ltd. (Central Press Photo Ltd)   Fig. 9

Museum of Art, Carnegie Institute, Pittsburgh   Fig. 34

L. B. Powell   Fig. 76 (World Wide Photos)

Department of English, University of Reading   Fig. 45 (E. O. Hoppé)

Royal Academy of Arts, London   [35, 134, 138]

S & G   Fig. 98

Evelyn Silber   [5, 28, 62, 77, 82, 83, 91, 105, 115, 144, 145, 147, 158, 171, 180].   Figs 47, 77, 78, 85 (PL), 90

Syndication International (Daily Herald Copyright, courtesy National Museum of Photography, Bradford)   Figs 1 (JJ), 41 (Sayers), 74 (JJ), 86 (JJ), 88

Tate Gallery, London   [14, 24, 48, 70, 71, 72, 90].   Fig. 75

Art Gallery of Ontario, Toronto   [55]

Victoria and Albert Museum, London   [101]

National Museum of Wales (by permission)   [34]

Walsall Museum and Art Gallery (Garman-Ryan Collection)   [4, 7, 10, 26, 30, 47, 66, 161, 162]

West Park Studios, Leeds   [13, 16, 40, 86, 117, 118, 119, 120, 121, 122, 124, 125, 126, 128, 129, 153, 170].   Figs 12, 91

Hans Wild   [160]

Gareth Winters, London   [38, 116, 156, XV]

4,000 copies printed in March 1987
2,000 copies reprinted in May 1989

© 1987, 1989
The Henry Moore Centre
for the Study of Sculpture,
Leeds City Art Galleries
and the authors as listed

ISBN 0 901286 21 4

Catalogue designed by Peter McGrath
and printed in Great Britain
by W. S. Maney and Son Limited
Hudson Road, Leeds LS9 7DL